American Culture and the Media

Reading, Writing, Thinking

As part of Houghton Mifflin's ongoing commitment to the environment, this text has been printed on recycled paper.

American Culture and the Media

Reading, Writing, Thinking

Anne Cassebaum
Elon College

Rosemary Haskell
Elon College

Houghton Mifflin Company
Boston   New York

Sponsoring Editor: Renée Deljon
Senior Development Editor: Ellen Darion
Senior Project Editor: Fred Burns
Senior Designer: Henry Rachlin
Production/Design Coordinator: Jennifer Waddell
Senior Manufacturing Coordinator: Priscilla Bailey
Marketing Manager: Nancy Lyman

Cover design: Diana Coe
Cover image: © 1996 Photodisc Inc.

Acknowledgments begin on page 471.

Copyright © 1997 by Houghton Mifflin Company. All rights reserved.

No part of this work may be reproduced or transmitted in any form or by any means, electronic or mechanical, including photocopying and recording, or by any information storage or retrieval system without the prior written permission of the copyright owner unless such copying is expressly permitted by federal copyright law. With the exception of non-profit transcription in Braille, Houghton Mifflin is not authorized to grant permission for further uses of copyrighted selections reprinted in this text without the permission of their owners. Permission must be obtained from the individual copyright owners as identified herein. Address requests for permission to make copies of Houghton Mifflin material to College Permissions, Houghton Mifflin Company, 222 Berkeley Street, Boston, MA 02116-3764.

Printed in the U.S.A.

Library of Congress Catalog Card Number: 96-76876

Student Edition ISBN: 0-395-72769-3

Instructor's Edition ISBN: 0-395-72770-7

123456789 - DH - 00 99 98 97 96

Contents

Preface   xi

Section I:
Reading and Writing about American Culture and the Media   1

1. Shaping Forces: Culture and Mass Media   3

Customs   CLYDE KLUCKHOHN   6
The Cruel Logic of Teenage Violence   WILLIAM O'BRIEN   9
Teenage Truths and Tribulations Across Cultures: Degrassi Junior High and Beverly Hills 90210   MARIE-CLAIRE SIMONETTI   12
Sex, Lies and Advertising   GLORIA STEINEM   21
The Effects of Television on Family Life   MARIE WINN   29
Tuning Out Network Bias   ISHMAEL REED   32
Don't Ask, Don't Tell: What You Didn't Hear on the 6 O'Clock News   CRAIG McLAUGHLIN AND BARRY YEOMAN   35
Television Power and American Values   WILLIAM LEE MILLER   43
Now Playing: Real Life, the Movie   NEAL GABLER   46
Writing Assignments   56

2. Work   59

A Driving Fear   ELLEN GOODMAN   62
Covering the Cops   JON KATZ   64
Working-Class Heroes No More   BARBARA EHRENREICH   72
Who Built the Pyramids?   STUDS TERKEL   76
My Young Men Shall Never Work   CHIEF SMOHALLA   83
The Price of Success   SAM KEEN   85
Writing Assignments   89

3. Diversity   93

White Privilege: Unpacking the Invisible Knapsack   PEGGY McINTOSH   96
The Media's Image of Arabs   JACK G. SHAHEEN   102

Just Walk on By: A Black Man Ponders His Power to Alter Public Space   BRENT STAPLES   105

TV's Black World Turns—But Stays Unreal
  HENRY LOUIS GATES, JR.   109

Portrayals of Latinos in and by the Media   DEBRA GERSH   114

Why They Excel   FOX BUTTERFIELD   118

Writing Assignments   124

4. Gender Roles   127

From Mary to Murphy   VICTORIA A. REBECK   129

The Other Difference Between Boys and Girls
  RICHARD M. RESTAK   133

In Harness: The Male Condition   HERB GOLDBERG   138

The Great Person-Hole Cover Debate   LINDSY VAN GELDER   144

Black Women and Feminism   BELL HOOKS   147

Can We End Media Bias Against Gays?   CRAIG DAVIDSON   151

Writing Assignments   159

5. Sports   163

Strong in the Blood but Perhaps Not in the Future
  WILLIAM C. RHODEN   165

Let's Stop Glorifying Bullies   JOSÉ CHEQUI TORRES   169

Outside Shot   PAT AUFDERHEIDE   173

What We Are Watching: The View from the Couch
  DAVID KLATELL AND NORMAN MARCUS   177

Joe Louis   MAYA ANGELOU   182

Media, Sports and Gender   JAY J. COAKLEY   185

Writing Assignments   192

6. Poverty and Wealth   195

What Is Poverty?   JO GOODWIN PARKER   198

There's Simply Not Enough Food   FRANCES MOORE LAPPÉ
  AND JOSEPH COLLINS   202

Freedom of Speech for the Wealthy   JERRY MANDER   207

Hunger in Africa: A Story Untold Until Too Late   JANE HUNTER
  AND STEVE ASKIN   210

A Society Without Poverty   KATHERINE VAN WORMER   217

Where Have You Been?   CAROL BRADLEY SHIRLEY   224

Writing Assignments   227

7. Violence   231

Public Enemy Number One?   MIKE MALES   234
Get to the Root of Violence: Militarism   JEAN PROKOPOW   241
On Rap, Symbolism and Fear   JON PARELES   243
Why We Crave Horror Movies   STEPHEN KING   249
TV Violence: The Shocking New Evidence   EUGENE H. METHVIN   252
Battered Justice   JOAN MEIER   257
Writing Assignments   266

8. The Environment   269

Are Today's Kids Detached from Nature?   RICHARD LOUV   271
TV's Capture of the Mind   JERRY MANDER   278
Our Land Is More Valuable Than Your Money
     BLACKFEET CHIEF   282
Seeing   ANNIE DILLARD   283
Technology Is the Answer (But What Was the Question?)
     AMORY B. LOVINS   286
The Media and Misinformation   SUSAN MCDONALD   291
Writing Assignments   296

Section II
Working on Your Paper: A Guide to Writing   299

9. Coming Up with Ideas   301

Brainstorming to Find Your Ideas   303
Freewriting to Find Your Ideas   304
Using Questions to Turn Up Ideas   305
Talking Ideas Out   311
Finding a Focus   313

10. Keeping a Journal   315

Why Keep a Journal?   315

The Personal Journal 317
The Media Journal 318

11. Making the Most of Your Reading 321
What Is Reading? 321
A Quick Course in Reading 322
Demonstration of a Reading 325

12. Analysis: Going Deeper to Come Up with Ideas 331
What Is Analysis? 332
Why Analyze the Media? 333
How to Do Analysis 333

13. Interviewing: Using Other People's Brains 341
Preparation 341
The Interview 343
After the Interview 343
Writing Up the Interview 344

14. Working the Library 345
What Is Research? 345
Finding Sources 347
Source Notes: Answers to Seven Basic Questions 349

15. Organizing: Getting Your Ideas Together 357
What Is Organizing? 357
Using Focus to Organize Your Paper 360
Using Audience to Organize Your Paper 361
Using Purpose to Organize Your Paper 361
Using Questions to Organize Your Paper 365

16. Writing the First Draft 371
Getting Started 371
What Is a Draft? 373
Writing from an Outline 374

17. Revising 377
What Is Revising? 377
Revising Your Focus 380
Revising for Your Audience 381
Revising Your Purpose 382
Revising Your Organization 385
Revising Your Style 386

18. Getting and Giving Good Criticism 403
What Is Criticism? 404
Four Ways to React to a Paper 405
Some Critics at Work 408
Writing Conferences 412

19. Editing: The Final Polish 415
How Important Is Correctness? 415
What Standards of Correctness Do We Need? 416
Dealing with Errors 417
The Most Common and Unwanted Errors 419
Punctuation Problems 419
Spelling Problems 430
Usage and Grammar Problems 438

20. Writing on the Spot 449
Five Ways to Avoid Panic: Writing Well on the Spot 449
Typical Essay Questions 450

21. Making Gains for the Next Paper 453
Writing Memos: A Way of Getting Good Criticism from Your Instructor 453
Reading and Reacting to Grades and Comments 455
Keeping Records of Past Papers 457
Finale 457

Appendixes 459

A - Record Forms for Making Gains on Your Writing 461

B - Answers to Practice Checks 465

Acknowledgments 471

Index 476

Preface

American Culture and the Media is based on our belief that reading and writing skills are best taught together and in the context of high-interest subject matter. In Section I, the mass media—TV, movies, magazines, radio, newspapers—and contemporary culture form a familiar and reassuring, yet rich and complex, subject for exploration and analysis. Section II, the rhetoric and brief handbook, gives advice and information for students to use as they work on their papers.

Organization

After an introductory chapter that shows culture and the mass media as shaping forces in our lives, each of the remaining seven chapters in Section I addresses a particular aspect of American culture in conjunction with its media representations: violence, gender roles, work, poverty and wealth, the environment, sports, and diversity.

Each chapter is organized to model a variety of ways to analyze any subject. Chapters open with two "Key Questions" followed by quotations about the topic. Then the student is invited to respond, in writing or orally, to questions under three headings: "Starting Out: Finding Out What You Already Know"; "Learning More Through Observation: Taking a Look Around You and Talking to People"; and "Questioning: Deciding What Else You Would Like to Know." The reading selections following have diverse authors and viewpoints and are accompanied by questions designed to help reading comprehension, to connect reading to a "writing skill" lesson, and to help the student make connections between the ideas in different articles. Each chapter closes with four "Writing Assignments" suggestions for longer papers, with commentary that can help students develop a heuristic for any writing assignment.

Section II, "Working on Your Paper: A Guide to Writing" offers a rhetoric focused on helping students with invention, research, drafting, revising, and editing. It includes a brief trouble-shooting handbook on the most common punctuation, spelling, and grammar errors as well as some basic instruction on library research and documentation methods. Your students should be able to move easily between the two sections of the book, using the *Guide to Writing* as they work on their own writing assignments—either in class or on their own. Cross-references from Section I to Section II are designed to encourage this movement.

Key Features of this Text

Section I: Reading and Writing about American Culture and the Media

- Fifty thematically unified high-interest readings in Section I.
- Questions, quotations, and introductions at the start of each chapter to focus and stimulate thinking.

- Invention exercises built into topic chapters to prepare students for writing assignments.
- Pre- and post-reading questions designed to stimulate thinking and help comprehension.
- "Connecting" questions after each reading to help students relate ideas in different articles.
- A brief section after each reading connects writing and reading by emphasizing one writing skill to be learned from each reading.
- Assignments for longer papers in each chapter.

Section II: Working on Your Paper: A Guide to Writing
- An accessible, encouraging style, designed with students' writing anxieties and attitudes in mind.
- A full chapter on analytical thinking, emphasizing media analysis, explains to students the methods of analysis we too often assume they know.
- A chapter on "Making the Most of Your Reading" outlines and models for students the main steps of active reading.
- Examples of student writing are used throughout the *Guide to Writing*.
- A handbook focused only on the most common student errors accompanied by clear explanations.
- A final chapter to help students with overall evaluation of their writing.

Ancillaries

- Instructor's Manual with summaries of each reading selection, commentary on each reading, and teaching suggestions for both the reader and the rhetoric.
- The Dictionary deal. *The American Heritage College Dictionary* may be shrinkwrapped with the text at a substantial savings.

Acknowledgments

We would like to express our gratitude to the Research and Development Committee of Elon College, which awarded us released time from teaching to work on this book. Among our many remaining debts of gratitude to our colleagues at Elon and other colleges, we owe most to Linda Martindale, who was generous with her time and ingenious in her ability to get our manuscripts ready for deadlines. We would also like to thank Ellen Darion, our editor at Houghton Mifflin. Her advice, enthusiasm, and support were invaluable. Finally, we thank our families—John, Willy and Vega Herold; and Bill, Brendan, and Henry Gargan—for living with us through this lengthy enterprise.

In addition, we would like to express our gratitude to the following reviewers who offered many helpful suggestions:

Deborah Barberousse, Coker College, South Carolina
Allan Carter, College of DuPage, Illinois
Connie Eggers, Western Washington University, Washington
Patricia Falk, Nassau County Community College, New York
Joan Gagnon, Honolulu Community College, Hawaii
Charles Hood, Antelope Valley College, California
Patricia A. Malinowski, Finger Lakes Community College, New York
E. Jane Melendez, East Tennessee State University, Tennessee
Judith L. Merrell, Community College of Allegheny County—Boyce Campus, Pennsylvania
Faye Parker, Dyersburg State Community College, Tennessee
Karen J. Patty-Graham, Southern Illinois University at Edwardsville, Illinois
Jayne Decker Taber, University of Maine at Farmington, Maine

SECTION I

Reading and Writing about American Culture and the Media

Introduction

We've organized all chapters around two subjects you already know a lot about—American culture and the mass media—because *knowing* a lot about a subject will help you to *write* better about it. All of us know about American culture, because we have lived in it. And most of us have logged a good number of hours tuned into mass media like television or radio, or reading magazines and watching movies. The readings of this text will help you to step back and analyze what we see, hear, and read and to ask questions such as what is the role of the mass media in our culture? Is television news fair or accurate? Is American culture violent in the way television suggests it is? How do magazine advertisements affect our stereotypes of people? These are some of the questions that this book will raise.

And raising questions is the main intention of this book. It invites you to ask, and answer, questions about American culture and the media. It offers readings with competing opinions and ideas for you to consider, but not to accept as final answers. And chapters end with suggested paper topics so you can develop your own ideas in writing for others to consider.

In Section I, each chapter is set up to help you investigate a topic and prepare for the writing you are going to do on it. Use the opening features of each chapter to get yourself thinking and questioning. Chapters start with two key questions on the main topic. These are followed by questions in the sections "Starting Out" and "Learning More Through Observation" that will help you explore in detail, in writing or discussion, what you already know and what you might discover about the topic—whether it's work, diversity, gender roles, sports, poverty, violence, or the environment. Readings follow to give other people's ideas on the issues each chapter raises. Questions and comments with each reading selection will help you to read closely and think about your own reaction to what you've read, as well as how a particular essay connects to other readings. You'll also get the chance to learn about writing from your reading by focusing on specific strategies writers use in each essay. At the end of each chapter are four possible assignments to respond to, with suggestions to help you get started on your thinking about each topic, to find a focus among your ideas, to organize them, and to tailor your paper to a particular audience. We think that by the end of each chapter you will find that there is a lot you want to write about, and the problem may be making a choice among several possibilities. As you work on these assignments—and other writing projects—you should consult Section II, *Working on Your Papers: A Guide to Writing,* which begins on p. 299.

Chapter 1

Shaping Forces: Culture and Mass Media

KEY QUESTIONS
How has American culture shaped you to be the person you are?
How much impact do the mass media have on us and our culture?

. . . .

Sometimes people call me an idealist. Well, that is the way I know I am an American. America is the only idealistic nation in the world.
—Woodrow Wilson

Being an American means never having to say you're sorry.
—Kurt Vonnegut

*O brave new world,
That has such people in it!*
—from William Shakespeare's *The Tempest*

When will America be America again?
—Langston Hughes

The press is so powerful in its image-making role, it can make a criminal look like he's the victim and make the victim look like he's the criminal. If you aren't careful, the newspapers will have you hating the people who are being oppressed and loving the people who are doing the oppressing.
—Malcolm X

Ours is the first society in history of which it can be said that life has moved inside the media.
—Jerry Mander

Shaping Forces

How has American culture shaped you to be the person you are? And what is the role of the mass media in our society? In this book, *American Culture and the Media,* you will explore different aspects of American culture and media to consider the values and attitudes that are dominant and their effect on us all. We'll begin by defining our key concepts, culture and media.

A Definition of Culture

Let's start with what we mean by *culture.* Most standard definitions of culture suggest that it is the sum total of what most people in a large group have in the way of material objects and possessions; what their customs and rituals are; and what they value or think is important. In his essay "Customs" social scientist Clyde Kluckhohn argues that studying culture is something we should all do, in order to understand just what values and attitudes we are likely to have by living in the United States. American culture's *objects and possessions* include our shopping malls, dishwashers, stereos, cars, and, yes, our denim jeans. Our culture also encompasses *customs and rituals:* everyday ways of greeting people, of eating dinner, or watching television; special events like birthday parties, funerals, weddings, graduation ceremonies, New Year's Eve celebrations, football games, and prom nights. But what do these objects and rituals reveal about how we feel and about what we think is important?

Even with America's vast diversity, most people would argue that there are certain *values and attitudes* that characterize Americans: freedom, equality, materialism, individualism, belief in technology and individual success, for example. An essay in this chapter, William O'Brien's "The Cruel Logic of Teenage Violence," highlights the dominance of violence in American culture, whereas Marie-Claire Simonetti in "Teenage Truths and Tribulations Across Cultures," argues that the TV series "Beverly Hills 90210" reveals the central American value of individualism.

Are Americans really more individualist, more self- rather than group-oriented than people of other cultures? That's a tough question, partly because our culture is so familiar to us that we hardly notice that it's there. However, comparing cultures can help us see more clearly our own attitudes and values.

The Mass Media

Mass media include television, movies, radio, compact disks, newspapers and magazines—any and all sources that can reach masses of people at one time. And any medium that can claim the attention of millions of people must have some impact on our culture. To begin with, mass media influence our basic daily activities, as Marie Winn argues in "The Effects of Television on Family Life," or, as Neal Gabler argues in "Now Playing: Real Life, the Movie," they distract us from our "real" lives. More positive are William Lee Miller's comments ("Television Power and American Values") on the way television can bring information and entertainment to people who might otherwise lack these things. Television, magazines, newspapers, and movies also transmit cultural messages to us: about what to value, how to feel about things, and even what to think about. Ninety-eight percent of U.S. households watch television for an average of seven hours a day; so that flickering screen may represent the biggest single cultural influence in our lives. And television is only *one* of the mass media.

To test the impact of media messages on your own life, you might ask whether you would be wearing your denim (designer?) jeans if TV or magazine advertising hadn't emphasized them so much. Or, you might ask how, and how often, TV network news tells us that freedom and equality are American values, particularly in contrast with other countries' values. You might also speculate on how much of your feeling about New Year's Eve comes from the TV screen's pictures of Times Square celebrations and how much from your own actual experience.

Who Decides What We See and Hear in the Media?

Who controls what we get to see and hear on the mass media? This is another question raised in this chapter. The answers to the question tell us even more about what our culture thinks is important. Gloria Steinem's answer, in "Sex, Lies, and Advertising," is very direct: advertisers. She assesses their influence on editors' decisions about what stories to include and exclude in a publication. In doing so, Steinem shows how *Ms.* magazine itself reveals the influence of one American value: materialism. In "Don't Ask, Don't Tell: What You Didn't Hear on the Six O'Clock News" Craig McLaughlin and Barry Yeoman look at a report on major news stories that *weren't* covered, to show how the news media shape our perceptions of what our important national issues actually are. These omitted stories raise the question of who decided *not* to cover them, and why.

And what about the news stories that *do* make it onto screen or page? Are they accurate? Are they fair? Ishmael Reed ("Tuning out Network Bias") worries about the stereotypes of minorities emerging from some media coverage of crime and their impact on our attitudes in the real world.

The readings in this chapter ask you to look at the way the mass media interact with our culture. They also encourage you to analyze words and images and sounds. Certainly, the study of your culture and the media should make you more aware of who you are and why you have absorbed—or chosen—the values and attitudes you now have.

Starting Out: Finding Out What You Already Know

1. Given what you know firsthand or from other sources, how do American customs and values differ from those of other countries?
2. Make a list of what Americans value.
3. Write down the main forces in your life that have shaped you to be the way you are.

4. List the mass media that you come into contact with everyday and the time you spend with each one.
5. Freewrite for a few minutes on how your life might be different without television.

Learning More Through Observation: Taking a Look Around You and Talking to People

1. Interview someone who has recently arrived in this country. Ask the person to describe what is different about American culture.
2. Observe some part of our culture (a mall, a drive-through bank, a fast-food place, a sporting event, a church service) and describe what it tells you about what most Americans think is important.
3. Choose a TV show and freewrite your response to the question "What, if anything, does this show tell me about real life in our culture?"
4. Stop watching television or reading the newspapers for seven days straight. Take notes during the week about how this change affects you.
5. Keep a log of advertisers or sponsors whose names appear on your TV screen. What connections can you make between the sponsor (and its product) and the show itself?

Questioning: Deciding What Else You Would Like to Know

List five questions that you still have about American culture and the mass media.

CLYDE KLUCKHOHN

Customs

Clyde Kluckhohn, an anthropologist, writes about the differences and similarities among the customs of different cultures.

BEFORE YOU READ

1. What customs do you think are particularly American?
2. What customs from other countries have shocked or surprised you? Why?

1   Why do the Chinese dislike milk and milk products? Why would the Japanese die willingly in a Banzai charge that seemed senseless to Americans? Why do some nations trace descent through the father, others

through the mother, still others through both parents? Not because different peoples have different instincts, not because they were destined by God or Fate to different habits, not because the weather is different in China and Japan and the United States. Sometimes shrewd common sense has an answer that is close to that of the anthropologist: "because they were brought up that way." By "culture" anthropology means the total life way of a people, the social legacy the individual acquires from his group. Or culture can be regarded as that part of the environment that is the creation of man.

2 This technical term has a wider meaning than the "culture" of history and literature. A humble cooking pot is as much a cultural product as is a Beethoven sonata. In ordinary speech a man of culture is a man who can speak languages other than his own, who is familiar with history, literature, philosophy, or the fine arts. In some cliques that definition is still narrower. The cultured person is one who can talk about James Joyce, Scarlatti, and Picasso. To the anthropologist, however, to be human is to be cultured. There is culture in general, and then there are the specific cultures such as Russian, American, British, Hottentot, Inca. The general abstract notion serves to remind us that we cannot explain acts solely in terms of the biological properties of the people concerned, their individual past experience, and the immediate situation. The past experience of other men in the form of culture enters into almost every event. Each specific culture constitutes a kind of blueprint for all of life's activities.

3 One of the interesting things about human beings is that they try to understand themselves and their own behavior. While this has been particularly true of Europeans in recent times, there is no group which has not developed a scheme or schemes to explain man's actions. To the insistent human query "why?" the most exciting illumination anthropology has to offer is that of the concept of culture. Its explanatory importance is comparable to categories such as evolution in biology, gravity in physics, disease in medicine. A good deal of human behavior can be understood, and indeed predicted, if we know a people's design for living. Many acts are neither accidental nor due to personal peculiarities nor caused by supernatural forces nor simply mysterious. Even those of us who pride ourselves on our individualism follow most of the time a pattern not of our own making. We brush our teeth on arising. We put on pants—not a loincloth or a grass skirt. We eat three meals a day—not four or five or two. We sleep in a bed—not in a hammock or on a sheep pelt. I do not have to know the individual and his life history to be able to predict these and countless other regularities, including many in the thinking process, of all Americans who are not incarcerated[1] in jails or hospitals for the insane.

4 To the American woman a system of plural wives seems "instinctively" abhorrent.[2] She cannot understand how any woman can fail to be jealous and uncomfortable if she must share her husband with other women. She feels it "unnatural" to accept such a situation. On the other hand, a Koryak woman of

---

[1] Imprisoned.

[2] Repulsive.

Siberia, for example, would find it hard to understand how a woman could be so selfish and so undesirous of feminine companionship in the home as to wish to restrict her husband to one mate.

5   Some years ago I met in New York City a young man who did not speak a word of English and was obviously bewildered by American ways. By "blood" he was as American as you or I, for his parents had gone from Indiana to China as missionaries. Orphaned in infancy, he was reared by a Chinese family in a remote village. All who met him found him more Chinese than American. The facts of his blue eyes and light hair were less impressive than a Chinese style of gait,[3] Chinese arm and hand movements, Chinese facial expression, and Chinese modes of thought. The biological heritage was American, but the cultural training had been Chinese. He returned to China.

6   Another example of another kind: I once knew a trader's wife in Arizona who took a somewhat devilish interest in producing a cultural reaction. Guests who came her way were often served delicious sandwiches filled with a meat that seemed to be neither chicken nor tuna fish yet was reminiscent[4] of both. To queries she gave no reply until each had eaten his fill. She then explained that what they had eaten was not chicken, not tuna fish, but the rich, white flesh of freshly killed rattlesnakes. The response was instantaneous—vomiting, often violent vomiting. A biological process is caught in a cultural web.

7   A highly intelligent teacher with long and successful experience in the public schools of Chicago was finishing her first year in an Indian school. When asked how her Navaho pupils compared in intelligence with Chicago youngsters, she replied, "Well, I just don't know. Sometimes the Indians seem just as bright. At other times they just act like dumb animals. The other night we had a dance in the high school. I saw a boy who is one of the best students in my English class standing off by himself. So I took him over to a pretty girl and told them to dance. But they just stood there with their heads down. They wouldn't even say anything." I inquired if she knew whether or not they were members of the same clan. "What difference would that make?"

8   "How would you feel about getting into bed with your brother?" The teacher walked off in a huff, but, actually, the two cases were quite comparable in principle. To the Indian the type of bodily contact involved in our social dancing has a directly sexual connotation. The incest taboos between members of the same clan are as severe as between true brothers and sisters. The shame of the Indians at the suggestion that a clan brother and sister should dance and the indignation of the white teacher at the idea that she should share a bed with an adult brother represent equally nonrational responses, culturally standardized unreason.

9   All this does not mean that there is no such thing as raw human nature. The very fact that certain of the same institutions are found in all known societies

---

[3] Way of walking.
[4] Similar to; brought the others to mind.

indicates that at bottom all human beings are very much alike. The files of the Cross-Cultural Survey at Yale University are organized according to categories such as "marriage ceremonies," "life crisis rites," "incest taboos." At least seventy-five of these categories are represented in every single one of the hundreds of cultures analyzed. This is hardly surprising. The members of all human groups have about the same biological equipment. All men undergo the same poignant life experiences such as birth, helplessness, illness, old age, and death. The biological potentialities of the species are the blocks with which cultures are built. Some patterns of every culture crystallize around focuses provided by the inevitables of biology: the difference between the sexes, the presence of persons of different ages, the varying physical strength and skill of individuals. The facts of nature also limit culture forms. No culture provides patterns for jumping over trees or for eating iron ore.

REACTING

1. Pick one of the customs from other cultures described by Clyde Kluckhohn and explain what you find particularly "foreign" about it.
2. Do you agree with Kluckhohn that culture has such a strong influence on us?

CONNECTING

1. This reading helps us answer one of this chapter's key questions, "How has American culture shaped you to be the person you are?" Write about, or discuss, your own responses to it.
2. Read William O'Brien's article "The Cruel Logic of Teenage Violence" below. How might Kluckhohn comment on it?

LEARNING ABOUT WRITING FROM READING

Kluckhohn uses the simple statement + support pattern to organize his ideas very effectively. He makes an early statement that people who are brought up in different cultures will deal with common human experiences differently. Then he supports that statement with several well-developed examples: the "system of plural wives"; the young man confused by New York City; the Chicago woman and her Navaho pupils. The last paragraph draws the significance of all these examples together again as the writer reminds us of their relationship to his initial thesis, or statement.

WILLIAM O'BRIEN

The Cruel Logic of Teenage Violence

William O'Brien, writing for the Sonoma County Peace Press, *focuses on the relationship between violence and some important values in American culture.*

BEFORE YOU READ

1. What explanations do you have for rising rates of teenage violence?
2. In what senses might it be "logical" in our culture (as the title suggests) for teenagers to be violent?

1   A scene in modern-day America: a teenager, who has illicitly acquired a gun, shoots and kills another teenager. Later, after being arrested, he admits with little remorse that he wanted his victim's tennis shoes.

2   A horrifying story, but not fantasy. Youth violence is an integral part of the moral landscape of the U.S. in 1994. A few short years ago the image of gun-toting kids was unthinkable. Yet these appalling stories are becoming a staple of the morning's news: last summer's slaying of a homeless man in Florida by a teenager who wanted his piece of pizza; this summer's gangland-style execution by an eleven-year-old in Chicago, who himself was later killed; in Philadelphia, a group of teenagers who shot an elderly, mentally ill homeless man.

3   A homicide committed by a teenager usually betrays a complex nexus[1] of dynamics. Poverty, social alienation, race and class divisions, the collapse of healthy families and communities, and the breakdown of traditional moral codes may all play a role in the pulling of the trigger, and all of these demand serious societal attention. But I am convinced that the most terrifying factor is precisely that such killings are not individual aberrations or the problems of a particular community. When a teen shoots another for tennis shoes (or for other seemingly preposterous reasons), he is manifesting, however perversely, certain general cultural values that he has learned.

4   One of those values is violence. Only recently is this society waking up to the pervasiveness of the violence that plagues us, a violence that is deeply woven into our cultural ethos. The teenage gun-toter is acting out of that very ethos, which embraces violence as acceptable, noble, valued, even entertaining.

5   All his life, the American teenager has been enthralled by fighting and bloodletting. (The grisly video game Mortal Kombat is, after all, simply a technologically advanced updating of John Wayne.) He has absorbed a popular mythology that shows heroes solving problems by killing—from Arnold Schwarzenegger to the "turkey shoot" in Kuwait where thousands of retreating Iraqi soldiers are slaughtered by our military.

6   Like most Americans, this teenager has internalized the paradigm that violence is manly, that might makes right, that lethal force will overcome all obstacles. How shocking is it, then, when he picks up a gun?

7   Nor is it surprising that he should value lives less than even paltry material gain. Such motivation emerges out of another deeply rooted cultural value: the hallowed American tradition of materialism.

8   Materialism in this culture is more than the simple acquisition of money and possessions. It is an all-embracing worldview that values those possessions as an ultimate end. Economically, culturally, and psychologically, Americans

---

[1] Link or connection.

operate in a system permeated by what theologian and social analyst Cornel West has called "market culture." Possessions are the ultimate measure of a person's worth. Upward mobility and consumption absorb our energies and define our goals. Exchange of commodities takes precedence over relationships. Advertising and relentless marketing of goods are the predominant and influential form of social discourse. Shopping malls are the new public arenas and sacred spaces.

9   Like the pervasive messages of violence, materialism infuses our culture, blunting our capacity to discern other kinds of meaning. We venerate the lives of the rich and famous and the value system "trickles down" to our youth, who are fed the lie that their ultimate worth as human beings depends on having $100 tennis shoes. (It is not irrelevant to note that advertising geared to youth was once heavily regulated by the FCC; such regulations were gutted by the Reagan Administration, creating an unprecedented torrent of youth-directed marketing in the 1980s and 1990s.)

10   When a teenager shoots another teenager for drug money or tennis shoes or gold jewelry, he is not an aberration. He is acting out the cruel logic of modern U.S. culture: life is cheap, possessions are the ultimate value, and violence is the way to achieve your ends.

11   We must grapple with the many complex social dynamics that feed into youth violence—the economic, social, family, and community issues. But we must also recognize the deeper spiritual task of conversion—conversion of ourselves as persons and conversion of the fundamental fabric of our culture. Until we undertake that work, until we effectively transform the moral logic that venerates violence and materialism, kids will continue to kill kids. We owe our children a more sane and less deadly set of values—but we will first need to learn them ourselves.

REACTING

1. Do you agree with William O'Brien's explanations for teenage violence? Why or why not?
2. Talk or write about what values O'Brien might have in mind when he says: "We owe our children a more sane and less deadly set of values."

CONNECTING

1. Use O'Brien's ideas to help you respond to one of this chapter's key questions: "How much impact do the mass media have on us and our culture?"
2. Turn to page 21 and read Gloria Steinem's "Sex, Lies, and Advertising." What connections do you find between O'Brien's and Steinem's ideas?

LEARNING ABOUT WRITING FROM READING

One of the marks of a good writer is the ability to use the short, simple sentence effectively. O'Brien gives a nice example of how to employ a series of short, simple sentences to emphasize a single point about the role of materialism in American culture:

> Possessions are the ultimate measure of a person's worth. Upward mobility and consumption absorb our energies and define our goals. Exchange of commodities takes precedence over relationships. Advertising and relentless marketing of goods are the predominant and influential form of social discourse. Shopping malls are the new public arenas and sacred spaces.

Notice how the paragraph gains in rhythm and clarity as the reader keys in to the simple sentence pattern of subject + verb and is able almost to predict what's coming next. Of course, you cannot write whole pages of prose in this way: knowing when repetition is no longer helpful and has become merely boring is another mark of the good writer.

MARIE-CLAIRE SIMONETTI

Teenage Truths and Tribulations Across Cultures: Degrassi Junior High and Beverly Hills 90210

Marie-Claire Simonetti, graduate student in the field of film and television criticism, gives a comparative analysis of Canadian and American TV shows for teenagers.

BEFORE YOU READ

1. *Tribulations* means trials or difficulties. List the tribulations of teenage life in America, using your own experiences as a guide.
2. Describe a typical episode of "Degrassi Junior High," "Beverly Hills 90210," or some other show for and about teenagers.

1   Canada, like a clumsy adolescent, has been experiencing growth pangs and searching for an identity for the last century. Partly due to historical events,

it has felt overshadowed and intimidated by its flashier, self-confident southern neighbor. As Canadian scholar Northrop Frye notes,

> American students have been conditioned from infancy to think of themselves as citizens of one of the world's great powers. Canadians are conditioned from infancy to think of themselves as citizens of a country of uncertain identity, a confusing past, and a hazardous future. (57)

2   Although Frye refers to the differences in education between the two cultures, his comment applies to the media, another institution that shapes the ideology of a culture (Fiske, "British" 256). Television shows, in particular, play a vital role in the conditioning of American and Canadian youth. America's *Beverly Hills 90210* and Canada's *Degrassi Junior High*, for instance, both touch on problems of teens maneuvering from the carefree days of childhood to the responsibilities of adulthood. Although similar in content, the stories not only impart but also shape different cultural perceptions of the world. Walter Fisher's narrative paradigm,[1] which examines how symbols are created and communicated through stories ("Narration" 6), sheds light on the American and Canadian worldviews as they appear in *Beverly Hills 90210* and *Degrassi Junior High*, respectively.

Wheels (Neil Hope), Joey (Pat Mastroianni), the aspiring musician, and Snake (Stefan Brogren) in *Degrassi Junior High.*

---

[1] An example or model.

The cast of *Beverly Hills, 90210*. The characters are now enrolled in college.

Teenspeak on the Tube

3   The two shows *Beverly Hills 90210* and *Degrassi Junior High* deal unflinchingly with identical teenage concerns in the same honest approach. They confront not only such common issues as peer pressure, friendships, and sexual relations, but also a litany of social issues such as teen pregnancy and motherhood, abortion, AIDS, child abuse, animal rights, homosexuality, alcoholism, bulimia/anorexia, sexism, epilepsy, drugs, parental neglect, cancer, and death.

4   Clearly, both shows, as most stories, strike a careful balance between pleasure and instruction (Szanto 17). They entertain, yet offer a wealth of information on current topics. Charles Rosin, executive producer of *Beverly Hills 90210*, hopes that "We can have some impact (a) to entertain and (b) when it's over, to get them [the audience] to think about what they have seen, for maybe about five seconds" ("The Summer"). *Degrassi Junior High* executive producer Linda Schuyler shares a similar belief regarding the informational/educational value of her program: "We feel our mandate is to present as many options as possible to our viewers. It's up to the audience to decide what they would do in that situation" ("Degrassi").

5   Thus, on *Beverly Hills 90210*, Brenda thinks she might be pregnant and makes an appointment with a doctor. Waiting for her first gynecologic exami-

nation, she wonders what the stirrups on the examining table are for. By the same token, a lecture on AIDS at Degrassi creates an opportunity to inform teen audiences about the disease. Students ask questions ranging from "What's abstinence?" to whether mosquitoes can transmit the virus.

6. In addition, both programs are careful not to oversimplify issues. Their story lines faithfully depict the conflicting perceptions, values, or prejudices at stake in complex controversies. For example, when a West Beverly teacher is suspended for sexual harassment, the audience discovers that although the victim lied, the teacher is not completely innocent either. Similarly, Degrassi's animal rights activists realize that cosmetics companies test their products on animals for economic reasons, thereby affecting jobs and the lives of real people.

7. Both shows endorse comparable moral values such as truth, honesty, trust, responsibility, reliability, and respect for elders. Because they sanction basic goodness and denounce confusion, error, and evil, they may be considered "true art" (Gardner 106; Fisher, "Narrative" 362).

8. Neither show is above moralizing. For instance, after her pregnancy scare, Brenda says, "I guess I shouldn't have sex if I can't take the consequences." By the same token, in *Degrassi Junior High,* the death of Alex's parents comes across as a form of retribution for his complaints about their good-natured discipline and for his ignoring their curfew.

9. Here stop the similarities. Significantly, the differences between the shows arise from their distinct cultural backgrounds. In *Continental Divide,* Seymour Lipset found that Canadians are more traditional, tolerant, law abiding, egalitarian, collectively oriented, and multicultural than Americans. Americans, in contrast, are more entrepreneurial,[2] individualistic, materialistic, and religious (15, 17, 26). Most of these cultural differences are immediately evident in the opening credit sequence of the programs.

Two Cultures, Two Tales

10. *Beverly Hills 90210*'s credit sequence opens with a group of teens gathering and posing for a "snap-shot." Then each teen is introduced individually with a short clip revealing something about him or her and ending with a closeup and credit. The Beach Boys' music, beach scenery, and surfboards suggest an atmosphere of leisure and group fun. Meanwhile, *Degrassi Junior High* opens with shots of students in class, in the hallways, and on the school grounds. One scene blends into another through visual "wipes" reminiscent of a blackboard being cleaned. Although the camera offers glimpses of the main characters, they are not individually introduced.

11. The openings reflect two distinctive spirits. *Beverly Hills 90210*'s beach theme invites audiences to a moment of escape. Actors strike a pose and look

---

[2] Risk taking; enterprising.

straight at the camera. The acknowledgment of the camera's presence implies that the characters are about to play in a story, whereas *Degrassi Junior High*'s school shots hit at its underlying didacticism, while its documentary-style opening conveys the show's aspirations at realism.

12   Such different presentations reflect cultural differences in audience expectations: American teens firmly believe in dreams, whereas their Canadian counterparts believe in life's sobering lessons. As Lipset shows, dreams fuel American entrepreneurialism, whereas life's lessons inspire traditional Canadian caution.

13   Rather than a typically American focus on individual characters as in *Beverly Hills 90210*, *Degrassi Junior High*'s opening prefers an ensemble approach. This distinction is maintained throughout its narrative structure, which foregrounds a few of the major characters one week and barely acknowledges them the next. *Beverly Hills 90210*, in contrast, keeps all of its main characters in focus, even if they are involved in different subplots. Such narrative structures are in keeping with Lipset's findings that Americans value individualism and Canadians are collectively oriented.

14   *Beverly Hills 90210* celebrates glamour, wealth, and other hegemonic[3] values. Thus, class divisions arise when one teen complains to another about her housekeeper; racial tensions are implied by the absence of visible minorities in school; sexism is blatant in the fact that boys will be boys (with their desire to watch strippers and obsession with sports) and girls will be girls (with their interest in dance, gossip, and fashion). In contrast, there are no class distinctions in *Degrassi Junior High*. Students share a nondescript middle-class lifestyle. The multicultural tableau of characters ranges from WASPy Caitlin to a black nicknamed B.L.T., and Yik, an earring-clad boat person from Vietnam.

15   Moreover, *Degrassi Junior High* defies hegemony in its unfailing criticism of patriarchy, double standards, systemic sexism, and gender-defined expectations. For example, Lucy risks losing a dream date with the captain of the boys' basketball team when she stands up for the practice rights of her volleyball team. Her reward: The jerk dumps her, but she wins the respect and interest of a progressive guy.

16   Whereas persistence and idealistic pursuits pay off in *Beverly Hills 90210*, they are discouraged in *Degrassi Junior High*. Thus, when Donna wishes to meet her favorite band and is about to abandon her quest, Kelly quips, "If we quit now, we're pretty pathetic." Giving up means losing, and losing is just not part of American lore. Similarly, Brandon's fight against racism almost turns sour when members of a predominantly black school accept his invitation to West Beverly's dance. Threats of a racial clash vanish, however, when blacks and whites start to dance together to rap music. The bottom line: Be true to your dreams and all will be well.

17   While obstacles melt away in front of Americans, they keep Canadian dreams in check. In *Degrassi Junior High*, would-be musician Joey repeatedly submits his tape recording to the local radio station—to no avail. His insistence is portrayed as somewhat pathetic; even his friends dismiss him as "just a dreamer."

---

[3] Dominant.

18 In that sense, both shows' narratives translate the values of their respective cultures: The American Dream conquers odds, whereas the Canadian ethos[4] cautions against the very same odds.

19 Despite its setting in Beverly Hills, which evokes avant-garde lifestyles, the show centers on the Walshes, a traditional, *Leave It To Beaver* style family in which parents and children live harmoniously. The Walshes provide an occasional haven to other teens shaken by tempestuous, modern lifestyles. The show's story implies that only a two-parent family can adequately meet teenagers' craving for stability. In contrast, several Degrassi kids live happily with their single parents. *Degrassi Junior High*'s two-parent families do not guarantee happiness. In one episode, Glenn's parents reject him when he tells them he is homosexual. Despite the preponderance of extended families in the States, the American ideal remains the two-parent family, married once and forever. It is perhaps Canada's lack of collective dream that explains its tolerance for diversity and its respect for individual norms. Paradoxically, this tolerance has come to be associated with Canadian identity.

20 Although *Beverly Hills 90210* and *Degrassi Junior High* deal with the same issues, they weave them into their narratives in different ways. On *Beverly Hills 90210*, bad things happen to minor characters only. If they do affect main characters, they either happened to them in an extra-diegetic[5] past (as in Dylan's alcoholism) or almost happen to them. For example, the topic of teenage pregnancy is treated with Brenda's pregnancy scare. Meanwhile, on *Degrassi Junior High,* Spike and Erica really become pregnant.

21 Both shows examine the various options available to teen moms: keeping the baby, giving it up for adoption, or having an abortion. *Degrassi Junior High*'s message is more powerful, however, in that it bears all the credibility and weight of reality. Audiences actually see the fear experienced by expectant teen mothers. *Beverly Hills 90210,* on the other hand, is stuck in the conditional tense. What ifs, no matter how scary they are, do not match the power of real situations.

22 Moreover, *Beverly Hills 90210* conveys the unsettling message that heroes, or "good people," manage somehow to stay out of trouble. On *Degrassi Junior High,* however, life spares no one. Being a story's main player does not confer immunity against life's woes; quite the opposite, major characters are liable to experience issues firsthand, just for the narrative's didactic purposes. For instance, Erica has an emotional encounter with pro-lifers protesting in front of the abortion clinic, and Spike worries about her premature baby girl.

23 It is significant that in terms of narrative probability and fidelity, both shows score high in their respective cultures. This is evidenced by the shows' success: *Beverly Hills 90210* reaches 50 percent of the teens watching television at that time (James), and *Degrassi Junior High* has won several Geminis (the Canadian equivalent of the Emmy). *Degrassi Junior High* and *Beverly Hills*

---

[4] Character; values.

[5] Not in the present story.

90210 both have narrative probability because their characters are consistent with their actions: Punkers behave as punkers; fans are committed to meeting the object of their admiration; and aspiring musicians get caught up in their art. More important, characters experience turmoil in the face of adversity, especially when they need to overcome their prejudices in order to mature.

24   Regarding narrative fidelity, although both shows meet their respective audiences' truth, they might not fare well cross-culturally. Indeed, where American teen audiences identify with Brandon's admirable faith in dreams, Canadian teens, taught to focus on obstacles, may dismiss him as idealistic and unrealistic. By the same token, to American teens who are not used to seeing major players in turmoil, *Degrassi Junior High*'s troubled characters may seem gross exaggerations, or worse, parodies of teenage ills.

25   This cultural clash is evidenced in *Degrassi Junior High*'s being shown on the American PBS network only (instead of a commercial channel) and in *Beverly Hills 90210*'s lukewarm reception in Canada (Godfrey). Moreover, the glamorous lifestyles tend to irk[6] Canadians, who prefer a context to which they can relate. *Globe and Mail* journalist Mark Foss remembers the lack of Canadian shows "back then that spoke to my experience as a teen. . . . Although I didn't know it at the time, my nationalistic soul craved a teenage drama that was both contemporary and Canadian" (C1).

26   The shows' distinctive types of closure also diminish their cross-cultural narrative fidelity: *Beverly Hills 90210* episodes have narrative closure, whereas *Degrassi Junior High* shows are often left open-ended.

27   *Beverly Hills 90210* generally ends up with a complete resolution of the crisis of the day, thereby providing a reassuring, upbeat ending. Such closure is in keeping with the American belief that the realization of one's dreams must be—and can be—part of one's lifetime achievements. For instance, not only does Donna meet her favorite band, they also sing for her at her favorite hangout.

28   *Degrassi Junior High* episodes, however, remain unresolved, stressing the overwhelming continuity of life. As Frye says, Canadians are taught that the future is hazardous (57). Unlike Americans, the future doesn't belong to Canadians. Elements beyond Canadians' control keep their dreams in check, forcing them to improvise their lives continuously. Thus, after telling his parents he's gay, Glenn must leave home. When his younger brother inquires when they will see each other again, Glenn answers, "When I'm welcome here again." In other words, their next meeting depends on their parents' whim, not on the brothers' will.

29   A dispute between PBS network executives and *Degrassi Junior High* creators further illustrates the differences in worldviews between Americans and Canadians. The quarrel arose when PBS decided to modify the ending of one episode dealing with abortion. In the original Canadian ending, the camera follows Erica as she carves a path through a sea of pro-life protesters gathered

---

[6] Irritate; annoy.

in front of the abortion clinic. There are shouts of "killer, murderer" as a closeup dwells on a realistic plastic replica of a fetus that is brandished by one of the pro-lifers. In the words of the critic, it is "an extraordinarily powerful scene" (Haslett Cuff).

30 PBS, however, decided to cut the episode at the point when the girl begins to walk toward the crowd. The tampered-with ending incensed the show's creator Kit Wood, who charged, "This changes the whole thing. What they've done gives it an American ending, happy, and safe" (Haslett Cuff).

31 The PBS version made Erica's ordeal seem simple and painless: It ignored her journey through the protest and, in particularly, the sight of the plastic fetus, which rekindles the guilt feelings she managed to suppress. In contrast, the original ending provided insight into Erica's moral dilemma and emotional turmoil.

Conclusion

32 As popular teen programs, *Beverly Hills 90210* and *Degrassi Junior High* honestly address identical contemporary topics that are of interest to their audiences. Although their basic moral tenets[7] (truthfulness, honesty, parental respect, goodness, etc.) are similar, their worldviews differ drastically. The shows tell distinct stories that reflect and construct two different perspectives of the world. *Beverly Hills 90210* celebrates the pursuit of dreams, persistence, individualism, hegemony, and materialism; *Degrassi Junior High* extols caution, tolerance, collectivism, multiculturalism, and egalitarianism.

33 Such divergent values might collide in a cross-cultural context. *Degrassi Junior High* fans might dismiss *Beverly Hills 90210* as unrealistically glamorous and superficial, while *Beverly Hills 90210* aficionados might deem *Degrassi Junior High* as too didactic and contrived. In other words, cultural boundaries may limit the shows' narrative fidelity.

34 In short, the two programs bear the ideological[8] imprint of their respective cultures. The application of the narrative paradigm to *Beverly Hills 90210* and *Degrassi Junior High* confirms what Lipset and Frye have said: Americans and Canadians may share the same continent, but they do not share the same outlooks on life.

Works Cited

"Degrassi Finds Formula for Success." *Calgary Herald* 4 Jan. 1988: B8.

Fisher, Walter, "Narration as a Human Communication Paradigm: The Case of Public Moral Argument." *Communication Monographs* 51 (Mar. 1984): 1–22.

———. "The Narrative Paradigm: An Elaboration." *Communication Monographs* 52 (Dec. 1985): 347–66.

---

[7] Principles.

[8] Relating to ideas, values, and attitudes.

Fiske, John. "British Cultural Studies." *Channels of Discourse.* Ed. Robert C. Allen. Chapel Hill: U of North Carolina P, 1987. 254–90.

———. *Understanding Popular Culture.* Cambridge: Unwin Hyman, 1989.

Foss, Mark. "A Certain Canadianness and Resistance to Formula Set Degrassi Apart." *Globe and Mail* 11 Feb. 1991: C1.

Frye, Northrop. *Divisions on a Ground: Essays on Canadian Culture.* Toronto: House of Anansi, 1982.

Gardner, John. *On Moral Fiction.* New York: Basic Books, 1978.

Godfrey, Stephen. "The Young and the Feckless." *Globe and Mail* 14 Nov. 1992: C1.

Haslett Cuff, John. "Degrassi High Creators Up in Arms Over PBS Cuts to Abortion Episode." *Globe and Mail* 3 Nov. 1989: C11.

James, Caryn. "90210 Goes to the Head of the Class." *New York Times* 4 Aug. 1991: 11:29.

Leitch, Thomas M. *What Stories Are: Narrative Theory and Interpretation.* University Park: Pennsylvania State UP, 1986.

Lipset, Seymour Martin. *Continental Divide.* New York: Routledge, 1990.

"The Summer Rerun of '92." *The Toronto Star Starweek* 10 July 1992: 4.

Szanto, George. *Narrative Taste and Social Perspectives: The Matter of Quality.* London: Macmillan, 1987.

REACTING

1. Respond to Marie-Claire Simonetti's list of differences between Canadian and American cultures. What would you add to or subtract from her list?

2. Explain and discuss Simonetti's claim (last paragraph) that "the two programs bear the ideological imprint of their respective cultures."

CONNECTING

1. Turn to p. 9 and read William O'Brien's essay ("The Cruel Logic of Teenage Violence") and add to the list of American cultural values that Simonetti's article provides. Now compare this list with the one you created earlier in "Reacting."

2. Use Simonetti's article to help you respond to one or both of this chapter's key questions: "How has American culture shaped you to be the person you are?" and "How much impact do the mass media have on us and our culture?"

LEARNING ABOUT WRITING FROM READING

Simonetti uses a standard comparison and contrast pattern to organize her ideas: the so-called "point-by-point" method. In other words, instead of telling you everything about "Degrassi Junior High" and then everything about "Beverly Hills 90210," she takes one issue (or point) at a time, and relates it to both shows. Then she moves on to her next point and relates it to both shows, and so on.

Here's an example of a typical comparative paragraph:

> Both shows examine the various options available to teen moms: keeping the baby, giving it up for adoption, or having an abortion. *Degrassi Junior High's* message is more powerful, however, in that it bears all the credibility and weight of reality. Audiences actually see the fear experienced by expectant teen mothers. *Beverly Hills 90210, on the other hand,* is stuck in the conditional tense. What ifs, no matter how scary they are, do not match the power of real situations. [Paragraph 21]

The simple, but neat, switch from one show to the other is achieved with the useful phrase "on the other hand."

GLORIA STEINEM

Sex, Lies, and Advertising

Gloria Steinem, co-founder of Ms. *magazine, looks at how an editor deals with the powerful influence of advertising in the publishing world.*

BEFORE YOU READ

1. Do we have a free press in this country? Explain your answer.
2. As an advertiser in a magazine, what would you expect or demand from the publishers in return for your money?

1   About three years ago, as *glasnost* was beginning and *Ms.* seemed to be ending, I was invited to a press lunch for a Soviet official. He entertained us with anecdotes about new problems of democracy in his country. Local Communist leaders were being criticized in their media for the first time, he explained, and they were angry.

2   "So I'll have to ask my American friends," he finished pointedly, "how more *subtly* to control the press." In the silence that followed, I said, "Advertising."

3   The reporters laughed, but later, one of them took me aside: How *dare* I suggest that freedom of the press was limited? How dare I imply that his newsweekly could be influenced by ads?

4   I explained that I was thinking of advertising's media-wide influence on most of what we read. Even newsmagazines use "soft" cover stories to sell ads, confuse readers with "advertorials," and occasionally self-censor on subjects known to be a problem with big advertisers.

5   But, I also explained, I was thinking especially of women's magazines. There, it isn't just a little content that's devoted to attracting ads, it's almost all

of it. That's why advertisers—not readers—have always been the problem for *Ms*. As the only women's magazine that didn't supply what the ad world euphemistically[1] describes as "supportive editorial atmosphere" or "complementary copy" (for instance, articles that praise food/fashion/beauty subjects to "support" and "complement" food/fashion/beauty ads), *Ms*. could never attract enough advertising to break even.

6 "Oh, *women's* magazines," the journalist said with contempt. "Everybody knows they're catalogs—but who cares? They have nothing to do with journalism."

7 I can't tell you how many times I've had this argument in 25 years of working for many kinds of publications. Except as moneymaking machines—"cash cows" as they are so elegantly called in the trade—women's magazines are rarely taken seriously. Though changes being made by women have been called more far-reaching than the industrial revolution—and though many editors try hard to reflect some of them in the few pages left to them after all the ad-related subjects have been covered—the magazines serving the female half of this country are still far below the journalistic and ethical standards of news and general interest publications. Most depressing of all, this doesn't even rate an exposé.

8 If *Time* and *Newsweek* had to lavish praise on cars in general and credit General Motors in particular to get GM ads, there would be a scandal—maybe a criminal investigation. When women's magazines from *Seventeen* to *Lear's* praise beauty products in general and credit Revlon in particular to get ads, it's just business as usual.

1

9 When *Ms*. began, we didn't consider *not* taking ads. The most important reason was keeping the price of a feminist magazine low enough for most women to afford. But the second and almost equal reason was providing a forum where women and advertisers could talk to each other and improve advertising itself. After all, it was (and still is) as potent a source of information in this country as news or TV and movie dramas.

10 We decided to proceed in two stages. First, we would convince makers of "people products" used by both men and women but advertised mostly to men—cars, credit cards, insurance, sound equipment, financial services, and the like—that their ads should be placed in a women's magazine. Since they were accustomed to the divisions between editorial and advertising in news and general interest magazines, this would allow our editorial content to be free and diverse. Second, we would add the best ads for whatever traditional "women's products" (clothes, shampoo, fragrance, food, and so on) that surveys showed *Ms*. readers used. But we would ask them to come in *without* the usual quid pro quo of "complementary copy."

11 We knew the second step might be harder. Food advertisers have always demanded that women's magazines publish recipes and articles on entertaining

---

[1] Using an inoffensive term.

(preferably ones that name their products) in return for their ads; clothing advertisers expect to be surrounded by fashion spreads (especially ones that credit their designers); and shampoo, fragrance, and beauty products in general usually insist on positive editorial coverage of beauty subjects, plus photo credits besides. That's why women's magazines look the way they do. But if we could break this link between ads and editorial content, then we wanted good ads for "women's products," too.

12   By playing their part in this unprecedented[2] mix of *all* the things our readers need and use, advertisers also would be rewarded: Ads for products like cars and mutual funds would find a new growth market; the best ads for women's products would no longer be lost in oceans of ads for the same category; and both would have access to a laboratory of smart and caring readers whose response would help create effective ads for other media as well.

13   I thought then that our main problem would be the imagery in ads themselves. Car makers were still draping blondes in evening gowns over the hoods like ornaments. Authority figures were almost always male, even in ads for products that only women used. Sadistic, he-man campaigns even won industry praise. (For instance, *Advertising Age* had hailed the infamous Silva Thin cigarette theme, "How to Get a Woman's Attention: Ignore Her," as "brilliant.") Even in medical journals, tranquilizer ads showed depressed housewives standing beside piles of dirty dishes and promised to get them back to work.

14   Obviously, *Ms.* would have to avoid such ads and seek out the best ones—but this didn't seem impossible. *The New Yorker* had been selecting ads for aesthetic reasons for years, a practice that only seemed to make advertisers more eager to be in its pages. *Ebony* and *Essence* were asking for ads with positive black images, and though their struggle was hard, they weren't being called unreasonable.

15   Clearly, what *Ms.* needed was a very special publisher and ad sales staff. I could think of only one woman with experience on the business side of magazines—Patricia Carbine, who recently had become a vice president of *McCall's* as well as its editor in chief—and the reason I knew her name was a good omen. She had been managing editor at *Look* (really *the* editor, but its owner refused to put a female name at the top of his masthead) when I was writing a column there. After I did an early interview with Cesar Chavez, then just emerging as a leader of migrant labor, and the publisher turned it down because he was worried about ads from Sunkist, Pat was the one who intervened. As I learned later, she had told the publisher she would resign if the interview wasn't published. Mainly because *Look* couldn't afford to lose Pat, it *was* published (and the ads from Sunkist never arrived).

16   Though I barely knew this woman, she had done two things I always remembered: put her job on the line in a way that editors often talk about but rarely do, and been so loyal to her colleagues that she never told me or anyone outside *Look* that she had done so.

---

[2] Something not done before; new.

17   Fortunately, Pat did agree to leave *McCall's* and take a huge cut in salary to become publisher of *Ms*. She became responsible for training and inspiring generations of young women who joined the *Ms*. ad sales force, many of whom went on to become "firsts" at the top of publishing. When *Ms*. first started, however, there were so few women with experience selling space that Pat and I made the rounds of ad agencies ourselves. Later, the fact that *Ms*. was asking companies to do business in a different way meant our saleswomen had to make many times the usual numbers of calls—first to convince agencies and then client companies besides—and to present endless amounts of research. I was often asked to do a final ad presentation, or see some higher decision-maker, or speak to women employees so executives could see the interest of women they worked with. That's why I spent more time persuading advertisers than editing or writing for *Ms*. and why I ended up with an unsentimental education in the seamy underside of publishing that few writers see (and even fewer magazines can publish).

18   Let me take you with us through some experiences, just as they happened:

19   • In the *Ms*. Gazette, we do a brief report on a congressional hearing into chemicals used in hair dyes that are absorbed through the skin and may be carcinogenic. Newspapers report this too, but Clairol, a Bristol-Myers subsidiary that makes dozens of products—a few of which have just begun to advertise in *Ms*.—is outraged. Not at newspapers or newsmagazines, just at us. It's bad enough that *Ms*. is the only women's magazine refusing to provide the usual "complementary" articles and beauty photos, but to criticize one of their categories—*that* is going too far.

20   We offer to publish a letter from Clairol telling its side of the story. In an excess of solicitousness, we even put this letter in the Gazette, not in Letters to the Editors where it belongs. Nonetheless—and in spite of surveys that show *Ms*. readers are active women who use more of almost everything Clairol makes than do the readers of any other women's magazine—*Ms*. gets almost none of these ads for the rest of its natural life.

21   Meanwhile, Clairol changes its hair-coloring formula, apparently in response to the hearings we reported.

22   • When *Ms*. begins, the staff decides not to accept ads for feminine hygiene sprays or cigarettes: they are damaging and carry no appropriate health warnings. Though we don't think we should tell our readers what to do, we do think we should provide facts so they can decide for themselves. Since the antismoking lobby has been pressing for health warnings on cigarette ads, we decide to take them only as they comply.

23   Philip Morris is among the first to do so. One of its brands, Virginia Slims, is also sponsoring women's tennis and the first national polls of women's opinions. On the other hand, the Virginia Slims theme, "You've come a long way, baby," has more than a "baby" problem. It makes smoking a symbol of progress for women.

24   We explain to Philip Morris that this slogan won't do well in our pages, but they are convinced its success with some women means it will work with *all* women. Finally, we agree to publish an ad for a Virginia Slims calendar as a test. The letters from readers are critical—and smart. For instance: Would you show

a black man picking cotton, the same man in a Cardin suit, and symbolize the antislavery and civil rights movements by smoking? Of course not. But instead of honoring the test results, the Philip Morris people seem angry to be proven wrong. They take away ads for *all* their many brands.

25   This costs *Ms.* about $250,000 the first year. After five years, we can no longer keep track. Occasionally, a new set of executives listens to *Ms.* saleswomen, but because we won't take Virginia Slims, not one Philip Morris product returns to our pages for the next 16 years.

26   Gradually, we also realize our naiveté in thinking we *could* decide against taking cigarette ads. They became a disproportionate support of magazines the moment they were banned on television, and few magazines could compete and survive without them; certainly not *Ms.*, which lacks so many other categories. By the time statistics in the 1980s showed that women's rate of lung cancer was approaching men's, the necessity of taking cigarette ads has become a kind of prison.

27   • We hear in 1980 that women in the Soviet Union have been producing feminist *samizdat* (underground, self-published books) and circulating them throughout the country. As punishment, four of the leaders have been exiled. Though we are operating on our usual shoestring, we solicit individual contributions to send Robin Morgan to interview these women in Vienna.

28   The result is an exclusive cover story that includes the first news of a populist peace movement against the Afghanistan occupation, a prediction of *glasnost* to come, and a grassroots, intimate view of Soviet women's lives. From the popular press to women's studies courses, the response is great. The story wins a Front Page award.

29   Nonetheless, this journalistic coup[3] undoes years of efforts to get an ad schedule from Revlon. Why? Because the Soviet women on our cover *are not wearing make-up*.

30   • Four years of research and presentations go into convincing airlines that women now make travel choices and business trips. United, the first airline to advertise in *Ms.*, is so impressed with the response from our readers that one of its executives appears in a film for our ad presentations. As usual, good ads get great results.

31   But we have problems unrelated to such results. For instance: Because American Airlines flight attendants include among their labor demands the stipulation that they could choose to have their last names preceded by "Ms." on their name tags—in a long-delayed revolt against the standard, "I am your pilot, Captain Rothgart, and this is your flight attendant, Cindy Sue"— American officials seem to hold the magazine responsible. We get no ads.

32   There is still a different problem at Eastern. A vice president cancels subscriptions for thousands of copies on Eastern flights. Why? Because he is offended by ads for lesbian poetry journals in the *Ms.* Classified. A "family airline," as he explains to me coldly on the phone, has to "draw the line somewhere."

---

[3] A masterstroke; something brilliantly done.

33   It's obvious that *Ms.* can't exclude lesbians and serve women. We've been trying to make that point ever since our first issue included an article by and about lesbians, and both Suzanne Levine, our managing editor, and I were lectured by such heavy hitters as Ed Kosner, then editor of *Newsweek* (and now of *New York Magazine*), who insisted that *Ms.* should "position" itself *against* lesbians. But our advertisers have paid to reach a guaranteed number of readers, and soliciting new subscriptions to compensate for Eastern would cost $150,000, plus rebating money in the meantime.

34   Like almost everything ad-related, this presents an elaborate organizing problem. After days of searching for sympathetic members of the Eastern board, Frank Thomas, president of the Ford Foundation, kindly offers to call Roswell Gilpatrick, a director of Eastern. I talk with Mr. Gilpatrick, who calls Frank Borman, then the president of Eastern. Frank Borman calls me to say that his airline is not in the business of censoring magazines: *Ms.* will be returned to Eastern flights.

35   • Women's access to insurance and credit is vital, but with the exception of Equitable and a few other ad pioneers, such financial services address men. For almost a decade after the Equal Credit Opportunity Act passes in 1974, we try to convince American Express that women are a growth market—but nothing works.

36   Finally, a former professor of Russian named Jerry Welsh becomes head of marketing. He assumes that women should be cardholders, and persuades his colleagues to feature women in a campaign. Thanks to this 1980s series, the growth rate for female cardholders surpasses that for men.

37   For this article, I asked Jerry Welsh if he would explain why American Express waited so long. "Sure," he said, "they were afraid of having a 'pink' card."

38   • Women of color read *Ms.* in disproportionate numbers. This is a source of pride to *Ms.* staffers, who are also more racially representative than the editors of other women's magazines. But this reality is obscured by ads filled with enough white women to make a reader snowblind.

39   Pat Carbine remembers mostly "astonishment" when she requested African American, Hispanic, Asian, and other diverse images. Marcia Ann Gillespie, a *Ms.* editor who was previously the editor in chief of *Essence,* witnesses ad bias a second time: Having tried for *Essence* to get white advertisers to use black images (Revlon did so eventually, but L'Oréal, Lauder, Chanel, and other companies never did), she sees similar problems getting integrated ads for an integrated magazine. Indeed, the ad world often creates black and Hispanic ads only for black and Hispanic media. In an exact parallel of the fear that marketing a product to women will endanger its appeal to men, the response is usually, "But your [white] readers won't identify."

40   In fact, those we are able to get—for instance, a Max Factor ad made for *Essence* that Linda Wachner gives us after she becomes president—are praised by white readers, too. But there are pathetically few such images.

41   • By the end of 1986, production and mailing costs have risen astronomically, ad income is flat, and competition for ads is stiffer than ever. The 60/40 pre-

ponderance of edit over ads that we promised to readers becomes 50/50; children's stories, most poetry, and some fiction are casualties of less space; in order to get variety into limited pages, the length (and sometimes the depth) of articles suffers; and, though we do refuse most of the ads that would look like a parody in our pages, we get so worn down that some slip through. Still, readers perform miracles. Though we haven't been able to afford a subscription mailing in two years, they maintain our guaranteed circulation of 450,000.

42 Nonetheless, media reports on *Ms.* often insist that our unprofitability must be due to reader disinterest. The myth that advertisers simply follow readers is very strong. Not one reporter notes that other comparable magazines our size (say, *Vanity Fair* or *The Atlantic*) have been losing more money in one year than *Ms.* has lost in 16 years. No matter how much never-to-be-recovered cash is poured into starting a magazine or keeping one going, appearances seem to be all that matter. (Which is why we haven't been able to explain our fragile state in public. Nothing causes ad flight like the smell of nonsuccess.)

43 My healthy response is anger. My not-so-healthy response is constant worry. Also an obsession with finding one more rescue. There is hardly a night when I don't wake up with sweaty palms and pounding heart, scared that we won't be able to pay the printer or the post office; scared most of all that closing our doors will hurt the women's movement.

44 Out of chutzpah[4] and desperation, I arrange a lunch with Leonard Lauder, president of Estée Lauder. With the exception of Clinique (the brainchild of Carol Phillips), none of Lauder's hundreds of products has been advertised in *Ms.* A year's schedule of ads for just three or four of them could save us. Indeed, as the scion of a family-owned company whose ad practices are followed by the beauty industry, he is one of the few men who could liberate many pages in all women's magazines just by changing his mind about "complementary copy."

45 Over a lunch that costs more than we can pay for some articles, I explain the need for his leadership. I also lay out the record of *Ms.*: more literary and journalistic prizes won, more new issues introduced into the mainstream, new writers discovered, and impact on society than any other magazine; more articles that became books, stories that became movies, ideas that became television series, and newly advertised products that became profitable; and, most important for him, a place for his ads to reach women who aren't reachable through any other women's magazine. Indeed, if there is one constant characteristic of the ever-changing *Ms.* readership, it is their impact as leaders. Whether it's waiting until later to have first babies, or pioneering PABA as sun protection in cosmetics, *whatever* they are doing today, a third to a half of American women will be doing three to five years from now. It's never failed.

46 But, he says, *Ms.* readers are not *our* women. They're not interested in things like fragrance and blush-on. If they were, *Ms.* would write articles about them.

---

[4] Boldness; brazenness.

47 On the contrary, I explain, surveys show they are more likely to buy such things than the readers of, say, *Cosmopolitan* or *Vogue*. They're good customers because they're out in the world enough to need several sets of everything: home, work, purse, travel, gym, and so on. They just don't need to read articles about these things. Would he ask a men's magazine to publish monthly columns on how to shave before he advertised Aramis products (his line for men)?

48 He concedes that beauty features are often concocted[5] more for advertisers than readers. But *Ms.* isn't appropriate for his ads anyway, he explains. Why? Because Estée Lauder is selling a "kept-woman mentality."

49 I can't quite believe this. Sixty percent of the users of his products are salaried, and generally resemble *Ms.* readers. Besides, his company has the appeal of having been started by a creative and hardworking woman, his mother, Estée Lauder.

50 That doesn't matter, he says. He knows his customers, and they would *like* to be kept women. That's why he will never advertise in *Ms.*

51 In November 1987, by vote of the Ms. Foundation for Education and Communication (*Ms.*'s owner and publisher, the media subsidiary of the Ms. Foundation for Women), *Ms.* was sold to a company whose officers, Australian feminists Sandra Yates and Anne Summers, raised the investment money in their country that *Ms.* couldn't find in its own. They also started *Sassy* for teenage women.

52 In their two-year tenure, circulation was raised to 550,000 by investment in circulation mailings, and, to the dismay of some readers, editorial features on clothes and new products made a more traditional bid for ads. Nonetheless, ad pages fell below previous levels. In addition, *Sassy,* whose fresh voice and sexual frankness were an unprecedented success with young readers, was targeted by two mothers from Indiana who began, as one of them put it, "calling every Christian organization I could think of." In response to this controversy, several crucial advertisers pulled out.

53 Such links between ads and editorial content was a problem in Australia, too, but to a lesser degree. "Our readers pay two times more for their magazines," Anne explained, "so advertisers have less power to threaten a magazine's viability."

54 "I was shocked," said Sandra Yates with characteristic directness. "In Australia, we think you have freedom of the press—but you don't."

55 Since Anne and Sandra had not met their budget's projections for ad revenue, their investors forced a sale. In October 1989, *Ms.* and *Sassy* were bought by Dale Lang, owner of *Working Mother, Working Woman,* and one of the few independent publishing companies left among the conglomerates. In response to a request from the original *Ms.* staff—as well as to reader letters urging that *Ms.* continue, plus his own belief that *Ms.* would benefit his other magazines by blazing a trail—he agreed to try the ad-free, reader-supported *Ms.* . . . and to give us complete editorial control.

---

[5] Designed; put together.

REACTING

1. After reading this article, will you look differently at the advertisements you see in magazines? How?
2. Does advertising work to limit free speech? How does your view compare to Gloria Steinem's? How might advertisers respond to her article?

CONNECTING

1. Turn to p. 32 and read Ishmael Reed's "Tuning Out Network Bias." Both Reed and Steinem write about media bias and stereotypes. How might they agree or disagree on what to do about it?
2. What answer does this article give to the question "Who decides what we read, see and hear in the mass media?"

LEARNING ABOUT WRITING FROM READING

Steinem starts with a story and a personal experience that focus on the point of her whole article. This particular introduction catches our interest for three reasons: it uses a question and answer, it is controversial, and it is personal. Look at how dramatically and quickly she frames the issue in paragraph 2:

> "So I'll have to ask my American friends," he [the Russian official] finished pointedly, "how more *subtly* to control the press." In the silence that followed, I said, "Advertising."

This anecdote works well too because it emphasizes the main point of the article for the reader.

MARIE WINN

The Effects of Television on Family Life

Marie Winn, author of The Plug-In Drug, *a book on television from which this essay is taken, here examines the impact of television on American family life.*

BEFORE YOU READ

1. Imagine what your family's life might have been like without television. What would have been different? What would have stayed the same?
2. Does television have an effect on your family life that is mainly negative or mainly positive? Give examples.

1. Television's contribution to family life has been an equivocal[1] one. For while it has, indeed, kept the members of the family from dispersing, it has not served to bring them *together*. By its domination of the time families spend together, it destroys the special quality that distinguishes one family from another, a quality that depends to a great extent on what a family *does*, what special rituals, game, recurrent jokes, familiar songs, and shared activities it accumulates.

2. "Like the sorcerer of old," writes Urie Bronfenbrenner, "the television set casts its magic spell, freezing speech and action, turning the living into silent statues so long as the enchantment lasts. The primary danger of the television screen lies not so much in the behavior it produces—although there is danger there—as in the behavior it prevents: the talks, the games, the family festivities and arguments through which much of the child's learning takes place and through which his character is formed. Turning on the television set can turn off the process that transforms children into people."[2]

3. Yet parents have accepted a television-dominated family life so completely that they cannot see how the medium is involved in whatever problems they might be having. A first-grade teacher reports:

4. "I have one child in the group who's an only child. I wanted to find out more about her family life because this little girl was quite isolated from the group, didn't make friends, so I talked to her mother. Well, they don't have time to do anything in the evening, the mother said. The parents come home after picking up the child at the babysitter's. Then the mother fixes dinner while the child watches TV. Then they have dinner and the child goes to bed. I said to this mother, 'Well, couldn't she help you fix dinner? That would be a nice time for the two of you to talk,' and the mother said, 'Oh, but I'd hate to have her miss "Zoom." It's such a good program!'"

5. Even when families make efforts to control television, too often its very presence counterbalances the positive features of family life. A writer and mother of two boys aged 3 and 7 described her family's television schedule in *The New York Times:*

6. We were in the midst of a full-scale war. Every day was a new battle and every program was a major skirmish. We agreed it was a bad scene all around and were ready to enter diplomatic negotiations. . . . In principle we have agreed on 2 1/2 hours of TV a day, "Sesame Street," "Electric Company" (with dinner gobbled up in between) and two half-hour shows between 7 and 8:30 which enables the grown-ups to eat in peace and prevents the two boys from destroying one another. Their pre-bedtime choice is dreadful, because, as Josh recently admitted, "There's nothing much on I really like." So . . . .

---

[1] Doubtful; uncertain.

[2] Urie Bronfenbrenner, "Who Cares for America's Children?" Address presented at the Conference of the National Association for the Education of Young Children, 1970.

it's "What's My Line" or "To Tell the Truth." .... Clearly there is a need for first-rate children's shows at this time. ....[3]

7   Consider the "family life" described here: Presumably the father comes home from work during the "Sesame Street"–"Electric Company" stint. The children are either watching television, gobbling their dinner, or both. While the parents eat their dinner in peaceful privacy, the children watch another hour of television. Then there is only a half-hour left before bedtime, just enough time for baths, getting pajamas on, brushing teeth, and so on. The children's evening is regimented with an almost military precision. They watch their favorite programs, and when there is "nothing much on I really like," they watch whatever else is on—because *watching* is the important thing. Their mother does not see anything amiss with watching programs just for the sake of watching; she only wishes there were some first-rate children's shows on at those times.

8   Without conjuring up memories of the Victorian era with family games and long, leisurely meals, and large families, the question arises: isn't there a better family life available than this dismal, mechanized arrangement of children watching television for however long is allowed them, evening after evening?

9   Of course, families today still do *special* things together at times: go camping in the summer, go to the zoo on a nice Sunday, take various trips and expeditions. But their *ordinary* daily life together is diminished—that sitting around at the dinner table, that spontaneous[4] taking up of an activity, those little games invented by children on the spur of the moment when there is nothing else to do, the scribbling, the chatting, and even the quarreling, all the things that form the fabric of a family, that define a childhood. Instead, the children have their regular schedule of television programs and bedtime, and the parents have their peaceful dinner together.

10   The author of the article in the *Times* notes that "keeping a family sane means mediating between the needs of both children and adults." But surely the needs of adults are being better met than the needs of the children, who are effectively shunted away and rendered untroublesome, while the parents enjoy a life as undemanding as that of any childless couple. In reality, it is those very demands that young children make upon a family that lead to growth, and it is the way parents accede to those demands that builds the relationships upon which the future of the family depends. If the family does not accumulate its backlog of shared experiences, shared *everyday* experiences that occur and recur and change and develop, then it is not likely to survive as anything other than a caretaking institution.

---

[3] Eleanor Dienstag, "What Will the Kids Talk About? Proust?" *The New York Times,* December 24, 1972.

[4] Unplanned; impulsive.

REACTING

1. What point did you find most disturbing in Marie Winn's essay? Why?
2. Do you agree with Winn's assessment of television's impact on family life? What evidence and examples do you find most convincing? What ones unconvincing?

CONNECTING

1. Turn to p. 43 and read William Lee Miller's "Television Power and American Values." How would Miller most likely react to Winn's article?
2. What effects do the mass media have on our lives? Does Winn talk about the effects of particular programs to answer that question?

LEARNING ABOUT WRITING FROM READING

As readers, we usually hope that first paragraphs will guide us through the rest of an essay or article. Sometimes we look for a "thesis statement," also called a "main point" or a "main idea." Winn's first paragraph does in fact contain such a statement, about what television does to the family: "For while it [television] has, indeed, kept the members of the family from dispersing, it has not served to bring them *together*." This main idea is then supported with evidence and illustration as the essay proceeds. Winn's essay fulfills the promise of the opening statement and tries to prove that television gathers people together in front of the screen but stops them from communicating with one another—particularly children with their parents.

As writers, we should try to signal the topic of our paper, as Winn does, to make our readers' lives easier. It is also worth noting how this main idea is also in the title of the essay *and* explains the opening (and more difficult) sentence: "Television's contribution to family life has been an equivocal one." Both the title and this sentence provide additional helpful signals to the reader about what's coming later.

ISHMAEL REED

Tuning Out Network Bias

Ishmael Reed, author of an essay collection entitled Writin' Is Fightin', *examines stereotypes about African Americans that are found in regular television news coverage.*

BEFORE YOU READ

1. In just a couple of sentences, explain what the article's title means to you.
2. What bias, if any, have you noticed in television news coverage?

1   In 1989, during a panel discussion at the Bumbershoot Arts Festival in Seattle, I expressed dismay at television's relentlessly negative news coverage of African Americans and Hispanic Americans. Half-seriously, I suggested that a boycott[1] of prime-time network news might be in order. I was shocked by the sustained applause that greeted this remark from an audience that was predominantly white.

2   Now, I and my colleagues at PEN Oakland, a branch of the International writers group that fights censorship, and writers in 13 cities are boycotting prime-time network news for the month of April. These programs are the chief source of information that Americans receive about the world. More often than

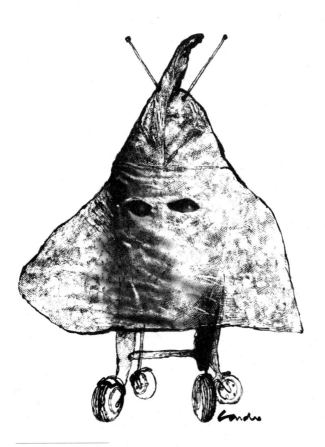

[1] Decision not to use or be involved with.

not, they associate black and Hispanic people exclusively with drugs, crime, unwed parenthood, welfare, homelessness, child abuse and rape, although the majority of the people involved in these circumstances are white.

3   The networks' reasoning seems to be that if blacks weren't here, the United States would be a paradise where people would work 24 hours a day, drink milk, go to church and be virgins until marriage. Yet, to cite but one example, a *USA Today* poll showed that 15 percent of the drug users in America are black, while 70 percent are white. According to *Black Entertainment News*, however, television news associates drugs with blacks 50 percent of the time while only 32 percent of the drug stories focus on whites.

4   Last month, NBC and CNN used blacks exclusively to illustrate Justice Department statistics about both black and white crime. On NBC's report, a white family was used to show the vulnerability of Americans to crime. At the end of the segment, black children were seen dancing in the street while a reporter commented on youthful drug dealers. Whether their participation was staged or whether these kids were engaged in the drug trade was unclear.

5   Recently Ed Turner, executive vice president of CNN, said that black faces go with drug stories because journalists "rely upon local police forces when busts are going to be made, and don't get calls saying there's going to be a bust of a high school in a white neighborhood." But when Home Box Office—not a network organization—did a feature called "Crack U.S.A.," it located a number of white crack users.

6   Many blacks were offended by CBS's widely seen "48 Hours on Crack Street," which seemed to attribute the crack problem to blacks, stigmatizing an entire class of people. Similarly, in a regular feature on ABC World News Tonight called "The American Agenda," blacks are disproportionately associated with "underclass" activities.

7   There is another problem that we minority citizens have with network news. If I have a beef with newspaper coverage, I can always write a letter, which may get published. And newspapers, to their credit, often print stories that reveal that some of their emotional and sensational Op-Ed writers and columnists are pushing myths about minority citizens.

8   Local television stations include community programs moderated by black, Hispanic and Asian American people. Radio stations include call-in programs that are as close to participatory democracy as you're likely to get from the electronic media.

9   Network news organizations, however, provide no opportunity to challenge their stories. With the elimination of the fairness doctrine, they aren't obligated to provide equal time to opposing viewpoints. The exclusion of a variety of viewpoints and the inability to respond to unbalanced stories are just as much a censorship problem as is the suppression of books and writers in other countries.

10 Alix Christie, a columnist for *The Oakland Tribune*, described the kick-off meeting for the PEN boycott as "the truest town meeting I've seen." The main purpose of the boycott is to educate the public in a way that the studies, articles

and reports about bias in network news coverage have apparently failed to do. So far, NBC, ABC and CNN have taken an interest in our complaints; I hope we continue a dialogue. But if the situation doesn't improve, we will come back in 1992 with a new boycott. We might even complain to their sponsors.

REACTING

1. Is your view of network news bias the same as Ishmael Reed's? Explain.
2. What other kinds of bias do you find on television news, both local and network?

CONNECTING

1. How are the ethnic stereotypes described by Reed similar to the sexist stereotypes described by Gloria Steinem in "Sex, Lies, and Advertising" (p. 21)?
2. How might Reed answer the question "Who controls what we see, read, and hear in the mass media?"

LEARNING ABOUT WRITING FROM READING

This article shows how a writer can inject his own personality into his writing without becoming too aggressive or overbearing in tone. Notice that Reed uses the first-person singular pronoun "I" in his article, particularly in the first two paragraphs and then again toward the end: "I expressed dismay," "I suggested," and "I was shocked" all occur in the first paragraph, and he concludes with "I hope we continue a dialogue" in the last paragraph.

Student writers (and others) often ask if it is all right to use "I" in their papers. Reed shows that use of the first-person pronoun can help to show the writer's commitment to his topic as long as it isn't overdone and as long as it doesn't lead the writer into too many statements of the obvious, such as "I think," or "I feel," or "I am going to write about."

CRAIG MCLAUGHLIN AND BARRY YEOMAN

Don't Ask, Don't Tell: What You Didn't Hear on the Six O'Clock News

The authors, both journalists, sum up an annual report on important stories missed or underreported by the press.

BEFORE YOU READ

1. Write down the ten news stories that you think got the most media coverage last year.
2. Write down the ten most important problems we face today. What does a comparison of the two lists suggest to you?

1   Nine out of 10 children slain in industrialized countries are slain in the United States.

2   That shameful statistic should be embedded in our brains. But when the United Nations released that and other damning facts in its report, *The Progress of Nations,* last September, its findings went unheralded by the U.S. media. They apparently didn't consider it particularly newsworthy that people between the ages of 15 and 24 in this country suffer a homicide rate five times that of any other industrialized country.

3   Project Censored, a nationwide media criticism project, hopes to focus attention on this issue by naming it the top underreported news story of 1993. The project cites a Sept. 25 front page *Dallas Morning News* article by reporter Gayle Reaves as its primary source.

4   "We had done a series about violence against women earlier that was worldwide in scope," said Reaves, "and because of that we were paying more attention to questions about violence than other people."

5   The project also cites a June 16 *USA Today* article about a Tufts University report that found that 12 million U.S. children go hungry.

6   "The story appeared in *USA Today,* but it was not picked up and it died right there and then," said Project Censored's founder and director Carl Jensen. Of the United Nations report, he said, "It blew me away when I read nine out of 10. That's news, and yet it didn't take off."

7   Since 1976, Jensen and his students at California's Sonoma State University have researched each year the hundreds of nominated stories they receive. They then forward their 25 recommendations to a panel of nationally known journalists, academics and social activists—including *20/20* host Hugh Downs, *Backlash* author Susan Faludi, and Massachusetts Institute of Technology professor Noam Chomsky—who rank the stories and select the "censored" Top 10.

8   The project has been steadily gaining in exposure and stature in recent years. Last year, a printing of 10,000 copies of its yearbook sold out before all the initial orders could be filled.

9   This year's winners include such diverse subjects as U.S. oil interests in Somalia, businesses profiting from poverty in the United States, and the contamination of groundwater by selenium in California.

10   "I think the list covers a very broad spectrum, and I like that," said Jensen. "The media mix should be broad."

11   The list of sources is also broad, and includes many mainstream media—*Sports Illustrated,* for example, and the *Los Angeles Times.* Project Censored

judges compare the coverage an issue received to the coverage they think it deserved.

12   Jensen has developed a broad definition of censorship to guide the project: "the suppression of information, whether purposeful or not, by any method—including bias, omission, underreporting or self-censorship—which prevents the public from fully knowing what is happening in the world."

13   Few of the stories would qualify as censored under a strict definition. With some stories, editors did not recognize their importance. With others, digging out the information was too much work.

14   Robert Boyle, who wrote an article about widespread contamination of the Western U.S. water supply for *Sports Illustrated*, described to Project Censored how he spent almost two years trying to interest editors without success. Then, at the 1992 *Sports Illustrated* Christmas party, managing editor Mark Mulvoy, who had never seen the piece, told Boyle he wanted a strong environmental article for the March 22 issue.

15   "Mark, I sent one in a year and a half ago," Boyle told him.

16   Boyle's anecdote, according to Jensen, illustrates how arbitrary the process of getting stories out to the public can be.

17   There are, however, instances when people with political and economic clout actively work to keep newsworthy events out of the press.

18   For example, the Bush administration asked Sandia Labs to study U.S. education. The government was looking for ammunition for its attack on public schools, but Sandia found that the educational system was performing steadily or even improving according to nearly every measure used. When Sandia presented its results in 1991, the government suppressed the report. Its findings never entered into the then-active debate over education reform.

19   Sandia researcher Robert Huelskamp finally wrote about the report for the May 1993 *Phi Delta Kappan*. However, Jensen said Huelskamp now refers calls about the report to the lab's public-information office, which downplays the study's significance.

20   "Obviously something came back and bit them," Jensen said. "Sandia to this day just doesn't want the story to get out. I believe this is censorship in the truest sense."

21   Lowenthal said that despite the diversity of both the subject matter of the Project Censored stories and the reasons they were underreported, there are some common themes.

22   "Many of these stories are not complete mysteries to the public," Lowenthal said. "Yet some of the more serious aspects of them have not been covered. Somalia comes to mind. Gallons and gallons of ink have been spilled on Somalia, but there have only been a few mentions of the major oil concession the four multi-national oil companies are poised to exploit as soon as stability returns."

23   Because many of the stories have been covered, if only incompletely, the media cannot rely on the most common excuse for not providing better coverage, he said.

24. "They used to say, 'Hey, we can't get everything,' and, 'Sorry, that's the limitations of the media.' This year, I don't think they can say that in many cases. It exhibits either an alarming degree of ignorance on the part of editors or a willful ignorance."

25. Lowenthal also said that in many of the stories the antagonists are powerful interests and the protagonists are members of disenfranchised groups, like children and the poor. Many of the stories, he added, "question and examine institutions, and that's something the press is reluctant to do. It's much easier and much more concise to focus on personalities and individual cases."

26. Project Censored's complete findings on media censorship in 1993 are contained in its 1994 yearbook, *Censored: The News That Didn't Make the News—And Why*, released last month by Four Walls Eight Windows.

27. Here's a list of the 10 stories we didn't hear enough about last year.

One

28. **The United States is killing its young.** The U.S. poverty rate for children is twice that of any other industrial country's. During the past 20 years, as other countries have been reducing the number of impoverished children, the United States and Great Britain have been losing ground. What's more, 90 percent of all children slain in industrialized nations were Americans.

29. "The plight of our children does not appear to be a function of our recently declining economy but rather one of misguided priorities," the Project Censored report explained. While "the economic problems that have affected the United States in the last decade have affected much of the world too," other countries have created programs and adopted policies to help children out of poverty and protect them from crime. The United States has not.

30. In September, the United Nations Children's Fund released a "strident warning" that the lives of American children were in danger. Only Gayle Reaves of the *Dallas Morning News* picked it up.

31. "It probably would benefit the public to understand that the rest of the world does not have the problems with societal, peacetime violence that the United States has," Reaves said. "It is important for people to know that we are not the norm, by far."

Two

32. **Why are we really in Somalia?** Is it really for humanitarian reasons? According to the *Los Angeles Times*, *Propaganda Review* and *Extra!* magazine, the real reason behind our military adventure is more selfish.

33. "Far beneath the surface of the tragic drama of Somalia, four major U.S. oil companies are quietly sitting on a prospective fortune in exclusive concessions to explore and exploit tens of millions of acres of Somali countryside," wrote the *Times*. "This land, in the opinion of geologists and industry sources, could yield significant amounts of oil and natural gas if the U.S.-led military mission can restore peace to the impoverished East African nation."

34   Reporter Mark Fineman explained that almost two-thirds of Somalia was divvied among Conoco, Amoco, Chevron and Phillips before Somalia's pro-American president Mohamed Said Barre was overthrown. The oil giants are "well positioned to pursue Somalia's most promising potential oil reserves the moment the nation is pacified."

Three

35   **The Sandia Report on Education:** When the Bush administration wanted ammunition for school reform, it asked the Sandia National Laboratory to study the U.S. educational system. But since 1991, the government has suppressed Sandia's findings that the system is not performing as poorly as superficial statistics imply.

36   The Sandia report concluded that on nearly every measure, American schools were improving slightly or holding steady. Overall, the American high-school graduation rate, 85 percent, ranks among the world's highest. One-fourth of all young Americans will receive a bachelor's degree. And while average SAT scores are falling, that's because more students are taking the test.

37   Why is this information so threatening? In short, by revealing that most public schools aren't so bad after all, the Sandia report had the potential to weaken the movements to "deregulate" public education and institute "school choice."

38   "The Sandia report is so threatening to the anti-public school lobby that those supporting school choice initiatives still refuse to acknowledge its existence," wrote Project Censored. In fact, only three publications—*Phi Delta Kappan, The Education Digest* and *U.S. News & World Report*—wrote about the report.

Four

39   **The real welfare cheats—America's corporations:** While the mainstream media goes after individuals on welfare, it ignores handouts to corporations.

40   Ralph Nader's *Multimedia Monitor* documented five types of government giveaways to big business. One is a scheme allowing corporations to keep the patents and profits on products developed with government funds.

41   "One glaring example is the AIDS-fighting drug AZT," noted Project Censored. "While AZT was developed with public funds and was in the public domain since 1964, the FDA gave the patent away to Burroughs Wellcome . . . which has earned over $300 million in sales over the last two years with no royalties going to U.S. taxpayers." Burroughs Wellcome is based in Research Triangle Park [N.C.].

Five

42   **The hidden tragedy of Chernobyl:** According to Ukrainian physicist Vladimir Chernousenko, hailed as a hero for helping clean up after the Chernobyl nuclear accident, the plant's failure was caused by a design flaw present in other reactors,

not operator error. What's more, the accident released 80 percent of the reactor's radioactive core, not 3 percent, as previously claimed.

It gets worse. According to *The Nation,* "Some 15,000 of the 30,000 young conscripts who were unnecessarily exposed to incredibly high radiation levels in order to permit the other three Chernobyl reactors to continue operations . . . have died since 1986. Because 100,000 square kilometers of unproductive land has become permanently uninhabitable, contaminated food from these areas has been widely shipped to other areas of the former Soviet Union and consumed by an estimated 65 million persons, with varying degrees of consequent damage to their immune response."

Six

U.S. Army quietly resumes biowarfare testing: Claiming to be working on defenses against biowarfare, the Army has resumed working with highly toxic organisms at a Dugway, Utah, site it closed in 1983 because of safety concerns.

"Ten years ago, residents of western Utah breathed a heavy sigh of relief when the Army discontinued testing biological warfare agents at its Dugway Proving ground," explained Project Censored. "The reason given was that the Army's testing facility was getting old, and its safety—its ability to prevent potentially deadly diseases from escaping into the air outside the facility and thence to the rest of the world—could no longer be guaranteed. Now the deadly bugs are back."

While the Army says it's taking better precautions this time around, there's still reason for worry: Last September, Utah officials cited the Dugway Proving Ground for 22 violations of state hazardous-waste regulations.

Three newspapers ran the story: *The Salt Lake Tribune, High Country News* and *High Desert Advocate.*

Seven

Selenium—The disaster that challenges the Exxon Valdez: Dying ducks at Kesterson National Wildlife Refuge briefly made the news, but continuing, widespread contamination of the Western water supply has been widely ignored.

"It's hard to believe, but the ecological disasters caused by the oil spills . . . in Prince William Sound . . . and . . . off Scotland's Shetland Island . . . seem to pale when compared with the chronic environmental nightmare being wrought by selenium-contaminated drainwater flowing from irrigated lands in California and 13 other Western states," warned Robert Boyle in *Sports Illustrated.*

In 1983, a wildlife biologist named Harry Ohlendorf found thousands of dead nesting birds at the Kesterson Refuge, where a canal dumps drainwater from farms in the San Joaquin Valley. The carnage included dead adults and embryos, along with deformed young coots, ducks, eared grebes, black-necked stilt and killdeers. When he reported his findings to the U.S. Fish and Wildlife

Service, he was told the subject was "totally out of context—does not lend anything but a red flag to people." The problem has continued unabated.

51 Boyle offered the story to *The New Yorker* and *Harper's* before *Sports Illustrated* finally published it.

Eight

52 **America's deadly doctors:** Five to 10 percent of U.S. doctors are poorly trained, incompetent, or physically or mentally impaired, and their negligence kills or injures 150,000 to 300,000 Americans a year—yet many continue to practice.

53 According to writer Sue Browder, who broke the story in *Woman's Day*, mainstream newspapers only report on incompetent doctors after a patient has won a million-dollar lawsuit. For instance, the *Hartford Courant* wrote about a doctor who gave a woman an abortion without her knowledge—but no one wrote about the same doctor when he lost his license in New York for inept care.

54 "It's not so much that this subject needs *wider* exposure so much as it needs *earlier* exposure," she said.

Nine

55 **There's a lot of money to be made in poverty:** Major U.S. corporations are cashing in on "fringe banks"—pawn shops and check-cashing services—and joining second-mortgage companies, used-car dealers, rent-to-own stores and others on the long list of poverty profiteers.

56 Interest on pawn-shop loans often runs beyond 200 percent, while check-cashers often charge up to 10 percent of a check's value. Those are just two examples of a growing "poverty industry" that targets low-income, blue-collar and minority consumers—especially in the South—for fraud, exploitation and price-gouging.

57 If this story sounds familiar, it's because you read it here first. "Poverty, Inc." was a collaboration between *Southern Exposure* magazine and *The Independent*. It won the prestigious Sidney Hillman Foundation award and was nominated for a National Magazine Award.

58 "The nation's news media have largely ignored the story and its ramifications," said Mike Hudson, the series editor. "No one has called the 'poverty industry' what it is—a huge, multi-billion-dollar collection of companies fueled by Wall Street funding and propped up by a new veneer of corporate respectability."

Ten

59 **Haiti—Drugs, thugs, the CIA and the deterrence of democracy:** The military leaders of Haiti, who overthrew President Aristide and help smuggle four tons of cocaine into the United States each month, have been trained and supported by the CIA.

60. Some of the military officials involved in the coup were on the CIA's payroll starting in the mid-1980s. According to one government official, "Several of the principal players of the current situation were compensated by the U.S. government."

61. What's more, the CIA "tried to intervene in Haiti's election with a covert-action program that would have undercut the political strength" of Aristide, according to one article. A Senate committee blocked that action, which was authorized by the Reagan administration.

62. The Pacifica News Services' Dennis Bernstein had to break the story before *The New York Times* and *Los Angeles Times* picked it up. Bernstein co-authored an article on the same topic in the *San Francisco Bay Guardian*.

63. "Democracy doesn't exist without a free and unfettered press that isn't afraid to ask the difficult questions . . . without checking informally with the State Department and the CIA," Bernstein said. "The press's continuing failure to report adequately on illegal intelligence operations and CIA-sponsored drug-running and assassination coup teams may ultimately lead to the end of democracy, not only in Haiti but in the U.S."

REACTING

1. Would you agree that these ten stories are major news items? Why?
2. Why do you think these stories did not receive extensive media coverage?

CONNECTING

1. Imagine a conversation between Ishmael Reed ("Tuning Out Network Bias," p. 32) and Gloria Steinem ("Sex, Lies and Advertising," p. 21) about why these stories weren't covered. How might each explain it?
2. Based on this report, who would you say controls the news media?

LEARNING ABOUT WRITING FROM READING

In their magazine article McLaughlin and Yeoman are summing up a long report and have to make the point about each "untold story" sharp and clear. In the last sentence of each "untold story," they do that, telling you why that story matters:

1. About U.S. children and violence—"It is important for people to know that we are not the norm, by far."
2. About our military intervention in Somalia—"The oil giants are 'well positioned to pursue Somalia's most promising potential oil reserves the moment the nation is pacified.'"

Brevity—getting right to the point—is a quality that readers often appreciate and need in order to understand the author's main idea.

WILLIAM LEE MILLER

Television Power and American Values

William Lee Miller, author of several books about American culture, often criticizes the role of television in our lives. But in this excerpt, taken from a longer and generally more negative essay, he examines some of its positive effects.

BEFORE YOU READ

1. What would you lose of value if your television were taken away?
2. What does the title suggest about the likely content of this piece?

1   I am as old as radio; our oldest child is as old as television. She and her younger siblings have a hard time imagining a world, a home, an evening, in which there is no television. It is even a little hard for me to remember life before television. Stephen Leacock wrote that he had long years of experience in the bank field—as a depositor. I have an analogous[1] experience in the television field, from watching Milton Berle to watching "Saturday Night Live"; from finding a bar with a TV set in Chicago to watching Murrow's program on Joseph McCarthy to taping Walter Cronkite's interview with Miss Lillian.

2   The interpretation of American television at the most general level is like that of other "advances" of modern technology, the so-called "progress" since the Industrial Revolution. These advances are accompanied by enormous costs and dangers. And of course the full effect is not that of one invention alone but of the complex whole; television is inextricably interwoven with the rest of modern technological society.

3   But television, like modern technological society, is not the total monster that some, partly in reaction to the opposite view, see it to be: writers like Jacques Ellul, agrarian romantics, returners to the soil. With all of the costs, these developments in industrial productivity, in transportation, and in communication represent net gains in the life of the broad populace. Modern technology, particularly television, has values that are peculiarly difficult for the articulate to appreciate and dangers that are peculiarly difficult for the general public to perceive.

4   As to the articulate classes, we dictate our denunciations of "impersonal," "dehumanizing" modern technology onto transcribing machines; they are typed on electric typewriters; they are "published" by the earliest of the decisive technological advances, the printing press; they are transmitted (to the allegedly alienated public) by modern means of transportation and communication. We

---

[1] Similar; parallel.

will discuss our books denouncing television on television talk shows, if any one will invite us to appear on them. Jacques Ellul's excoriation of technology is available in paperback in small Midwestern cities; to bring about that result requires a whole series of uses of the technology the book denounces.

5   More important, the daily life of the ordinary man is concretely improved in mundane ways. People in what used to be called the underdeveloped countries are busily striving to attain what literati in the advanced nations busily denounce. Television shares to some extent, ambiguously, in that mundane improvement in the daily life of millions that is more obvious in other technological advances—central heating, motor cars, penicillin, modern plumbing, the telephone. These are not what poets sing about, but they are what people latch onto. The justification of mass television is not, first of all, the occasional "good" program but just the addition to the life of the ordinary person of another, more complete and accessible and varied source of entertainment and information than had hitherto been available. Proposition: Life is more *interesting* for the elderly poor, for people living alone, for patients in hospitals (you walk down the corridor and quickly learn what is on all three networks), for residents of Gnaw Bone, Indiana, and Skyline, Wyoming, for working class and poor people, the forest of TV aerials over whose homes the critics used to deplore[2]—life is more interesting for the broad public, and especially for the poorer, and more remote, the disabled, disconnected, and disadvantaged, than it was before the advent of television. I was struck by this aside in Kenneth Tynan's article on Johnny Carson in *The New Yorker*: "Between April and September, the numbers dip, but this reflects a seasonal pattern by which all TV shows are affected. A top NBC executive explained to me, with heartless candor, 'People who can afford vacations go away in the summer. It's only the poor people who watch us all the year round.'"

6   I wasn't poor, but I never saw Hank Luisetti shoot a jump shot nor did I know what Art Tatum looked like, much as I admired them, in my culturally deprived youth before television. My son has seen Julius Erving, Walt Frazier, and Bill Walton of the NBA on CBS. The defense rests.

7   Neither unambiguous progress nor monster, television is not "neutral" either. Television, like technology generally, is not *simply* an instrument or tool which extends human powers, to be used according to one's choice for good or for evil. The giant levers of modernity have a particularly powerful shape—each one, and the collection of all of them. Taken together, they make the simultaneous centripetal and centrifugal forces that Mannheim described: great new centers (30 Rock, hard rock, Black Rock, Fred Silverman) combined with wider and wider "mass democratization" (99 percent of households with a set; 78 percent color sets; 46 percent more than one set); on an "average" Sunday night—the biggest night—97 million viewers; on other nights, 80 million, 30 million and more watching the same program; 104 million watching Super Bowl XII; 111 million watching Nixon's resignation; 75 million watching at least part of the Carter-Ford debates).

---

[2] Dislike intensely; condemn.

8   As the automobile eliminated the Sunday-night church service and the use of the parlor for courting and helped to create the suburb, so television will have its own string of *unintended* side effects in the shaping of a social order. Television, like technology, is neither an unequivocal good nor an unequivocal evil, nor yet simply neutral, but an enormously powerful phenomenon[3] with quite particular traits, about which the society needs to make conscious social decisions, recognizing the mammoth dangers and kinds of damage those traits can represent.

9   Television is a condition of our present social life, irreversible; it is an aspect of the perennial human struggle that never ends. Obviously it was an enormous mistake that this potent[4] instrument was allowed simply to grow out of radio and given over therefore to commercial control. It did not require the sponsorship of Maxwell House coffee or the billion-dollar annual revenues for three commercial networks in order for life to be a little more interesting in Gnaw Bone.

REACTING

1. Would you agree with William Miller that television makes life more interesting for many people? Explain your answer.
2. Does Miller describe the way you see television benefiting you personally?

CONNECTING

1. How might Marie Winn ("The Effects of Television on Family Life," p. 29) reply to Miller's list of the virtues of television?
2. When a technology like television is everywhere, how much can we control its effect on us? What would Winn say about this?

LEARNING ABOUT WRITING FROM READING

Students often ask, "Can I use 'I' in my paper?" It's a good question, because teachers have different views on it. Here, Miller uses "I" from the very start and brings in his own experience in ways that make his article clearer and more interesting. Look at his first sentence:

> I am as old as radio; our oldest child is as old as television. She and her younger siblings have a hard time imagining a world, a home, an evening, in which there is no television. It is even a little hard for me to remember life before television.

Miller is able to use his own life to illustrate how dramatically television has changed our lives. Because his experience is both personal and typical, it fits

---

[3] Observable characteristic or quality.
[4] Powerful.

well here, and the use of "I" creates a warmer, more conversational tone for the reader.

Neal Gabler

Now Playing: Real Life, the Movie

Neal Gabler, writer for Video Review, *looks at the tendency of the mass media to distract us from our "real" lives.*

BEFORE YOU READ

1. Why do you, or why does someone you know, want to be on television or get some kind of celebrity attention from the media?
2. When you vote for candidates, are you persuaded more by their views on issues or by your sense of what kind of person the candidate is?

1   *Fade in* on New York Harbor off the Battery on a muggy June day. A young man jumps from a launch into the roiling water and disappears beneath the surface. Within seconds divers in scuba gear plunge in after him. Boats converge on the scene. A helicopter hovers overhead. But the man never surfaces.

2   *Fade in* on five toughs rampaging down the mean streets of Washington one night. The gang encircles a dazed man. One of them rears back and unleashes a savage punch. The victim falls stiffly, like a tree being felled.

3   *Fade in* on a snowy slope in fashionable Aspen. We see two figures in ski parkas silhouetted against the sky: a man and a woman. Suddenly, another woman appears. She wheels on the first woman and hisses, "Stay away from my husband!"

4   These are all scenes from recent movies, but you wouldn't have seen any of them at your local theater. The first was a rescue drill conducted by the New York Harbor Police; according to some accounts, the policeman playing the victim had foregone a life jacket to make the rescue look more authentic for a German television crew shooting the action. The young man drowned. The second was a video made by a gang of Washington youths during a so-called wilding. And the third was the famous confrontation on the slopes between Ivana Trump and Marla Maples. The reason you wouldn't have seen any of these scenes at your local theater is that they were playing on a different kind of screen. These movies were playing on the screen of *life*.

5   Reality has always had a way of challenging fiction and frequently outflanking it. But by the "screen of life" I mean something much more self-consciously theatrical than chance invention. I mean that life itself is gradually being transformed into a medium all its own like television, radio, and print.

And we are becoming both performance artists in and audiences for a grand, ongoing entertainment that is often richer, more complex and more compelling than anything in the conventional media. Or, as Philip Roth put it in his story "On the Air": "What if the world is some kind of—of *show!* . . . What if we are all only talent assembled by the Great Talent Scout Up Above! The Great Show of Life! Starring Everybody! Suppose entertainment is the Purpose of Life!"

6   Philip Roth was writing more than twenty years ago, but the evidence has steadily mounted ever since that politics, religion, news, education, warfare, crime, *everything* are really branches of, well, call it show biz. Everywhere the fabricated, the inauthentic and the theatrical have gradually driven out the natural, the genuine, and the spontaneous until there is no distinction between real life and stagecraft. In fact, one could argue that the theatricalization of American life is the major cultural transformation of this century. Devoured by artifice[1], life is a movie.

Reality Management: Enter Fantasy, Riding a TV Set

7   It is difficult to pinpoint precisely when the process began. Surely as soon as America first emerged as a mass industrial society there were individuals who saw no reason to let the vagaries of life govern when one could orchestrate life to one's benefit. Soon public relations experts were manufacturing events and manipulating reality, and over decades these small contrivances, established on a thousand fronts from business to news to politics, metastasized[2]. Before long everyone in public life had a PR rep and everything in public life seemed the product of premeditation.

8   It was this sort of image-mongering and reality management that the historian Daniel Boorstin deplored in his path-breaking 1961 study "The Image: A Guide to Pseudo-Events in America." For Mr. Boorstin, Americans increasingly lived in a "world where fantasy is more real than reality." And he warned, "We risk being the first people in history to have been able to make their illusions so vivid, so persuasive, so 'realistic' that they can live in them." Mr. Boorstin believed that by letting artifice displace experience, we were debasing our culture. Still, he assumed that if one lifted the scrim, one would find a reality behind the counterfeit. What he could not have foreseen was that the scrim would become the reality.

9   Partly, he underestimated the extent of the theatrical in America because he underestimated the power of television to dictate the terms of our discourse. As Neil Postman has observed in his powerfully argued screed against television, "Amusing Ourselves to Death: Public Discourse in the Age of Show Business," "We are now a culture whose information, ideas, and epistemology are given form by television, not by the printed word." And Mr. Postman went on to say

---

[1] Clever trick or device.

[2] Grew and spread like a cancer.

that television, unlike print, "has made entertainment itself the natural format for the representation of all experience." Television not only welcomes artifice, it demands it. Inherently visual, inherently visceral[3], television abhors dead air. It requires that everyone on it—newsmakers, authors, generals, criminals, academicians—keep us entertained or we'll tune out.

10 Television certainly has contributed to the frenzy of role-playing in America, if only because the lone standard to which television holds anyone is the standard of performance. (Mr. Postman says that Richard Nixon was done in by television not because he was a liar but because he *looked* like one.)

11 In a famous commercial a few years back, a soap opera star announced, "I'm not a doctor but I play one on TV." Today, when it seems everyone is engaged in one sort of performance or another, that could serve as the nation's motto. "I'm not a hero but I play one," says Oliver North. "I'm not a football star but I play one," says Brian Bosworth. "I'm not a journalist but I play one," says the local news anchor. "I'm not a president but I play one," says Ronald Reagan.

12 Since the media transmit these performances, it is tempting to blame them for the theatricalization. But doing so is mistaking symptoms for causes. Life is the medium, television an important but component part. And life hasn't become a form of entertainment because PR men learned to stroke our cultural G-spots or because wily television executives learned how to lobotomize us into grinning idiots. We have been complicit in the whole process and for good reason. It works.

13 If theatricalization accelerated at roughly the same time that America was emerging as a mass industrial society, it was also a time when American life was becoming less manageable, more complex. With the old verities of nineteenth-century small-town America suddenly under siege, people needed techniques to help them understand the changing social order and possibly dominate it.

14 A painless way to make sense of this new world was suggested by one of the modernizing forces itself: the movies. The movies offered many forms of guidance to confused Americans, particularly to immigrant urban dwellers; they became a virtual manual for acculturation. But one of the most important and most subtle services for the movies offered was to serve as a popular model of narrative coherence. If reality was overwhelming, one could always carve it into a story, as the movies did. One could bend life to the familiar and comforting formulas one saw in the theater.

15 Beginning in the 1920s, the tabloids and then magazines and television provided dozens of real-life plots, from kidnappings and murders to political scandals, to crimes in executive suites, to election campaigns, to World War II, to the cold war, to Watergate, to the recent Soviet coup attempt. Today, virtually all the news assumes a narrative configuration[4] with cause and effect, villain and

---

[3] Instinctive, from the gut.
[4] Shape.

hero, beginning, middle, and provisional end, and frequently a moral. Events that don't readily conform, the savings and loan scandal, for example, seem to drift in foggy limbo like a European art film rather than a sleek commercial American hit.

16   That is why reading the news is just like watching a series of movies: a hostage crisis is a thriller, the Milwaukee serial murders a morbidly fascinating real-life *Silence of the Lambs,* the Kennedy Palm Beach case a soap opera, a fire or hurricane a disaster picture.

17   One even suspects that Americans were riveted by the Clarence Thomas-Anita Hill hearings last week not because of any sense of civic duty but because it was a spellbinding show—part *Rashomon,* part *Thelma and Louise,* part *Witness for the Prosecution.*

18   But as with movies, if "formalizing" reality is a way of domesticating it, it is also a means of escaping it. Michael Wood, in his book *America in the Movies,* described our films as a "rearrangement of our problems into shapes which tame them, which disperse them to the margins of our attention" where we can forget about them. By extending this function to life itself, we convert everything from the kidnapping of the Lindbergh baby to the marital misadventures of Elizabeth Taylor into distractions, cheap entertainments that transport us from our problems.

19   But before disapproving too quickly, one is almost compelled to admit that turning life into escapist entertainment has both a perverse logic and a peculiar genius. Why worry about the seemingly intractable problems of society when you can simply declare, "It's morning in America" and have yourself a long-running Frank Capra movie right down to an aw-shucks president? Why fret over America's declining economic might when you can have an honest-to-goodness war movie that proves your superiority? Movies have always been a form of wish fulfillment. Why not life?

20   When life is a movie, it poses serious questions for those things that were not traditionally entertainment and now must accommodate themselves. Politics, for instance. Much has already been made of the fact that Ronald Reagan came to the White House after a lifetime as a professional actor. Lou Cannon, in his biography of Mr. Reagan, *President Reagan: The Role of a Lifetime,* details just how central this was to Mr. Reagan's concept of the presidency and what it suggests about the new political landscape.

Performance Politics: Good Vibes from the Oval Office

21   "What he wanted to be, and what he became, was an accomplished presidential performer," writes Mr. Cannon. Everything was scripted for Mr. Reagan, from press conferences to quips; even in personal conversations he read from note cards. When the president did wing it, he was vague and often incoherent.

22   Of course President Reagan was not the first politician to have been a consummate performer. One thinks immediately of Franklin Roosevelt. But for

Roosevelt the performance was always a function of the presidency—a means to sell his policies. For Mr. Reagan, the presidency was a function of the performance. What the administration was selling was what movies sell: good vibes.

23   None of this was lost on Mr. Reagan's advisers. They knew that his primary function was to star in the movie of his presidency and offer genial reassurance that everything would be OK. In this escapist entertainment there would be no racial divisiveness, no economic calamity, no education crisis, no AIDS.

24   We acquiesced[5] not because we were deluded[6] but because it was a pretty good movie as movies go: well executed, thematically sound, deeply satisfying, fun. "You believed it because you wanted to believe it," President Reagan once told a columnist who insisted he had seen the young actor on the set of the movie *Brother Rat,* even though Mr. Reagan had not been there. "There's nothing wrong with that. I do it all the time."

25   Psychologically speaking, the president may have been right. Politically speaking, though, the presidential movie is a far more vexing proposition for a democracy. In the first place, turning the presidency into performance art changes the way we measure the presidency from the efficaciousness of the administration's policies to the power of its performance—that old TV gauge. In this the media were happy to collaborate. Throughout the Reagan years one heard ad nauseam about the effectiveness of the president's delivery, about his popularity, about his charm until, as Professor Kiku Adatto noted of the press corps during the 1988 Bush-Dukakis campaign, the reporters had become theater critics, dissecting the stagecraft of the campaign rather than its substance.

26   In the second place, if performance art turns the presidency into a movie, it also turns Americans into an audience. "You like the audience," Mr. Reagan once mused after his presidency. "You want to please the audience." But audiences, unlike citizens, have neither responsibilities nor obligations. There are no minority rights either. The majority rules, and if you don't enjoy the movie you can just skedaddle. Anyone who has the temerity[7] to stand up during the show and criticize it for not being relevant is likely to seem irrelevant himself. This movie isn't *about* relevancy. This movie is about escape.

27   Were President Reagan the author of this phenomenon, one might pass it off as a weird blip on the political screen. But, again, Mr. Reagan is the symptom, not the cause. From now on every president will be drafting the script of his presidency. For President Bush it is the story of a self-effacing American Everyman, half Yankee, half Texan, whose common demeanor belies a steely toughness.

---

[5] Went along.
[6] Fooled.
[7] Nerve, courage.

War, the Miniseries: Casting for the Gulf Was Impeccable

28 Just as every movie blockbuster comes with its own set pieces, the movie within the movie, so the Bush administration devised *its* set piece: a staggeringly successful miniseries called the Gulf War, which demonstrated on an unprecedented scale how events might be given the narrative shape and heady rush of a good action picture.

29 It is odd, unseemly even, to describe a war as "telegenic," but that is precisely what the Gulf War was. Each network introduced its war coverage with music, a logo, and a title—*Crisis in the Gulf* on ABC; *Showdown in the Gulf* on CBS before the hostilities and *War in the Gulf* after the hostilities had begun; *America at War* on NBC. For them it was a new series, and even the correspondents, notably CNN's Peter Arnett and Wolf Blitzer and NBC's "Scud stud" Arthur Kent gained a star's celebrity.

30 Certainly the Gulf War was a lot more telegenic than Vietnam. Vietnam was a long logy hallucination of a movie—the good guys indistinguishable from the bad, the plot dribbling away to entropy. The Pentagon had learned that if it were to control the media front it couldn't let that happen again. The next war was going to be short, sharp, its narrative lineaments clean, happily unconfused as to heroes and villains. The next war was going to be an entertainment.

31 The casting was impeccable. Articulate, brilliant, rugged, sensitive, heroic H. Norman Schwarzkopf was a figure of Herculean proportions, especially when placed beside the Vietnam commanders William Westmoreland and Creighton Abrams. On the other hand, Saddam Hussein resembled the evil mastermind from a Saturday afternoon serial. As for actual combat, the action we saw, primarily bombs hitting targets, were antiseptic and precise.

32 Formulated like a World War II movie, the Gulf War even ended like a World War II movie, with the troops marching triumphantly down Broadway or Main Street bathed in the gratitude of their fellow Americans while the final credits rolled. Nor did the movie analogy end with the parades. The Gulf War, like *Star Wars*, had its ancillary markets: trading cards, T-shirts, videocassettes of the action.

33 Nevertheless, there is one distinction between this "movie" and the conventional movies that helped keep the home fires burning during World War II, other than the obvious one that those played in theaters and this one played in the medium of life. Those movies had a purpose besides entertainment. They were designed to mobilize support and forge a consensus for the real war being fought overseas. But when the war itself is a movie, when its real-life objectives are murky and mercurial,[8] the war "movie" mobilizes support for . . . what?

34 For itself, one supposes, which is why the real point of this war may not have been to liberate Kuwait, ensure the flow of oil or eliminate Mr. Hussein. It may have been to restore our confidence, to make us feel good—which is, of

---

[8] Rapidly changing.

course, traditionally not the function of warfare but of the movies or TV. "General Sherman had it all wrong," editorialized the *Nation* earlier this year. "War ain't hell—it's entertainment."

When Life Upstages Art: Elizabeth Taylor's Celebrity Theory

35   When life itself is an entertainment medium it also forces adjustments from the stars of films, TV, records, and the rest of the conventional media. How do you hold your own life in the movie when the president, businessmen like Donald Trump, alleged mobsters like John Gotti, the Kennedys, even mass murderers compete for public attention? When everything is entertainment, what can you provide that these new entertainers cannot?

36   The answers come from an unlikely source: Elizabeth Taylor, who may be as close to a theorist of the life movie as there is. Ms. Taylor's life has long seemed like real-life soap opera of the most lurid hue. A childhood in Hollywood, marriage after marriage, the tragic death of her one true love, bouts with illness, obesity, drug addition, recovery—the list goes on.

37   All these things had kept Ms. Taylor in the public view. More, they had kept her a first-rank celebrity. In fact, Ms. Taylor's life was so much more entertaining than anything she could do on screen that she didn't have to work in the movies or TV to hold our interest. She just had to live.

38   In "The Image," Mr. Boorstin noted that the celebrity "will be destroyed, as he was made, by publicity," the idea being that publicity is perishable; once the celebrity passes from public view there are no lasting accomplishments to survive him. But Elizabeth Taylor understood that one never need pass from that view; that one could keep unraveling the long skein of one's life; that one could make of one's own life a movie and that so long as it was entertaining, one would never be passé. "I am my own industry," she once declared, and she was absolutely right. (A marketing executive recently described an in-store promotional movie Ms. Taylor made for her new White Diamonds perfume as "a theatrical event," complete with tickets and popcorn.) When was the last time you went to see a *real* Elizabeth Taylor movie? When was the last time you *read* about her?

39   In the old days of celebrity, we seldom went to see a movie solely because we were curious about a star we had read about; on the contrary, we were curious about stars because we had gone to see their movies. Today the life is almost always a teaser for the work—when there is any work to tease. No one I know rushes out to see a Mickey Rourke picture, few were tempted by the recent Farrah Fawcett-Ryan O'Neal sitcom, and Dolly Parton hardly rivals Madonna's popularity—to name some recent cover subjects of *Vanity Fair*, the chronicle of the celebrity life movie. But they each have stories to tell and lives to sell.

40   Demi Moore, the actress-wife of Bruce Willis, didn't even have a picture in release at the time of her controversial *Vanity Fair* cover, but the magazine aptly described her yet-unborn child as "her next project." Julia Roberts did have a movie in release when she suddenly aborted her impending marriage to the

actor Kiefer Sutherland. The picture, *Dying Young,* did disappointing business. But as Caryn James pointed out in these pages, Ms. Robert's *life movie* was booming. The tabloids and *People* got everyone gossiping about the young woman's romances just as they once did about Ms. Taylor's.

41   In effect, the life now is always usurping the work just as one suspects that for the celebrities themselves the life movie is always usurping whatever "real" life there is. "It's not easy being Cary Grant," the actor was once alleged to have said, meaning, presumably, that it isn't easy for an ordinary mortal to live up to his screen image. Grant was assuming, of course, that there was a difference between the man and the image. It is much easier being, say, Cher, because that assumption doesn't hold. When life is a movie, image and life conflate. The stars aren't projecting anymore. They seem to be living for us, opening their lives to public inspection, letting us in on their secrets, *entertaining* us.

42   But "entertainment" may be too limiting a word for these life movies. As mindlessly voyeuristic as all this may sound, the stars are also providing a kind of art as well as entertainment. Semioticians who study language and signs have long held that culture itself could be "read" as a vast text. Similarly, lives can have themes as well as plots, and these themes can be a major part of their appeal: the content that informs the story.

43   One of the appeals of Elizabeth Taylor's life is that it forcefully conveys the theme of survival. No matter what happens to Liz, she always triumphs. One of the appeals of Cher's life is that it conveys the idea of self-renewal: from a motley-dressed rock-and-roll star to a sex object to a serious actress. Sylvester Stallone's life has had the thematic amplitude[9] of a Greek myth. He is the shepherd (actually deli waiter) who becomes the gods' (actually Hollywood's) favorite and then, succumbing to his overweening pride and to Circe (actually Brigitte Nielsen), must be punished for his hubris. Now, according to last year's *Vanity Fair* profile, "Sly's Cry From the Heart," he is chastened and newly sensitive.

44   No doubt stars could keep recycling the formulas if there weren't someone to push the edge of the celebrity envelope. Madonna's life is as soap operatic as the best of them, and it is ripe with thematic possibilities: sexual role reversal, hedonism[10] with impunity, the wages of celebrity, to name a few. But Madonna has added a brilliant Pirandellian wrinkle to the old formula. She has made her life work *about* her life movie.

45   In the documentary *Truth or Dare,* Madonna admits that she is not the best singer, dancer, or actress and adds disingenuously, "Who do I think I am, trying to pull this off?" But Madonna knows exactly who she is. She is a conceptual performance artist whose truest art is the art of manipulation. That alone might not make her any different from Cher, Mr. Stallone, Ms. Taylor, or the rest, save

---

[9] Fullness.
[10] Philosophy of the pursuit of pleasure.

this: Madonna gleefully reveals her manipulation to us. She luxuriates in it. Like the magicians Penn and Teller, who are constantly debunking their magic, she invites us to see the mechanisms behind the tricks, until all we see are the mechanisms. It is the shamelessness of it that makes her so appealing to her fans.

46   "She doesn't want to *live* off-camera, much less talk," her then-boyfriend, the actor Warren Beatty, complains in *Truth or Dare*. Mr. Beatty himself has always pretended to be secretive. He lurks at the edges of the frame here as he has lurked at the edges of the press for decades. Yet lurk he does. Not for nothing do we know not only Mr. Beatty's romantic entanglements, but even his love-making techniques. It is part of his life movie as legendary Lothario.[11] What he cannot see is that Madonna is Mr. Beatty without the hypocrisy.

47   In fairness, though, not even Madonna always gets it. In *Truth or Dare*, Kevin Costner saunters backstage to pay his respects after a concert. Flashing that big lopsided Costner grin, he tells her the concert was "neat," then apologizes for having to get back home to the kids. No sooner has Mr. Costner left than Madonna is sneering incredulously, "Neat?" and sticking her finger down her throat to gag. Madonna didn't seem to realize that she had momentarily become a guest star in Mr. Costner's life movie, believing instead that he was a guest star in hers. "Neat" was deliberate and probably ironic. It is the sort of thing one expects Mr. Costner to say. And the excuse about getting back to the children is as central to the Costner "movie" as sex is to the Beatty "movie."

48   Life couldn't be a movie if it were limited to the famous and powerful. Americans have always emulated[12] their stars in fashion, behavior, attitude. Now, consciously or not, they are emulating the stars' theatricalization. Recently I heard about a party where the hosts' eight-year-old daughter roamed about with a video camera. As the party was breaking up, the girl called the guests to attention, popped a cassette in the deck, and showed them the edited video version of their party, complete with titles, effects, and soundtrack.

Ordinary People
Cultural Footprints Exit into the Video

49   And a recent article in the *Times* reported what must surely be the frontier of this domestic theatricalization: a young man asked his divorced parents to step in front of the camcorder and reenact happier times so that their granddaughter could see how it was before the breakup.

50   These are the new entertainments and the new arts, spun in life from life. It is even conceivable that these, more than our novels, films, and paintings, may be the cultural footprints we leave behind. Someday, perhaps, future generations will be retelling the sagas of Elizabeth Taylor, the Kennedys, Nancy

---

[11] A great lover.

[12] Admired and copied.

Reagan, Donald Trump, and Sylvester Stallone, or watching the videos of that divorced couple playing themselves in better days. Someday they may be parsing the meanings of these narratives as we interpret Greek myths.

Meanwhile, we edge ever closer to Philip Roth's dark, prophetic vision—ever closer to the time when entertainment will be the only purpose of life and everything else will be dispersed to the margins and forgotten.

REACTING

1. Would you agree with Neal Gabler that too often we are lulled into being entertained when actually we should be asking critical questions about issues?
2. Did we treat the Gulf War as entertainment? Why would you agree or disagree?

CONNECTING

1. Ishmael Reed ("Tuning Out Network Bias," p. 32) and Gabler both talk about the power of images. Would they agree about how images distort reality?
2. William Miller ("Television Power and American Values," p. 43) argues that life is better in Gnaw Bone (small town) America because television adds interest to it. How might Gabler respond to that view?

LEARNING ABOUT WRITING FROM READING

In this long article on several topics, Gabler needs to pull his ideas together for the reader. He does this by referring to the same idea from Philip Roth both at the beginning and end of his article. After his opening three examples, Gabler quotes Philip Roth: "What if the world is some kind of—of *show!* . . . What if we are all only talent assembled by the Great Talent Scout Up Above! The Great Show of Life! Starring Everybody! <u>Suppose entertainment is the Purpose of Life!</u>"

The underlined words sum up Gabler's main concern about how images can lead us astray, and he repeats his and Philip Roth's point in the close:

> Meanwhile, we edge ever closer to Philip Roth's dark, prophetic vision—ever closer to the time when entertainment will be the only purpose of life and everything else will be dispersed to the margins and forgotten.

This ending reminds us of the main point and brings us back to the beginning to give a sense of completion.

WRITING ASSIGNMENTS

ASSIGNMENT I
HOW WOULD YOUR LIFE BE DIFFERENT WITHOUT TELEVISION?

Coming Up with Ideas and a Focus

There is a lot that could be covered here, so you need to select your focus carefully. Your paper might examine specific parts of your life and how they might be without television: daily life on your own or with family, friends, and roommates; education; work; relationships with people outside your family; hobbies; and activities outside work are just a few examples.

Organizing Your Ideas

Consider organizing your ideas using a comparison-contrast pattern: life with versus life without television. Or you might use narrative, where you tell the story of a day in the life of someone without television.

(For help with comparison-contrast papers, see pp. 310 and 367–368; for help with narrative papers, see pp. 306 and 366.)

Audience

Try writing for an audience of confirmed television watchers: people for whom television is a permanent and necessary part of life. With this audience in mind, you should be looking for the chance to make surprising and interesting points about how life might be different. Telling details of description can help your readers enter into this unusual experience.

ASSIGNMENT II
EVALUATE A NEWS STORY. EXAMINE A NEWS ARTICLE OR TAPED COVERAGE OF A TELEVISION NEWS REPORT. THEN RESEARCH THAT NEWS ITEM IN DEPTH TO DECIDE HOW FAIR, COMPLETE, AND INSIGHTFUL THE NEWS REPORT IS.

Coming Up with Ideas and a Focus

Your TV or newspaper analysis and your own research will provide a lot of information, and the question itself spells out some of the issues you need to focus on as you work through all your data. Ask yourself how fair, how complete, and how insightful the news article or TV news report is, given what you know about the topic from your own research. Your answers to these questions will provide the main points for your paper.

Organizing Your Ideas

It might be helpful to make an early statement about your evaluation of the article or TV report. Then back it up with evidence on the issues of fairness, completeness, and insightfulness. (For help with statement-support papers, see pp. 305 and 365–366.)

Audience

You might try addressing your paper as a letter to the editor of the newspaper or magazine or to the producer of the TV news program. If you have this audience in mind, you will be encouraged to make your comments very clear and your own evaluation very thorough and fair, because your readers may become defensive about any criticisms you may have.

ASSIGNMENT III
IF YOU HAVE LIVED OR TRAVELED OUTSIDE THE UNITED STATES, EXPLAIN WHAT WAS SIGNIFICANTLY DIFFERENT ABOUT THE CULTURE YOU ENCOUNTERED.

Coming Up with Ideas and a Focus

As you begin work on this paper, try freewriting or talking about your experiences before focusing on specific differences between American culture and the other culture. The challenge is to select the most interesting and revealing differences as your focus.

Organizing Your Ideas

The assignment itself, by asking you to focus on differences between two cultures, suggests that a variation of the comparison-contrast pattern might be useful.
 (For help with comparison-contrast papers, see pp. 310 and pp. 367–368.)

Audience

You might try writing this for people who are thinking of traveling to the place you are describing. Imagine that they need to know what will cause "culture shock" when they arrive.

ASSIGNMENT IV
IS AMERICAN INDIVIDUALISM A STRENGTH OR A PROBLEM IN OUR CULTURE?

Coming Up with Ideas and a Focus

Before trying to respond to the question, spend some time freewriting and talking about what you mean by "American individualism," perhaps thinking of people and situations where you saw individualism in action. Find a focus for this paper by talking and writing about how you feel about these examples of individualism, so that you can arrive at a judgment about whether, overall, it is a strength or a weakness.

Organizing Your Ideas

One way to organize your ideas is to open the paper with a statement of your position on the issue of American individualism. Back this statement up with detailed reasons.

(For help with statement-support papers, see pp. 305 and 365–366.)

Audience

You might try directing your paper to people who are thinking of immigrating to the United States. Inform them carefully about a key value in a culture they know little about. Decide what you want to say about its strengths and weaknesses. Will you be warning or encouraging these potential immigrants about the opportunities that await them on American shores?

Chapter 2

Work

KEY QUESTIONS
What are the rewards of working?
How are work and its rewards seen in the media?

- -

We all have a basic need to be active, engaged in meaningful pursuits, and valued by other people. In an important sense, these things constitute the true value of work more than money or power.
—Brad Edmondson, "Remaking a Living"

Two out of three businessmen [on TV] are portrayed as criminal, evil, greedy, or foolish; almost one-half of all work-related activities performed by businessmen involve illegal acts . . . and television almost never portrays business as a socially or economically useful activity.
—Leonard J. Theberge, Crooks, Conmen and Clowns: Businessmen in TV Entertainment

Workers of the world, unite. You have nothing to lose but your chains.
—Karl Marx, Communist Manifesto

Annual Vacation Time (in weeks)

	By Law	By Bargaining Agreement
Austria	4	4–5
Denmark	—	5
Finland	5	5–6
France	5	5–6
Germany	3	4–6
Greece	4	
Ireland	3	4
Italy	—	4–6
Netherlands	3	4–5
Portugal	4	
Spain	5	5
Sweden	5	5–8
Switzerland	4	4–5
United States	—	2–4
United Kingdom	—	4–6

"Reduction of Working Time in Europe," *European Industrial Relations Review*, quoted in *Utne Reader* (July/August 1991).

Introduction

Work. Few smile at the sound of that word. Why do so many Americans have mixed feelings, at best, about work and its rewards? Work can be a source of pleasure and fulfillment. It is work that allows us to develop our talents, be connected to our neighbors and community, and, of course, earn what we need to live. But some work can stifle our talents and development, leave us with too little time and energy for family and friends, or fail to give us enough to live on. Sometimes work doesn't give us enough control over our lives; sometimes we cannot even get work to do.

Mahatma Gandhi, the famous Indian leader, once told a journalist that happiness comes from loving your work. Do Americans love their work? Can they? In this chapter you will read about Mike Lefevre, who was interviewed by Studs Terkel in "Who Built the Pyramids?" He gives us one American's view of his life's work.

Our culture certainly seems to place a high value on hard work. The Protestant "work ethic" equation—hard work equals success equals a sign of God's favor and our own salvation—is a formula many of us perhaps still believe in. Many Americans see work as the route to success. But what does "success" mean? Is it satisfaction in work well done and in the public recognition gained? Is it the acquisition of more consumer goods? Our modern salvation might look more like a consumers' paradise than our Puritan founders intended. In "A Driving Fear," Ellen Goodman says we work because we have a fear of falling from our social and financial positions. Perhaps it is just this idea of work that Chief Smohalla is objecting to in "My Young Men Shall Never Work."

Clearly some Americans, maybe many, expect—and find—a great deal of satisfaction in their work: but perhaps too much, and perhaps at too high a price, as Sam Keen argues in "The Price of Success." His description of the typical high-powered corporate executive who has achieved "success" should make everyone pause for thought.

What do the mass media tell us about work in American culture? What sort of work is portrayed or talked about, and in what ways? How often does television show us people hard at work as opposed to people enjoying the pleasures of free time, either spending money or relaxing at home? Are advertisements the source of our messages about work and its rewards? One of this chapter's articles, Barbara Ehrenreich's "Working-Class Heroes No More," claims that blue-collar workers and labor issues are pretty much ignored by television and the movies—both in the news and in entertainment.

"Covering the Cops," by Jon Katz, is about both television and newspaper coverage of police officers' work. Katz gives limited praise to the "unfiltered reality" of the television show "Cops" because it is a better alternative to the extremes of unquestioning acceptance or absurdly harsh criticism implied by other media coverage of police work.

In conclusion, consider work in relation to the other chapters in this book: Do women and men work differently and for different rewards? Is sports a kind of work? Why are people who work full-time still poor? How do the different races and ethnic groups in America experience work? Work is a huge part of our culture and our lives, so there is a lot to explore when you consider how work itself, and the rewards it may bring, are portrayed by the mass media.

Starting Out: Finding Out What You Already Know

1. Jot down a list of words that you associate with the word *work*.
2. What do you think are the "rewards of working"?
3. Do men and women view work and its rewards differently?
4. Which TV occupations seem to you to be the most and the least attractive? Why?
5. Would you say that workers in the United States are treated well, decently, or exploited? Why?

Learning More Through Observation: Taking a Look Around You and Talking to People

1. List five TV shows or movies that portray people at work. Choose one and freewrite about it, focusing on how attractive or unattractive the job seems to be on screen.

2. List five popular TV shows. Which jobs are portrayed on them? Jot down a list in your journal.
3. Interview someone older than you, or someone from another culture, or someone who is in a different situation from you, asking what the person thinks the rewards of working are and what his or her ideal job would be.
4. Is the idea of work the same for all the different groups that make up American culture? List any differences you see.
5. Interview five people and ask them what two things they like best and dislike most about work. Compare your responses to others in class and see what patterns you find.

Questioning: Deciding What Else You Would Like to Know

List five questions that you still have about work and its rewards in American culture.

ELLEN GOODMAN

A Driving Fear

Ellen Goodman, journalist and newspaper columnist, analyzes that "school-starts-tomorrow" feeling we all know so well.

BEFORE YOU READ

1. How do *you* feel on Sunday nights before the school week or workweek begins? Do you feel the same way at the end of the summer holidays?
2. What motivates you to get up and go to school or work?

1   The geese are overhead, flying south in vee formations as crisp as a sharpened pencil. We watched them from the porch in a Maine light transformed by September clarity. Now we follow their lead, proceeding on our own annual migration.

2   The path we take also heads south, along parallel highway lines. We pass the exit to Kennebunkport where George Bush has spent his vacation in the presidential triathlon: fishing at 10, tennis at 11, horseshoes at noon.

3   Within an hour of home, the roads become clogged with our own species: back-to-school, back-to-work creatures.

4   With jars of wild blackberry jam wrapped carefully in T-shirts and towels, we are returning to the real world, although why we call it "real" I cannot tell you.

5   Is reality hard-edged and harried while fantasy is soft and leisurely? Is the real world one of obligations and the fantasy world one of pleasures?

6   Our migration takes only a few hours, but as we reach the city a familiar feeling comes out of its August hibernation. The rush that comes from being rushed.

7   A lick of anxiety accompanies us through the traffic to the airport where, in some adult variation of the old car pool, I leave my once-child on her way back to college.

8   And as I watch her, books, bags, guitar and all, the familiar watchword of the real world comes back into my mind: Hurry. The new year has begun. Hurry.

9   This is what I associate with September as much as clean notebooks and new shoes. We learn all over again to trade our own rhythms for those of school and work, and, in turn, we teach that to our children.

10 In millions of homes there is the same sudden nagging jump-start to the year. It is the sound of our own voices commanding ourselves and our kids: Stop dawdling.

11 On the streets today, there are kids with straight parts in their hair and lunch in their Batman boxes. Behind these kids there is a private tutor, at least one parent whose alarm bell precedes the school bell, whose workday begins with the urgent morning job of getting everyone out of the house. Someone who wages a small battle against the sleepy summer tug of leisure, or its evil twin, sloth.

12 This is what morning is like in America. Not the image of ripe Reaganesque fields and flags, but of pressed parents who may regret the sound of their own impatience sprinkling the breakfast cereal. It is the image of kids collected in buses and cars, delivered to buildings and redistributed to teachers and classrooms. Americans on schedule, on line, productive.

13 There is no mystery to why we trade our inner peace for a workaday lockstep. There is no living to be made on the sand.

14 Nor is there any mystery to why we become our children's trainers in this pattern. We are driven for the most part by what Barbara Ehrenreich calls succinctly[1] in her new book title "The Fear of Falling."

15 Even the middle class in America, or especially the middle class in America, is insecure about its economic future and its children's future. That's more true now in an era when the middle is shrinking and many are slipping down or scrambling up.

16 The fear of falling attaches itself to another anxiety—"a fear of inner weakness," as Ehrenreich observes, "of growing soft, of failing to strive, of losing discipline and will."

17 We fight these anxieties in ourselves by making a virtue out of necessity; hard work. We fight it in our children by driving out daydreams with discipline. Our own days speed up and we teach, even compel, our children to keep up.

18 If we are very lucky, we find work we like and schools where our children are happy. But it's only when we step aside for a time, a week or a summer, that the pace becomes daunting, unnatural.

---

[1] Clearly and briefly.

19   Pretty soon, I know, long before we have emptied the last jar of blackberry jam, it will seem routine again.

20   To the children on my street the school year that crackles with a fresh start will grow as worn and familiar as a chalkboard eraser. Workaday life will seem as normal as wearing a necktie instead of a T-shirt, heels instead of sneakers.

21   But today, having just left the ocean for the city, I am most aware of the deliberate, even dutiful, way we prepare our children to lead the exact life that we find so rushed. The pressure is on. Hurry, kids.

REACTING

1. Does Ellen Goodman describe a feeling you recognize?
2. Do you agree that "fear of falling" is a major reason why people work?

CONNECTING

1. Do the media generally represent this "driving fear" described by Goodman?
2. Are there other authors in this chapter on work and its rewards who discuss motivation for working? Compare their ideas with Goodman's.

LEARNING ABOUT WRITING FROM READING

Goodman uses specific and concrete words to convey the abstract idea of a "driving fear" very vividly to her readers. For example, she talks of the anxiety of the new work year in terms of

pressed parents

kids with straight parts

with their lunch in Batman boxes

On the other hand, disappearing summer relaxation is made concrete in "the last jar of blackberry jam." This technique is important if you want to make your readers feel the experience you are describing. You need to give them images they can relate to, rather than making them guess what (in this case) a "driving fear" really means.

JON KATZ

Covering the Cops

Jon Katz, journalist and media critic, examines the TV show "Cops," focusing on its portrayal of police work and on the journalists whose work it is to create that portrait.

BEFORE YOU READ

1. What fictional police TV shows are you familiar with? What is your opinion of them?
2. What would be the challenges of "covering the cops" if you were a television reporter or a newspaper journalist?

1 Perhaps the most mythologized figure of modern journalism is the urban police reporter, that tough-talking, street-savvy wise-ass who matched cops drink for drink and wisecrack for wisecrack, and who got rewrite from Sweetheart.

2 But that reporter looked a lot better in *The Front Page* than *on* it. Coming, most likely, from a working class background, he identified with and protected the men he covered, becoming their ideological comrade-in-arms rather than watchdog or chronicler. Rarely did he report on police racism, brutality, and corruption and therefore, for middle-class America, such evils hardly existed. These days, the stereotypical police reporter has virtually vanished from the country's newsrooms, while the police are often shown to be corrupt, brutal, and bigoted.

3 Today's upper middle-class, college-educated journalists have little in common with the police, and are frequently to the left of them politically. Brutal police response to antiwar demonstrations and the civil rights movement shook idealized notions of law enforcement. Officer Murphy, twirling his baton and occasionally cuffing an errant rascal for the lad's own good, was replaced by Bull Connor—or, more recently, his heirs on the LAPD. Meanwhile, police seem increasingly isolated, abandoned by journalists and everyone else as they try to deal with horrifying levels of social decay, hatred, and bloodshed. They seem to have turned inward, talking to and trusting no one but their lawyers and each other.

4 Against this backdrop comes *Cops,* perhaps the inevitable television appropriation of the police reporter's role. Syndicated nationwide by Fox television, *Cops* is one of the most successful of the gritty new telecasts that offer Americans more reality than they ever imagined possible. Taped by crews carrying mobile shoulder-held video cameras, shows like *Cops* are what producers call "unfiltered" television—a new wave of reality-based entertainment with serious implications for a news media already reeling from the invasion of talk shows, tabloid telecasts, newsmagazines, and cable-casts.

5 No reporter or producer narrates *Cops;* no equivalent of the journalist offers a detached perspective. The cameras ride with the police in their patrol cars, following the officers and picking up the sounds of jangling keys and handcuffs, squawking radios and creaking leather as they arrest drunk drivers, rush into vicious bar brawls, quell[1] domestic disputes, chase burglars onto rooftops, arrive at murder and accident scenes, pursue kids in stolen cars at hair-raising speeds, and get punched, kicked, run over, spat upon, stabbed, and

---

[1] Quiet; pacify.

sometimes shot at by the people they confront. Those old-time police reporters would keel over in shock.

6 Some departments—in Los Angeles and New York City, for example—have declined to allow *Cops* cameras in their police cars, citing legal concerns or fears for the safety of camera crews. Many, including those in Kansas City, Hoboken, San Diego, Pittsburgh, Houston, and Boston, have agreed to be subjects for the broadcast. Needless to say, the officers selected by their departments to participate are articulate, meticulously professional, sometimes even laughably solicitous. On *Cops*, the police thank drunk drivers profusely for cooperating and hand out quarters to teenagers caught driving without licenses so they can call Mom and Dad to come pick them up.

7 But the officers on *Cops* are nonetheless revealing, often poignantly so. They almost pleadingly make their case to a public they know is skeptical. An officer in New Jersey wonders how the wailing grandchildren of the woman he has just arrested will feel about the police who searched their grandmother's apartment and arrested her on drug charges. A California policeman frets about court rulings that allow lawsuits against individual police officers as well as the municipalities they work for, endangering everything he owns. An officer in Kansas City talks about how serious the consequences of a policeman's mistake may be—far more serious than mistakes made by other American workers.

8 What is striking about these sometimes-eloquent voices is that they rarely are heard in the conventional press.

9 The cameras recording *Cops* probably would not catch a Rodney King-style beating. The officers would know better than to behave like that; even if they didn't, it's unclear whether the broadcast's producers would show it, since the program depends on the voluntary cooperation of the police. As with the old police reporters, the police point of view is what the audience sees and hears.

10 But *Cops* can be riveting, as it is when the camera moves into a woman's house minutes after she's been murdered and lies in a pool of blood, or when it looks over an officer's shoulder as he or she prowls through a pitch-black attic in search of a man they've been told has a gun. In one episode, officers rush to surround a woman who, a caller to 911 has said, is carrying an Uzi submachine gun. As the officers frantically scream for her to put her hands up, a machine gun protrudes visibly from her rear pocket. It turns out to be a realistic-looking plastic toy. The viewer can't help but wonder what would have happened to the woman—and the officers—if she had reached suddenly for her pocket or had not understood English or had been drunk or high on drugs.

11 The media have made it clear that members of minority groups fear and resent the way they're treated by some officers, especially whites from other communities. What *Cops* reminds us is how dangerous, terrifying, and complex a police officer's job is, and how unseemly it is for journalists sitting in safe and comfortable newsrooms to make self-righteous snap judgements about police work.

12 *As angry young men screamed "assassins" at police in Washington Heights yesterday, the sisters of a man killed by a police officer wailed and fainted in the*

Cameras ride with the police in their patrol cars, following the officers as they rush into bar brawls, chase burglars onto rooftops, and get punched, kicked, spat upon, and stabbed.

hallway where their brother's blood still stains the walls. "Oh God, Oh God," the sisters of Jose Garcia, 24, yelled in Spanish as they collapsed in the hallway at 505 W. 162nd St., their voices echoing in the room overcrowded with screaming spectators.

—*New York Newsday,* July 6, 1992

13   In Los Angeles, New York City, Miami, Detroit, and scores of other cities and towns, police behavior has led to bitter condemnations and sometimes to rioting, destruction, and killing. Typically, the officer confronts a young male in an urban neighborhood, is or feels threatened, and wounds or kills the young man. If the officer is white and the youth black or Hispanic, the community and the media—sometimes both—explode.

14   The shooting of Jose "Kiko" Garcia in New York City's teeming Washington Heights last summer is a case in point, not only embodying the tensions between minority groups and the police, but also posing serious questions about how the media cover them.

15   According to the police, on the night of July 3 plainclothes detective Michael O'Keefe and two other officers spotted Jose Garcia on a crowded street and thought they saw a gun in his pocket. O'Keefe became separated from his partners and confronted Garcia alone. Within minutes, O'Keefe was shrieking for help on his police radio; by the time other officers arrived, Garcia lay dead.

16   For days, local newspapers, but especially local television, aired account after account suggesting that Garcia had been killed for no reason. A deputy mayor was widely quoted as saying that Garcia had no arrest record and never carried a gun, and that O'Keefe had been "abusing people for a long time. There was no reason to kill Kiko." The Garcia family's lawyer said pretty much the same thing.

17   On the night of the shooting, an unidentified man told WNBC-TV that O'Keefe had beaten Garcia "until he couldn't stand up, and then just pulled out a gun and killed him. No reason." The reporter, shaking his head sympathetically, never questioned his account in any way.

18   Other eyewitnesses told reporters that O'Keefe beat and kicked Garcia through the inner hallways and lobby of the apartment building into which he had pursued him, then shot him three times as he lay helpless on the floor. Several people said they saw O'Keefe using his radio to beat Garcia and heard Garcia screaming "Mommy" and "Why are you doing this to me?" in Spanish. "He's laying on his face in blood, and then the cop takes out his gun," one supposed eyewitness told *New York Newsday*. "I ran back to my apartment, and then I heard the shots." Some neighbors claimed that O'Keefe was not only a brutal cop, but that he had a reputation for stealing from drug dealers.

19   Not surprisingly, the shooting and its subsequent coverage sparked several days of disorder, looting, and destruction. O'Keefe was burned in effigy, and Washington Heights residents threw trash cans, bottles, and rocks at officers, smashed windows, and burned police cars.

20   Two months later, a Manhattan grand jury cleared Officer O'Keefe of any wrongdoing in the shooting of Garcia, who, it turned out, did have a criminal record involving drugs. The shooting occurred in a building sometimes used by drug dealers. Garcia did have a gun, said the grand jury, and O'Keefe was justified in feeling that his life was in danger during the violent struggle between the two men. Pathologists found cocaine in Garcia's system at the time of his

death. There were no bruises or marks on Garcia's body to suggest a beating, nor were there any signs that O'Keefe's radio had been used to beat Garcia.

21   The audio tapes of a panicked O'Keefe shouting for help were shockingly at odds with accounts that had O'Keefe mercilessly beating Garcia. Moreover, the grand jury found, those eyewitness accounts would have been impossible given lighting, sight lines, and the witnesses' supposed locations. Other witnesses wouldn't testify, recanted their original testimony, or disappeared. Nor did the grand jury find any evidence to support charges that O'Keefe was brutal or corrupt.

22   The most detailed media account of O'Keefe's version of events did not appear until two months after he had been exonerated by the grand jury. In a November 2, 1992, interview in *New York* magazine, O'Keefe described being cut off from his partners in a brutal battle with Garcia that saw the two men fighting desperately for Garcia's gun, O'Keefe screaming for help over his radio as Garcia pointed the barrel of his gun into the officer's face. "I thought I was going to die," O'Keefe told the magazine. The officer said he grabbed Garcia's wrist, drew his gun, and fired a shot at point-blank range into Garcia's stomach.

23   Two days after the shooting, in an effort to calm the Washington Heights community (the Democratic National Convention was only a week away), Mayor David Dinkins visited Garcia's family, enraging many of the city's police officers. The mayor's call for an all-civilian review board enraged them further: in September, more than 10,000 cops and supporters demonstrated at city hall in protest. Some of the officers and their off-duty supporters staged, in effect, their own riot, storming police barricades, blocking the Brooklyn Bridge, shoving reporters and photographers. Some were overheard shouting racial slurs.

24   The protest touched off another wave of condemnation of the police from politicians, community critics, and journalists. THUGS IN BLUE was one tabloid headline. Columnists and editorial writers cited the cops' behavior as yet another example of why minority groups were right to distrust and fear the police. "All those years when we gave police the benefit of the doubt seemed extraordinarily naive in retrospect," wrote Anna Quindlen in *The New York Times*.

25   The media's outrage was certainly appropriate. But no New York City news organization acknowledged that it would also have been appropriate to point out the errors of its coverage of the Garcia shooting, apologize to O'Keefe, or explain to readers and viewers why much of their reporting had been false and misleading.

26   Everything about the shooting—the time of year, the place it occurred, the ethnicity of the officer and of the person he shot—cried out for journalistic restraint. Reporters know that eyewitnesses at crime scenes are often unreliable, excitable advocates for one side or another, sometimes so anxious to be on television that their accounts become more melodramatic than what they actually saw. Reporters also know that some politicians exploit police-community tensions. Besides, police brutality lawsuits can involve enormous amounts of money—some damage settlements have reached into the millions—so that

27 Add the threat of violence and civil disorder and there are lots of reasons for reporters and editors to be extraordinarily cautious about explosive eyewitness accounts of police-community confrontations offered in the heat of the moment. New York's media, prodded by the city's first black mayor, had helped to squelch rumors and maintain calm in the wake of the L.A. riots last spring. But there seems to be less restraint or caution when police shootings are involved.

28 "So what were the Washington Heights riots all about?" *The New York Times* disingenuously wondered in an editorial following the grand jury report. The editorial cited a number of factors that might have led to the unrest—drug gangs trying to force a police retreat, past complaints of police brutality. Coverage of the shooting was not on the list.

29 Among the questions the press faces in dealing with its coverage of the police is whether or not the overwhelming focus on brutality and racism obscures fundamental issues about urban policing:

30 • Has violence in some urban neighborhoods escalated beyond the ability of police departments to cope with it? In Newark, young—sometimes pre-adolescent—thieves in stolen cars ram police cruisers for kicks. They taunt police officers, who are prohibited from engaging in high speed chases. In November, four people were killed in one night by joy-riding kids whose stolen cars crashed. In New York City, 430 children under the age of sixteen had been shot in the first ten months of 1992, 73 of them bystanders. In the first seven months, according to city officials, 51 children under sixteen became homicide victims.

31 • How should police best deal with inner-city males in areas where violence has escalated dramatically? Gun control advocates say there are as many as 150 million guns in America. Scholars and authors like Andrew Hacker (*Two Nations*) and Christopher Jencks (*Rethinking Social Policy*) have begun to document the conditions that overwhelm many urban police departments. The new statistics hardly excuse police brutality, but they at least partly explain why police officers and young males are increasingly confronting one another in violent situations: more kids have more guns and are using them more frequently.

32 Federal researchers report that by the late 1980s, as the drug epidemic swept America's cities, more teen-aged males in urban neighborhoods began dying from gunshot wounds than from any other cause. Death from guns among all U. S. teenagers shot up by 61 percent from 1979 to 1989, but among black teen-aged males in major cities the increase was a staggering 233 percent. A study by the National Crime Analysis Project at Northeastern University found that from 1985 to 1991 the number of sixteen-year-olds arrested for murder climbed by 158 percent, while homicide arrests of fifteen-year-olds more than tripled.

33 • Can white police officers who live in outlying areas control minority urban communities? Should cities enact police residency requirements, thus increasing the number of minority officers? Should different kinds of policing and

patrolling be considered, using neighborhood security aides, social workers, parent-training programs, school-based tutoring, parents, even teen-agers?

34 • Should states of emergency be declared in neighborhoods where children are being slaughtered? Should federal troops or state militias reinforce beleaguered police departments? Should the media deploy more of their own resources to covering violence committed by and upon urban children, thus demonstrating—and pressuring the government to demonstrate—that their plight is as important a story as suburban car-jacking?

35 The police themselves often aren't much help. Cops may resent reporters, but journalists remain the best and most credible vehicle for exploring and explaining police work. Police departments need to be more forthcoming more quickly when their officers are involved in shootings and confrontations, not wait weeks or months for official reports, as happened in the Garcia case.

36 As *Cops* makes clear, the more the public sees of their work, the more comprehensible their work becomes. In October, a *New York Times* reporter, trying to explain the pressures that had led to the unruly police demonstration outside of city hall a month earlier, asked for permission to spend a week with the police in a Brooklyn neighborhood. But departmental officials would agree to allow only one night on radio car patrol and one day on foot patrol. Even though the reporter asked to be assigned to a tough, high-crime precinct, the department insisted that she be assigned to a safe, low-crime precinct. Even there, precinct commanders had to intervene before the reporter was permitted a second day on car patrol. Despite the limitations, the piece was revealing and compelling, in much the same way *Cops* is, belatedly conveying the violence and tensions of urban policing.

37 Broadcasts like *Cops* are moving into a vacuum that would be better filled by journalists. The press needs to move closer to where it belongs on one of the biggest and most important stories in American life: into the middle, prepared to challenge the police when appropriate, but also willing to capture and put into context the environments in which they work.

REACTING

1. How do you feel about an "unfiltered reality" or true-life broadcast like "Cops"? Is it fact or fiction, or both?
2. Can you find evidence from your own news and entertainment media experience that the police are, in fact, presented as "corrupt, brutal, and bigoted"? Describe some examples.

CONNECTING

1. The jobs of both police officer and journalist are mentioned by Jon Katz. What rewards do you think each job brings?

2. Read Barbara Ehrenreich's "Working-Class Heroes No More" below. Compare Katz's ideas about the media's treatment of police work with those of Ehrenreich about media coverage of blue-collar workers.

LEARNING ABOUT WRITING FROM READING

Katz's article contains some nice examples of sentences composed of long lists of distinct but parallel elements. Note, in the following sample, how three such lists are combined in a single long sentence:

> The cameras ride with the police in their patrol cars, following the officers and picking up the sounds of jangling keys and handcuffs, squawking radios and creaking leather as they arrest drunk drivers, rush into vicious bar brawls, quell domestic disputes, chase burglars onto rooftops, arrive at murder and accident scenes, pursue kids in stolen cars at hair-raising speeds, and get punched, kicked, run over, spat upon, stabbed, and sometimes shot at by the people they confront.

How does Katz keep his readers with him? Two ways: (1) he uses commas to separate each item so that we know to expect at least one more thing; and (2) he expresses all the items within each list in the same grammatical form. List one consists of adjective + noun pairs, governed by the phrase "picking up the sounds of." List two contains active verbs, and list three passive verbs, all governed by the subject "they."

BARBARA EHRENREICH

Working-Class Heroes No More

Barbara Ehrenreich, author of many studies of workers in the United States and abroad, looks at the media attention given to American blue-collar workers.

BEFORE YOU READ

1. What recent news items covering labor issues can you recall? List them.
2. Name some working-class heroes.

1   You may not have noticed it, but 50,000 American coal miners have been on strike for six months. The ten-state strike has featured the unprecedented[1] mass application of non-violent civil disobedience to a labor struggle:

---
[1] New; not done before.

Thousands of miners and members of their families were arrested for peacefully blocking mine entrances. Troops were called in; they even, in some instances, fired on the strikers.

2   It was possible, however, to read the daily newspapers with some diligence during the strike and completely miss the story. Meanwhile, the papers I read gave daily front-page coverage to the Soviet coal miners' strike. I do not begrudge a bit of this coverage to the brave miners of Siberia; there were more of them (500,000) and they inhabit a country that has until recently fancied itself to be governed by a "dictatorship of the proletariat." In fact, the Russian strike gave us an idea of what decent labor coverage might be like if the American media were to attempt it: The workers' demands were presented sympathetically; the larger ramifications of the strike were duly analyzed; and individual strike leaders were profiled generously.

3   The eclipse of the American coal miners reflects the media's usual preference for labor insurgency in foreign—ideally, Communist—societies, a preference stunningly illustrated by the ecstatic coverage granted to Solidarity in 1981, at the very moment American air-traffic controllers were being ground under the heel of the Reagan administration. But it also reflects an entirely local phenomenon: the disappearance of the American working class from the mind of the American middle class.

4   Two quick definitions: By "working class" I mean not only industrial workers in hard hats but all those people who are not professionals, managers, or entrepreneurs;[2] who work for wages rather than salaries; and who spend their working hours variously lifting, bending, driving, monitoring, inputting, cleaning, providing physical care for others, loading, unloading, cooking, serving, and the like. The working class, so defined, comprises 60 to 70 percent of the U.S. population.

5   By "middle class" I mean really the "professional middle class," the "professional-managerial class," or what intellectuals often call the "new class." This group includes the journalists, professors, and media executives who are responsible, in a day-to-day sense, for what we see or do not see in the media; what we understand or do not understand to be an "issue." The middle class, so defined, amounts to no more than 20 percent of the U.S. population.

6   So when I say the working class is disappearing, I am not referring to a particular minority group favored, for theoretical reasons, by the left. I mean the American majority. And I am laying the blame not only on the corporate sponsors of the media, who undoubtedly prefer that we think of everyone as either a capitalist or a "consumer," but also on many less wealthy and powerful people—people who, for example, work in the media.

7   The American working class has never received publicity in proportion to its numbers. In the 1950s and early 1960s, for example, the official myth was that America was a classless society, or alternately, "one big middle class." The working class did, however, enjoy a brief modishness in the 1970s, following its

---

[2] People engaged in business ventures.

"discovery" by the media in 1969. This discovery was in many ways parallel to the "discovery" of poverty six years earlier: A previously invisible group was suddenly showcased on the covers of national newsmagazines, examined on television specials, and seized upon by academics. As with the poor, the discovery of the working class brought with it the attention of Hollywood (*The Deer Hunter, Blue Collar, Saturday Night Fever*, etc.) and of journalists and academics (who produced dozens of articles and books on "work in America" and "the neglected majority").

8   Then, in the 1980s, the working class dropped from sight. Hollywood, smitten with the Reagan rich, lost interest; and prime-time television has led us to believe that most every family is supported by a doctor-lawyer team. In academia, the decline of the working class has been, if anything, more complete. As a professor friend explained to me, speaking of his academic colleagues, "Class is out of style." Even the Democratic party, supposed ally of the "little guy," has managed to eschew[3] almost all mention of America's growing class inequality—thus helping guarantee, according to some analysts, their ignominious defeats in 1984 and 1988.

9   So it is possible for a middle-class person today to read the papers, watch television, even go to college, without suspecting that America has any inhabitants other than white-collar operatives and, of course, the annoyingly persistent "black underclass." The producers of public-affairs talk shows do not blush when they serve up four upper-income professionals (all white, male, and usually conservative) to ponder the minimum wage or the need for national health insurance. Never, needless to say, do we hear from an uninsured breadwinner or an actual recipient of the minimum wage. Working-class people are likely to cross the screen only as witnesses to crime or sports events, never as commentators or—even when their own lives are under discussion—as "experts."

10   If anything, the natural solipsism[4] of the professional middle class has increased with the class-polarizing trends of the 1980s. Compared with the situation a decade ago, the classes are less likely to mix in college (with the decline of financial aid), in residential neighborhoods (with the gluttonous rise in real-estate prices), or even in the malls (with the segmentation of the retail industry into upscale and downscale components).

11   In the absence of real contact or communication, stereotypes march on unchallenged; prejudices easily substitute for knowledge. The most intractable stereotype is of the working class (which is, in the middle-class imagination, only white) as a collection of reactionaries and bigots—as reflected, for example, in the use of the terms *hard hat* and *redneck* as class slurs. (In reality, the working class is consistently *more* liberal than the middle class—in their opinions, voting behavior, and party affiliation.)

12   Even deeper than the stereotype of the hard-hat bigot lies the middle-class suspicion that the working class is dumb, inarticulate, and mindlessly loyal to

---

[3] Shun; avoid.

[4] Belief in the importance of the self.

archaic values. In the entertainment media, for example, the working class is usually a setting for macho exhibitionism (from *Saturday Night Fever* to, in cameo, *Working Girl*) or mental impairment (*Married . . . With Children*).

13   Finally, there is the prejudice that grows out of middle-class moralism about matters of taste. All privileged classes seek to differentiate themselves from the less privileged by the ways they dress, eat, and entertain themselves, and tend to see their own choices in these matters as inherently wiser, better, and more aesthetically inspired. For example, in the middle-class stereotype, the white working class is addicted to cigarettes, Budweiser, polyester, and network television. (In part, this is true, because Bud is cheaper than Dos Equis and polyester is cheaper than linen.) Furthermore, in the middle-class view, Budweiser and polyester are "tacky"—a code word for "lower class." Health issues, in addition to a certain reverence for the "natural" in matters of food and fiber, lend these middle-class prejudices a high-minded tone of moral indignation.

14   I do not raise these concerns to stir up guilt or to reinstate the working class as the "agent of revolution" in the classical Marxist sense. But I am alarmed by what seems to me to be the growing parochialism of the professional middle class—living in its own social and residential enclaves, condemned to hear only the opinions of its own members (or, of course, of the truly rich), and cut off from the lives and struggles and insights of the American majority. This parochialism is insidiously[5] self-reinforcing: The less "we" know about "them," the more likely "we" are to forget "them" altogether; and the more likely it is that the Democratic party, seeking to address a phantom middle-class majority, will lose its identity—and with it, the party's historically most loyal supporters.

REACTING

1. What, in fact, does Barbara Ehrenreich mean by "working class"?
2. Can you think of any TV shows and films that do portray these kinds of workers, and thus might change Ehrenreich's argument?

CONNECTING

1. Might Ehrenreich applaud the arrival of a TV show like "Cops"? (See Jon Katz's "Covering the Cops," p. 64.) Why or why not?
2. What labor issues do you consider most important?

LEARNING ABOUT WRITING FROM READING

Ehrenreich begins her argument with a comparison using two little stories, or anecdotes, about American press coverage of the U.S. and Siberian coal strikes. Ironically, Siberia's strikes got coverage but the U.S. strikes did not. Notice how

---

[5] Treacherously alluring but damaging.

she uses the two anecdotes to get us both focused and interested. These two examples show the basis of her argument about lack of coverage of American labor issues in the American media:

> You may not have noticed it, but 50,000 American coal miners have been on strike for six months. The ten-state strike has featured the unprecedented mass application of non-violent civil disobedience to a labor struggle. . . . It was possible, however, to . . . completely miss the story. Meanwhile, the papers I read gave daily front-page coverage to the Soviet coal miners' strike. . . .

STUDS TERKEL

Who Built the Pyramids?

Studs Terkel's book, Working, *is a series of interviews of American workers. In this excerpt, Mike Lefevre, steelworker, talks about his working life.*

BEFORE YOU READ

1. Freewrite on the topic "hard physical repetitive labor."
2. What television shows or films include characters like steelworkers or other blue-collar workers?

Who built the seven towers of Thebes?
The books are filled with the names of kings.
Was it kings who hauled the craggy blocks of stone?
In the evening when the Chinese wall was finished
Where did the masons go?
—BERTOLT BRECHT

Mike Lefevre

1   *It is a two-flat dwelling, somewhere in Cicero, on the outskirts of Chicago. He is thirty-seven. He works in a steel mill. On occasion, his wife Carol works as a waitress in a neighborhood restaurant; otherwise, she is at home, caring for their two small children, a girl and a boy.*

2   *At the time of my first visit, a sculpted statuette of Mother and Child was on the floor, head severed from body. He laughed softly as he indicated his three-year-old daughter: "She Doctor Spock'd it."*

3   I'm a dying breed. A laborer. Strictly muscle work . . . pick it up, put it down, pick it up, put it down. We handle between forty and fifty thousand

pounds of steel a day. (Laughs) I know this is hard to believe—from four hundred pounds to three- and four-pound pieces. It's dying.

4   You can't take pride any more. You remember when a guy could point to a house he built, how many logs he stacked. He built it and he was proud of it. I don't really think I could be proud if a contractor built a home for me. I would be tempted to get in there and kick the carpenter in the ass (laughs), and take the saw away from him. 'Cause I would have to be part of it, you know.

5   It's hard to take pride in a bridge you're never gonna cross, in a door you're never gonna open. You're mass-producing things and you never see the end result of it. (Muses) I worked for a trucker one time. And I got this tiny satisfaction when I loaded a truck. At least I could see the truck depart loaded. In a steel mill, forget it. You don't see where nothing goes.

6   I got chewed out by my foreman once. He said, "Mike, you're a good worker but you have a bad attitude." My attitude is that I don't get excited about my job. I do my work but I don't say whoopee-doo. The day I get excited about my job is the day I go to a head shrinker. How are you gonna get excited about pullin' steel? How are you gonna get excited when you're tired and want to sit down?

7   It's not just the work. Somebody built the pyramids. Somebody's going to build something. Pyramids, Empire State Building—these things just don't happen. There's hard work behind it. I would like to see a building, say, the Empire State, I would like to see on one side of it a foot-wide strip from top to bottom with the name of every bricklayer, the name of every electrician, with all the names. So when a guy walked by, he could take his son and say, "See, that's me over there on the forty-fifth floor, I put the steel beam in." Picasso can point to a painting. What can I point to? A writer can point to a book. Everybody should have something to point to.

8   It's the not-recognition by other people. To say a woman is *just* a housewife is degrading, right? Okay. *Just* a housewife. It's also degrading to say *just* a laborer. The difference is that a man goes out and maybe gets smashed.

9   When I was single, I could quit, just split. I wandered all over the country. You worked just enough to get a poke, money in your pocket. Now I'm married and I got two kids . . . (trails off). I worked on a truck dock one time and I was single. The foreman came over and he grabbed my shoulder, kind of gave me a shove. I punched him and knocked him off the dock. I said, "Leave me alone. I'm doing my work, just stay away from me, just don't give me the with-the-hands business."

10 Hell, if you whip a damn mule he might kick you. Stay out of my way, that's all. Working is bad enough, don't bug me. I would rather work my ass off for eight hours a day with nobody watching me than five minutes with a guy watching me. Who you gonna sock? You can't sock General Motors, you can't sock anybody in Washington, you can't sock a system.

11 A mule, an old mule, that's the way I feel. Oh yeah. See. (Shows black and blue marks on arms and legs, burns.) You know what I heard from more than one guy at work? "If my kid wants to work in a factory, I am going to kick the hell out of him." I want my kid to be an effete snob. Yeah, mm-hmm. (Laughs.) I want him to be able to quote Walt Whitman, to be proud of it.

12   If you can't improve yourself, you improve your posterity. Otherwise life isn't worth nothing. You might as well go back to the cave and stay there. I'm sure the first caveman who went over the hill to see what was on the other side—I don't think he went there wholly out of curiosity. He went there because he wanted to get his son out of the cave. Just the same way I want to send my kid to college.

13   I work so damn hard and want to come home and sit down and lay around. *But I gotta get it out.* I want to be able to turn around to somebody and say, "Hey, fuck you." You know? (Laughs.) The guy sitting next to me on the bus too. 'Cause all day I wanted to tell my foreman to go fuck himself, but I can't.

14   So I find a guy in a tavern. To tell him that. And he tells me too. I've been in brawls. He's punching me and I'm punching him, because we actually want to punch somebody else. The most that'll happen is the bartender will bar us from the tavern. But at work, you lose your job.

15   This one foreman I've got, he's a kid. He's a college graduate. He thinks he's better than everybody else. He was chewing me out and I was saying, "Yeah, yeah, yeah." He said, "What do you mean, yeah, yeah, yeah. Yes *sir.*" I told him, "Who the hell are you, Hitler? What is this *"Yes, sir"* bullshit? I came here to work, I didn't come here to crawl. There's a fuckin' difference." One word led to another and I lost.

16   I got broke down to a lower grade and lost twenty-five cents an hour, which is a hell of a lot. It amounts to about ten dollars a week. He came over—after breaking me down. The guy comes over and smiles at me. I blew up. He didn't know it, but he was about two seconds and two feet away from a hospital. I said, "Stay the fuck away from me." He was just about to say something and was pointing his finger. I just reached my hand up and just grabbed his finger and I just put it back in his pocket. He walked away. I grabbed his finger because I'm married. If I'd a been single, I'd a grabbed his head. That's the difference.

17   You're doing this manual labor and you know that technology can do it. (Laughs.) Let's face it, a machine can do the work of a man; otherwise they wouldn't have space probes. Why can we send a rocket ship that's unmanned and yet send a man in a steel mill to do a mule's work?

18   Automation? Depends how it's applied. It frightens me if it puts me out on the street. It doesn't frighten me if it shortens my work week. You read that little thing: what are you going to do when this computer replaces you? Blow up computers. (Laughs.) Really. Blow up computers. I'll be goddamned if a computer is gonna eat before I do! I want milk for my kids and beer for me. Machines can either liberate man or enslave 'im, because they're pretty neutral. It's man who has the bias to put the thing one place or another.

19   If I had a twenty-hour workweek, I'd get to know my kids better, my wife better. Some kid invited me to go on a college campus. On a Saturday. It was summertime. Hell, if I had a choice of taking my wife and kids to a picnic or going to a college campus, it's gonna be the picnic. But if I worked a twenty-hour week, I could go do both. Don't you think with that extra twenty hours people could really expand? Who's to say? There are some people in factories just by force of circumstance. I'm just like the colored people. Potential

Einsteins don't have to be white. They could be in cotton fields, they could be in factories.

20   The twenty-hour week is a possibility today. The intellectuals, they always say there are potential Lord Byrons, Walt Whitmans, Roosevelts, Picassos working in construction or steel mills or factories. But I don't think they believe it. I think what they're afraid of is the potential Hitlers and Stalins that are there too. The people in power fear the leisure man. Not just the United States. Russia's the same way.

21   What do you think would happen in this country if, for one year, they experimented and gave everybody a twenty-hour week? How do they know that the guy who digs Wallace today doesn't try to resurrect Hitler tomorrow? Or the guy who is mildly disturbed at pollution doesn't decide to go to General Motors and shit on the guy's desk? You can become a fanatic if you had the time. The whole thing is time. That is, I think, one reason rich kids tend to be fanatic about politics: they have time. Time, that's the important thing.

22   It isn't that the average working guy is dumb. He's tired, that's all. I picked up a book on chess one time. That thing laid in the drawer for two or three weeks, you're too tired. During the weekends you want to take your kids out. You don't want to sit there and the kid comes up: "Daddy, can I go to the park?" You got your nose in a book? Forget it.

23   I know a guy fifty-seven years old. Know what he tells me? "Mike, I'm old and tired *all* the time." The first thing happens at work: When the arms start moving, the brain stops. I punch in about ten minutes to seven in the morning. I say hello to a couple of guys I like, I kid around with them. One guy says good morning to you and you say good morning. To another guy you say fuck you. The guy you say fuck you to is your friend.

24   I put on my hard hat, change into my safety shoes, put on my safety glasses, go to the bonderizer. It's the thing I work on. They rake the metal, they wash it, they dip it in a paint solution, and we take it off. Put it on, take it off, put it on, take it off, put it on, take it off. . .

25   I say hello to everybody but my boss. At seven it starts. My arms get tired about the first half-hour. After that, they don't get tired any more until maybe the last half-hour at the end of the day. I work from seven to three thirty. My arms are tired at seven thirty and they're tired at three o'clock. I hope to God I never get broke in, because I always want my arms to be tired at seven thirty and three o'clock. (Laughs.) 'Cause that's when I know that there's a beginning and there's an end. That I'm not brainwashed. In between, I don't even try to think.

26   If I were to put you in front of a dock and I pulled up a skid in front of you with fifty hundred-pound sacks of potatoes and there are fifty more skids just like it, and this is what you're gonna do all day, what would you think about—potatoes? Unless a guy's a nut, he never thinks about work or talks about it. Maybe about baseball or about getting drunk the other night or he got laid or he didn't get laid. I'd say one out of a hundred will actually get excited about work.

27   Why is it that the communists always say they're for the workingman, and as soon as they set up a country, you got guys singing to tractors? They're singing

about how they love the factory. That's where I couldn't buy communism. It's the intellectuals' utopia, not mine. I cannot picture myself singing to a tractor, I just can't. (Laughs.) Or singing to steel. (Singsongs.) Oh whoop-dee-doo, I'm at the bonderizer, oh how I love this heavy steel. No thanks. Never hoppen.

28   Oh yeah, I daydream. I fantasize about a sexy blonde in Miami who's got my union dues. (Laughs.) I think of the head of the union the way I think of the head of my company. Living it up. I think of February in Miami. Warm weather, a place to lay in. When I hear a college kid say, "I'm oppressed," I don't believe him. You know what I'd like to do for one year? Live like a college kid. Just for one year. I'd love to. Wow! (Whispers) Wow! Sports car! Marijuana! (Laughs.) Wild, sexy broads. I'd love that, hell yes, I would.

29   Somebody has to do this work. If my kid ever goes to college, I just want him to have a little respect, to realize that his dad is one of those somebodies. This is why even on—(muses) yeah, I guess, sure—on the black thing . . . (Sighs heavily.) I can't really hate the colored fella that's working with me all day. The black intellectual I got no respect for. The white intellectual I got no use for. I got no use for the black militant who's gonna scream three hundred years of slavery to me while I'm busting my ass. You know what I mean? (Laughs.) I have one answer for that guy; go see Rockefeller. See Harriman. Don't bother me. We're in the same cotton field. So just don't bug me. (Laughs.)

30   After work I usually stop off at a tavern. Cold beer. Cold beer right away. When I was single, I used to go into hillbilly bars, get in a lot of brawls. Just to explode. I got a thing on my arm here (indicates scar). I got slapped with a bicycle chain. Oh, wow! (Softly) Mmm. I'm getting older. (Laughs.) I don't explode as much. You might say I'm broken in. (Quickly) No, I'll never be broken in. (Sighs.) When you get a little older, you exchange the words. When you're younger, you exchange the blows.

31   When I get home, I argue with my wife a little bit. Turn on TV, get mad at the news. (Laughs.) I don't even watch the news that much. I watch Jackie Gleason. I look for any alternative to the ten o'clock news. I don't want to go to bed angry. Don't hit a man with anything heavy at five o'clock. He just can't be bothered. This is his time to relax. The heaviest things he wants is what his wife has to tell him.

32   When I come home, know what I do for the first twenty minutes? Fake it. I put on a smile. I got a kid three years old. Sometimes she says, "Daddy, where've you been?" I say, "Work." I could have told her I'd been in Disneyland. What's work to a three-year-old kid? If I feel bad, I can't take it out on the kids. Kids are born innocent of everything but birth. You can't take it out on your wife either. This is why you go to a tavern. You want to release it there rather than do it at home. What does an actor do when he's got a bad movie? I got a bad movie every day.

33   I don't even need the alarm clock to get up in the morning. I can go out drinking all night, fall asleep at four, and bam! I'm up at six—no matter what I do. (Laughs.) It's a pseudo-death, more or less. Your whole system is paralyzed and you give all the appearance of death. It's an ingrown clock. It's a thing you just get used to. The hours differ. It depends. Sometimes my wife wants to do

something crazy like play five hundred rummy or put a puzzle together. It could be midnight, could be ten o'clock, could be nine thirty.

What do you do weekends?

34   Drink beer, read a book. See that one? *Violence in America*. It's one of them studies from Washington. One of them committees they're always appointing. A thing like that I read on a weekend. But during the weekdays, gee . . . I just thought about it. I don't do that much reading from Monday through Friday. Unless it's a horny book. I'll read it at work and go home and do my homework. (Laughs.) That's what the guys at the plant call it—homework. (Laughs.) Sometimes my wife works on Saturday and I drink beer at the tavern.

35   I went out drinking with one guy, oh, a long time ago. A college boy. He was working where I work now. Always preaching to me about how you need violence to change the system and all that garbage. We went into a hillbilly joint. Some guy there, I didn't know him from Adam, he said, "You think you're smart." I said What's your pleasure?" (Laughs.) He said, "My pleasure's to kick your ass." I told him I really can't be bothered. He said, "What're you, chicken?" I said, "No, I just don't want to be bothered." He came over and said something to me again. I said, "I don't beat women, drunks, or fools. Now leave me alone."

36   The guy called his brother over. This college boy that was with me, he came nudging my arm, "Mike, let's get out of here." I said, "What are you worried about?" (Laughs.) This isn't unusual. People will bug you. You fend it off as much as you can with your mouth and when you can't, you punch the guy out.

37   It was close to closing time and we stayed. We could have left, but when you go into a place to have a beer and a guy challenges you—if you expect to go in that place again, you don't leave. If you have to fight the guy, you fight.

38   I got just outside the door and one of these guys jumped on me and grabbed me around the neck. I grabbed his arm and flung him against the wall. I grabbed him here (indicates throat), and jiggled his head against the wall quite a few times. He kind of slid down a little bit. This guy who said he was his brother took a swing at me with a garrison belt. He just missed and hit the wall. I'm looking around for my junior Stalin (laughs), who loves violence and everything. He's gone. Split. (Laughs.) Next day I see him at work. I couldn't get mad at him, he's a baby.

39   He saw a book in my back pocket one time and he was amazed. He walked up to me and he said, "You read?" I said, "What do you mean, I read?" He said, "All these dummies read the sports pages around here. What are you doing with a book?" I got pissed off at the kid right away. I said, "What do you mean, all these dummies? Don't knock a man who's paying somebody's else's way through college." He was a nineteen-year-old effete snob.

Yet you want your kid to be an effete snob?

40   Yes, I want my kid to look at me and say, "Dad, you're a nice guy, but you're a fuckin' dummy." Hell yes, I want my kid to tell me that he's not gonna be like me . . .

41   If I were hiring people to work, I'd try naturally to pay them a decent wage. I'd try to find out their first names, their last names, keep the company as small as possible, so I could personalize the whole thing. All I would ask a man is a handshake, see you in the morning. No applications, nothing. I wouldn't be interested in the guy's past. Nobody ever checks the pedigree on a mule, do they? But they do on a man. Can you picture walking up to a mule and saying, "I'd like to know who his granddaddy was?"

42   I'd like to run a combination bookstore and tavern. (Laughs.) I would like to have a place where college kids came and a steelworker could sit down and talk. Where a workingman could not be ashamed of Walt Whitman and where a college professor could not be ashamed that he painted his house over the weekend.

43   If a carpenter built a cabin for poets, I think the least the poets owe the carpenter is just three or four one-liners on the wall. A little plaque: Though we labor with our minds, this place we can relax in was built by someone who can work with his hands. And his work is as noble as ours. I think the poet owes something to the guy who builds the cabin for him.

44   I don't think of Monday. You know what I'm thinking about on Sunday night? Next Sunday. If you work real hard, you think of a perpetual[1] vacation. Not perpetual sleep . . . What do I think of on a Sunday night? Lord, I wish the fuck I could do something else for a living.

45   I don't know who the guy is who said there is nothing sweeter than an unfinished symphony. Like an unfinished painting and an unfinished poem. If he creates this thing one day—let's say, Michelangelo's Sistine Chapel. It took him a long time to do this, this beautiful work of art. But what if he had to create this Sistine Chapel a thousand times a year? Don't you think that would even dull Michelangelo's mind? Or if da Vinci had to draw his anatomical charts thirty, forty, fifty, sixty, eighty, ninety, a hundred times a day? Don't you think that would even bore da Vinci?

Way back, you spoke of the guys who built the pyramids, not the pharaohs, the unknowns. You put yourself in their category?

46   Yes. I want my signature on 'em, too. Sometimes, out of pure meanness, when I make something, I put a little dent in it. I like to do something to make it really unique. Hit it with a hammer. I deliberately fuck it up to see if it'll get by, just so I can say I did it. It could be anything. Let me put it this way: I think God invented the dodo bird so when we get up there we could tell Him, "Don't you ever make mistakes?" and He'd say, "Sure, look." (Laughs.) I'd like to make my imprint. My dodo bird. A mistake, *mine*. Let's say the whole building is nothing but red bricks. I'd like to have just the black one or the white one or the purple one. Deliberately fuck up.

47   This is gonna sound square, but my kid is my imprint. He's my freedom. There's a line in one of Hemingway's books. I think it's from *For Whom the Bell Tolls*. They're behind the enemy lines, somewhere in Spain, and she's pregnant.

---

[1] Unending.

She wants to stay with him. He tells her no. He says, "if you die, I die," knowing he's gonna die. But if you go, I go. Know what I mean? The mystics call it the brass bowl. Continuum. You know what I mean? This is why I work. Every time I see a young guy walk by with a shirt and tie and dressed up real sharp, I'm lookin' at my kid, you know? That's it.

REACTING

1. Now that you've read the essay, tell why Mike Lefevre wants to ask the question "Who built the pyramids?"
2. What is your impression of Mike Lefevre and his views on work?

CONNECTING

1. Turn to p. 85 and read Sam Keen's portrait of successful corporate executives. Compare it with Mike Lefevre's account.
2. Jon Katz describes a TV show/documentary about policemen in "Covering the Cops" (p. 64). Imagine a similiar show about steelworkers. What would it be like?

LEARNING ABOUT WRITING FROM READING

"Who Built the Pyramids?" is an example of a particular kind of interview technique. Studs Terkel, the author and interviewer, has taken himself out of the interview and allowed Mike Lefevre to speak for himself with only occasional prompting questions. The result is almost a monologue. This interview format can be very effective if it sounds like natural talk and if the speaker is well focused. In the long first section of this interview, Mike Lefevre seems to be responding to the general question, "What is your work like and how do you feel about it?"

CHIEF SMOHALLA

My Young Men Shall Never Work

As told by Herbert J. Spinden.

Chief Smohalla was a Native American, a Nez Percé. Herbert Spinden's report of Chief Smohalla's words shows us a view of work that may be surprisingly different from our own.

BEFORE YOU READ

1. Look at the very first sentence of this short passage. What does that first sentence lead you to expect?

2. Think of your own reasons for arguing that "young men (and women) should never work."

> The Nez Percé are a tribe of American Indians formerly occupying much of the Pacific Northwest whose reservation is in Idaho.
>
> Because Native Americans resisted giving up their homes and nomadic way of life to become farmers, white people have often called them lazy, stubborn, and impractical. But to Indians, whose homes, land, and hunting were sacred, anything that threatened any one of these, threatened their whole system of beliefs and values, in short, their very life.

1. My young men shall never work. Men who work cannot dream and wisdom comes in dreams.
2. You ask me to plow the ground. Shall I take a knife and tear my mother's breast? Then when I die she will not take me to her bosom to rest.
3. You ask me to dig for stone. Shall I dig under her skin for bones? Then when I die I cannot enter her body to be born again.
4. You ask me to cut grass and make hay and sell it and be rich like white men. But how dare I cut off my mother's hair?
5. It is a bad law and my people cannot obey it. I want my people to stay with me here. All the dead men will come to life again. We must wait here in the house of our fathers and be ready to meet them in the body of our mother.

REACTING

1. Freewrite or discuss your immediate reactions to Chief Smohalla's reasons for not working.
2. Do his reasons make sense for people who are not of the Nez Percé culture? Try to translate them into your own cultural terms.

CONNECTING

1. Compare this article with Ellen Goodman's "A Driving Fear" (p. 62). Do they share any common ground? Discuss.
2. Think about the rewards of working from your own experience, and use them to respond to Chief Smohalla.

LEARNING ABOUT WRITING FROM READING

This short passage is an excellent example of the way that repeated sentence openings create a pattern that helps the reader not only to understand but also to *feel* the writer's position. The three "You ask me's" imply that the speaker is under pressure from another person, or people, who all want him to do something else. But Chief Smohalla has an answer for all of their demands.

Sam Keen

The Price of Success

Sam Keen, writer on men's issues, describes and analyzes one of the typical American success stories: the male corporate executive. Sam Keen wrote Fire in the Belly: On Being a Man *(1991), from which this excerpt is taken.*

BEFORE YOU READ

1. Try to answer the question asked in the first sentence of the article.
2. Offer your own definition of success.

1   At what cost to the life of our body and spirit do we purchase corporate and professional success? What sacrifices are we required to make to these upstart economic gods?

2   Here are some of the secrets they didn't tell you at the Harvard Business School, some of the hidden, largely unconscious, tyrannical, unwritten rules that govern success in professional and corporate life:

3   *Cleanliness is next to prosperity.* Sweat is lower class, lower status. Those who shower before work and use deodorant make more than those who shower after work and smell human throughout the day. As a nation we are proud that only three percent of the population has to work on the land—get soiled, be earthy—to feed the other ninety-seven percent.

4   *Look but don't touch.* The less contact you have with real stuff—raw material, fertilizer, wood, steel, chemicals, making things that have moving parts—the more money you will make. Lately, as we have lost our edge in manufacturing and production, we have comforted ourselves with the promise that we can prosper by specializing in service and information industries. Oh, so clean.

5   *Prefer abstractions.* The further you move up toward the catbird seat, the penthouse, the office with the view of all Manhattan, the more you live among abstractions. In the brave new world of the market you may speculate in hog futures without ever having seen a pig, buy out an airline without knowing how to fly a plane, grow wealthy without having produced anything.

6   *Specialize.* The modern economy rewards experts, men and women who are willing to become focused, concentrated, tightly bound, efficient. Or to put the matter more poignantly, we succeed in our professions to the degree that we sacrifice wide-ranging curiosity and fascination with the world at large, and become departmental in our thinking. The professions, like medieval castles, are small kingdoms sealed off from the outer world by walls of jargon. Once initiated by the ritual of graduate school, MBAs, economists, lawyers, and physicians speak only to themselves and theologians speak only to God.

7   *Sit still and stay indoors.* The world is run largely by urban, sedentary males. The symbol of power is the chair. The chairman of the board sits and manages. As a general rule those who stay indoors and move the least make the most money. Muscle doesn't pay. Worse yet, anybody who has to work in the sun and rain is likely to make the minimum wage. With the exception of quarterbacks, boxers, and race car drivers, whose bodies are broken for our entertainment, men don't get ahead by moving their bodies.

8   *Live by the clock.* Ignore your intimate body time, body rhythms, and conform to the demands of corporate time, work time, professional time. When "time is money," we bend our bodies and minds to the demands of EST (economic standard time). We interrupt our dreams when the alarm rings, report to work at nine, eat when the clock strikes twelve, return to our private lives at five, and retire at sixty-five—ready or not. As a reward we are allowed weekends and holidays for recreation. Conformity to the sacred routine, showing up on time, is more important than creativity. Instead of "taking our time" we respond to deadlines. Most successful men, and lately women, become Type A personalities, speed freaks, addicted to the rush of adrenaline, filled with a sense of urgency, hard driven, goal oriented, and stressed out. The most brutal example of this rule is the hundred-hour week required of physicians in their year of residency. This hazing ritual, like circumcision, drives home the deep mythic message that your body is no longer your own.

9   *Wear the uniform.* It wouldn't be so bad if those who earned success and power were proud enough in their manhood to peacock their colors. But no. Success makes drab. The higher you rise in the establishment the more colorless you become, the more you dress like an undertaker or a priest. Bankers, politicians, CEOs[1] wear black, gray, or dark blue, with maybe a bold pinstripe or a daring "power tie." And the necktie? That ultimate symbol of the respectable man has obviously been demonically designed to exile the head from the body and restrain

---

[1] *CEOs:* chief executive officers.

all deep and passionate breath. The more a corporation, institution, or profession requires the sacrifice of the individuality of its members, the more it requires uniform wear. The corp isn't really looking for a few good men. It's looking for a few dedicated Marines, and it knows exactly how to transform boys into uniform men. As monks and military men have known for centuries, once you get into the habit you follow the orders of the superior.

10 *Keep your distance, stay in your place.* The hierarchy of power and prestige that governs every profession and corporation establishes the proper distance between people. There are people above you, people below you, and people on your level, and you don't get too close to any of them. Nobody hugs the boss. What is lacking is friendship. I know of no more radical critique of economic life than the observation by Earl Shorris that nowhere in the vast literature of management is there a single chapter on friendship.

11 *Desensitize yourself.* Touch, taste, smell—the realm of the senses—receive little homage. What pays off is reason, will-power, planning, discipline, control. There has, of course, recently been a move afoot to bring potted plants and tasteful art to make corporate environments more humane. But the point of these exercises in aesthetics, like the development of communication skills by practitioners of organizational development, is to increase production. The bottom line is still profit, not pleasure or persons.

12 *Don't trouble yourself with large moral issues.* The more the world is governed by experts, specialists, and professionals, the less anybody takes responsibility for the most troubling consequences of our success-failure. Television producers crank out endless cop and killing tales, but refuse to consider their contribution to the climate of violence. Lawyers concern themselves with what is legal, not what is just. Physicians devote themselves to kidneys or hearts of individual patients while the health delivery system leaves masses without medicine. Physicists invent new generations of genocidal weapons which they place in the eager arms of the military. The military hands the responsibility for their use over to politicians. Politicians plead that they have no choice—the enemy makes them do it. Professors publish esoterica while students perish from poor teaching. Foresters, in cahoots with timber companies, clear-cut or manage the forest for sustained yield, but nobody is in charge of oxygen regeneration. Psychologists heal psyches while communities fall apart. Codes of professional ethics are for the most part, like corporate advertisements, high sounding but self-serving.

13 When we live within the horizons of the economic myth, we begin to consider it honorable for a man to do whatever he must to make a living. Gradually

we adopt what Erich Fromm[2] called "a marketing orientation" toward ourselves. We put aside our dreams, forget the green promise of our young selves, and begin to tailor our personalities to what the market requires. When we mold ourselves into commodities, practice smiling and charm so we will have "winning personalities," learn to sell ourselves, and practice the silly art of power dressing, we are certain to be haunted by a sense of emptiness.

14   Men, in our culture, have carried a special burden of unconsciousness, of ignorance of the self. The unexamined life[3] has been worth quite a lot in economic terms. It has enabled us to increase the gross national product yearly. It may not be necessary to be a compulsive extrovert to be financially successful, but it helps. Especially for men, ours is an outer-directed culture that rewards us for remaining strangers to ourselves, unacquainted with feeling, intuition, or the subtleties of sensation and dreams.

15   Many of the personality characteristics that have traditionally been considered "masculine"—aggression, rationality—are not innate or biological components of maleness but are products of a historical era in which men have been socially assigned the chief roles in warfare and the economic order. As women increasingly enter the quasimilitary world of the economic system they are likely to find themselves governed by the logic of the system. Some feminists, who harbor a secret belief in the innate moral superiority of women, believe that women will change the rules of business and bring the balm of communication and human kindness into the boardroom. To date this has been a vain hope. Women executives have proven themselves the equal of men in every way—including callousness. The difference between the sexes is being eroded as both sexes become defined by work. It is often said that the public world of work is a man's place and that as women enter it they will become increasingly "masculine" and lose their "femininity." To think this way is to miss the most important factor of the economic world. Economic man, the creature who defines itself within the horizons of work and consumption, is not man in any full sense of the word, but a being who has been neutralized, degendered, rendered subservient to the laws of the market. The danger of economics is not that it turns women into men but that it destroys the fullness of both manhood and womanhood.

REACTING

1. Think of some opposing viewpoints to rebut Sam Keen's statement: "Economic man, the creature who defines itself within the horizons of work and consumption, is not man in any full sense of the word, but a being who has been neutralized, degendered, rendered subservient to the laws of the market."

---

[2] *Erich Fromm:* German American psychologist and social critic (1900–1980).

[3] *the unexamined life:* in Plato's *Apology of Socrates,* Socrates says "the life which is unexamined is not worth living."

2. Choose one of the items on Keen's list of things you must do or be in order to become a successful professional. Describe some concrete examples of Keen's "rules," or some illustrations from professional work that undermine them.

CONNECTING

1. After reading Herb Goldberg's article "In Harness: The Male Condition" in the chapter on gender roles (p. 138), compare Keen's view of men in our culture with Goldberg's.
2. Do Sam Keen and Chief Smohalla ("My Young Men Shall Never Work," p. 83) share any common ground in their views on work?

LEARNING ABOUT WRITING FROM READING

Keen's article shows the power of the short, simple, declarative sentence: one without buts, becauses, althoughs, and howevers. Here's one example:

> Sit still and stay indoors. The world is run largely by urban, sedentary males. The symbol of power is the chair. The chairman of the board sits and manages. As a general rule those who stay indoors and move the least make the most money. Muscle doesn't pay.

Sentences 1, 2, 3, 4 and 6, in particular, are like bullets, getting quickly to the heart of the matter. But the sentences do not produce a confused, fragmentary effect. This is because the writer has been careful to build connections by employing synonyms or near-synonyms instead of conjunctions: *sedentary* in sentence 2 reminds us of *indoors* in sentence 1: *chairman* and *sits* remind us of *chair; muscle* reminds us of *move*—and so on. We are thus kept on track without the help of explicit joining words.

WRITING ASSIGNMENTS

ASSIGNMENT I
DESCRIBE THE WAY A TELEVISION SHOW PRESENTS A PARTICULAR OCCUPATION AND EVALUATE THE ACCURACY OF THE PORTRAYAL.

Coming Up with Ideas and a Focus

This assignment asks you to do two things: describe and evaluate for accuracy in relation to real life. Before you can choose a show, however, you need to review or find out about television shows that portray work of some kind. Then select a show and do some close analysis to come up with ideas about the way an occupation is portrayed.

Here are some questions to bear in mind as you watch:

What exactly is the job? Be sure you can name it.

What work activities are shown on screen? Writing, telephoning, giving orders, making something, and making decisions are some examples.

What rewards are shown?

What do you learn about the worker outside the workplace (e.g., family, social life, personality)?

Your notes on questions like these should give you plenty of ideas to write about. (For help with analyzing, see pp. 331–340.)

Organizing Your Ideas

One way to organize your ideas is to follow the question's own two-part outline: describe the television portrayal of the occupation and then evaluate it. Some kind of guiding statement, early on in the paper, about what the portrayal is like and how accurate it is will help your readers to stay on track with you.

Audience

If you imagine that you have to present this paper to people who actually work in the occupation you describe, you may find that you will be more aware of the need for careful and accurate description of what's on the screen and of the need for accurate knowledge of the same occupation in the real world. Otherwise, it will be tough to persuade your readers that your evaluation is a sound one.

ASSIGNMENT II
WHY SHOULD WE WORK? WRITE A RESPONSE TO CHIEF SMOHALLA'S SPEECH "MY YOUNG MEN SHALL NEVER WORK."

Coming Up with Ideas and a Focus

This is such an unusual question that, at first, you may have no ideas at all until you start talking or writing about why we should or should not work. Or you may be absolutely certain of your answer, but be unable to explain why: "Yes—work is good!" (So why do I always feel so exhausted?) Or "No—we should be free of work!" (But what would be the alternative?) In a single paper you will have room to focus only on a few important reasons for your response. Think of incidents related to your work experience and your leisure-time activities to support your position.

Organizing Your Ideas

One format to think about here might be cause and effect. The question "Why should we work?" invites a yes or no response and then *because*. . . . Then consider the order of presentation of your reasons: most important first? lead up to the most important?

Audience

The assignment invites you to address Chief Smohalla, or someone who holds ideas like his, with ideas about work that may be different from those of most Americans. What can you say to persuade him that we should indeed work? Or how can you show that you agree with him, but perhaps for different reasons?

ASSIGNMENT III
DESCRIBE A JOB YOU WOULD LIKE TO HAVE AND DECIDE IF THE MEDIA HAVE INFLUENCED YOU TO WANT THIS JOB.

Coming Up with Ideas and a Focus

As you begin work on this paper, try making notes on your "dream" job and then making notes on any television, movie, or press coverage of it. The assignment suggests two focuses for the paper: the job itself and the impact of media coverage. You'll want to figure out from your notes on media coverage how big a role the media have played in shaping your feelings about the job.

Organizing Your Ideas

The comments on focus also suggest a two-part outline: (1) describe the job you'd like to have, and why; and (2) explain the media's influence on your attitude toward the job. Note that part 2 actually breaks down into two subparts: a description of media coverage plus an explanation of its impact on your opinions about the job. In order to keep your readers with you as they move through your ideas, make some kind of very brief guiding statement, or main point, early on in your paper, about why you like the job and how much the media have influenced you.

Audience

Try addressing your paper to your classmates. If everyone is writing the same kind of paper, pool your responses and see if you can generalize about popular occupations and the influence of the media on work choices. Remember that your classmates may never have considered the job or the media examples you have chosen, so you will need to inform them clearly and concisely about both issues.

ASSIGNMENT IV
WATCH SEVEN DAYS' WORTH OF NETWORK NEWS. WRITE A REPORT ON THAT WEEK'S LEVEL OF TV NEWS INTEREST IN LABOR ISSUES, COMMENTING ON THE SIGNIFICANCE OF WHAT YOU HAVE FOUND.

Coming Up with Ideas and a Focus

Coming up with ideas for this assignment will mean watching television with notebook in hand. (You may even want to create a chart for easier recording of data.) You are asked here to analyze what you see by focusing on what appears, how often, and for how long. Your final paper will summarize your findings in a report. You may also choose to record information about *how* labor issues were portrayed: what positive or negative terms were used, how the people looked or behaved, and so on. (For help with analyzing, see pp. 331–340.)

Organizing Your Ideas

One format to try out is the pattern of many research reports:

- Investigating questions (what you wanted to find out)
- Methods of research (how you found out your data)
- The actual research data (what you found)
- Conclusions (what your data mean)

Many researchers also briefly show their conclusions at the beginning of their report, with the rest of their information supporting that statement.

Audience

Who might read this kind of report? Try directing the introduction and conclusion, which frame your research data, to an audience concerned about labor issues. See if you can awaken their interest in your project—a systematic study of what the audience may have half-noticed but never really analyzed. Be sure to include a clear summary of your findings for them to think about.

Chapter 3

Diversity

KEY QUESTIONS
Is the "melting pot" working?
How do the media portray America's ethnic and racial groups?

• •

America is God's crucible, the great melting pot, where all the races of Europe are melting and reforming!
—Israel Zangwill, The Melting Pot

There is little connection between the lives of black Americans and the images of blacks that Americans view daily.
—Henry Louis Gates, Jr., "TV's Black World Turns—But Stays Unreal"

Do I really want to be integrated into a burning house?
—James Baldwin, The Fire Next Time

Introduction

What defines America? Surely racial and ethnic diversity must be part of the answer. We are proud of our diversity: the variety of people enriching America with their energy, in contrast to the "sameness" of other countries. We think of our Statue of Liberty still welcoming the "huddled masses," the exhausted immigrants from the Old World. On a less exalted level, we savor our rich global mix of foods—pizzas, egg rolls, burritos, blintzes—as evidence of our diversity. These things are part of our patriotic feeling that the American experience and historical experiment are good and have somehow worked—that diversity really does enrich and strengthen our country.

On the other hand, is America really the harmonious melting pot portrayed in the history books? Prejudice and racism in their many forms are still major forces in the United States. Simply considering our other chapters—on work, gender roles, poverty, violence, and environment—in relation to different racial and ethnic groups may indicate the uneasiness of our diversity. Do all our culture's groups experience these things in the same ways? Writers in this chapter offer some opinions on these issues. Peggy McIntosh's essay, "White Privilege: Unpacking the Invisible Knapsack," takes a look at how racism resembles sexism in its ability to recognize the unearned advantages that accompany whiteness and maleness in our society. Brent Staples's essay, "Just Walk On By: A Black Man Ponders His Power to Alter Public Space," suggests that even a visit to a jewelry store can be a different experience for members of different races.

Equality, integration: these are virtues for most Americans. But sometimes we may question exactly how equal we really are—and how integrated. Some people might even wonder if equality and integration—the traditional "melting pot" virtues—are always desirable. What happens when the result of integration is a dull sameness rather than varieties of excellence? Fox Butterfield's "Why They Excel" examines an ethnic group whose success may be a result of its resistance to integration into a rather mediocre mainstream American culture.

Television, the movies, and newspapers, as parts of that culture, help to shape our views of ourselves and others. Think for a minute about how African, Anglo, Asian, Hispanic, and Italian Americans are represented on the screen and in print. Jack Shaheen gives us some very personal responses to portrayals of his own ethnic group in "The Media's Image of Arabs." Henry Louis Gates, in "TV's Black World Turns—But Stays Unreal," notes the presence of African Americans on the television screen but doesn't look there for a vision of a racially equal society. More optimistically, Debra Gersh's "Portrayals of Latinos in and by the Media" claims that the media have the power, if only they will use it, to bring about another "civil rights movement"—only this time with Latinos/Hispanic Americans at the center.

So take a look at what images are presented by the mass media, how stereotyped or realistic those images are, how closely the media represent real life, and what role, if any, the media play in unifying—or dividing—American culture. In doing so, you'll be addressing a question that challenges the notion of this entire text: Is there a single American culture that we can study as a unit, or do many groups within the United States feel more tightly bound to their own cultures than to the so-called "American" culture of this book's title?

Starting Out: Finding Out What You Already Know

1. What stereotypes do you frequently hear about your own racial or ethnic group?
2. How many different groups were you aware of in your neighborhood when you were growing up? Do a journal entry on your memories of ethnic and racial diversity (or lack of it) at school or at home.
3. Freewrite your thoughts on one of the quotations listed at the beginning of this chapter.
4. List from memory any television programs or films that feature characters outside mainstream white America.
5. What do you associate with the phrase "America's melting pot"?

Learning More Through Observation: Taking a Look Around You and Talking to People

1. Look in *TV Guide* and list those programs that feature different racial and ethnic groups.
2. Choose a suitable magazine advertisement and freewrite your response to the way the picture and the copy deal with assumptions about racial and ethnic groups.
3. Interview someone from a different racial or ethnic group and ask the person what he or she thinks about the melting pot idea. Has it worked for that person? Does he or she want it to work?
4. Find out how any or all of the following vary among different racial and ethnic groups: death rate, education levels, income levels, occupation types, incarceration rate.
5. List some general release movies that feature nonwhite or non-Anglo characters. Choose one and freewrite on your response to the way it presents minority characters.

Questioning: Deciding What Else You Would Like to Know

List five questions that you have about America's diversity.

Peggy McIntosh

White Privilege: Unpacking the Invisible Knapsack

Peggy McIntosh, author of Experiencing Race, Class and Gender in the United States, *analyzes and compares the attitudes of two privileged groups in American culture.*

BEFORE YOU READ

1. Write or talk about what the title of this article suggests to you. (How do you unpack a knapsack that's invisible? What can this mean?)
2. List the privileges that you think a particular ethnic group enjoys.

1 Through work to bring materials from Women's Studies into the rest of the curriculum, I have often noticed men's unwillingness to grant that they are over-privileged, even though they may grant that women are disadvantaged. They may say they will work to improve women's status, in the society, the university, or the curriculum, but they can't or won't support the idea of lessening men's. Denials which amount to taboos surround the subject of advantages which men gain from women's disadvantages. These denials protect male privilege from being fully acknowledged, lessened or ended.

2 Thinking through unacknowledged male privilege as a phenomenon[1], I realized that since hierarchies in our society are interlocking, there was most likely a phenomenon of white privilege which was similarly denied and protected. As a white person, I realized I had been taught about racism as something which puts others at a disadvantage, but had been taught not to see one of its corollary aspects, white privilege, which puts me at an advantage.

3 I think whites are carefully taught not to recognize white privilege, as males are taught not to recognize male privilege. So I have begun in an untutored way to ask what it is like to have white privilege. I have come to see white privilege as an invisible package of unearned assets which I can count on cashing in each day, but about which I was "meant" to remain oblivious. White privilege is like an invisible weightless knapsack of special provisions, maps, passports, codebooks, visas, clothes, tools and blank checks.

4 Describing white privilege makes one newly accountable. As we in Women's Studies work to reveal male privilege and ask men to give up some of their

---

[1] Notable characteristic.

power, so one who writes about having white privilege must ask, "Having described it, what will I do to lessen or end it?"

5 After I realized the extent to which men work from a base of unacknowledged privilege, I understood that much of their oppressiveness was unconscious. Then I remembered the frequent charges from women of color that white women whom they encounter are oppressive. I began to understand why we are justly seen as oppressive, even when we don't see ourselves that way. I began to count the ways in which I enjoy unearned skin privilege and have been conditioned into oblivion about its existence.

6 My schooling gave me no training in seeing myself as an oppressor, as an unfairly advantaged person, or as a participant in a damaged culture. I was taught to see myself as an individual whose moral state depended on her individual moral will. My schooling followed the pattern my colleague Elizabeth Minnich has pointed out: whites are taught to think of their lives as morally neutral, normative,[2] and average, and also ideal, so that when we work to benefit others, this is seen as work which will allow "them" to be more like "us."

7 I decided to try to work on myself at least by identifying some of the daily effects of white privilege in my life. I have chosen those conditions which I think in my case *attach somewhat more to skin-color privilege* than to class, religion, ethnic status, or geographical location, though of course all these other factors are intricately intertwined. As far as I can see, my African American co-workers, friends and acquaintances with whom I come into daily or frequent contact in this particular time, place, and line of work cannot count on most of these conditions.

1. I can if I wish arrange to be in the company of people of my race most of the time.
2. If I should need to move, I can be pretty sure of renting or purchasing housing in an area which I can afford and in which I would want to live.
3. I can be pretty sure that my neighbors in such a location will be neutral or pleasant to me.
4. I can go shopping alone most of the time, pretty well assured that I will not be followed or harassed.
5. I can turn on the television or open to the front page of the paper and see people of my race widely represented.
6. When I am told about our national heritage or about "civilization," I am shown that people of my color made it what it is.
7. I can be sure that my children will be given curricular materials that testify to the existence of their race.
8. If I want to, I can be pretty sure of finding a publisher for this piece on white privilege.

---

[2] Setting a standard.

9. I can go into a music shop and count on finding the music of my race represented, into a supermarket and find the staple foods which fit with my cultural traditions, into a hairdresser's shop and find someone who can cut my hair.
10. Whether I use checks, credit cards, or cash, I can count on my skin color not to work against the appearance of financial reliability.
11. I can arrange to protect my children most of the time from people who might not like them.
12. I can swear, or dress in second hand clothes, or not answer letters, without having people attribute these choices to the bad morals, the poverty, or the illiteracy of my race.
13. I can speak in public to a powerful male group without putting my race on trial.
14. I can do well in a challenging situation without being called a credit to my race.
15. I am never asked to speak for all the people of my racial group.
16. I can remain oblivious of the language and customs of persons of color who constitute the world's majority without feeling in my culture any penalty for such oblivion.
17. I can criticize our government and talk about how much I fear its policies and behavior without being seen as a cultural outsider.
18. I can be pretty sure that if I ask to talk to "the person in charge," I will be facing a person of my race.
19. If a traffic cop pulls me over or if the IRS audits my tax return, I can be sure I haven't been singled out because of my race.
20. I can easily buy posters, postcards, picture books, greeting cards, dolls, toys, and children's magazines featuring people of my race.
21. I can go home from most meetings of organizations I belong to feeling somewhat tied in, rather than isolated, out-of-place, outnumbered, unheard, held at a distance, or feared.
22. I can take a job with an affirmative action employer without having co-workers on the job suspect that I got it because of race.
23. I can choose public accommodation without fearing that people of my race cannot get in or will be mistreated in the places I have chosen.
24. I can be sure that if I need legal or medical help, my race will not work against me.
25. If my day, week, or year is going badly, I need not ask of each negative episode or situation whether it has racial overtones.
26. I can choose blemish cover or bandages in "flesh" color and have them more or less match my skin.

8   I repeatedly forgot each of the realizations on this list until I wrote it down. For me white privilege has turned out to be an elusive[3] and fugitive subject. The pressure to avoid it is great, for in facing it I must give up the myth of meritocracy.[4] If these things are true, this is not such a free country; one's life is not what one makes it; many doors open for certain people through no virtues of their own.

9   In unpacking this invisible knapsack of white privilege, I have listed conditions of daily experience which I once took for granted. Nor did I think of any of these perquisites as bad for the holder. I now think that we need a more finely differentiated taxonomy[5] of privilege, for some of these varieties are only what one would want for everyone in a just society, and others give license to be ignorant, oblivious, arrogant and destructive.

10   I see a pattern running through the matrix of white privilege, a pattern of assumptions which were passed on to me as a white person. There was one main piece of cultural turf; it was my own turf, and I was among those who could control the turf. *My skin color was an asset for any move I was educated to want to make.* I could think of myself as belonging in major ways, and of making social systems work for me. I could freely disparage, fear, neglect, or be oblivious to anything outside of the dominant cultural forms. Being of the main culture, I could also criticize it fairly freely.

11   In proportion as my racial group was being made confident, comfortable, and oblivious, other groups were likely being made inconfident, uncomfortable, and alienated. Whiteness protected me from many kinds of hostility, distress, and violence, which I was being subtly trained to visit in turn upon people of color.

12   For this reason, the word "privilege" now seems to me misleading. We usually think of privilege as being a favored state, whether earned or conferred by birth or luck. Yet some of the conditions I have described here work to systematically overempower certain groups. Such privilege simply *confers dominance* because of one's race or sex.

13   I want, then, to distinguish between earned strength and unearned power conferred systematically. Power from unearned privilege can look like strength when it is in fact permission to escape or to dominate. But not all of the privileges on my list are inevitably damaging. Some, like the expectation that neighbors will be decent to you, or that your race will not count against you in court, should be the norm in a just society. Others, like the privilege to ignore less powerful people, distort the humanity of the holders as well as the ignored groups.

14   We might at least start by distinguishing between positive advantages which we can work to spread, and negative types of advantages which unless rejected will always reinforce our present hierarchies. For example, the feeling that one

---

[3] Hard to pin down.

[4] A system where advancement is based on merit or achievement.

[5] Classification.

belongs within the human circle, as Native Americans say, should not be seen as privilege for a few. Ideally it is an *unearned entitlement*. At present, since only a few have it, it is an *unearned advantage* for them. This paper results from a process of coming to see that some of the power which I originally saw as attendant on being a human being in the U.S. consisted [of] *unearned advantage and conferred dominance.*

15   I have met very few men who are truly distressed about systemic, unearned male advantage and conferred dominance. And so one question for me and others like me is whether we will be like them, or whether we will get truly distressed, even outraged, about unearned race advantage and conferred dominance and if so, what we will do to lessen them. In any case, we need to do more work in identifying how they actually affect our daily lives. Many, perhaps most, of our white students in the U.S. think that racism doesn't affect them because they are not people of color; they do not see "whiteness" as a racial identity. In addition, since race and sex are not the only advantaging systems at work, we need similarly to examine the daily experience of having age advantage, or ethnic advantage, or physical ability, or advantage related to nationality, religion, or sexual orientation.

16   Difficulties and dangers surrounding the task of finding parallels are many. Since racism, sexism, and heterosexism are not the same, the advantaging associated with them should not be seen as the same. In addition, it is hard to disentangle aspects of unearned advantage which rest more on social class, economic class, race, religion, sex and ethnic identity than on other factors. Still, all of the oppressions are interlocking, as the Combahee River Collective[6] Statement of 1977 continues to remind us eloquently.

17   One factor seems clear about all of the interlocking oppressions. They take both active forms which we can see and embedded forms which as a member of the dominant group one is taught not to see. In my class and place, I did not see myself as a racist because I was taught to recognize racism only in individual acts of meanness of members of my group, never in invisible systems conferring unsought racial dominance on my group from birth.

18   Disapproving of the systems won't be enough to change them. I was taught to think that racism could end if white individuals changed their attitudes. [But] a "white" skin in the United States opens many doors for whites whether or not we approve of the way dominance has been conferred on us. Individual acts can palliate, but cannot end, these problems.

19   To redesign social systems we need first to acknowledge their colossal unseen dimensions. The silences and denials surrounding privilege are the key political tool here. They keep the thinking about equality or equity incomplete, protecting unearned advantage and conferred dominance by making these taboo subjects. Most talk by whites about equal opportunity seems to me now to be about equal opportunity to try to get into a position of dominance while denying that *systems* of dominance exist.

---

[6] A group of black feminist women in Boston from 1974 to 1980.

20   It seems to me that obliviousness[7] about white advantage, like obliviousness about male advantage, is kept strongly inculcated in the United States so as to maintain the myth of meritocracy, the myth that democratic choice is equally available to all. Keeping most people unaware that freedom of confident action is there for just a small number of people props up those in power, and serves to keep power in the hands of the same groups that have most of it already.

21   Though systemic change takes many decades, there are pressing questions for me and I imagine for some others like me if we raise our daily consciousness of the perquisites of being light-skinned. What will we do with such knowledge? As we know from watching men, it is an open question whether we will choose to use unearned advantage to weaken hidden systems of advantage, and whether we will use any of our arbitrarily-awarded power to try to reconstruct power systems on a broader base.   [1989]

REACTING

1. What most surprised and interested you in Peggy McIntosh's list of privileges that white people can expect in everyday life? Add to the list.
2. Do you agree that racism and sexism resemble each other in the way that McIntosh suggests? Explain.

CONNECTING

1. Turn to p. 105 and read Brent Staples's "Just Walk On By: A Black Man Ponders His Power to Alter Public Space." In his essay Staples gives insights into life as an African American man. What would he have to say about McIntosh's discussion of male privilege?
2. Turn to p. 118 and read Fox Butterfield's "Why They Excel." What might McIntosh say about the Asian American experience? Does it fit her basic argument? Why or why not?

LEARNING ABOUT WRITING FROM READING

McIntosh uses the first-person pronoun "I" throughout her essay. Is this all right, we often ask? The answer is yes, usually, but you need to think about its impact on your readers.

In this case the author uses her own identity as a white woman to add power to her argument that not only white men but also white women can be seen as oppressors. This is quite an unusual angle on the race and gender argument: it gets our attention and adds to our feeling that the author is personally committed to her thesis.

---

[7] State of forgetfulness or unawareness.

For example, when McIntosh writes:
> I began to count the ways in which I enjoy unearned skin privilege and have been conditioned into oblivion about its existence. My schooling gave me no training in seeing myself as an oppressor, as an unfairly advantaged person. . . .

we can connect with her personal discovery, even participate in it ourselves. In this way she perhaps wins us over to her point of view.

JACK G. SHAHEEN

The Media's Image of Arabs

Jack Shaheen's article describes the American media's portrayal of an often-overlooked minority group.

BEFORE YOU READ

1. What images come to mind when you hear the word *Arab*?
2. Name three television shows or films with an Arab character. Describe that character.

1 America's bogyman is the Arab. Until the nightly news brought us TV pictures of Palestinian boys being punched and beaten, almost all portraits of Arabs seen in America were dangerously threatening. Arabs were either billionaires or bombers—rarely victims. They were hardly ever seen as ordinary people practicing law, driving taxis, singing lullabies or healing the sick. Though TV news may portray them more sympathetically now, the absence of positive media images nurtures suspicion and stereotype. As an Arab-American, I have found that ugly caricatures[1] have had an enduring impact on my family.

2 I was sheltered from prejudicial portraits at first. My parents came from Lebanon in the 1920s; they met and married in America. Our home in the steel city of Clairton, Pa., was a center for ethnic sharing—black, white, Jew and gentile. There was only one major source of media images then, at the State movie theater where I was lucky enough to get a part-time job as an usher. But in the late 1940s, Westerns and war movies were popular, not Middle Eastern dramas. Memories of World War II were fresh, and the screen heavies were the Japanese

---
[1] Cartoon-like drawings; oversimplified pictures.

and the Germans. True to the cliché[2] of the times, the only good Indian was a dead Indian. But when I mimicked or mocked the bad guys, my mother cautioned me. She explained that stereotypes blur our vision and corrupt the imagination. "Have compassion for all people, Jackie," she said. "This way, you'll learn to experience the joy of accepting people as they are, and not as they appear in films. Stereotypes hurt."

3   Mother was right. I can remember the Saturday afternoon when my son, Michael, who was seven, and my daughter Michele, six, suddenly called out: "Daddy, Daddy, they've got some bad Arabs on TV." They were watching that great American morality play, TV wrestling. Akbar the Great, who liked to hear the cracking of bones, and Abdullah the Butcher, a dirty fighter who liked to inflict pain, were pinning their foes with "camel locks." From that day on, I knew I had to try to neutralize the media caricatures.

4   It hasn't been easy. With my children, I have watched animated heroes Heckle and Jeckle pull the rug from under "Ali Boo-Boo, the Desert Rat," and Laverne and Shirley stop "Sheik Ha-Mean-Ie" from conquering "the U.S. and the world." I have read comic books like the "Fantastic Four" and "G.I. Combat" whose characters have sketched Arabs as "lowlifes" and "human hyenas." Negative stereotypes were everywhere. A dictionary informed my youngsters that an Arab is a "vagabond, drifter, hobo and vagrant." Whatever happened, my wife wondered, to Aladdin's good genie?

5   To a child, the world is simple: good versus evil. But my children and others with Arab roots grew up without ever having seen a humane Arab on the silver screen, someone to pattern their lives after. Is it easier for a camel to go through the eye of a needle than for a screen Arab to appear as a genuine human being?

6   Hollywood producers must have an instant Ali Baba kit that contains scimitars[3], veils, sunglasses and such Arab clothing as *chadors*[4] and *kufiyahs*[5]. In the mythical "Ay-rabland," oil wells, tents, mosques, goats and shepherds prevail. Between the sand dunes, the camera focuses on a mock-up of a palace from "Arabian Nights"—or a military air base. Recent movies suggest that Americans are at war with Arabs, forgetting the fact that out of 21 Arab nations, America is friendly with 19 of them. And in "Wanted Dead or Alive," a movie that starred Gene Simmons, the leader of the rock group Kiss, the war comes home when an Arab terrorist comes to the United States dressed as a rabbi and, among other things, conspires with Arab-Americans to poison the people of Los Angeles. The movie was released last year.

7   The Arab remains American culture's favorite whipping boy. In his memoirs, Terrel Bell, Ronald Reagan's first secretary of education, writes about an

---

[2] Overused phrase or word.

[3] Curved swords.

[4] Women's loose black robes, covering head to toe.

[5] Men's cloth headcoverings.

"apparent bias among mid-level, right-wing staffers at the White House" who dismissed Arabs as "sand niggers." Sadly, the racial slurs continue. At a recent teacher's conference, I met a woman from Sioux Falls, S.D., who told me about the persistence of discrimination. She was in the process of adopting a baby when an agency staffer warned her that the infant had a problem. When she asked whether the child was mentally ill, or physically handicapped, there was silence. Finally, the worker said: "The baby is Jordanian."

8   To me, the Arab demon of today is much like the Jewish demon of yesterday. We deplore the false portrait of Jews as a swarthy[6] menace. Yet a similar portrait has been accepted and transferred to another group of Semites—the Arabs. Print and broadcast journalists have started to challenge this stereotype. They are now revealing more humane images of Palestinian Arabs, a people who traditionally suffered from the myth that Palestinian equals terrorist. Others could follow that lead and retire the stereotypical Arab to a media Valhalla.

9   It would be a step in the right direction if movie and TV producers developed characters modeled after real-life Arab-Americans. We could then see a White House correspondent like Helen Thomas, whose father came from Lebanon, in "The Golden Girls," a heart surgeon patterned after Dr. Michael DeBakey on "St. Elsewhere," or a Syrian-American playing tournament chess like Yasser Seirawan, the Seattle grandmaster.

10   Politicians, too, should speak out against the cardboard caricatures. They should refer to Arabs as friends, not just as moderates. And religious leaders could state that Islam like Christianity and Judaism maintains that all mankind is one family in the care of God. When all imagemakers rightfully begin to treat Arabs and all other minorities with respect and dignity, we may begin to unlearn our prejudices.

REACTING

1. Does Jack Shaheen's account of media images of Arabs match your own sense of how this group is portrayed?
2. What emotional impact does his essay have on you? Explain what you feel.

CONNECTING

1. Turn to p. 109 and read Henry Louis Gates's "TV's Black World Turns—But Stays Unreal." Compare Shaheen's and Gates's reasons for criticizing the media.
2. Read Brent Staples's "Just Walk On By: A Black Man Ponders His Power to Alter Public Space" (p. 105). Are Shaheen's concerns the same as Staples's? Explain your answer.

---

[6] Dark-skinned.

LEARNING ABOUT WRITING FROM READING

Most writers complain about how difficult it is to organize their ideas. Shaheen's article demonstrates some simple but effective organizational patterns: chronological and statement + support.

> *Chronological.* Shaheen starts with his early childhood and moves through time to explore his own children's experiences.
>
> *Statement and support.* Within this chronological framework, Shaheen provides examples of media portrayals of Arabs. These examples support his main idea about the general nature of the portrayals.

BRENT STAPLES

Just Walk On By: A Black Man Ponders His Power to Alter Public Space

Brent Staples, a journalist who has a doctorate in psychology, gives an account of his own experiences as an African-American man in contemporary America.

BEFORE YOU READ

1. What do you think the author might mean by "altering public space"?
2. In what ways do you think members of different social groups—racial, ethnic, sexual—"alter public space"?

1   My first victim was a woman—white, well dressed, probably in her early twenties. I came upon her late one evening on a deserted street in Hyde Park, a relatively affluent neighborhood in an otherwise mean, impoverished section of Chicago. As I swung onto the avenue behind her, there seemed to be a discreet, uninflammatory distance between us. Not so. She cast back a worried glance. To her, the youngish black man—a broad six feet two inches with a beard and billowing hair, both hands shoved into the pockets of a bulky military jacket—seemed menacingly close. After a few more quick glimpses, she picked up her pace and was soon running in earnest. Within seconds she disappeared into a cross street.

2   That was more than a decade ago. I was 22 years old; a graduate student newly arrived at the University of Chicago. It was in the echo of that terrified woman's footfalls that I first began to know the unwieldy inheritance I'd come into—the ability to alter public space in ugly ways. It was clear that she thought herself the quarry of a mugger, a rapist, or worse. Suffering a bout of insomnia,

however, I was stalking sleep, not defenseless wayfarers. As a softy who is scarcely able to take a knife to a raw chicken—let alone hold it to a person's throat—I was surprised, embarrassed, and dismayed all at once. Her flight made me feel like an accomplice in tyranny. It also made it clear that I was indistinguishable from the muggers who occasionally seeped into the area from the surrounding ghetto. That first encounter, and those that followed, signified that a vast unnerving gulf lay between nighttime pedestrians—particularly women—and me. And I soon gathered that being perceived as dangerous is a hazard in itself. I only needed to turn a corner into a dicey situation, or crowd some frightened, armed person in a foyer somewhere, or make an errant move after being pulled over by a policeman. Where fear and weapons meet—and they often do in urban America—there is always the possibility of death.

3   In that first year, my first away from my hometown, I was to become thoroughly familiar with the language of fear. At dark, shadowy intersections in Chicago, I could cross in front of a car stopped at a traffic light and elicit the *thunk, thunk, thunk, thunk* of the driver—black, white, male, or female—hammering down the door locks. On less traveled streets after dark, I grew accustomed to but never comfortable with people who crossed to the other side of the street rather than pass me. Then there were the standard unpleasantries with police, doormen, bouncers, cab drivers, and others whose business it is to screen out troublesome individuals *before* there is any nastiness.

4   I moved to New York nearly two years ago and I have remained an avid night walker. In Central Manhattan, the near-constant crowd cover minimizes tense one-on-one street encounters. Elsewhere—visiting friends in SoHo, where sidewalks are narrow and tightly spaced buildings shut out the sky—things can get very taut indeed.

5   Black men have a firm place in New York mugging literature. Norman Podhoretz in his famed (or infamous) 1963 essay, "My Negro Problem—And Ours," recalls growing up in terror of black males; they "were tougher than we were, more ruthless," he writes—and as an adult on the Upper West Side of Manhattan, he continues, he cannot constrain his nervousness when he meets black men on certain streets. Similarly, a decade later, the essayist and novelist Edward Hoagland extols a New York where once "Negro bitterness bore down mainly on other Negroes." Where some see mere panhandlers, Hoagland sees "a mugger who is clearly screwing up his nerve to do more than just *ask* for money." But Hoagland has "the New Yorker's quick-hunch posture for broken-field maneuvering," and the bad guy swerves away.

6   I often witness that "hunch posture," from women after dark on the warren-like streets of Brooklyn where I live. They seem to set their faces on neutral and, with their purse straps strung across their chests bandolier style, they forge ahead as though bracing themselves against being tackled. I understand, of course, that the danger they perceive is not a hallucination. Women are particularly vulnerable to street violence, and young black males are drastically overrepresented among the perpetrators of that violence. Yet these truths are no solace against the kind of alienation that comes of being ever the suspect, against being set apart, a fearsome entity with whom pedestrians avoid making eye contact.

7   It is not altogether clear to me how I reached the ripe old age of 22 without being conscious of the lethality nighttime pedestrians attributed to me. Perhaps it was because in Chester, Pennsylvania, the small, angry industrial town where I came of age in the 1960s, I was scarcely noticeable against a backdrop of gang warfare, street knifings, and murders. I grew up one of the good boys, had perhaps a half-dozen fist fights. In retrospect, my shyness of combat has clear sources.

8   Many things go into the making of a young thug. One of those things is the consummation of the male romance with the power to intimidate. An infant discovers that random flailings send the baby bottle flying out of the crib and crashing to the floor. Delighted, the joyful babe repeats those motions again and again, seeking to duplicate the feat. Just so, I recall the points at which some of my boyhood friends were finally seduced by the perception of themselves as tough guys. When a mark cowered and surrendered his money without resistance, myth and reality merged—and paid off. It is, after all, only manly to embrace the power to frighten and intimidate. We, as men, are not supposed to give an inch of our lane on the highway; we are to seize the fighter's edge in work and in play and even in love; we are to be valiant in the face of hostile forces.

9   Unfortunately, poor and powerless young men seem to take all this nonsense literally. As a boy, I saw countless tough guys locked away; I have since buried several, too. They were babies, really—a teenage cousin, a brother of 22, a childhood friend in his mid-twenties—all gone down in episodes of bravado played out in the streets. I came to doubt the virtues of intimidation early on. I chose, perhaps even unconsciously, to remain a shadow—timid, but a survivor.

10   The fearsomeness mistakenly attributed to me in public places often has a perilous flavor. The most frightening of these confusions occurred in the late 1970s and early 1980s when I worked as a journalist in Chicago. One day, rushing into the office of a magazine I was writing for with a deadline story in hand, I was mistaken for a burglar. The office manager called security and, with an ad hoc[1] posse, pursued me through the labyrinthine halls, nearly to my editor's door. I had no way of proving who I was. I could only move briskly toward the company of someone who knew me.

11   Another time I was on assignment for a local paper and killing time before an interview. I entered a jewelry store on the city's affluent Near North Side. The proprietor excused herself and returned with an enormous red Doberman pinscher straining at the end of a leash. She stood, the dog extended toward me, silent to my questions, her eyes bulging nearly out of her head. I took a cursory look around, nodded, and bade her good night. Relatively speaking, however, I never fared as badly as another black male journalist. He went to nearby Waukegan, Illinois, a couple of summers ago to work on a story about a murderer who was born there. Mistaking the reporter for the killer, police hauled him from his car at gunpoint and but for his press credentials would probably

---

[1] For a specific purpose.

have tried to book him. Such episodes are not uncommon. Black men trade tales like this all the time.

12   In "My Negro Problem—And Ours," Podhoretz writes that the hatred he feels for blacks makes itself known to him through a variety of avenues—one being his discomfort with that "special brand of paranoid touchiness" to which he says blacks are prone. No doubt he is speaking here of black men. In time, I learned to smother the rage I felt at so often being taken for a criminal. Not to do so would surely have led to madness—via that special "paranoid touchiness" that so annoyed Podhoretz at the time he wrote the essay.

13   I began to take precautions to make myself less threatening. I move about with care, particularly late in the evening. I give a wide berth to nervous people on subway platforms during the wee hours, particularly when I have exchanged business clothes for jeans. If I happen to be entering a building behind some people who appear skittish, I may walk by, letting them clear the lobby before I return, so as not to seem to be following them. I have been calm and extremely congenial on those rare occasions when I've been pulled over by the police.

14   And on late-evening constitutionals along streets less traveled by, I employ what has proved to be an excellent tension-reducing measure: I whistle melodies from Beethoven and Vivaldi and the more popular classical composers. Even steely New Yorkers hunching toward nighttime destinations seem to relax, and occasionally they even join in the tune. Virtually everybody seems to sense that a mugger wouldn't be warbling bright, sunny selections from Vivaldi's *Four Seasons*. It is my equivalent of the cowbell that hikers wear when they know they are in bear country.

REACTING

1. Have you ever felt that you have "altered public space"? If so, how?
2. What do you think of the author's solution to the problem he describes?

CONNECTING

1. How might Brent Staples respond to Peggy McIntosh's article ("White Privilege: Unpacking the Invisible Knapsack," p. 96) about the connections between white privilege and male privilege?
2. How does Brent Staples's article help you to respond to one of this chapter's key questions, "Is the melting pot working?"?

LEARNING ABOUT WRITING FROM READING

Ask yourself which parts of this article are most convincing and interesting.
    We (writing teachers) often say, in fact, that stories told from personal experience have the most punch and impact. Brent Staples tells several little stories, or *anecdotes*, from his own life to illustrate his main idea and make it convincing.

The key to successful anecdotes is the quick, clear, and vivid detailing of the event and the characters involved, so that they "make the point."

Read the following anecdote from Staples's article and decide for yourself why and how it tells you more about the writer's experience than a bland, general and abstract statement such as: "When I go to new places, people always suspect me of doing something wrong and are afraid of me."

> Another time I was on assignment for a local paper and killing time before an interview. I entered a jewelry store on the city's affluent Near North Side. The proprietor excused herself and returned with an enormous red Doberman pinscher straining at the end of a leash. She stood, the dog extended toward me, silent to my questions, her eyes bulging nearly out of her head. I took a cursory look around, nodded, and bade her good night.

HENRY LOUIS GATES, JR.

TV's Black World Turns—But Stays Unreal

Henry Louis Gates, Jr., a prominent Harvard literary scholar, analyzes and evaluates television's portrayal of African American lifestyles.

BEFORE YOU READ

1. Gates gives his thesis in the title. Try writing it in your own words.
2. How well does television reflect your ethnic group?

1   There is a telling moment in the 1986 film "Soul Man" when a young man explains to a friend why he has decided to down a bottle of tanning pills and turn himself black. The friend is skeptical: What's it actually going to be like, being black?

2   "It's gonna be great," the hero assures him. "These are the 80's, man. This is the 'Cosby' decade. America *loves* black people."

3   Alas, he soon discovers the gulf that separates the images of black people he sees on television and the reality that blacks experience every day.

4   Even black Americans sometimes need to be reminded about the deceptiveness of television. Blacks retain their fascination with black characters on TV: Many of us buy *Jet* magazine primarily to read its weekly television feature, which lists *every* black character (major or minor) to be seen on the screen that

week. Yet our fixation with the presence of black characters on TV has blinded us to an important fact that "Cosby," which began in 1984, and its offshoots over the years demonstrate convincingly: There is very little connection between the social status of black Americans and the fabricated images of black people that Americans consume each day. Moreover, the representation of blacks on TV is a very poor index to our social advancement or political progress.

5 But the young man is right about one thing: This is the "Cosby" decade. The show's unprecedented success in depicting the lives of affluent blacks has exercised a profound influence on television in the last half of the 80's. And, judging from the premier of this season's new black series—"Family Matters," "Homeroom" and "Snoops," as well as "Generations," an interracial soap opera—"Cosby's" success has led to the flow of TV sitcoms that feature the black middle class, each of which takes its lead from the "Cosby" show.

6 Historically, blacks have always worried aloud about the image that white Americans harbor of us, first because we have never had control of those images and, second, because the greater number of those images have been negative. And given television's immediacy, and its capacity to reach so many viewers so quickly, blacks, at least since "Amos 'n' Andy" back in the early 50's have been especially concerned with our images on the screen. I can remember as a child sitting upstairs in my bedroom and hearing my mother shout at the top of her voice that someone *"colored . . . colored!"* was on TV and that we had all better come downstairs at once. And, without fail, we did, sitting in front of our TV, nervous, full of expectation and dread, praying that our home girl or boy would not let the race down.

'White' Money vs. 'Colored' Money

7 Later, when American society could not successfully achieve the social reformation it sought in the 60's through the Great Society, television solved the problem simply by inventing symbols of that transformation in the 80's, whether it was Cliff Huxtable—whom we might think of as the grandson of Alexander Scott (played by Mr. Cosby in "I Spy," 1965–68)—or Benson (1979–86), the butler who transforms himself into a lieutenant governor.

8 Today, blacks are doing much better on TV than they are in real life, an irony underscored by the use of black public figures (Mr. Cosby, Michael Jackson, Michael Jordan, Bobby McFerrin) as spokesmen for major businesses. When Mr. Cosby, deadpan, faces the camera squarely and says, "E.F. Hutton. Because it's my money," the line blurs between Cliff Huxtable's successful career and Mr. Cosby.

9 This helps to explain why "Cosby" makes some people uncomfortable: As the dominant representation of blacks on TV, it suggests that blacks are solely responsible for their social conditions, with no acknowledgment of the severely constricted life opportunities that most black people face. What's troubling about the phenomenal success of "Cosby," then, is what was troubling about the earlier popularity of "Amos 'n' Andy": it's not the representation itself (Cliff

Huxtable, a child of college-educated parents, is altogether believable), but the role it begins to play in our culture, the status it takes on as being, well, truly representative.

10   As long as *all* blacks were represented in demeaning or peripheral[1] roles, it was possible to believe that American racism was, as it were, indiscriminate. The social vision of "Cosby," however, reflecting the minuscule integration of blacks into the upper middle class (having "white money," my mother used to say, rather than "colored" money) reassuringly throws the blame for black poverty back onto the impoverished.

11   This is the subliminal[2] message of America's weekly dinner date with the Huxtables, played out to a lesser extent in other weekly TV encounters with middle-class black families, such as "227," "A Different World," "Amen" (Sherman Helmsley is a lawyer), and with isolated black individuals, such as the dashing Blair Underwood on "L.A. Law" and Philip Michael Thomas on "Miami Vice." One principal reason for the failure of Flip Wilson's "Charlie & Company" was the ambiguity of his class status; Wilson's character, Charlie Richmond, was an office worker at the Department of Highways, his wife (Gladys Knight) a schoolteacher. Wilson once joked, acidly, that he was the star of the black version of "The Cosby Show," which may have been true in ways that he did not intend.

The Great 'Amos 'n' Andy' Debate

12   In 1933, Sterling Brown, the great black poet and critic, divided the full range of black character types in American literature into seven categories: the contented slave; the wretched freeman; the comic Negro; the brute Negro; the tragic mulatto[3]; the local color Negro; and the exotic primitive. It was only one small step to associate our public negative image in the American mind with the public negative social roles that we were assigned and to which we were largely confined. "If only they could be exposed to the *best* of the race," the sentiment went, "then they would see that we were normal human beings and treat us better."

13   Such a burdensome role for the black image led, inevitably, to careful monitoring and, ultimately, to censorship of our representations in literature, film, radio and later television. The historian W. E. B. Du Bois summarized this line of thinking among blacks: "We want," he said in 1925, "everything that is said about us to tell of the best and highest and noblest in us. We insist that our Art and Propaganda be one. We fear that the evil in us will be called racial while in others it is viewed as individual. We fear that our shortcomings are not merely human but foreshadowings and threatenings of disaster and failure." And the

---

[1] Secondary; away from the center of action.

[2] Unconscious; unarticulated.

[3] Mixed race.

genre about which we were most sensitive, Du Bois wrote, was comedy. "The more highly trained we become," he wrote in 1921, "the less we can laugh at Negro comedy."

14   One of my favorite pastimes is screening episodes of "Amos 'n' Andy" for black friends who think that the series was both socially offensive and politically detrimental. After a few minutes, even hardliners have difficulty restraining their laughter. "It's still racist," is one typical comment, "but it was funny."

15   The performance of those great black actors—Tim Moore, Spencer Williams and Ernestine Wade—transformed racist stereotypes into authentic black humor. The dilemma of "Amos 'n' Andy," however, was that these were the *only* images of blacks that Americans could see on TV. The political consequences for the early civil rights movement were thought to be threatening. The N.A.A.C.P. helped to have the series killed.

16   What lies behind these sorts of arguments is a belief that social policies affecting black Americans were largely determined by our popular images in the media. But the success of the "Cosby" show has put the lie to that myth: "Cosby" exposes more white Americans than ever before to the most nobly idealized blacks in the history of entertainment, yet social and economic conditions for the average black American have not been bleaker in a very long time.

17   To make matters worse, "Cosby" is also one of the most popular shows in apartheid South Africa, underscoring the fact that the relationship between how whites treat us and their exposure to "the best" in us is far from straightforward. (One can hear the Afrikaaner speaking to his black servants: "When you people are like Cliff and Clare, *then* we will abandon apartheid.")

18   There are probably as many reasons to like the "Cosby" show as there are devoted viewers—and there are millions of them. I happen to like it because my daughters (ages 9 and 7) like it, and I enjoy watching them watch themselves in the depictions of middle-class black kids, worrying about school, sibling rivalries and family tradition. But I also like "Cosby" because its very success has forced us to rethink completely the relation between black social progress and the images of blacks that American society fabricates, projects and digests.

19   But the "Cosby" vision of upper-middle-class blacks and their families is comparatively recent. And while it may have constituted the dominant image of blacks for the last five years, it is a direct reaction against the lower-class ghetto comedies of the 70's such as "Sanford and Son" (1972–77), "Good Times" (1974–79), "That's My Mama" (1974–75) and "What's Happening!!" (1976–79). The latter three were single-mother-dominated sitcoms. Although "Good Times" began with a nuclear family, John Amos—who had succeeded marvelously in transforming the genre of the black maternal household—was soon killed off, enabling the show to conform to the stereotype of a fatherless black family.

20   Even "The Jeffersons" (1975–85) conforms to this mold. George and Louise began their TV existence as Archie Bunker's working-class neighbors, saved their pennies, then "moved on up," as the theme song says, to Manhattan's East Side. "The Jeffersons" also served as a bridge between sitcoms depicting the ghetto and those portraying the new black upper class.

21   In fact, in the history of black images on television, character types have distinct pasts and, as is also the case with white shows, series seem both to lead to other series and to spring from metaphorical ancestors.

Is TV Depicting a Different World?

22   And what is the measure of the Huxtables' nobility? One of the reasons "Cosby" and its spin-off, "A Different World," are so popular is that the black characters in them have finally become, in most respects, just like white people.

23   While I applaud "Cosby's" success at depicting (at long last) the everyday concerns of black people (love, sex, ambition, generational conflicts, work and leisure) far beyond reflex responses to white racism, the question remains: Has TV managed to depict a truly "different world?" As Mark Crispin Miller puts it, "By insisting that blacks and whites are entirely alike, television denies the cultural barriers that slavery necessarily created; barriers that have hardened over years and years, and that still exist"—barriers that produced different cultures, distinct worlds.

24   And while "Cosby" is remarkably successful at introducing most Americans to traditional black cultural values, customs and norms, it has not succeeded at introducing America to a truly different world. The show that came closest—that presented the fullest range of black character types—was the 1987–88 series "Frank's Place," starring Tim Reid and his wife Daphne Maxwell Reid and set in a Creole restaurant in New Orleans.

25   Unfortunately, Mr. Reid apparently has learned his lesson: His new series, "Snoops," in which his wife also stars, is a black detective series suggestive of "The Thin Man." The couple is thoroughly middle-class: He is a professor of criminology at Georgetown; she is head of protocol at the State Department. "Drugs and murder and psychotic people," Mr. Reid said in a recent interview. "I think we've seen enough of that in real life."

26   But it is also important to remember that the early 70's ghetto sitcoms ("Good Times" and "Sanford") were no more realistic than "Cosby" is. In fact, their success made the idea of ghetto life palatable for most Americans, robbing it of its reality as a place of exile, a place of rage, and frustration, and death. And perhaps with "Cosby's" success and the realization that the very structure of the sitcom (in which every character is a type) militates against its use as an agent of social change, blacks will stop looking to TV for our social liberation. As a popular song in the early 70's put it, "The revolution will not be televised."

REACTING

1. Why do you think the *Cosby* show was so successful?
2. Now, after reading this essay, reconsider the question, "How well does television reflect your ethnic group?"

CONNECTING

1. Read Debra Gersh's "Portrayals of Latinos in and by the Media" below. Compare Gates's claim that "the revolution will not be televised" with the views expressed in Gersh's article. Would her sources agree with Gates?
2. Peggy McIntosh ("White Privilege: Unpacking the Invisible Knapsack," p. 96) talks about the "invisible knapsack" of white privilege. Could "The Cosby Show" help people recognize that bag of advantages?

LEARNING ABOUT WRITING FROM READING

Many of your assignments involve writing about TV shows. Look at how Gates manages to give us a quick sketch of a show's key points by using specific words:

> Even "The Jeffersons" (1975–85) conforms to this mold. George and Louise began their TV existence as Archie Bunker's working-class neighbors, saved their pennies, then "moved on up," as the theme song says, to Manhattan's East Side. "The Jeffersons" also served as a bridge between sitcoms depicting the ghetto and those portraying the new black upper class.

DEBRA GERSH

Portrayals of Latinos in and by the Media

Debra Gersh reports on a conference where media treatment of Latinos was a major topic of discussion.

BEFORE YOU READ

1. How are Hispanic Americans portrayed by television, movies, and newspapers? List some images that come to mind.
2. Why should members of different ethnic and racial groups care about how their group is portrayed in the media?

1   During hearings in Los Angeles on the events surrounding last year's rioting, part of the attention focused on the media.

2   "Several people asked me why we were interested in the media," said Cruz Reynoso, a member of the U.S. Commission on Civil Rights, which held the hearings.

3   "The media have everything to do with civil rights," he added, explaining that the media "set the national agenda for issues to be debated" and they define "who we are."

4   Speaking at a meeting devoted to "The News, Latinos and Civil Rights" during the National Association of Hispanic Journalists annual conference in Washington, Reynoso told of various portrayals of Latinos in and by the news media, as recounted by various witnesses.

5   What this means for the Civil Rights Commission, he said, is that it is vitally important for civil rights advocates and the media to work together.

6   While the Latino community in Los Angeles depends on the Spanish-language media, the mainstream media are still a source of great power, he said.

7   There is a need not just for Latino reporters but also writers and producers and others behind the scenes who make the decisions about what gets covered, he added.

8   Growing up, Reynoso said, there always were Spanish-language media in his home, but outside the home, in the mainstream press, "it was as if we were invisible."

9   The Spanish-language media, he added, is not enough to reach the consciousness of the community as a whole.

10 "In this country, we are in a great experiment," Reynoso stated, "to see how people who are different in race, language, ethnicity and other factors can live together."

11 Although it will be difficult, Reynoso thinks it is an experiment that can be won, with the help of the media.

12 "You are a vital part in making sure all of us recognize all Americans . . . [in] binding America together," Reynoso told the NAHJ attendees.

13 New York *Daily News* columnist Juan González said he has had many battles with editors during his 16 years as a journalist over his activism in the Puerto Rican community.

14 Even in the early years of the Puerto Rican civil rights movement in New York, which was "barely covered," González said, its leaders understood the "tremendous power and influence of the mass media to determine what people will think about."

15 "That power has been held closely," he added, noting that "the battle to open it up is one we must wage."

16 "Throughout your careers, there are editors and publishers and owners who will tell you differently, [that you] must be 'objective, above the fray,'" González said. "I am challenging that assumption."

17 González urged Latino journalists to continually "be concerned with what happens in our community" and to "insist that coverage be more equitable and balanced."

18 As one whose organization was the focus of media attention, Dolores Huerta, vice president of the United Farm Workers, said, "Mass-based organizations do not get the kind of coverage they should," especially when they are composed of minorities.

19 Huerta told the NAHJ that the only time the UFW could get coverage was when there was a strike, and even then, a peaceful action was portrayed as violent.

20   The media, she explained, "never really reported the type of organization going on or the benefits we were trying to achieve."

21   Further, portrayals of the workers often pictured them as illegal aliens and never told the "true story of the farm workers who go out and toil in the fields to feed the nation and they can't feed their own family."

22   Huerta told of stories that vilified the workers but never came down on the growers for refusing to negotiate or providing unreasonable working conditions.

23   She said it is "very painful when you see your own Latino reporters telling that story like the mainstream [media]. When we start mimicking the major press against our own people, it is a great disservice."

24   UFW founder Cesar Chavez understood the power of the media and started a newspaper and two radio stations to reach the union's constituency, Huerta explained.

25   The next step is television, she said, where there ought to be more dark-skinned people.

26   Racism is "very blatant. A lot of us feel it," she said. "We've got to start calling it what it is: racism."

27   "Civil rights are rights all people share. They are rights we all have and they are all the same rights," commented Guillermo Martínez, senior vice president/news, Univision, during a panel discussion following the speakers' remarks.

28   Referring to a newspaper article describing the tension between blacks and Hispanics over civil rights—since blacks have worked so hard for civil rights, can the Latinos just walk in and enjoy those protections as well?—Martínez pointed out that if you say you have civil rights and others do not, you are doing the same thing as those who would deny them to you.

29   "Journalists have an obligation that advocates who want to divide the community further do not get away with it because our people will suffer," he said.

30   Elvira Valenzuela Crocker, president of the Mexican American Women's National Association, noted that Latino journalists do a disservice to the Hispanic community if they do not know its history or its issues.

31   "The black civil rights movement did not occur because black journalists were not with them," she noted. "If ours is to happen, you have to be with us."

32   Alan Acosta, assistant metro editor of the *Los Angeles Times,* pointed out that not only do Latino journalists lack a sense of their history but also of their power.

33   "If you have power, you have to use it," he said, adding that when it comes to civil rights, each generation has to re-earn the gains made before it.

34   It was not until the riots in Washington, two years ago, that issues affecting the Latino community gained exposure, explained Pedro Avilés, executive director of the Washington-based Latino Civil Rights Task Force.

35   Coverage of Latino civil rights was infrequent, unfocused and often negatively biased, he said, adding that it also is not as "sexy" a story as the rioting.

36   Nevertheless, Avilés said, "Latino journalists have to play a more active and assertive role in discrimination coverage."

37   Some Latino journalists have been very supportive, he continued, but "unless people take bold actions, we don't have any attention from the media on [these] issues."

38   Avilés stressed that he was not advocating riots, but he did note that is how the Hispanic community in Washington got some attention.

39   "I hope in your role as journalists you will take a more active and assertive role," Avilés said. "Yes, we've been successful in getting our issues out, but that was because of the riot. If you want to avoid that, journalists need to play a more assertive role."

40   On Capitol Hill, perception is 98% of reality, and the media are important in shaping that perspective, explained Mario Moreno, director of the Washington office of the Mexican American Legal Defense and Educational Fund.

41   "Unfortunately, stereotypes prevail and on the Hill, civil rights is seen as a black issue," Moreno said, telling the NAHJ audience, "You have to turn that around."

42   Hispanic journalists "tend to shy away from covering Hispanic issues because they do not want to get pigeonholed," commented ABC News *Prime Time Live* correspondent John Quiñones, "Don't worry about that."

REACTING

1. Do you agree that "the media have everything to do with civil rights," as Cruz Reynoso says in this article? What can the media do to encourage racial and ethnic equality?

2. Should journalists from minority groups avoid covering news stories about their own group? Respond to John Quiñones's comment in the last paragraph.

CONNECTING

1. Compare Henry Louis Gates's view of the media's role in race relations ("TV's Black World Turns—But Stays Unreal," p. 109) with Debra Gersh's. Do these authors believe that television can help minority groups achieve equality?

2. How does this article help you to respond to the chapter's key question "Is the melting pot working?"?

LEARNING ABOUT WRITING FROM READING

Debra Gersh's article is mostly a report about what was said at a meeting held during a conference of the National Association of Hispanic Journalists. Gersh either quotes directly or summarizes what participants said about media coverage of Latinos.

Notice how in paragraphs 8 and 9 direct quotations are built into the reporter's sentence structure and the way *summary* (a condensed version of the original in the reporter's own words) can be used:

> Growing up, Reynoso said, there always were Spanish-language media in his home, but outside the home, in the mainstream press, "it was as if we were invisible."
>
> The Spanish-language media, he added, is not enough to reach the consciousness of the community as a whole.

a. In this example, the first letter of the direct quotation is *not* capitalized, because it needs to look like part of the entire sentence that begins "Growing up . . ."
b. The period is placed *inside* the closing quotation marks.
c. Without quotation marks to signal that her words come from some other source, the reporter is careful to indicate that she is summarizing another person's ideas by including "Reynoso said" and "he added," as the summary proceeds.

Fox Butterfield

Why They Excel

Fox Butterfield is the author of China: Alive in the Bitter Sea, *published in 1982, which won the American Book Award. As he writes in this article, he first became interested in the success of Asians when, as a journalist in Taiwan in 1969, he watched a team of boys from a poor mountain village win the Little League World Series.*

BEFORE YOU READ

1. Is talent or hard work likelier to make you successful? Explain your answer.
2. What is a stereotype? List some stereotypes that you are aware of in your own thinking.

1   Kim-Chi Trinh was just 9 in Vietnam when her father used his savings to buy a passage for her on a fishing boat. It was a costly and risky sacrifice for the family, placing Kim-Chi on the small boat, among strangers, in hopes she would eventually reach the United States, where she would get a good education and enjoy a better life. Before the boat reached safety in Malaysia, the supply of food and water ran out.

2   Still alone, Kim-Chi made it to the United States, coping with a succession of three foster families. But when she graduated from San Diego's Patrick Henry High School in 1988, she had a straight-A average and scholarship offers from Stanford and Cornell universities.

3   "I have to do well—it's not even a question," said the diminutive 19-year-old, now a sophomore at Cornell. "I owe it to my parents in Vietnam."

4   Kim-Chi is part of a tidal wave of bright, highly motivated Asian-Americans who are suddenly surging into our best colleges. Although Asian-Americans make up only 2.4 percent of the nation's population, they constitute 17.1 percent of the undergraduates at Harvard, 18 percent at the Massachusetts Institute of Technology and 27.3 percent at the University of California at Berkeley.

5   With Asians being the fastest-growing ethnic group in the country—two out of five immigrants are now Asian—these figures will increase. At the University of California at Irvine, a staggering 35.1 percent of the undergraduates are Asian-American, but the proportion in the freshman class is even higher: 41 percent.

6   Why are the Asian-Americans doing so well? Are they grinds, as some stereotypes suggest? Do they have higher IQs? Or are they actually teaching the rest of us a lesson about values we have long treasured but may have misplaced—like hard work, the family and education?

7   Not all Asians are doing equally well. Poorly educated Cambodian and Hmong refugee youngsters need special help. And Asian-Americans resent being labeled a "model minority," feeling that is just another form of prejudice by white Americans, an ironic reversal of the discriminatory laws that excluded most Asian immigration to America until 1965.

8   But the academic success of many Asian-Americans has prompted growing concern among educators, parents and other students. Some universities have what look like unofficial quotas, much as Ivy League colleges did against Jews in the 1920s and '30s. Berkeley Chancellor Ira Heyman apologized last spring for an admissions policy that, he said, had "a disproportionately negative impact on Asian-Americans."

9   I have wondered about the reason for the Asians' success since I was a fledgling journalist on Taiwan in 1969. That year, a team of boys from a poor, isolated mountain village on Taiwan won the annual Little League World Series at Williamsport, Pa. Their victory was totally unexpected. At the time, baseball was a largely unknown sport on Taiwan, and the boys had learned to play with bamboo sticks for bats and rocks for balls. But since then, teams from Taiwan, Japan or South Korea have won the Little League championship in 16 out of the 21 years. How could these Asian boys beat us at our own game?

10   Fortunately, the young Asians' achievements have led to a series of intriguing studies. "There is something going on here that we as Americans need to understand," said Sanford M. Dornbusch, a professor of sociology at Stanford. Dornbusch, in surveys of 7000 students in six San Francisco-area high schools, found that Asian-Americans consistently get better grades than any other group of students, regardless of their parents' level of education or their families'

social and economic status, the usual predictors of success. In fact, those in homes where English is spoken often, or whose families have lived longer in the United States, do slightly less well.

11 "We used to talk about the American melting pot as an advantage," Dornbusch said. "But the sad fact is that it has become a melting pot with low standards."

12 Other studies have shown similar results. Perhaps the most disturbing have come in a series of studies by a University of Michigan psychologist, Harold W. Stevenson, who has compared more than 7000 students in kindergarten, first grade, third grade and fifth grade in Chicago and Minneapolis with counterparts in Beijing; Sendai, Japan; and Taipei, Taiwan. On a battery of math tests, the Americans did worst at all grade levels.

13 Stevenson found no differences in IQ. But if the differences in performance are showing up in kindergarten, it suggests something is happening in the family, even before the children get to school.

14 It is here that the various studies converge: Asian parents are able to instill more motivation in their children. "My bottom line is, Asian kids work hard," said Professor Dornbusch.

15 In his survey of San Francisco-area high schools, for example, he reported that Asian-Americans do an average of 7.03 hours of homework a week. Non-Hispanic whites average 6.12 hours, blacks 4.23 hours and Hispanics 3.98 hours. Asians also score highest on a series of other measures of effort, such as fewer class cuts and paying more attention to the teacher.

16 Don Lee, 20, is a junior at Berkeley. His parents immigrated to Torrance, Calif., from South Korea when he was 5, so he could get a better education. Lee said his father would warn him about the dangers of wasting time at high school dances or football games. "Instead," he added, "for fun on weekends, my friends and I would go to the town library to study."

17 The real question, then, is how do Asian parents imbue their offspring with this kind of motivation? Stevenson's study suggests a critical answer. When the Asian parents were asked why they think their children do well, they most often said "hard work." By contrast, American parents said "talent."

18 "From what I can see," said Stevenson, "we've lost our belief in the Horatio Alger myth that anyone can get ahead in life through pluck and hard work. Instead, Americans now believe that some kids have it and some don't, so we begin dividing up classes into fast learners and slow learners, where the Chinese and Japanese believe all children can learn from the same curriculum."

19 The Asians' belief in hard work also springs from their common heritage of Confucianism, the philosophy of the 5th-century B.C. Chinese sage who taught that man can be perfected through practice. "Confucius is not just some character out of the past—he is an everyday reality to these people," said William Liu, a sociologist who directs the Pacific Asian-American Mental Health Research Center at the University of Illinois in Chicago.

20 Confucianism provides another important ingredient in the Asians' success. "In the Confucian ethic," Liu continued, "there is a centripetal family, an

orientation that makes people work for the honor of the family, not just for themselves." Liu came to the United States from China in 1948. "You can never repay your parents, and there is a strong sense of guilt," he said. "It is a strong force, like the Protestant Ethic in the West."

> ### A Tie That Binds
>
> Kim-Chi Trinh, 19, has not seen her parents since she left Vietnam 10 years ago and has not received a letter from them in three years. "They could be dead, for all I know," she said. "But they are still very real to me." One tie that binds Kim-Chi to them is a legacy of Vietnamese proverbs and folk tales about virtuous children, which they would tell her before she fell asleep at night. "I still remember them," she said, "It is as if my parents willed me to be a good student and a good daughter."
>
> Here are two of Kim-Chi's favorite proverbs:
>
> - If you try hard enough, you can make a piece of iron into a needle.
> - If you don't study, you will never become anything. If you study, you will become what you wish.

21   Liu has found this in his own family. When his son and two daughters were young, he told them to become doctors or lawyers—jobs with the best guaranteed income, he felt. Sure enough, his daughters have gone into law, and his son is a medical student at UCLA, though he really wanted to become an investment banker. Liu asked his son why he picked medicine. The reply: "Ever since I was a little kid, I always heard you tell your friends their kids were a success if they got into med school. So I felt guilty. I didn't have a choice."

22   Underlying this bond between Asian parents and their children is yet another factor I noticed during 15 years of living in China, Japan, Taiwan and Vietnam. It is simply that Asian parents establish a closer physical tie to their infants than do most parents in the United States. When I let my baby son and daughter crawl on the floor, for example, my Chinese friends were horrified and rushed to pick them up. We think this constant attention is overindulgence and old-fashioned, but for Asians, who still live through the lives of their children, it is highly effective.

23   Yuen Huo, 22, a senior at Berkeley, recalled growing up in an apartment above the Chinese restaurant her immigrant parents owned and operated in Millbrae, Calif. "They used to tell us how they came from Taiwan to the United States for us, how they sacrificed for us, so I had a strong sense of indebtedness," Huo said. When she did not get all A's her first semester at Berkeley, she recalled, "I felt guilty and worked harder."

24   Here too is a vital clue about the Asians' success: Asian parents expect a high level of academic performance. In the Stanford study comparing white and

Yuen Huo, 22, with her parents, Peter and Shue Huo, at home in Millbrae, Calif. Yuen, a senior now, felt guilty when she didn't get all A's her first semester in college.

Asian students in San Francisco high schools, 82 percent of the Asian parents said they would accept only an A or a B from their children, while just 59 percent of white parents set such a standard. By comparison, only 17 percent of Asian parents were willing to accept a C, against 40 percent of white parents. On the average, parents of black and Hispanic students also had lower expectations for their children's grades than Asian parents.

25   Can we learn anything from the Asians? "I'm not naïve enough to think everything in Asia can be transplanted," said Harold Stevenson, the University of Michigan psychologist. But he offered three recommendations.

26   "To start with," he said, "we need to set higher standards for our kids. We wouldn't expect them to become professional athletes without practicing hard."

27   Second, American parents need to become more committed to their children's education, he declared. "Being understanding when a child doesn't do well isn't enough." Stevenson found that Asian parents spend many more hours really helping their children with homework or writing to their teachers. At Berkeley, the mothers of some Korean-American students move into their sons' apartments for months before graduate school entrance tests to help by cooking and cleaning for them, giving the students more time to study.

28   And, third, schools could be reorganized to become more effective—without added costs, said Stevenson. One of his most surprising findings is that Asian students, contrary to popular myth, are not just rote learners subjected to intense pressure. Instead, nearly 90 percent of Chinese youngsters said they actually enjoy school, and 60 percent can't wait for school vacations to end. These are vastly higher figures for such attitudes than are found in the United States. One reason may be that students in China and Japan typically have a recess after each class, helping them to relax and to increase their attention spans. Moreover, where American teachers spend almost their entire day in front of classes, their Chinese and Japanese counterparts may teach as little as three hours a day, giving them more time to relax and prepare imaginative lessons.

29   Another study, prepared for the U.S. Department of Education, compared the math and science achievements of 24,000 13-year-olds in the United States and five other countries (four provinces of Canada, plus South Korea, Ireland, Great Britain and Spain). One of the findings was that the more time students spent watching television, the poorer their performance. The American students watched the most television. They also got the worst scores in math. Only the Irish students and some of the Canadians scored lower in science.

30   "I don't think Asians are any smarter," said Don Lee, the Korean-American at Berkeley. "There are brilliant Americans in my chemistry class. But the Asian students work harder. I see a lot of wasted potential among the Americans."

REACTING

1. How do you account for the success of Asian Americans that Fox Butterfield describes? Do you agree with his reasons?
2. Would you say that Butterfield is stereotyping Asian Americans in this article? Consider the evidence he offers to support his generalizations and explain your answer.

CONNECTING

1. Does this article give a good argument against those who want America to be a melting pot? Compare it with other articles in this chapter.
2. Butterfield quotes Kim-Chi Trinh's favorite proverb: "If you study, you will become what you wish." Do you believe this? What proverb would you offer to explain individual success?

LEARNING ABOUT WRITING FROM READING

Whether you were convinced by this article or not, notice that Butterfield cites several kinds of evidence to support his main idea:

a. Personal stories that are interesting, easy reading
b. Data compiled from research, for example, the percentages of Asian American students at major universities, to show their high success rate
c. Ideas from experts in education about why Asian Americans do so well
d. His own ideas and reasons

All of these are good sources of evidence to support his main idea, although they are not proof. Furthermore, having more than one type of support can strengthen an argument.

WRITING ASSIGNMENTS

ASSIGNMENT I
WRITE A REVIEW OF A TELEVISION SHOW OR MOVIE THAT YOU FEEL DEALS FAIRLY WITH MINORITY ISSUES.

Coming Up with Ideas and a Focus

One way to try this assignment is to make a list of TV shows or movies that deal with minority issues. Choosing which show or movie to discuss will play a large part in finding your focus. Watch your choice carefully, making notes about your ideas on its treatment of minority issues. Reviewing your notes, you will then need to decide what kind of statement you want to make about how fair the movie or show is. You will also need to define for your readers what your guidelines are for determining what makes a show "fair." (For help with analyzing, see Chapter 12.)

Organizing Your Ideas

Perhaps the most likely organization pattern will be statement-support, but you may want to try a comparison-contrast pattern instead. To demonstrate the show's fairness, compare parts of the show to your life or to the lives of people you know or to information you've researched about a particular ethnic or racial group. In each case your ability to describe scenes from the screen will be very important. (For help with statement-support papers, see pp. 305 and 365. For help with comparison-contrast papers, see pp. 310 and 367.)

Audience

To sharpen your descriptive and persuasive skills, try directing your review to readers of a specific magazine or paper that runs reviews. What will you need to do to interest and persuade them?

ASSIGNMENT II
IN AN INTERVIEW, EXPLORE THE QUESTION "IS AMERICA A MELTING POT?"

Coming Up with Ideas and a Focus

Before you try to focus on specific interview questions, it's a good idea to define your own understanding of the melting pot. What does it mean? Have you any experience of it? What interests you about it? What do you want to know? These last two questions in particular will help you to find your focus among the mass of ideas suggested by the assignment itself. (For help with interviewing, see p. 341.)

Organizing Your Ideas

As with all interview assignments, you will be basing your paper on the answers to the questions you ask your interviewee. Some articles based on interviews follow a chronological pattern, keeping the rough order of the answers as they were given during the interview. Others group material according to particular topic headings, no matter when in the interview the answer was given.

Audience

It might make sense to have your classmates in mind as your audience. The challenge is to write in clear and vivid detail, with the purpose of helping them get to know the person you interviewed as well as you do. Direct quotations, anecdotes, and other details often give a strong flavor of the interviewee's personality. Including them will help you to inform your audience about someone else's point of view, as well as entertain them.

ASSIGNMENT III
ARE YOU SEPARATED FROM OTHER RACIAL AND ETHNIC GROUPS IN AMERICAN CULTURE? TELL YOUR OWN STORY OF SEPARATION OR INTEGRATION.

Coming Up with Ideas and a Focus

Researching your own mind and memory—in freewriting, journals, and conversations—may be the best way to get started. The focus of your story should be your own experiences with integration or separation, perhaps both. Everything you tell your reader should center on this central issue. You might relate several stories, as Brent Staples does in "Just Walk On By: A Black Man Ponders His Power to Alter Public Space," (p. 105), or tell about one incident in detail.

Organizing Your Ideas

You might see the pattern of organization as a statement about separation or integration supported by evidence from your own experience. Or it might be a narrative, or story, of a single experience. (For help with statement-support papers, see pp. 305 and 365. For help with narrative papers, see pp. 306 and 366.)

In any case, your evidence will most likely involve both narrative and description. You may need to tell little stories, or anecdotes, packed with telling details about your experiences, that support your statement about how you felt.

Audience

Try writing this paper for a group of interested foreigners: people who would like to know more about the diverse culture of the United States (so different from that of most other countries) and about the impact it has on the people who live in it. Your paper should enable these readers to sympathize with your experiences and to understand why you felt connected or disconnected from people around you.

ASSIGNMENT IV
SHOW HOW A TELEVISION SHOW, MOVIE, COMMERCIAL, OR POPULAR SONG STEREOTYPES A GROUP THAT YOU YOURSELF BELONG TO.

Coming Up with Ideas and a Focus

Most of us belong to a social group that at least one of the mass media has stereotyped. After listing the groups you belong to, generate ideas by writing down several examples of media stereotyping one group. Then find your focus by choosing the most interesting of these examples, and go from there.

Organizing Your Ideas

This assignment asks you for one main thing: an analysis of media treatment of a selected social group. (For help with analysis, see p. 331.) An analysis of media stereotypes might be organized like a statement-support paper: you make a claim about the way the group is stereotyped and support it with details and examples.

Audience

Your classmates are an excellent audience for this paper because they would very likely be interested in hearing about the stereotypes other people face in their lives. You might also want to think of this paper as a guest editorial for a newspaper, alerting others to how it feels to be stereotyped by the media and persuading them to consider the impact of the media in shaping their own views of themselves and others.

Chapter 4

Gender Roles

KEY QUESTION
Do gender roles, in real life and in the media, help or hinder us?

• •

If there's a sleazy character in an ad, 100 percent of the ones we found were men. If there's an incompetent character, 100 percent of them in the ads are male.
—Fred Hayward, quoted by Bernard R. Goldberg in "TV Insults Men, Too"

The "other America" is a changing neighborhood: men are moving out and their children are moving in. . . . Today, three-quarters of the poor are women and children.
—Diana Pearce, "The Feminization of Ghetto Poverty," The Gender Reader

Amendment XIX to the Constitution of the United States:
The right of citizens of the United States to vote shall not be denied or abridged by the United States or by any State on account of sex.

Introduction

Why do men and women behave differently? *Do* they behave differently? Have you ever wondered why little boys play with trucks and little girls often don't? This chapter may give you some things to think about.

Sociologists, in particular, are interested in the way our culture influences men and women to behave in certain gender-linked ways. The influence may come from church, school, parents, friends, and of course, the mass media. Even our language shapes our thinking about men and women, Lindsy Van Gelder argues in "The Great Person-Hole Cover Debate," and needs to be changed to eliminate bias. If you want to say, "Yes, but men and women are actually born different," then you've gotten to the heart of what is know as the nature *versus* nurture debate. This debate centers on whether men and women are bound to behave differently and to have different roles by their nature, or whether any differences come from the cultural environment in which they were brought up or nurtured. Richard Restak's "The Other Difference Between Boys and Girls" is on the "nature" side of the fence. Boys and girls actually do show biological differences, he argues.

Whether or not we like the roles we've got, however we got them, and whether or not they help or harm us, are other questions. Herb Goldberg, in his essay "In Harness: The Male Condition," certainly feels that American culture in general has handed men a basically destructive and limiting gender role. Other authors here argue that the mass media do in fact shape our gender roles in important ways. Craig Davidson's "Can We End Media Bias Against Gays?" opposes what Davidson sees as negative presentation of gays and lesbians in the press and on television. On the other hand, Victoria Rebeck, in "From Mary to Murphy," feels that at least some progress has been made in the presentation of women on television since "The Mary Tyler Moore Show" first aired in the 1960s.

How important are gender issues anyway? Bell hooks, in "Black Women and Feminism," says that feminists should not ignore issues of class and race. You may feel that gender roles have changed dramatically in the last generation and that men and women now have much more similar lives than they once did. Indeed, some things have certainly changed; but just placing the word *men* or *women* next to a few of our chapter headings raises questions: Do men and women work in the same jobs for the same rewards? Do they experience poverty in the same way? Do they play and watch the same sports? Are they violent in the same way? Do they experience racial discrimination in the same way? And if they don't, what is the reason for the difference?

Still, it's not always clear what effect the media really have: Do they shape or reflect "real" life? Are they ahead of or behind the times? No matter what conclusions your own reading and observation lead you to, the roles of men and women in American culture cannot fail to interest all of us: nobody is unaffected by this issue.

Starting Out: Finding Out What You Already Know

1. List what comes to mind when you hear the phrases "a real man" and "a real woman."

2. List the advantages of being your sex.
3. List the advantages of being the opposite sex. Compare your list with those of your classmates, grouping yourself by sex.
4. Freewrite about any instances when you felt limited by your sex.
5. Write about when you felt liberated by being male or female.

Learning More Through Observation: Taking a Look Around You and Talking to People

1. Interview people older than you and ask them what has changed for men and women since they were teenagers.
2. List as many characters in TV drama of your own sex as you can recall. (Check the *TV Guide* if you need a memory jog.) Pick the one you would most like to be and the one you would least like to be. Say why.
3. Pick a character from a movie or television show who seems to occupy a traditional sex role. List the things that make the role "traditional" in your view.
4. Do a journal entry on someone you know who seems to have avoided traditional male or female gender roles.
5. Do popular songs sung by women tend to be different from those sung by men? If so, how?

Questioning: Deciding What Else You Would Like to Know

List five questions that you still have about gender roles in American culture.

VICTORIA A. REBECK

From Mary to Murphy

Victoria Rebeck, a reviewer for The Christian Century, *compares two successful TV shows that have women in leading roles.*

BEFORE YOU READ

1. List some TV shows that you think give an outdated view of the roles of men or women. Are these reruns or recent productions?
2. Do you think that television programs can change the way we feel about what it means to be male or female in American culture?

1. Mary Tyler Moore played the model woman of the 1970s. In the role of Mary Richards on "The Mary Tyler Moore Show" (reruns are still showing in some markets), she was an attractive, bright, competent and single career woman. She was also—particularly in the earlier episodes—extremely self-conscious and self-effacing, which was supposed to be part of her charm.

2. In one episode Mary complains to her close friend Rhoda Morgenstern that she hates to eat alone in public: "Where do you look? How do you turn the page of your newspaper without spilling your coffee—and then *everyone* is looking at you?" Above all, Mary is *nice*. In this case that means overly modest; she all but invites people to take advantage of her. In the first season the theme song began, "How will you make it on your own?" (The next year it instead asked rhetorically, "Who can turn the world on with her smile?")

3. In addiction therapy parlance, Mary Richards is a classic enabler codependent. As associate producer of a news program, she acts as lackey to the gruff, hard-drinking producer Lou Grant. Mary is the only staff member who calls him "Mr. Grant." Though Lou frequently and publicly insults the vain and vacuous[1] news anchor Ted Baxter, he depends on Mary to relay any really bad news. Lou doesn't even have to ask. All he has to do is summon Mary into his office. "You want me to tell him, don't you?" she prompts. Lou aims to intimidate people, but he avoids genuine confrontation. That task is left to Mary, who wears her insecurity on her sleeve. Mary enables Lou to continue this denial-and-avoidance approach; she tacitly agrees to smooth things over and straighten things out for him and assume the responsibility and attendant guilt herself.

4. A good example is the episode in which Mary, Lou and newswriter Murray Slaughter are served by an inept waitress. Though Mary is usually ready to excuse such people, this time she gets up the gumption to complain gently to the manager. Since he had already heard similar complaints, the manager decides to fire the waitress. This sends Mary into one of her agonized guilt trips. Though the waitress was truly incompetent (and unrepentant), Mary feels responsible for the firing. When the woman appears a few days later seeking employment at the station, Mary feels obliged to hire her as a secretary even though she lacks appropriate skills. Since *she* had gotten the woman fired, Mary moans that she is responsible for getting her another job.

5. The stronger female character in the program is the wisecracking Rhoda Morgenstern. Her apparent punishment for this trait is that she is unable to land a steady boyfriend. The scriptwriters knew that, however successful Mary and Rhoda are in their careers, what these women really need and want is a man to validate their femininity.

6. In the late 1980s, there is another woman starring in a newsroom sitcom. She has moved up to be coanchor of a news-features program. Played by Candice Bergen, the character talks tough and has the streetwise name of Murphy Brown.

---

[1] Stupid; empty-headed.

7   Unlike Mary Richards, Murphy is self-confident, a seasoned professional who's seen some rough action. Like Mary, she is surrounded by eccentric supporting characters. Taking the Ted Baxter role is the perky Corky Sherwood. She is much smarter than Ted, but every bit as image-conscious and easily flattered. She liberally doles out maternalistic advice (à la home economist Sue Ann Nivens, a later "MTM" habitué[2])—and coy chidings ("Somebody is not pulling her weight around here, and her initials are M.B."). Ted's officious baritone voice is assumed by another co-worker, Jim Dial, who is nonetheless much more than a talking head. The team is rounded out by Frank Fontana, a sensible Murray Slaughter-clone complete with receding hairline. Young and insecure Miles Silverberg, their self-important producer (*executive* producer, he would correct me), is not nearly as intimidating as Lou Grant.

8   Murphy does not suffer fools gladly. She complains vigorously to the personnel department for failing to provide her with an adequate secretary. In one episode the network tests an up-and-coming talent named Miller Redfield, a master of happy talk. ("You be careful out there," he calls out merrily to Jim, who is being threatened by armed guards while reporting from outside of Qaddafi's headquarters.) Just before he and Murphy are to broadcast their first show, Redfield advises her to engage in "friendly repartee" with him between stories. "I don't engage in friendly repartee," she retorts. "It would be unpleasant for both of us."

9   Murphy is straightforward and often brusque, but she is not portrayed as less of a woman for it. She is stronger and more sure of herself than Mary Richards, but we like her no less than we did Mary. She does not, like Rhoda, bemoan an open social calendar. In fact, her romantic life seems immaterial. Many of the episodes take place at her workplace and focus on the relationships there. She is not sexless, however; she is always stylishly clad and well coiffed.

10   Whereas Mary Richards is a codependent, Murphy Brown, as it happens, is a recovering alcoholic. The difference is evident in the two characters' behavior. Mary lacks the self-esteem to differentiate between what is truly her responsibility and what is out of her control. Her self-deprecation reflects her sense of ladylike demeanor. Murphy, on the other hand, having come to grips with her dependency on alcohol, expresses her feelings openly and accepts the consequences. She does not assume the guilt imposed on her by others.

11   In an October episode, Murphy relates the crisis of her alcohol dependency. She tells a scoop-hungry junior-high journalism student about how she admitted herself to a substance-abuse treatment center. She had been assigned to interview Mañuel Noriega, and feeling the pressure of the task had begun drinking "to get ahead of the panic." On the day she was to board a plane for Panama she retreated into her office where she pulled out a bottle of Scotch "to calm my nerves." She remembered nothing after that except waking up at home several hours later, having missed her flight to Central America. She planned a trip to the Betty Ford Clinic instead.

---

[2] Inhabitant; here, a regular character.

12 "Murphy Brown" is a comedy, and so this story is followed up with a wisecrack from the budding reporter ("That's not a big story—these days celebrities going to Betty Ford is strictly page three stuff"). But Murphy offers her own share of sarcastic rejoinders. She is not necessarily the straight woman or apologist in the joke-making, like Mary. She is self-aware, responsible for her own behavior but not others'. She does not take pains to soften her sharp comments.

13 Murphy Brown does not necessarily depict the ultimate feminist vision (she is beautiful and white, surely for the sake of ratings). Her addiction problem probably reflects the writers' desire to be trendy in a time when celebrity drug-abuse confessions flourish on the newsstand. She is not necessarily a role model; she is sometimes too biting and makes her share of mistakes. But at least she is off the pedestal. And given Murphy's advance over Mary, we can hope that the star of a '90s newsroom sitcom will achieve full recovery from the dysfunction of sexism.

REACTING

1. Do you agree with Victoria Rebeck that the movement from "Mary to Murphy" is progress?
2. Compare your own reactions to these two shows with those of Rebeck.

CONNECTING

1. In your opinion, which female role model is the more "helpful" in today's society, Mary or Murphy? Explain your answer. What would a feminist role model be like?
2. Respond to former Vice President Dan Quayle's argument that "Murphy Brown" conveys destructive values.

LEARNING ABOUT WRITING FROM READING

This essay is a good demonstration of how to use comparisons to make your point. Rebeck doesn't mention the character Murphy Brown in the first half, but look at the way she connects her with Mary Tyler Moore in the second part. Key words used to compare, or link, the two shows are "on the other hand," "unlike," "like," and "whereas."

Paragraph 10 shows some of these connectors at work:

> <u>Whereas</u> Mary Richards is a codependent, Murphy Brown, as it happens, is a recovering alcoholic. The <u>difference</u> is evident in the two characters' behavior. Mary lacks the self-esteem to differentiate between what is truly her responsibility and what is out of her control. Her self-deprecation reflects her sense of

ladylike demeanor. Murphy, <u>on the other hand,</u> having come to grips with her dependency on alcohol, expresses her feelings openly and accepts the consequences. She does not assume the guilt imposed on her by others.

RICHARD M. RESTAK

The Other Difference Between Boys and Girls

Richard Restak, a Washington, D.C., neurologist, offers his conclusions about the functioning of men's and women's brains.

BEFORE YOU READ

1. In what ways, if any, do men and women think differently? Make a list.
2. Do you expect to agree or disagree with an article about differences between the sexes? Why or why not?

1   Boys think differently from girls. Recent research on brain behavior makes that conclusion inescapable, and it is unrealistic to keep denying it.

2   I know how offensive that will sound to feminists and others committed to overcoming sexual stereotypes. As the father of three daughters, I am well aware of the discrimination girls suffer. But social equality for men and women really depends on recognizing these differences in brain behavior.

3   At present, schooling and testing discriminate against both boys and girls in different ways, ignoring differences that have been observed by parents and educators for years. Boys suffer in elementary school classrooms, which are ideally suited to the way girls think. Girls suffer later on, in crucial ways, taking scholarship tests that are geared for male performance.

4   Anyone who has spent time with children in a playground or school setting is aware of differences in the way boys and girls respond to similar situations. Think of the last time you supervised a birthday party attended by five-year-olds. It's not usually the girls who pull hair, throw punches or smear each other with food.

5   Usually such differences are explained on a cultural basis. Boys are expected to be more aggressive and play rough games, while girls are presumably encouraged to be gentle, nonassertive and passive. After several years of exposure to such expectations, the theory goes, men and women wind up with widely

varying behavioral and intellectual repertoires.[1] As a corollary to this, many people believe that if child-rearing practices could be equalized and sexual stereotypes eliminated, most of these differences would eventually disappear. As often happens, however, the true state of affairs is not that simple.

6   Undoubtedly, many of the differences traditionally believed to exist between the sexes are based on stereotypes. But despite this, evidence from recent brain research indicates that many behavioral differences between men and women are based on differences in brain functioning that are biologically inherent and unlikely to be modified by cultural factors alone.

7   The first clue to brain differences between the sexes came from observations of male and female infants. From birth, female infants are more sensitive to sounds, particularly to their mother's voice. In a laboratory, if the sound of the mother's voice is displaced to another part of the room, female babies will react while male babies usually seem oblivious to the displacement. Female babies are also more easily startled by loud noises. In fact, their enhanced hearing performance persists throughout life, with females experiencing a fall-off in hearing much later than males.

8   Tests involving girls old enough to cooperate show increased skin sensitivity, particularly in the fingertips, which have a lower threshold for touch identification. Females are also more proficient at fine motor performance. Rapid tapping movements are carried out quickly and more efficiently by girls than by boys.

9   In addition, there are differences in what attracts a girl's attention. Generally, females are more attentive to social contexts—faces, speech patterns and subtle vocal cues. By four months of age, a female infant is socially aware enough to distinguish photographs of familiar people, a task rarely performed well by boys of that age. Also at four months, girls will babble to a mother's face, seemingly recognizing her as a person, while boys fail to distinguish between a face and a dangling toy, babbling equally to both.

10 Female infants also speak sooner, have larger vocabularies and rarely demonstrate speech defects. Stuttering, for instance, occurs almost exclusively among boys.

11 Girls can also sing in tune at an earlier age. In fact, if we think of the muscles of the throat as muscles of fine control—those in which girls excel—then it should come as no surprise that girls exceed boys in language abilities. This early linguistic bias often prevails throughout life. Girls read sooner, learn foreign languages more easily and, as a result, are more likely to enter occupations involving language mastery.

12 Boys, in contrast, show an early visual superiority. They are also clumsier, performing poorly at something like arranging a row of beads, but excel at other activities calling on total body coordination. Their attentional mechanisms are also different. A boy will react to an inanimate object as quickly as he

---

[1] Range or collection.

will to a person. A male baby will often ignore the mother and babble to a blinking light, fixate on a geometric figure and, at a later point, manipulate[2] it and attempt to take it apart.

13   A study of nursery preschool children carried out by psychologist Diane McGuinness of Stanford University found boys more curious, especially in regard to exploring their environment. McGuinness' studies also confirmed that males are better at manipulating three-dimensional space. When boys and girls are asked to mentally rotate or fold an object, boys overwhelmingly outperform girls. "I folded it in my mind" is a typical male response. Girls, when explaining how they perform the same task, are likely to produce elaborate verbal descriptions which, because they are less appropriate to the task, result in frequent errors.

14   In an attempt to understand the sex differences in spatial ability, electroencephalogram (EEG) measurements have recently been made of the accompanying electrical events going on within the brain.

15   Ordinarily, the two brain hemispheres produce a similar electrical background that can be measured by an EEG. When a person is involved in a mental task—say, subtracting 73 from 102—the hemisphere that is activated will demonstrate a change in its electrical background. When boys are involved in tasks employing spatial concepts, such as figuring out mentally which of three folded shapes can be made from a flat, irregular piece of paper, the right hemisphere is activated consistently. Girls, in contrast, are more likely to activate both hemispheres, indicating that spatial ability is more widely dispersed in the female brain.

16   When it comes to psychological measurements of brain functioning between the sexes, unmistakable differences emerge. In 11 subtests of the most widely used test of general intelligence, only two subtests reveal similar mean scores for males and females. These sex differences have been substantiated across cultures and are so consistent that the standard battery of this intelligence test now contains a masculinity-femininity index.

17   Further support for sex differences in brain functioning comes from experience with subtests that eventually had to be omitted from the original test battery. A cube-analysis test, for example, was excluded because, after testing thousands of subjects, a large sex bias appeared to favor males. In all, over 30 tests eventually had to be eliminated because they discriminated in favor of one or the other sex. One test, involving mentally working oneself through a maze, favored boys so overwhelmingly that, for a while, some psychologists speculated that girls were totally lacking in a "spatial factor."

18   Most thought-provoking of all is a series of findings by Eleanor Maccoby and Carol Nagly Jacklin of Stanford on personality traits and intellectual achievement. They found that girls whose intellectual achievement is greatest tend to be unusually active, independent, competitive and free of fear or anxiety,

---

[2] Handle; move by hand.

while intellectually outstanding boys are often timid, anxious, not overtly aggressive and less active.

19   In essence, Maccoby and Jacklin's findings suggest that intellectual performance is incompatible with our stereotype of femininity in girls or masculinity in boys.

20   Research evidence within the last six months indicates that many of these brain sex differences persist over a person's lifetime. In a study at the University Hospital in Ontario that compared verbal and spatial abilities of men and women after a stroke, the women did better than men in key categories tested. After the stroke, women tended to be less disabled and recovered more quickly.

21   Research at the National Institute of Mental Health is even uncovering biochemical differences in the brains of men and women. Women's brains, it seems, are more sensitive to experimentally administered lights and sounds. The investigator in charge of this research, Dr. Monte Buchsbaum, speculates that the enhanced response of the female brain depends on the effect of sex hormones on the formation of a key brain chemical. This increased sensibility to stimuli[3] by the female brain may explain why women more often than men respond to loss and stress by developing depression.

22   It's important to remember that we're not talking about one sex being generally superior or inferior to another. Rather, psychobiological research is turning up important functional differences between male and female brains. The discoveries might possibly contribute to further resentments and divisions in our society. But must they? Why are sex differences in brain functioning disturbing to so many people? And why do women react so vehemently[4] to findings that, if anything, indicate enhanced capabilities in the female brain?

23   It seems to me that we can make two responses to these findings on brain-sex differences. First, we can use them to help bring about true social equity. One way of doing this might be to change such practices as nationwide competitive examinations. If boys, for instance, truly do excel in right-hemisphere tasks, then tests such as the National Merit Scholarship Examination should be radically redesigned to assure that both sexes have an equal chance. As things now stand, the tests are heavily weighted with items that virtually guarantee superior male performance.

24   Attitude changes are also needed in our approach to "hyperactive" or "learning disabled" children. The evidence for sex differences here is staggering: More than 95 percent of hyperactives are males. And why should this be surprising in light of the sex differences in brain function that we've just discussed?

25   The male brain learns by manipulating its environment, yet the typical student is forced to sit still for long hours in the classroom. The male brain is primarily visual, while classroom instruction demands attentive listening. Boys are clumsy in fine hand coordination, yet are forced at an early age to express

---

[3] Plural of *stimulus:* something that causes a response.
[4] Forcefully; passionately.

themselves in writing. Finally, there is little opportunity in most schools, other than during recess, for gross motor movements or rapid muscular responses. In essence, the classrooms in most of our nation's primary grades are geared to skills that come naturally to girls but develop very slowly in boys. The results shouldn't be surprising: a "learning disabled" child who is also frequently "hyperactive."

26 "He can't sit still, can't write legibly, is always trying to take things apart, won't follow instructions, is loud, and, oh yes, terribly clumsy," is a typical teacher description of male hyperactivity. We now have the opportunity, based on emerging evidence of sex differences in brain functioning, to restructure elementary grades so that boys find their initial educational contacts less stressful.

27 At more advanced levels of instruction, efforts must be made to develop teaching methods that incorporate verbal and linguistic approaches to physics, engineering and architecture (to mention only three fields where women are conspicuously underrepresented and, on competitive aptitude tests, score well below males).

28 The second alternative is, of course, to do nothing about brain differences and perhaps even deny them altogether. Certainly there is something to be said for this approach too. In the recent past, enhanced social benefit has usually resulted from stressing the similarities between people rather than their differences. We ignore brain-sex differences, however, at the risk of confusing biology with sociology, and wishful thinking with scientific facts.

29 The question is not, "Are there brain-sex differences?" but rather, "What is going to be our response to these differences?" Psychobiological research is slowly but surely inching toward scientific proof of a premise first articulated by the psychologist David Wechsler more than 20 years ago:

30 "The findings suggest that women seemingly call upon different resources or different degrees of like abilities in exercising whatever it is we call intelligence. For the moment, one need not be concerned as to which approach is better or 'superior.' But our findings do confirm what poets and novelists have often asserted, and the average layman long believed, namely, that men not only behave, but 'think' differently from women."

REACTING

1. Do you find Richard Restak's argument about male and female differences convincing? Why or why not? In particular, how do you react to the first paragraph?
2. Which "difference" did you find most interesting, surprising, or disturbing? Why?

CONNECTING

1. How does Restak's information affect the way you answer the chapter's key question about gender roles helping or hindering us?

2. Turn to p. 147 and read bell hooks's "Black Women and Feminism." How might hooks respond to Restak's claims that men and women are inherently (biologically) different?

LEARNING ABOUT WRITING FROM READING

Restak's opening paragraphs demonstrate one way to begin an essay or article. He comes out with guns blazing, no holds barred:

> Boys think differently from girls . . . it is unrealistic to keep denying it.

Readers certainly know from this dramatic statement where the author stands. But the risk is that they will be so hostile to these opening words that they will stop reading. Restak recognizes that risk, so his second paragraph acknowledges the hostility of some of his readers and qualifies the black-and-white sharpness of his first paragraph:

> I know how offensive that will sound to feminists and others committed to overcoming sexual stereotypes. . . . But social equality for men and women really depends on recognizing these differences in brain behavior.

People are more likely to keep reading if they think that their objections will be dealt with in a reasonable way. Restak gives them cause to think that this will be the case.

HERB GOLDBERG

In Harness: The Male Condition

Herb Goldberg, a writer on men's issues, writes about what it's like to be a man in contemporary American society.

BEFORE YOU READ

1. What does the title lead you to expect? Use the word *harness* to help you here: What do you associate with that word, and what does it have to do with "the male condition"?
2. What do you think it means to be male in America?

1   Most men live in harness. Richard was one of them. Typically he had no awareness of how his male harness was choking him until his personal and professional life and his body had nearly fallen apart.

2   Up to that time he had experienced only occasional short bouts of depression that a drink would bring him out of. For Richard it all crashed at an

early age, when he was thirty-three. He came for psychotherapy with resistance, but at the instruction of his physician. He had a bad ulcer, was losing weight, and, in spite of repeated warnings that it could kill him, he was drinking heavily.

3   His personal life was also in serious trouble. He had recently lost his job as a disc jockey on a major radio station because he'd been arrested for drunk driving. He had totaled his car against a tree and the newspapers had a picture of it on the front page. Shortly thereafter his wife moved out, taking with her their eight-year-old daughter. She left at the advice of friends who knew that he had become violent twice that year while drunk.

4   As he began to talk about himself it became clear that he had been securely fitted into his male harness early in his teens. In high school he was already quite tall and stronger than most. He was therefore urged to go out for basketball, which he did, and he got lots of attention for it.

5   He had a deep, resonant voice that he had carefully cultivated. He was told that he should go into radio announcing and dramatics, so he got into all the high school plays. In college he majored in theater arts.

6   In his senior year in college he dated one of the most beautiful and sought-after girls in the junior class. His peer group envied him, which reassured Richard that he had a good thing going. So he married Joanna a year after graduating and took a job with a small radio station in Fresno, California. During the next ten years he played out the male role; he fathered a child and fought his way up in a very competitive profession.

7   It wasn't until things had fallen apart that he even let himself know that he had any feelings of his own, and in therapy he began to see why it had been so necessary to keep his feelings buried. They were confusing and frightening.

8   More than anything else, there was a hypersensitive concern over what others thought about him as a "man." As other suppressed feelings began to surface they surprised him. He realized how he had hated the pressures of being a college basketball player. The preoccupation with being good and winning had distorted his life in college.

9   Though he had been to bed with many girls before marriage and even a few afterward, he acknowledged that rarely was it a genuine turn-on for him. He liked the feeling of being able to seduce a girl but the experience itself was rarely satisfying, so he would begin the hunt for another as soon as he succeeded with one. "Some of those girls were a nightmare," he said, "I would have been much happier without them. But I was caught in the bag of proving myself and I couldn't seem to control it."

10   The obsessive preoccupation in high school and college with cultivating a deep, resonant "masculine" voice he realized was similar to the obsession some women have with their figures. Though he thought he had enjoyed the attention he got being on stage, he acknowledged that he had really disliked being an entertainer, or "court jester," as he put it.

11   When he thought about how he had gotten married he became particularly uncomfortable. "I was really bored with Joanna after the first month of dating but I couldn't admit it to myself because I thought I had a great thing going. I

married her because I figured if I didn't one of the other guys would. I couldn't let that happen."

Richard had to get sick in his harness and nearly be destroyed by role-playing masculinity before he could allow himself to be a person with his own feelings, rather than just a hollow male image. Had it not been for a bleeding ulcer he might have postponed looking at himself for many years more.

Like many men, Richard had been a zombie,[1] a daytime sleepwalker. Worse still, he had been a highly "successful" zombie, which made it so difficult for him to risk change. Our culture is saturated with successful male zombies, businessmen zombies, golf zombies, sports car zombies, playboy zombies, etc. They are playing by the rules of the male game plan. They have lost touch with, or are running away from, their feelings and awareness of themselves as people. They have confused their social masks for their essence and they are destroying themselves while fulfilling the traditional definitions of masculine-appropriate behavior. They set their life sails by these role definitions. They are the heroes, the studs, the providers, the warriors, the empire builders, the fearless ones. Their reality is always approached through these veils of gender expectations.

When something goes seriously wrong, they discover that they are shadows to themselves as well as to others. They are unknown because they have been so busy manipulating and masking themselves in order to maintain and garner more status that a genuine encounter with another person would threaten them, causing them to flee or to react with extreme defensiveness.

Men evaluate each other and are evaluated by many women largely by the degree to which they approximate the ideal masculine model. Women have rightfully lashed out against being placed into a mold and being related to as a sex object. Many women have described their roles in marriage as a form of socially approved prostitution. They assert that they are selling themselves out for an unfulfilling portion of supposed security. For psychologically defensive reasons the male has not yet come to see himself as a prostitute, day in and day out, both in and out of the marriage relationship.

The male's inherent survival instincts have been stunted by the seemingly more powerful drive to maintain his masculine image. He would, for example, rather die in the battle than risk living in a different way and being called a "coward" or "not a man." He would rather die at his desk prematurely than free himself from his compulsive patterns and pursuits. As a recently published study concluded, "A surprising number of men approaching senior citizenship say they would rather die than be buried in retirement."

The male in our culture is at a growth impasse. He won't move—not because he is protecting his cherished central place in the sun, but because he *can't* move. He is a cardboard Goliath precariously balanced and on the verge of toppling over if he is pushed even ever so slightly out of his well-worn path. He lacks the fluidity of the female who can readily move between the traditional

---

[1] Automaton; the living dead.

definitions of male or female behavior and roles. She can be wife and mother or a business executive. She can dress in typically feminine fashion or adopt the male styles. She will be loved for having "feminine" interests such as needlework or cooking, or she will be admired for sharing with the male in his "masculine" interests. That will make her a "man's woman." She can be sexually assertive or sexually passive. Meanwhile, the male is rigidly caught in his masculine pose and, in many subtle and direct ways, he is severely punished when he steps out of it.

18   Unlike some of the problems of women, the problems of men are not readily changed through legislation. The male has no apparent and clearly defined targets against which he can vent his rage. Yet he is oppressed by the cultural pressures that have denied him his feelings, by the mythology of the woman and the distorted and self-destructive way he sees and relates to her, by the urgency for him to "act like a man" which blocks his ability to respond to his inner promptings both emotionally and physiologically, and by a generalized self-hate that causes him to feel comfortable only when he is functioning well in harness, or when he lives for joy and for personal growth.

19   The prevalent "enlightened" male's reaction to the women's liberation movement bears testimony to his inability to mobilize himself on his own behalf. He has responded to feminist assertions by donning sack cloth, sprinkling himself with ashes, and flagellating[2] himself—accusing himself of the very things she is accusing him of. An article entitled "You've Come a Long Way, Buddy" perhaps best illustrates the male self-hating attitude. In it, the writer said,

20   The members of the men's liberation movement are . . . a kind of embarrassing vanguard, the first men anywhere on record to take a political stand based on the idea that what the women are saying is right—men are a bunch of lazy, selfish, horny, unhappy oppressors.

21   Many other undoubtedly well-intentioned writers on the male condition have also taken a basically guilt- and shame-oriented approach to the male, alternately scolding him, warning him, and preaching to him that he better change and not be a male chauvinist pig anymore. During many years of practice as a psychotherapist, I have never seen a person grow or change in a self-constructive, meaningful way when he was motivated by guilt, shame, or self-hate. That manner of approach smacks of old-time religion and degrades the male by ignoring the complexity of the binds and repressions that are his emotional heritage.

22   Precisely because the tenor and mood of the male liberation efforts so far have been one of self-accusation, self-hate, and a repetition of feminist assertions, I believe it is doomed to failure in its present form. It is buying the myth that the male is culturally favored—a notion that is clung to despite the fact that every critical statistic in the area of longevity, disease, suicide, crime,

---

[2] Beating; punishing.

accidents, childhood emotional disorders, alcoholism, and drug addiction shows a disproportionately higher male rate.

23   Many men who join male liberation groups do so to please or impress their women or to learn how to deal with and hold onto their recently liberated wives or girlfriends. Once in a male liberation group they intellectualize their feelings and reactions into lifelessness. In addition, the men tend to put each other down for thinking like "typical male chauvinists" or using words like "broad," "chick," "dyke," etc. They have introjected the voices of their feminist accusers and the result is an atmosphere that is joyless, self-righteous, cautious, and lacking in a vitalizing energy. A new, more subtle kind of competitiveness pervades the atmosphere: the competition to be the least competitive and most free of the stereotyped version of male chauvinism.

24   The women's liberation movement did not effect its astounding impact via self-hate, guilt, or the desire to placate[3] the male. Instead it has been energized by anger and outrage. Neither will the male change in any meaningful way until he experiences his underlying rage toward the endless, impossible binds under which he lives, the rigid definitions of his role, the endless pressure to be all things to all people, and the guilt-oriented, self-denying way he has traditionally related to women, to his feelings, and to his needs.

25   Because it is so heavily repressed, male rage only manifests itself indirectly and in hidden ways. Presently it is taking the form of emotional detachment, interpersonal withdrawal, and passivity in relationship to women. The male has pulled himself inward in order to deny his anger and to protect himself and others from his buried cascade[4] of resentment and fury. Pathetic, intellectualized attempts not to be a male chauvinist pig will *never* do the job.

26   There is also a commonly expressed notion that men will somehow be freed as a by-product of the feminist movement. This is a comforting fantasy for the male but I see no basis for it becoming a reality. It simply disguises the fear of actively determining his own change. Indeed, by responding inertly and passively, the male will be moved, but not in a meaningful and productive direction. If there is to be a constructive change for the male he will have to chart his own way, develop his own style and experience his own anxieties, fear, and rage because *this time mommy won't do it!*

27   Recently, I asked a number of men to write to me about how they see their condition and what liberation would mean to them. A sense of suffocation and confusion was almost always present.

28   A forty-six-year-old businessman wrote: "From what do I need to be liberated? I'm too old and tired to worry about myself. I know that I'm only a high-grade mediocrity. I've come to accept a life where the dreams are now all revealed as unreality. I don't know how my role or my son's role should change. If I knew I suppose it would be in any way that would make my wife happier and less of a shrew."

---

[3] Please, pacify.
[4] Waterfall; sequence of events that follow one another swiftly.

29   A thirty-nine-year-old carpenter discussing the "joys" of working responded: "I contend that the times in which it is fun and rewarding in a healthy way have been fairly limited. Most of the time it has been a question of running in fear of failure." Referring to his relationships, he continued. "There is another aspect of women's and men's lib that I haven't experienced extensively. This is the creation of close friendships outside of the marriage. My past experiences have been stressful to the point where I am very careful to limit any such contact. What's the fear? I didn't like the sense of insecurity developed by my wife and the internal stresses that I felt. It created guilt feelings."

30   A fifty-seven-year-old college professor expressed it this way: "Yes, there's a need for male lib and hardly anyone writes about it the way it really is, though a few make jokes. My gut reaction, which is what you asked for, is that men—the famous male chauvinist pigs who neglect their wives, underpay their women employees, and rule the world—are literally slaves. They're out there picking that cotton, sweating, swearing, taking lashes from the boss, working fifty hours a week to support themselves and the plantation, only then to come back to the house to do another twenty hours a week rinsing dishes, toting trash bags, writing checks, and acting as butlers at the parties. It's true of young husbands and middle-aged husbands. Young bachelors may have a nice deal for a couple of years after graduating, but I've forgotten, and I'll never again be young! Old men. Some have it sweet, some have it sour.

31   "Man's role—how has it affected my life? At thirty-five, I chose to emphasize family togetherness and income and neglect my profession if necessary. At fifty-seven, I see no reward for time spent with and for the family, in terms of love or appreciation. I see a thousand punishments for neglecting my profession. I'm just tired and have come close to just walking away from it and starting over; just research, publish, teach, administer, play tennis, and travel. Why haven't I? Guilt. And love. And fear of loneliness. How should the man's role in my family change? I really don't know how it can, but I'd like a lot more time to do my thing."

32   The most remarkable and significant aspect of the feminist movement to date has been woman's daring willingness to own up to her resistances and resentment toward her time-honored, sanctified roles of wife and even mother. The male, however, has yet to fully realize, acknowledge, and rebel against the distress and stifling aspects of many of the roles he plays—from good husband, to good daddy, to good provider, to good lover, etc. Because of the inner pressure to constantly affirm his dominance and masculinity, he continues to act as if he can stand up under, fulfill, and even enjoy all the expectations placed on him no matter how contradictory and devitalizing[5] they are.

33   It's time to remove the disguises of privilege and reveal the male condition for what it really is.

---

[5] Deadening, life-removing.

REACTING

1. Would you agree with Herb Goldberg about what American culture asks men to be?
2. Do Goldberg's examples convince you that men in our culture are "in harness"? Why or why not?

CONNECTING

1. Who else in this chapter on gender roles in American culture would agree with Goldberg? What ideas do they have in common?
2. Turn to p. 151 and read Craig Davidson's "Can We End Media Bias Against Gays?" Imagine Goldberg and Davidson conversing about how men's ideas about masculinity have become what they are.

LEARNING ABOUT WRITING FROM READING

A word about stories. Remember how you loved stories when you were a child? "Tell me a story" sounds childish, but the truth is that we love to hear stories all our lives. Soap operas have a huge following, and they are nothing but stories about people's lives. The parables from the Bible are what we remember most easily, and they, too, are stories, or anecdotes (brief stories). Stories are one of the best ways we have of communicating with our readers.

What does Richard's story do for this essay? Try imagining this essay without it. How would its absence have changed the essay's effect on you?

LINDSY VAN GELDER

The Great Person-Hole Cover Debate

Lindsy Van Gelder, prolific journalist and a self-described "feminist anarchist," examines the messages our language sends about what it means to be male or female.

BEFORE YOU READ

1. What is your reaction to the following changes in the Gettysburg Address?

    Four score and seven years ago, our foremothers brought forth on this continent a new nation conceived in liberty and dedicated to the proposition that all women are created equal. Gettysburg Address, Mary Todd Lincoln

2. Try to guess just from the title what this article is about and what the author's point of view is.

1. I wasn't looking for trouble. What I was looking for, actually, was a little tourist information to help me plan a camping trip to New England.

2. But there it was, on the first page of the 1979 edition of the State of Vermont *Digest of Fish and Game Laws and Regulations:* a special message of welcome from one Edward F. Kehoe, commissioner of the Vermont Fish and Game Department, to the reader and would-be camper, *i.e.,* me.

3. This person (*i.e.,* me) is called "the sportsman."

4. "We have no 'sportswomen, sportspersons, sportsboys, or sportsgirls,'" Commissioner Kehoe hastened to explain, obviously anticipating that some of us sportsfeminists might feel a bit overlooked. "But," he added, "we are pleased to report that we do have many great sportsmen who are women, as well as young people of both sexes."

5. It's just that the Fish and Game Department is trying to keep things "simple and forthright" and to respect "long-standing tradition." And anyway, we really ought to be flattered, "sportsman" being "a meaningful title being earned by a special kind of dedicated man, woman, or young person, as opposed to just any hunter, fisherman, or trapper."

6. I have heard this particular line of reasoning before. In fact, I've heard it so often that I've come to think of it as The Great Person-Hole Cover Debate, since gender-neutral manholes are invariably brought into the argument as evidence of the lengths to which humorless, Newspeak-spouting feminists will go to destroy their mother tongue.

7. Consternation about woman-handling the language comes from all sides. Sexual conservatives who see the feminist movement as a unisex plot and who long for the good olde days of *vive la différence,*[1] when men were men and women were women, nonetheless do not rally behind the notion that the term "mankind" excludes women.

8. But most of the people who choke on expressions like "spokesperson" aren't right-wing misogynists,[2] and this is what troubles me. Like the undoubtedly well-meaning folks at the Vermont Fish and Game Department, they tend to reassure you right up front that they're only trying to keep things "simple" and to follow "tradition," and that some of their best men are women, anyway.

9. Usually they wind up warning you, with great sincerity, that you're jeopardizing the worthy cause of women's rights by focusing on "trivial" side issues. I would like to know how anything that gets people so defensive and resistant can possibly be called "trivial," whatever else it might be.

---

[1] Let difference flourish.

[2] People who hate women.

10   The English language is alive and constantly changing. Progress—both scientific and social—is reflected in our language, or should be.

11   Not too long ago, there was a product called "flesh-colored" Band-Aids. The flesh in question was colored Caucasian. Once the civil rights movement pointed out the racism inherent in the name, it was dropped. I cannot imagine reading a thoughtful, well-intentioned company policy statement explaining that while the Band-Aids would continue to be called "flesh-colored" for old time's sake, black and brown people would now be considered honorary whites and were perfectly welcome to use them.

12   Most sensitive people manage to describe our national religious traditions as "Judeo-Christian," even though it takes a few seconds longer to say than "Christian." So why is it such a hardship to say "he or she" instead of "he"?

13   I have a modest proposal for anyone who maintains that "he" is just plain easier: since "he" has been the style for several centuries now—and since it really includes everybody anyway, right?—it seems only fair to give "she" a turn. Instead of having to ponder over the intricacies³ of, say, "Congressman" versus "Congress person" versus "Representative," we can simplify things by calling them all "Congresswoman."

14   Other clarifications will follow: "a woman's home is her castle" . . . "a giant step for all womankind". . . "all women are created equal" . . . "Fisherwoman's Wharf." . . .

And don't be upset by the business letter that begins "Dear Madam," fellas. It means you, too.

REACTING

1. What is Lindsy Van Gelder's proposal? Do you agree with it?
2. What kind of person does the author seem to be? Do you like her tone of voice? Why or why not?

CONNECTING

1. Describe how Herb Goldberg ("In Harness: The Male Condition," p. 138) would respond to the proposal that we make our language nonsexist.
2. How would Van Gelder respond to the key question "Do gender roles help or hinder us?"?

---

³ Complexities, details.

LEARNING ABOUT WRITING FROM READING

Van Gelder makes her point with voice, humor, and even at times a sarcastic tone. Note the lively way she ends her essay—not with a clear but dull summary but with one more example of sexist language, delivered with irony and sting:

> And don't be upset by the business letter that begins "Dear Madam," fellas. It means you, too.

Van Gelder uses this particular example to sum up her attack on sexist language. Consider ending one of your papers with an example rather than an explanation.

BELL HOOKS

Black Women and Feminism

Bell hooks, feminist writer and critic, examines the impact on African American women of the white-dominated American feminist movement.

BEFORE YOU READ

1. Consider the connections you see between racism and sexism. What do they have in common? Where do they differ?
2. Speculate about the meaning of the title "Black Women and Feminism." What do you predict the article will be about?

1   For ten years now I have been an active feminist. I have been working to destroy the psychology of dominance that permeates Western culture and shapes female/male sex roles and I have advocated[1] reconstruction of U.S. society based on human rather than material values. I have been a student in women's studies classes, a participant in feminist seminars, organizations, and various women's groups. Initially I believed that the women who were active in feminist activities were concerned about sexist oppression and its impact on women as a collective group. But I became disillusioned as I saw various groups of women appropriating feminism to serve their own opportunistic[2] ends. Whether it was women university professors crying sexist oppression (rather than sexist discrimination) to attract attention to their efforts to gain promotion; or women using feminism to mask their sexist attitudes; or women writers

---

[1] Championed; strongly recommended.
[2] Selfishly capitalizing on an opportunity or chance occurrence.

superficially exploring feminist themes to advance their own careers, it was evident that eliminating sexist oppression was not the primary concern. While their rallying cry was sexist oppression, they showed little concern about the status of women as a collective group in our society. They were primarily interested in making feminism a forum for the expression of their own self-centered needs and desires. Not once did they entertain the possibility that their concerns might not represent the concerns of oppressed women.

2   Even as I witnessed the hypocrisy of feminists, I clung to the hope that increased participation of women from different races and classes in feminist activities would lead to a re-evaluation of feminism, radical[3] reconstruction of feminist ideology, and the launching of a new movement that would more adequately address the concerns of both women and men. I was not willing to see white women feminists as "enemies." Yet as I moved from one women's group to another trying to offer a different perspective, I met with hostility and resentment. White women liberationists saw feminism as "their" movement and resisted any efforts by non-white women to critique, challenge, or change its direction.

3   During this time, I was struck by the fact that the ideology of feminism, with its emphasis on transforming and changing the social structure of the U.S., in no way resembled the actual reality of American feminism. Largely because feminists themselves, as they attempted to take feminism beyond the realm of radical rhetoric into the sphere of American life, revealed that they remained imprisoned in the very structures they hoped to change. Consequently, the sisterhood we talked about has not become a reality. And the women's movement we envisioned would have a transformative effect on U.S. culture has not emerged. Instead, the hierarchical[4] pattern of sex-race relationships already established by white capitalist patriarchy merely assumed a different form under feminism. Women liberationists did not invite a wholistic analysis of woman's status in society that would take into consideration the varied aspects of our experience. In their eagerness to promote the idea of sisterhood, they ignored the complexity of woman's experience. While claiming to liberate women from biological determinism, they denied women an existence outside that determined by our sexuality. It did not serve the interest of upper and middle class white feminists to discuss race and class. Consequently, much feminist literature, while providing meaningful information concerning women's experiences, is both racist and sexist in its content. I say this not to condemn or dismiss. Each time I read a feminist book that is racist and sexist, I feel a sadness and an anguish of spirit. For to know that there thrives in the very movement that has claimed to liberate women endless snares that bind us tighter and tighter to old oppressive ways is to witness the failure of yet another potentially radical, transformative movement in our society.

---

[3] Thoroughgoing, extreme.

[4] Organized according to rank.

4   Although the contemporary feminist movement was initially motivated by the sincere desire of women to eliminate sexist oppression, it takes place within the framework of a larger, more powerful cultural system that encourages women and men to place the fulfillment of individual aspirations above their desire for collective change. Given this framework, it is not surprising that feminism has been undermined by the narcissism, greed, and individual opportunism of its leading exponents. A feminist ideology[5] that mouths radical rhetoric about resistance and revolution while actively seeking to establish itself within the capitalist patriarchal system is essentially corrupt. While the contemporary feminist movement has successfully stimulated an awareness of the impact of sexist discrimination on the social status of women in the U.S., it has done little to eliminate sexist oppression. Teaching women how to defend themselves against male rapists is not the same as working to change society so that men will not rape. Establishing houses for battered women does not change the psyches of the men who batter them, nor does it change the culture that promotes and condones their brutality. Attacking heterosexuality does little to strengthen the self-concept of the masses of women who desire to be with men. Denouncing housework as menial labor does not restore to the woman houseworker the pride and dignity in her labor she is stripped of by patriarchal devaluation. Demanding an end to institutionalized sexism does not ensure an end to sexist oppression.

5   The rhetoric of feminism with its emphasis on resistance, rebellion, and revolution created an illusion of militancy and radicalism that masked the fact that feminism was in no way a challenge or a threat to capitalist patriarchy. To perpetuate the notion that all men are creatures of privilege with access to a personal fulfillment and a personal liberation denied women, as feminists do, is to lend further credibility to the sexist mystique of male power that proclaims all that is male is inherently superior to that which is female. A feminism so rooted in envy, fear, and idealization of male power cannot expose the dehumanizing effect of sexism on men and women in American society. Today, feminism offers women not liberation but the right to act as surrogate men. It has not provided a blueprint for change that would lead to the elimination of sexist oppression or a transformation of our society. The women's movement has become a kind of ghetto or concentration camp for women who are seeking to attain the kind of power they feel men have. It provides a forum for the expression of their feelings of anger, jealousy, rage, and disappointment with men. It provides an atmosphere where women who have little in common, who may resent or even feel indifferent to one another can bond on the basis of shared negative feelings toward men. Finally, it gives women of all races, who desire to assume the imperialist, sexist, racist positions of destruction men hold a platform that allows them to act as if the attainment of their personal aspirations and their lust for power is for the common good of all women.

---

[5] System of beliefs and values.

6   To me feminism is not simply a struggle to end male chauvinism or a movement to ensure that women will have equal rights with men; it is a commitment to eradicating[6] the ideology of domination that permeates[7] Western culture on various levels—sex, race, and class, to name a few—and a commitment to reorganizing U.S. society so that the self-development of people can take precedence over imperialism, economic expansion, and material desires. Writers of a feminist pamphlet published anonymously in 1976 urged women to develop political consciousness:

7   In all these struggles we must be assertive and challenging, combating the deep-seated tendency in Americans to be liberal, that is, to evade struggling over questions of principle for fear of creating tensions or becoming unpopular. Instead we must live by the fundamental dialectical principle: that progress comes only from struggling to resolve contradictions.

8   It is a contradiction that white females have structured a women's liberation movement that is racist and excludes many non-white women. However, the existence of that contradiction should not lead any woman to ignore feminist issues. Oftentimes I am asked by black women to explain why I would call myself a feminist and by using that term ally myself with a movement that is racist. I say, "The question we must ask again and again is how can racist women call themselves feminists." It is obvious that many women have appropriated[8] feminism to serve their own ends, especially those white women who have been at the forefront of the movement; but rather than resigning myself to this appropriation I choose to re-appropriate the term "feminism," to focus on the fact that to be "feminist" in any authentic sense of the term is to want for all people, female and male, liberation from sexist role patterns, domination, and oppression.

9   Today masses of black women in the U.S. refuse to acknowledge that they have much to gain by feminist struggle. They fear feminism. They have stood in place so long that they are afraid to move. They fear change. They fear losing what little they have. They are afraid to openly confront white feminists with their racism or black males with their sexism, not to mention confronting white men with their racism and sexism. I have sat in many a kitchen and heard black women express a belief in feminism and eloquently critique the women's movement explaining their refusal to participate. I have witnessed their refusal to express these same views in a public setting. I know their fear exists because they have seen us trampled upon, raped, abused, slaughtered, ridiculed and mocked. Only a few black women have rekindled the spirit of feminist struggle that stirred the hearts and minds of our 19th century sisters. We, black women

---

[6] Rooting out, removing.
[7] Spreads, penetrates.
[8] Adopted, taken up.

who advocate feminist ideology, are pioneers. We are clearing a path for ourselves and our sisters. We hope that as they see us reach our goal—no longer victimized, no longer unrecognized, no longer afraid—they will take courage and follow.

REACTING

1. What was the most interesting or most surprising point bell hooks made? Explain your answer.
2. How does the article answer this chapter's key question?

CONNECTING

1. Read Craig Davidson's "Can We End Media Bias Against Gays?" on this page. What might Davidson say in response to the following argument (paragraph 6):

    [F]eminism is not simply a struggle to end male chauvinism or a movement to ensure that women will have equal rights with men; it is a commitment to eradicating the ideology of domination that permeates Western culture on various levels—sex, race, and class, to name a few.

2. Would bell hooks see the progress in Victoria Rebeck's "From Mary to Murphy" (p. 129)?

LEARNING ABOUT WRITING FROM READING

Hooks uses both the first-person singular pronoun "I" and the first-person plural pronoun "we" in this passage. Why? Students often ask if it's all right to use "I" in their writing. The answer is yes, as long it's not overdone and is appropriate for the kind of writing you are doing. People don't usually worry about using "we," but the same rules apply.

Hooks is fine on both counts. She uses "I" in a few sentences at the beginning of the passage to establish her own personal experiences as a black feminist. But at the end of the passage she uses "we" to make the connection between herself and the members of the much larger group to which she belongs.

CRAIG DAVIDSON

Can We End Media Bias Against Gays?

Craig Davidson, a writer on gay and lesbian issues, discusses the problems he sees with media portrayals of homosexuals.

BEFORE YOU READ

1. How would you answer the title question?
2. What images of gay men and women have you noticed on television or in the press?

1   Not so long ago, an editor at the *Columbia Journalism Review* rejected a manuscript about anti-gay and -lesbian prejudice in the newsroom with the terse observation that the issues raised in the piece were problems "a few years ago, but not now." Would that it were so. While there is less overt defamation of gay people in respectable news reporting than there used to be—the Dan Rathers of the world know not to call gays perverts or child molesters—that was always just the tip of the iceberg.

2   Anti-gay prejudice in the media occurs not just as vicious slander, but also as casual bias, perpetuation of negative stereotypes, deference to the prejudice of others, and lesbian and gay invisibility. Problems with media coverage of the lesbian and gay community are rooted as much in heterosexism (the attitude that heterosexuals are important and homosexuals are not) as in homophobia (fear and loathing of gay people).

3   **Vicious slander.** Relatively few gay or gay-sympathetic persons seem to be aware of the extent to which vicious anti-gay name-calling and stereotyping still are broadcast. Virtually every city has one or two radio personalities whose stock in trade is outrageous behavior and insults. Often, they ridicule many minorities, but reserve their most vicious attacks for lesbians and gays.

4   Current examples are talk-show host Rush Limbaugh and "shock jock" Howard Stern, both nationally syndicated, who use "fag" and "dyke" freely and are particularly fond of so-called "comedy" routines about AIDS. A variation on their theme is Bob Grant, whose talk show on WABC in New York is the area's most popular program. Marketed as a serious, conservative political commentator, he is, in fact, an extremist, particularly on lesbian, gay, and AIDS issues. Broadcasting from a mobile booth at City Hall on the day the New York City gay rights bill was debated, Grant invited a lesbian caller to come down to the booth so he could "punch [her] nose right down [her] throat."

5   The op-ed page of most newspapers is another frequent source of vicious homophobia. Patrick Buchanan and William F. Buckley, Jr., are the best known of a large lineup of columnists who regularly attack homosexuals as "sodomites" and "pederasts," and who refuse to acknowledge the gay community's overwhelmingly positive response to AIDS. Around the country, many Buchanan and Buckley clones also serve as publisher or editor of their local newspaper, positions from which their biases influence news reporting as well.

6   Many assume that a reasonable op-ed page and talk-show balance between "conservatives" and "liberals" provides fairness on lesbian, gay, and AIDS

issues, but that is not the case. While Buchanan and his cronies attack gays regularly, major liberal columnists such as Anthony Lewis, Tom Wicker, and James Reston virtually ignore gay issues and often are ignorant or prejudiced themselves. The best that Tom Braden, the liberal on "Crossfire," could think to say about gay people on one show, for example, was "They're all dying anyway, so leave them alone."

7   The recording industry—music and comedy—is a third major source of vicious homophobia in the media. Sam Kinison's "comedy" routine about gays having brought AIDS to America after "f—king monkeys in Africa" is a vivid case in point. So was a Damon Wayans skit broadcast on HBO as part of a live comedy hour. "Everybody does it," he said. "And the fags ain't fighting back." Homophobic insults also are cropping up more and more in the lyrics of heavy metal bands like Guns 'n Roses, and a number of rap groups are equally offensive to gays and lesbians.

8   **Casual prejudice.** Overt homophobes at least are straightforward about their prejudices. More problematic are the celebrities, producers, and reporters who claim to have nothing against gays—or even to support them—but who nevertheless think, speak, and behave in ways that rely on and reinforce anti-gay attitudes.

9   Celebrities pose a particular problem in this regard. Andy Rooney probably was being honest when he claimed that his statement in a syndicated column that he "wouldn't want to spend much time in a small room" with a homosexual wasn't intended maliciously. Nonetheless, it delivered the message that gay people are offensive and to be avoided.

10   Rooney stated in his defense that he has many gay friends and that most of them didn't find his remark offensive. While Rooney and his friends are entitled to their odd interpersonal relations, the fact is that the millions of others exposed to Rooney's anti-gay comments don't know him personally. For these people, his comments served to reinforce prejudices and ultimately feed anti-gay discrimination and violence.

11   Other examples of casual celebrity homophobia include Zsa Zsa Gabor's remarks that she didn't want to go to jail because she feared being accosted by lesbians, and Bob Hope's comment that a loud tie sported by someone on "The Tonight Show" would have been worn by a "fag" 20 years earlier. Intellectually, it is easy to dismiss these comments as unimportant. However, as many Americans get their information about the world from Gabor's and Hope's regular forums—"The Tonight Show" and *The National Enquirer*—as from "Nightline" and *The Washington Post*. The latter may be more important in shaping public policy, but gays are more likely to be beaten up on the street by readers of the *Enquirer* than by policy analysts. Also, people tend to accept information reinforcing their preconceptions and to reject anything that challenges them. A bigoted comment from Zsa Zsa Gabor can have as much impact as a dispassionate discussion about gay people by an unknown expert.

12   A pernicious form of casual homophobia that recurs in news reporting is the inclusion of homosexuality in laundry lists of social evils. Many reporters

whom, if asked, would claim not to have anything against gay people blithely list "drugs, crime, and homosexuality" as evidence of social decline, or "gratuitous sex, violence, and homosexuality" in television as examples of "trash TV." Whether reporters consciously are expressing anti-gay sentiments or simply unthinkingly repeating litanies of "bad things" they learned as children, these associations reinforce the social prejudice against gay people.

Negative stereotypes

13   Both the entertainment and news media continue to promote negative stereotypes of lesbians and gay men. Recent examples on television include an episode of "Quantum Leap" that featured a lesbian who murdered her lover because the latter was "going straight"; the much-publicized "Midnight Caller" episode in which a bisexual man wantonly spread AIDS; and a "Mr. Belvedere" show in which the serious and legitimate issue of sexual exploitation of children was presented unfairly only in the male adult/male child context. The hit movie "No Way Out" and the 1990 releases, "Darkman" and "After Dark, My Sweet," provide examples from Hollywood. In many cases, characters who are emotionally imbalanced and criminal also are gay—for no apparent reason other than that being gay added to their menace.

14   These plots are not implausible, of course, but they are completely—and dangerously—unrepresentative of our community. At least until lesbians and gay men are represented in all of their diversity, television and movie producers have an obligation not to perpetuate dangerous stereotypes.

15   News reporters and editors also help emphasize negative lesbian and gay images. If a heterosexual rape results in murder, for example, newspaper headlines about the incident never refer to a "heterosexual murderer"; instead, the facts speak for themselves. If the incident involves gay people, however, the headline almost inevitably will refer to a "gay killing." Similarly, the sexual orientation of a gay murderer, rapist, or child molester almost always is identified, while that of a gay philanthropist or good Samaritan is not mentioned. The result of these patterns is the constant association of gayness with badness.

16   Other stereotypes—such as effeminacy in men, masculinity in women, and "flamboyance" generally—also are common. Gays don't complain about media reliance on them *per se*.[1] They do object, however, to the tendency to focus on them exclusively, rather than represent the gay community's diversity.

17   **Deference to the prejudice of others.** Homophobia often is identified as the last publicly acceptable prejudice. While this is not precisely true—as disabled people, among others, know—homophobia clearly is more acceptable than racism, anti-Semitism, and sexism. Television public affairs show host Robert Novak put this sentiment bluntly, saying of the Andy Rooney affair: "You can

---

[1] *per se* (Latin) in and of itself; for its own sake.

say anything you want about homosexuals, and I do," but racist remarks "cross the line."

18 The relative acceptability of homophobia has its impact felt in the editing room. Every media outlet has standards of acceptability and engages in self-censorship, but guidelines for rejecting homophobic material are much weaker than those applied to racist, anti-Semitic, or sexist content. For example, HBO vigorously defended its decision to broadcast Damon Wayans' fag-bashing routine by appealing to freedom of artistic expression. However, a similar black-, Jew-, or women-bashing routine never would have been allowed to air.

A double standard

19 Media response to the Andy Rooney affair provided another example of this double standard. The media were generally indifferent to Rooney's series of anti-gay remarks. Yet, one disputed racist remark garnered national news attention immediately. While the NAACP was besieged with calls, most reporters failed to contact the Gay & Lesbian Alliance Against Defamation (GLAAD) at any time. Rooney himself, commenting on his suspension after his return to "60 Minutes," devoted virtually his entire commentary to defending himself against the charge of racism—as if his homophobia didn't matter.

20 A particularly appalling feature of the coverage was the frequency with which commentators defended Rooney's homophobia on the ground that "most people agree." Even if that were true—and gays don't concede it—since when can bigotry be justified by public referendum?

21 Talk shows provide particularly pernicious examples of indifference to anti-gay prejudice. Lesbian and gay activists almost never are asked onto these programs to discuss their issues dispassionately.[2] Instead, they inevitably are paired with representatives of the far right and forced to defend themselves against charges of moral depravity. In contrast, when was the last time a black or Jewish person was asked to defend himself or herself from personal attack by a member of the Ku Klux Klan as a condition of appearing on the air?

22 A variation on this problem is the extent to which reporters regularly seek out highly vocal, virulently homophobic "experts" to "balance" stories about the gay community. Viewed through the eyes of editors and reporters who themselves harbor conscious or unconscious anti-gay feelings, objectively balanced articles appear to be "pro-gay," and "imbalanced" becomes a code word for "insufficiently anti-gay."

23 A recent incident at *The New York Times* provides a classic example of anti-lesbian stereotyping and reliance on "experts." Assigned to write an article about lesbian mothers and their children, a *Times* reporter submitted a story which mentioned that virtually all available studies show no psychological harm

---

[2] Coolly; without emotion.

to children from having lesbian parents and that most experts concur with the studies. Notwithstanding the article's balance and careful identification of references, a nighttime editor at the *Times*—without notice to the reporter—simply made up and added to the article a reference to some unnamed clinicians' "speculation" that children will, in fact, be harmed by their lesbian mothers' hostility to men. This incident was too much even for the not very self-critical *Times*, which published a correction several days later.

24 **Invisibility.** The forms of anti-gay prejudice in the media discussed above are made worse by the general invisibility of lesbians and gay men in the mainstream media. With good news not reported and positive lesbian and gay characters virtually nonexistent, there is nothing to balance the slander and the stereotypes.

25 The invisibility problem affects lesbians and people of color particularly profoundly, since the few positive depictions of gays almost always are white and male. For example, with the exception of the lesbian nurse-practitioner in ABC's "Heartbeat," every recurring gay character introduced into a television sit-com or drama in the last few years was a white man (ABC's "Hooperman" and "thirtysomething," and CBS's "Doctor, Doctor").

26 Lesbian and gay invisibility is a serious problem in how the news is reported. Judgements about the newsworthiness of events in the gay community inextricably are linked to the value of gays as people. The current wave of lesbian and gay media activism largely was provoked by two extreme cases of media invisibility: the media's failure to cover AIDS during the first four years of the epidemic when it was affecting "just" gay men; and the 1987 March on Washington for Lesbian and Gay Rights, the largest civil rights demonstration in Washington in 20 years, which both *Time* and *Newsweek* ignored.

27 Invisibility is compounded by reporters' reluctance to let lesbians and gay men speak for themselves. A *Los Angeles Times* article, for example, reported as true the Centers for Disease Control's contention that a volleyball league for gay men they had set up was the first of its kind. A single call to one of the many lesbian and gay sports clubs in Los Angeles County would have proven this untrue.

28 A related problem is the media's failure to acknowledge gay and lesbian institutions. In news coverage of the fundamentalist attack on gay characters on television, for example, reporters virtually always identify by name the anti-gay American Family Association and its executive director, Donald Wildmon, but with equal regularity fail to specify who is on the other side (GLAAD or the National Gay & Lesbian Task Force, for instance). At best, they are referred to generically as "gay organizations" or "militant homosexual groups."

29 Smaller-scale, but also important, examples of gay invisibility include a still-common refusal to list gay or lesbian survivors in obituaries and skittishness about mentioning the homosexuality of historical figures in reference works and elsewhere.

30 There is no quick fix to media bias against lesbians and gay men. After all, producers, editors, and reporters are mostly non-gay and themselves products

Some Positive Images of Alternative Lifestyles on Television in the Nineties

Show	Character
All My Children ABC	Michael Delaney teaches high school history, and in a lesson on the Holocaust, he revealed his sexual orientation. The parents protested, but enough stood by him for him to retain his job.
Beverly Hills 90210 FOX	A resident of a hospice where Kelly works, Jerry accidentally exposed Kelly to the HIV virus in a kitchen accident. He convinced her to go to the doctor and went with her to lend support. Through his action, Kelly realized that she has been at risk in her own behavior with her boyfriends.
Chicago Hope CBS	Dr. Sutton, the obstetrician-gynecologist, is confronted by two of his ex-wives who are now living together in a lesbian relationship. They have decided he should be the father of their child.
Friends NBC	Carol Willig is the ex-wife of Ross and the mother of his son. She is in a relationship with Susan Bunch, who plans to help raise the child. Carol and Susan wed in the 1995/96 season.
General Hospital ABC	Jon Hanley served as confidant to Stone Cates, a heterosexual teenage boy diagnosed with HIV. Jon's character had and ultimately died of AIDS.
Melrose Place FOX	Matt Fielding has worked as a social worker at a runaway shelter. Sympathetic and friendly, he has survived "gay bashings" and the loss of employment due to his sexual orientation.
My So-Called Life ABC	Enrique "Rickie" Vasquez is a gay teenager who lost his home after he admitted his sexual orientation. He shows that gay teenagers don't always suffer loss of friends
NYPD ABC	The character of John Irvin was originally a temporary role on the show. He became popular and continues in his role as secretary for the precinct.
Northern Exposure CBS	Ron Bantz and Erik Hillman own and operate a bed and breakfast in Cicely, Alaska; they married in 1994.
One Life to Live ABC	Billy Douglas, a teenager, hid his orientation from everyone, including himself. At a service for the AIDS quilt, Billy confessed his secret to all and found support from his mother, his best friend Joey Buchanan, and others.
Party of Five FOX	Ross, Claudia's violin teacher, teaches her both music and how to accept others who think and act differently.
Roseanne ABC	Leon announced his love for his lover Scott and they married in 1995. Leon, with Roseanne and her sister, is part-owner of the restaurant.

Linda Martindale compiled this chart using material found on the GLAD SFBA Page (http://www.ccnet.com/gaytrek/glaad.html). Martindale is writing a book dealing with social issues on daytime drama.

of our homophobic and heterosexist society. Gays believe progress can be made, however, and have identified three basic strategies. The first is to respond aggressively and loudly to instances of overt prejudice in an effort to shape an environment where public homophobia is considered as unacceptable as racism and anti-Semitism. The second is to educate media professionals about the gay community so they won't be afraid to come directly to it for more information. The third is to identify and pursue opportunities for getting lesbian and gay voices directly into the mainstream media. For now, this strategy mostly involves demanding equal time when the gay community has been defamed. In the long run, as time and resources allow, it should involve affirmative strategies such as encouraging the professional development of openly lesbian or gay newspaper columnists and working with management to develop affirmative action programs for lesbian and gay reporters.

REACTING

1. How likely are Craig Davidson's three solutions for fixing media bias (last paragraph) to succeed?
2. Why does the kind of media bias described by Davidson matter?

CONNECTING

1. Compare Davidson's discussion of media treatment of gays and lesbians with Victoria Rebeck's discussion of media treatment of women in "From Mary to Murphy" (p. 129).
2. How much do Davidson's concerns about gays and lesbians have in common with bell hooks's concerns about black women in "Black Women and Feminism" (p. 147)?

LEARNING ABOUT WRITING FROM READING

Davidson uses an opening strategy worth studying. Paragraph 1 contains a micro-anecdote (a very short story) about an editor rejecting a manuscript about lesbians and gays. Paragraph 2 lists five kinds of media distortion: "vicious slander, . . . casual bias, perpetuation of negative stereotypes, deference to the prejudice of others, and lesbian and gay invisibility." These five topics turn out to be the subheadings that organize the rest of the article. The list in paragraph 2 provides a map for us to follow, helping us to anticipate where Davidson is headed with his argument.

It's evident that, merely in terms of clarity, Davidson could have begun without the anecdote and relied on his useful list of topics in paragraph 2. What has he gained, however, by including paragraph 1?

WRITING ASSIGNMENTS

ASSIGNMENT I
DESCRIBE THE MAIN MESSAGES YOUR CULTURE HAS GIVEN YOU ABOUT WHAT MEN OR WOMEN ARE LIKE. EXPLAIN WHO, OR WHAT, IN OUR CULTURE HAS GIVEN YOU THESE MESSAGES.

Coming Up with Ideas and a Focus

You might begin by asking yourself what our culture has told you about how to be a man or a woman. Try listing the main messages you have received, along with their sources in the culture: parents, church, school, television, song lyrics, and the like. To find a focus, you will need to decide which messages are the most interesting and significant.

Organizing Your Ideas

Your paper might open with a statement about the main messages about male or female gender roles that different parts of your culture have given you. Support and illustrate that statement with examples from different parts of our culture and narratives or descriptions from your own experience. (For help with statement-support papers, see pp. 305 and 365.)

Audience

If other people in your class are writing on this same assignment, try informing each other about your own experiences in the culture you all share. Then see if you can generalize from the different papers in your group about the most common American cultural messages on maleness and femaleness. Is there any agreement about what parts of the culture are responsible for sending the strongest gender messages?

ASSIGNMENT II
DESCRIBE, ANALYZE, AND COMMENT ON A MAGAZINE ADVERTISEMENT OR A TELEVISION COMMERCIAL. WHAT ARE ITS OBVIOUS AND HIDDEN MESSAGES ABOUT MEN OR WOMEN? WHAT ARE YOUR COMMENTS ON THESE MESSAGES?

Coming Up with Ideas and a Focus

After making and reviewing a list of TV or magazine advertisements, choose one or two and freewrite, focusing on "gender messages." Keep going until you find an example that sparks lots of ideas and interest. (What *does* that ad for disposable diapers really say about men and fatherhood?)

Organizing Your Ideas

The assignment invites a three-part outline of description, analysis, and commentary:

1. Tell what the details of the ad actually are.
2. Show what messages they give about men or women.
3. Say how you feel about those messages and comment on their place in our culture.

Audience

Imagine a group of people who have not seen the ad itself, people who are also somewhat skeptical about the whole idea of "hidden" media messages. Your job is to persuade them that such messages do exist.

ASSIGNMENT III
WHAT ARE THE ADVANTAGES AND/OR DISADVANTAGES OF BEING MALE OR FEMALE IN THE UNITED STATES TODAY?

Coming Up with Ideas and a Focus

This very broad question asks you to take a position on the situation of men or women in our culture. Think about which sex you will discuss, and whether you will deal with advantages or disadvantages or both. Find a focus by making some choices among many points. You might start by asking what the best and worst things are about being male or female and go from there.

Organizing Your Ideas

There are two or three ways of visualizing this paper. You might set up a comparison and contrast between advantages and disadvantages. Or you might decide to make a general statement about what it's like to be male or female and then support that statement with evidence drawn from your knowledge of American culture. (For help with comparison-contrast papers, see pp. 310 and 367. For help with statement-support papers, see pp. 305 and 365.)

Audience

Sharpen your persuasive skills by writing this for an audience of men, if you are writing about women, and for women, if you are writing about men. An audience of the opposite sex may be more of a challenge to persuade: you may have to explain things they've never noticed. You will also need to engage their sympathies and interest.

ASSIGNMENT IV
COMPARE AND CONTRAST RACISM AND SEXISM IN AMERICAN CULTURE.

Coming Up with Ideas and a Focus

This assignment asks you to consider how sexism and racism are alike and different. Get started by listing as many points of similarity and difference as you can, no matter how outlandish they may seem. Do racism and sexism make their victims feel the same kinds of emotions? Do they spring from the same causes? Can they be solved in the same way? Do the mass media contribute to both attitudes in a similar fashion? You cannot address all points in a single paper, so you will need to focus on the most interesting.

Organizing Your Ideas

A likely organizational pattern is comparison-contrast. You will be making a statement about similarities and differences, supported by your information about racism and sexism. (For help with comparison-contrast papers, see p. 367.)

Audience

Because the paper's purpose is both informative and persuasive, you might want to target an audience who has never considered a relationship between racism and sexism. Your paper will illustrate some new ways of seeing the two, as well as persuading readers that your point of view is worth considering.

Chapter 5

Sports

KEY QUESTIONS
What do American sports reveal about our culture?
How do the media affect the way we see and value sports?

. . . *event sponsorship is the new way for companies to reach TV viewers, and the trend is clear. It should come as no surprise to anyone that one day we will find ourselves enjoying events on television that carry the FTD Rose Bowl, the Atlas World Series, and the Q-Tip Cottonbowl.*
—DAVID KLATELL AND NORMAN MARCUS,
SPORTS FOR SALE: TV, MONEY AND THE FANS

In fact, the habit of sports-watching has become so ingrained in the American psyche that the game itself may not actually matter.
—EDWIN DIAMOND, NEW YORK, 1990

Even if there is a dearth of traditional sports heroes and some cynicism among fans about the motives and behavior of contemporary professional athletes, fans still may envy or respect the mobility and financial success of the athletes. As long as there is an American Dream, upwardly mobile and rich athletes will symbolize a fulfillment of dreams held by the fans.
—HOWARD L. NIXON II, SPORT AND THE AMERICAN DREAM

Introduction

Sports are a way of celebrating life. In sports, we find challenge, excitement, frustration, play, laughter, tedium, physical exhilaration and exhaustion. Is it any wonder that Americans love sports? Your own experiences may tell you that we do. You may even come from a place like the one described by William Rhoden in "Strong in the Blood," where high school football, with its coaches, players, fans, and boosters, dominates the life of an entire community.

Sports are so much a part of American life that it is possible to find out a lot about the culture from studying both the various sports and the way the media deal with them. Some people have suggested that sports act like a sponge, soaking up the culture's tone and color, its values and attitudes. Do sports, in fact, illustrate our culture's competitiveness, love of success, attachment to violence, and celebration of the individual? Do sports tell us more about men's and women's roles in our culture? Are sports like work, leading to similar rewards?

A good test of the importance of sports in American culture is to ask the question: "What would American culture be like without sports?" Can we imagine what we would do with our spare time, what we would watch on television, what we would do with our children, or what we would talk about with our friends and acquaintances at work?

José Torres, in "Let's Stop Glorifying Bullies," argues that sports—even apparently violent ones like boxing—encourage self-control and "grace under pressure." Maya Angelou tells how boxer Joe Louis's success in the 1930s made her race proud. But Pat Aufderheide's "Outside Shot" complicates the link between sports and success by asking if the documentary sports film *Hoop Dreams* is the story of the great American dream or of a sports "business" that exploits young African American athletes.

Those of us who do not play or attend games ourselves get most of our sports experience from the mass media—the sports pages of newspapers and sports magazines and television especially. We might even say that sports are for most of us a media experience rather than a real one. So it's important to ask questions about the impact of media coverage of particular sports, not only on the sport itself but also on the people reading about and watching that sport.

David Klatell and Norman Marcus argue positively that television and sports are a terrific combination and that they serve each other well. But Jay Coakley, in his survey of television and newspaper sports coverage in the 1970s and 1980s, has a less enthusiastic view, suggesting that sports journalism has reinforced rather than questioned traditional gender roles in our culture. If Coakley's thesis is correct, then even people who don't play and don't care about sports should be concerned about the role of sports and of media coverage of sports in American culture. This chapter asks you to look at sports from new points of view.

Starting Out: Finding Out What You Already Know

1. Why do you like or dislike sports? List as many reasons as you can.

2. Freewrite about how you felt about sports when you were a child. (Remember making the team? Or not making it? Or being afraid of failing? Or looking stupid? Or . . . ?)
3. Imagine what your and your family's lives might be like if there were no sports anywhere—on television, in film, or in real life. Write a journal entry on the subject.
4. Compare being present at a sporting event with watching it on television.
5. What stereotypes do people have about student athletes and professional athletes?

Learning More Through Observation: Taking a Look Around You and Talking to People

1. List some TV sports programs. Freewrite on one, focusing on your likes and dislikes about the program.
2. List sports films. Freewrite on a particular film, focusing on what it says about the sport and the people who play it.
3. Talk to your friends about what they value when playing and watching sporting events. Why do they devote time to sports?
4. Ask someone much older or much younger than you are what he or she thinks the "all-American" sport is, and why.
5. Watch a sports event, then list the qualities of a good broadcaster or a good player in that particular sport.

Questioning: Deciding What Else You Would Like to Know

List five questions that you still have about sports and their place in American culture.

WILLIAM C. RHODEN

Strong in the Blood but Perhaps Not in the Future

William C. Rhoden, writing for The New York Times, *analyzes and illustrates the role of football in the life of a small Georgia town.*

BEFORE YOU READ

1. How important is high school football in your town?

2. What does the title's "strong in the blood" suggest about the likely content of the article?

1   VALDOSTA, Ga., Sept. 22—By 8 o'clock this morning the inner circle of the "coffee club" had already occupied its customary table in the back of Jackson Baywood Pharmacy. L. E. Deming, Bob Anderson, Bill Mizell and Laman Golivesky arrived at 7:30 and put in their orders. Soon, Mack Green and John Lastinger trickled in.

2   The conversation is seamless and, to an outsider, flows like a river that has no beginning or ending. Everybody speaks at once, everyone knows precisely what is being said in each conversation, and everyone comes together when the talk turns to Valdosta High School football.

3   All across America on Friday nights, high school football is the game. But in this community of 43,000 in the western part of the state near the Florida border, football is more: it has become a way of life, a thread connecting generations. And with the winningest high-school team in the nation (based on total victories), Valdosta's success and reputation was the reason why the National High School Football Hall of Fame will be built here next year.

4   Small wonder the city has nicknamed itself "Winnersville."

5   "This school's got a great tradition, second- and third-generation players," said Lastinger, the president of the chamber of commerce. "My dad played, I played, my son played. We've gotten used to excellence, and it filters throughout the community."

6   Valdosta football has forged a strong, sustaining bond between the members of the coffee club as well. All played on the team except for Mizell, who played on the junior varsity, and nearly all of them have sons who played for Valdosta, and some grandsons.

7   This morning, on the day before a big game with Columbia of Lake City, Fla., the topic of conversation is whether the passion for Valdosta football is waning. Ten years ago, the mere thought of lagging interest was blasphemous.[1] But last year the team lost four games, and last week, Nick Hyder, Valdosta's head coach since 1974, expressed concern about falling attendance even though the team had won its first three games.

8   "I don't think that's it," Lastinger said. "The people here probably accept defeat better than anyone I know of."

9   He thought for a moment. "I guess one reason is that we don't have to do it that much."

10   Tonight, a caravan of yellow school buses will make the hour-long drive to Lake City. In the old days, the town would rent Greyhound buses to travel to games. In many cases, the sight of 15 or so buses descending on a town, along with the reputation of the school, was enough to intimidate a rival.

---

[1] Irreverent; very disrespectful.

11   The entourage will include the school's marching band; cheerleaders; drill team; parents, teachers, and of course the 114 members of the Valdosta football team.

12   In many ways the school embodies the timeless ideal of high school athletics: competition, hard work, character, and community pride.

13   At another level, Valdosta football is emblematic of the spirit of south Georgia with its network of small intimate communities. Football is unparalleled king here and forms a link between elementary schools, the high school, the University of Georgia, which attracts some of Valdosta's best players, and Valdosta State University, which has emerged as a small-college power.

14   In Valdosta, the football team is more than just a point of civic pride. It is generally credited with helping to usher the city through the trauma of integration in the late 1960's. Whites resented the Federal mandate of forced integration; blacks, who saw their schools dismantled, resented the loss of positions as principals, teachers and coaches.

15   "The school was so successful that kids at the black school, Pineville, wanted to be part of it," said Lastinger. "Other schools had to change their colors, their nicknames, their songs. Valdosta continued to be the Wildcats."

16   The support remained even as the racial balance changed from what was once an all-white school. Today, the team is 70 percent black.

17   The architect of the team's success for the last 20 years has been Hyder. He was handpicked for the job in 1974 by Wright Bazemore, who coached the team from 1941 to 1971. Charley Greene was the coach in 1972 and '73, but stepped down after he lost three games in those two seasons.

18   Since taking over, Hyder has become the winningest coach in the state in 1-AAAA, the state's highest division. Valdosta has won seven state titles under him.

19   "We're concerned with all of the things like building character, school spirit and neighborhood," said Bill Aldrich, the Valdosta principal for the last 11 years. "But a coach who comes here must know in the back of his mind that a program which has had this kind of success over 75 years places a high premium on winning."

20   But now there are signs that the program, while not buckling, is straining under the weight of pressure forged by change.

21   Last season Valdosta finished 6–4, the first time in 20 years it lost more than two games and the first time in 15 years it failed to make the playoffs. Some members of the powerful Touchdown Club inadvertently[2] refer to last year as a "losing season."

22   "The expectations are on a high level here," Hyder, 59, said. "I understand that, I understood it since I've been here. We've gone 15–0 here and those same people weren't happy—I can probably name them. I welcome that—you have to welcome the opposition."

23   It may be as simple as his choice of quarterbacks.

---

[2] Inattentively; accidentally.

24   Valdosta had had black quarterbacks the last five seasons, and last season Hyder and some supporters sensed that some of the boosters wanted a white player to be given a chance.

25   "I think the people who want a change want one for that one element right there," Hyder said. "They don't like the fact that I'm going to play the one who deserves it."

26   This season, Hyder began with Kareem Wilson at quarterback. Despite a 3–0 start, Hyder said there have been grumblings. "Some of the people do not like the fact that our quarterback is black, that one position," he said.

27   Aldrich, the principal, who coached under Hyder before going into administration, disagrees that race had anything to do with discontent over last season. He also pointed out that Valdosta's history with black football players—which began with John Copeland in 1966—was never tumultuous.

28   "I think that any frustration from fans last year was that they could see indecision more than anything else," Aldrich said, referring to Hyder. "The team missed peer leadership. Not black, not white, there was just no leadership. This year coach Hyder made a decision early on. I don't think black and white had anything to do with it."

29   If passions for Valdosta football are cooling, it may have a lot to do with the town's growth and diversification. There is more to do than watch high school football.

30   Much to Hyder's chagrin, the Boys Club and local Y.M.C.A. have instituted fall baseball for youths ages 10 to 14. Hyder feels the league will dilute interest in football at the crucial youth levels, which have been the backbone of Valdosta's success. "If you give a mother a choice between her son playing football and baseball, she's going to choose baseball," he said.

31   Valdosta State University, which achieved university status last year, is rapidly turning this city into a college town. The university's enrollment has grown from 500 in 1957 to its current level of 9,500. The university is riding on the success of its football team, which plays at the Division II level and is currently ranked seventh nationally.

32   "Valdosta High used to be the only game in town," Bill Mizell said. "Now the college team is drawing away from the high school team. I had a friend who used to go to the 'Cats game every Friday night; now he opts to go just to the V.S.U. games."

33   What may be of even greater significance is that with changing demographics, the traditional Valdosta community is no longer tied to the school as it once was.

34   "This place has grown a little bit," Green said. "We don't know all the players like we used to, and all the families—and their dogs."

35   Even so, the coffee club will be in Lake City tonight, cheering mightily, for memories past and present.

36   "If you cut me," Mizell said, "I'll still bleed Gold and Black."

REACTING

1. What's good and what's bad about high school football being so important in a small town like Valdosta?
2. Based on this report, would you say sports promote harmony? Why?

CONNECTING

1. How does this article help you to answer the key question: "What do American sports reveal about our culture?"?
2. If you were making a film about Valdosta high school football (see Pat Aufderheide's description of the basketball film *Hoop Dreams,* p. 173), what would its main themes be? What would it be the "story" of?

LEARNING ABOUT WRITING FROM READING

This article contains a lot of direct quotations from the people William Rhoden interviewed. This gives us an opportunity to learn about the finer points of using quotation marks and the commas and periods that go with them. Here's an example:

> "This school's got a great tradition, second- and third-generation players," said Lastinger, the president of the chamber of commerce. "My dad played, I played, my son played. We've gotten used to excellence, and it filters throughout the community."

Note that a comma is needed at the end of the first quotation, to separate it from the *attribution,* the part that tells you who said the words. Note, also, that this comma, and the period at the end of the second quotation, are placed inside the closing quotation marks.

José Chegui Torres

Let's Stop Glorifying Bullies

José Torres, world light-heavyweight boxing champion in 1965–1966 and author of Fire and Fear: The Inside Story of Mike Tyson, *considers some issues relating to sports, especially boxing, and social violence.*

BEFORE YOU READ

1. Write or talk about your own definition of the term *bully.*

2. What do you know about boxing? What do you like or dislike about the sport?

In the midst of his 1992 rape trial, prizefighter Mike Tyson greets fans.

1   I have no idea whether O.J. Simpson actually committed the murders of his ex-wife and her friend, but I did hear the 911 tapes and saw the photos of his battered ex-wife. Obviously, at various times, O.J. Simpson used his physical superiority to control Nicole Brown Simpson. In other words, he bullied her.

2   I have a problem with people who stand on the sidelines and cheer this man as if he is some kind of hero. Being a champion athlete doesn't make someone a hero. He must also behave like a hero off the field.

3   I've known fighters—Mike Tyson, Carlos Monzón and Jake LaMotta, among others—who have beaten or abused their wives and other women. For me, their athletic ability is meaningless when measured against their bullying of

a vulnerable human being. That you can "whip" anyone in the world with your fists doesn't mean that you *should*.

4   Boxing champions are not expected to operate that way. They are masters of *controlled* violence. They always seem to know who, when and where to attack. They possess physical and psychological weapons designed to be used only in the ring or when in real danger—not against the defenseless. The boxer who strikes his wife is abusing his own talent just as surely as if he shot her with a firearm or stabbed her with a knife.

5   Ultimately, a bully is a coward. I have felt this way since childhood.

6   Bullies were despised in the streets of Puerto Rico, where I grew up during World War II. A typical bully took advantage of his size or his brutality or his willingness to use a club or a knife. He was an expert in spotting the feeble. If a boy hobbled from the effects of polio, the bully taunted him or struck him. If a boy wore glasses, the bully would knock them off, start shoving or slapping, and perhaps extort money or the boy's lunchbag. Bullies picked on girls, on old people, on the helpless.

7   A bully fought only when he was certain he would win. We thought he was the lowest form of human being.

8   Today, things are different. Bullies are often admired—and rewarded. In rap videos, the man most respected is often the "toughest," the one most armored with the disguises of *machismo*. He uses rap music to maintain his own sense of superiority by shouting insults at women, police officers, gays, ethnic groups, immigrants. The same music is sometimes used to encourage young boys to establish their manhood through the mouth of a gun.

9   Recently, some people—dazed by the Tyson and Simpson cases—have linked these athletes' abusive behavior not to their personalities but to the sports they practiced. But, despite the fact that boxing may be one of the most primitive contests known to man, it's also probably the mightiest builder of character and self-control in sports. And football may not be that much different.

10   Tyson and Simpson both established themselves as true champions. To do this, they had to be experts at self-control. They had to display consistently what Ernest Hemingway called "grace under pressure." As champions, they would have known how to turn their own fear—the bully's worst enemy—into their best friend. In the intensity of the contest, for example, they may have felt close to death, yet—aware that such a feeling is part of the game's normal hazard—they continued battling.

11   To say that boxers and football players are primed by their sports to burst into fits of rage at the slightest provocation is absurd.

12   In the boxing gym, a bully has no specific skin color, ethnic or religious background. Often, he may have been the *macho* man in his school and neighborhood because of his bulky size and big mouth. Typically, he comes to the gym to turn his physical attributes into fame and money. Trouble begins for him when he discovers that physical size and loudness make no impression in the gym. At once, his confidence starts to weaken.

13   Then a familiar scenario occurs: He is told—usually on a Friday—that his sparring sessions start the following Monday. Bewildered by his uncontrollable fright—and worried about being exposed for the coward he really is—he never returns to the gym again.

14   Instead, he most likely will continue to rummage around neighborhoods rich and poor, searching for victims. Bullies lack courage, compassion, self-discipline and a sense of responsibility. They are cowards. Let's stop glorifying them. Especially when they are famous.

Do You Know How to Stop a Bully?

WHAT DO *YOU* THINK? National statistics reveal that between 15 percent and 20 percent of all students in the United States experience some form of bullying. Children—especially the weakest or most vulnerable among them—are intimidated, verbally humiliated and physically attacked in their neighborhoods and on school grounds. They often suffer in silence, afraid to tell their parents and teachers about the bully.

But even when adults are aware of bullying, they may not know how to deal with it. Experienced counselors can help. So can hearing what other people have done in similar situations. Therefore, we'd like to put the question to you, our readers. Do you know how to stop a bully?

If you have ever been the victim of a bully—or even been a bully yourself—we'd like to hear about it.

PARENTS: Did you ever come up with a creative solution to protect your child from being terrorized by a bully?

TEACHERS: Were you ever forced to confront the problem of bullies? What did you find worked best? Have your students found successful solutions to the problem?

Send us your stories about bullies who were stopped, and we will publish a selection of them in a future issue. Your experience may help to put another bully out of business.

Letters should be sent to: Bullies, P.O. Box 4843, Grand Central Station, New York, NY 10163-4843. [This request originally appears in *Parade* magazine.]

REACTING

1. What do you think about José Torres's definition of the sport of boxing?
2. Do you think our culture does, in fact, glorify bullies? If so, why might that be?

CONNECTING

1. How does this article help you to answer one of this chapter's key questions: "What do American sports reveal about our culture?"?

2. Turn to p. 182 and read Maya Angelou's "Joe Louis." How might Angelou, who also writes about boxing, respond to José Torres's article?

LEARNING ABOUT WRITING FROM READING

Student writers often ask whether it's all right to use the first-person pronoun "I" in their papers. The answer they usually get is that it's fine to do so, as long as that choice fits in with other choices the writer has made about purpose, audience, and style, and their relationship to the paper's topic. José Torres uses "I" quite a lot in this article. By doing so, he establishes his own personal interest in the topic, reminds us that he, as a boxer himself, has direct knowledge of the sport and its champions, and that he understands what it's like to be in the ring as a fighter. All of these things add to his credibility and to the human interest of his argument.

PAT AUFDERHEIDE

Outside Shot

Pat Aufderheide, writing for the magazine In These Times, *discusses basketball, the subject of the successful film* Hoop Dreams, *and talks about the movie's production history.*

BEFORE YOU READ

1. What do you expect the article to be about, given its title?
2. Describe a sports movie you are familiar with. What story does it have? What does it tell you about sports in American culture?

1   Basketball, family, race and the American dream. No, it's not Ken Burns' next project. It's something so improbable and so good that it could shake your comfortable cynicism.

2   *Hoop Dreams*—the nearly three-hour documentary that became the hit of the Sundance Film Festival, the smash closer of the New York Film Festival, the spawner of a book and fiction feature film—is enough to restore your faith in independent filmmaking as a window on the American cultures we don't see "at the movies."

3   Producers Steve James, Peter Gilbert and Frederick Marx, working with executive producer Gordon Quinn of Chicago's venerable documentary house, Kartemquin Films, found two promising young black athletes on the street courts in Chicago. Over four and a half years, they followed Arthur Agee and

William Gates through high school and into their first year at college on athletic scholarships.

4   The thickly textured epic that emerges has a story line that couldn't be tighter if it were scripted. Arthur, lithe[1] and sassy, and William, big and shy, start out together at St. Joseph High School—Isiah Thomas' old alma mater. Arthur, seen as less talented, can't afford to stay at St. Joe's with a partial scholarship, and gets bumped back to a grim public school. Meanwhile, his parents split up, his dad loses his job and starts to deal drugs. William wings along, even excelling in academics, urged on by his brother Curtis, himself once a basketball star and now a security guard. Then his knee goes out, and he undergoes surgery to get back in the game.

5   The two boys' basketball careers over the next two years—full of amazing upsets and heart-stopping action—are almost unbearably suspenseful, because each contest is more than just a game. The boys, and much more so their families, pin whatever hopes they have on athletic success. When William loses a game, Curtis is not just chagrined but devastated. When Arthur's father gets himself off drugs and comes back to church and family, his son's success is at the center of his new life.

6   You can see the dark side of victory on the faces of the boys' mothers on the day they head off to college. Both are proud but anxious too, worried about their sons' ability to handle the challenges ahead.

7   You can look at *Hoop Dreams* as a movie that shows how amateur athletics exploits young kids for the benefit of professional sports. Or you can see it as a great family film—one that explores the struggle of working-class black families aspiring to the American dream. Watching them battle through their lives is at once inspiring and alarming. Their ability to endure, and even to hope, taxes credulity—and yet this is all real life. You have to wonder where the breaking point is, for them and so many others.

8   The urgency of this struggle is made plain by the film's highly crafted use of cinéma vérité[2] techniques. The saga of these kids, though emblematic of basic social conflicts in American culture, is also a story of these two particular people and their families. The vérité style provides a wealth of information—clothing, decor, casual gestures, the unexpected remark, the action in the background—that we depend on in daily life to form what we call intuition.

9   But daily life is inchoate.[3] The meaning of it always eludes us because we're too busy living the story to retell it. It takes an artist to make somebody else's daily life meaningful to us. That's the kind of work Kartemquin Films has been known for over the last 25 years, in which such vérité-style documentaries as *The Chicago Maternity Center Story*, *The Last Pullman Car* and *Golub* have emerged to controversy and acclaim. And so it's not surprising that James,

---

[1] Graceful.
[2] Realistic filmmaking.
[3] Confused; without clear form.

Gilbert and Marx found a natural home for their project at Kartemquin with Quinn. His career-long commitment to making public the drama of daily life was critical in shaping the project and then keeping it on course over the years. But, James notes, they still had to grow into the vérité style, as the first part of the film itself shows in its dependence on interviews rather than lived moments.

It also was not clear for the first two years what the film would be about—until the boys' on-court careers started going awry in their junior year. At first, the two athletes believed that the filmmakers would lose interest in them once the ugly prospect of failure loomed. When the filmmakers stuck with them, the boys and their families began to become friends of the filmmakers. Meanwhile, St. Paul public TV station KTCA had become convinced of the project's interest, and became a co-producer and an important guarantor during the long years of *Hoop Dreams'* maturation.

11   *Hoop Dreams'* big splash leaves most of the participants better off than they ever hoped. The big exceptions, ironically, are the film's subjects. The National Collegiate Athletic Association prohibits them or their families from benefiting financially from the film in any way—on pain of losing their scholarships. The *Hoop Dreams* team is working hard to win a waiver of the rules, which clearly were not designed for this rarest of surprise successes.

12   Will *Hoop Dreams,* now debuting in commercial theaters in selected cities, buck the fate of most documentaries? After all, the form is cursed with an image so dowdy that the filmmakers joke about remaking their documentary as a feature film called "Hoop Dreams: The Movie." But the film's superb craftsmanship of scene and narrative, combined with the instant appeal of family drama and basketball, ought to boost it out of the documentary's usual fate.

13   And once there, audiences will be as engaged by the usually unmentionable tensions of race and class as by the poignancy of the stories the movie tells. *Hoop Dreams* is about people who keep refusing to accept that they are living an American tragedy.

REACTING

1. Would you like to see the film *Hoop Dreams*? Explain your answer.
2. React to Pat Aufderheide's statement that "at first, the two athletes [in the film] believed that the filmmakers would lose interest in them once the ugly prospect of failure loomed."

CONNECTING

1. Turn to p. 182 and read Maya Angelou's "Joe Louis." Imagine how Angelou might comment on the connections between the information about African American athletes in "Outside Shot" and the victory of Joe Louis.
2. Compare the impact of a documentary sports film like *Hoop Dreams* with that of a fictional sports movie (for example, *Hoosiers*). Will the two types of film affect people differently? If so, why and how?

LEARNING ABOUT WRITING FROM READING

The author opens with a sentence fragment: "Basketball, family, race and the American dream." Yes, sentence fragments are sometimes allowed! Journalists, novelists and poets, in particular, seem to have a special license to break the rules. A *sentence fragment*—a group of words with no subject and no main verb—can sometimes quickly bring a topic into sharp focus, as it does here. But you need to be aware that you are using sentence fragments—and to use them sparingly. Otherwise your audience may start to have doubts about your credibility as a competent writer.

DAVID KLATELL AND NORMAN MARCUS

What We Are Watching: The View from the Couch

David Klatell and Norman Marcus, authors of the book Sports for Sale: TV, Money and the Fans, *from which this excerpt is taken, analyze and evaluate some aspects of television coverage of sports.*

BEFORE YOU READ

1. Try turning the article's title into a question. What would you expect as an answer to the question: "What are we watching on TV sports programming?"
2. What do you prefer: sports live or sports on screen? Why?

1   Rodney Dangerfield ought to be the patron saint of television sports—viewers and sports program producers alike get very little respect. Despite the fact that sports programming is among the most popular, original, and spontaneous forms of television worldwide, viewers are frequently characterized as low-brow, passive spectators, whose preference for sports programming is vaguely antisocial. The dedicated men and women who produce the programs are most often prophets without honor in their own companies. It is not uncommon to hear the Sports division of a network disparaged as "lightweight" because it is not so imposing as News, so creative as Entertainment, so profitable as afternoon Soaps, so important as Sales. Besides, it looks like such fun to work in Sports—lots of travel, weekdays off, attendance at exciting events, the chance to rub elbows with famous athletes—why, it's hardly like work at all.

2   This attitude galls the highly skilled professionals whose job it is to bring a unique version of sports to television viewers. It ought similarly to gall thoughtful viewers, because it denigrates their ability to perceive the differences among program formats and select attractive, interesting sports events. In how many households have sports viewers been told to shut off the "boob tube"? Why do television sports fans put up with being called "Joe six-pack" or "the couch potato"—often by members of their own family? Who decided that it is socially acceptable for intelligent adults to become hopelessly addicted to *Dallas*, or *Hill Street Blues*, or *As the World Turns*, but that equally compulsive baseball viewing is somehow childish?

3   Why, then, don't we give up and turn off the set? It is because of the personal experience of having seen for ourselves a tiny memorable moment which can be shared around office water-coolers for days—and replayed in our memories forever. The lawn will have to wait, because the next game, the next play, the next moment might be the magic one, and the suspense is killing us.

4   At its best, television sports is the finest programming television can offer. In many respects, sports may be the quintessential television program format, taking fullest advantage of the role television plays in our daily lives. Sports on television have visually attractive elements—splashy colors, attractive locations, motion and movement galore. They have expansive vistas, exquisite details, and larger-than-life images. Compared with the austere hush and "studio" sound of most programs, sports are alternately loud and brassy, and painfully hushed: you can tell the moment you hear the sound of the crowd what's going on. There is drama, tension, suspense, raw emotion, real anger, unvarnished joy, and a host of other responses. Most of all, you are watching real people compete for real, as unsure of the outcome as the viewer. The script, being written in front of you, is subject to few constraints common to the formulas of standard entertainment fare. In sports television the "bad guy" of the script often wins, unexpected things happen, virtue doesn't necessarily triumph, and goodness is not always rewarded.

5   Although many television program formats rely on the viewers to project their own fantasy of stepping through the screen to join the action, few do so as instinctively as sports. Many viewers of *Dallas* must have thought to themselves how wonderful it would be to be as rich as J.R. Ewing and to live his lifestyle. Few, however, ever believe even the most remote combination of circumstances could ever make such a dream reality. Sports viewers, on the other hand, share an almost universal sense of mutual interest and personal expertise in sports, and many, if not most, have played some. They commonly believe that were it not for unhappy circumstance, or childhood injury, or too-strict parents, or time constraints, they could have been the athletes now gracing the screen. Walter Mitty lives in all of us: "Boy, if I only got in shape, I could do that!" we think. On television we watch long stretches of unimaginable athletic excellence, hoping to catch an occasional reflection of some ability of our own.

6   The programs can also be viewed in a much more detached, almost casual manner. Sports are perfect for those drowsy weekend afternoons when one feels somewhere between taking a nap and cleaning out the attic. You can watch a bit, leave, come back, and watch some more. There's no dialogue to follow, no crucial scene to miss (in sports, you'll never miss all the replays), no complex serial plots from last week's show. Sports can be a sort of visual Muzak, playing quietly in the background, while other activities dominate your attention. When something of particular note happens, you will be alerted by the announcers, or the crowd noise. By and large, the competitors and events are familiar and need neither explanation nor rapt attention. They go on for hours, so what's the harm in a ten-minute lapse of attention? In short, you can watch sports just about any way you feel on a particular day. You can control the relationship between program producer and audience, simply by the way you choose to watch.

7   The drama inherent in athletic competition is sometimes taken for granted, usually by non-sports fans. To them, all baseball games look the same, all announcers sound the same, all crowds act the same. They have no sense of the pride, passion, and pain embodied in the competitors; no sense of the theatrical performance witnessed by the stadium crowd; no sense of the reporters and

announcers describing simultaneous snippets from a dozen or so biographies unfolding in public. And no sense of having witnessed one of those rare, transcendental moments when sports really do become an allegory for life. As in many other areas, some sports clichés are actually true. There really is a thrill of victory, an agony of defeat, as ABC's Wide World of Sports mentions every week. The gritty realities of competition convey an underlying passion that no scripted television drama—no matter how carefully crafted—can regularly bring to the small screen.

8   Sports transforms itself into dance, into song, into drama, into comedy, into news—often when one least expects it. It embodies aspects of ethnic, community, regional, and national pride. It produces heroes and villains, rule-makers and law-breakers. It magnifies the striving accomplishments and tribulations of athletes raised high and fallen low. It is often candid, sometimes voyeuristic; often reassuring, sometimes disturbing. On some occasions, you can't turn away, on others you do so readily. Such moments are most special when they happen unexpectedly, when you want to call out to others, "Hey, come in here and watch this!" How often does this happen in any other television program format. . . .

9   The production of a major live sports event can be television at its most exhilarating. It can also be an enormous, and frequently unrecognized, challenge to the resources, expertise, and daring of the production crew. They must extract, from an unscripted and unrehearsed event, sufficient entertainment, news and information to satisfy a knowledgeable and demanding audience. Frequently working under daunting physical conditions, they must incorporate complex technological innovations without the benefit of real field-testing. They must attract and hold the interest of an audience large enough to be profitable, sometimes when the event itself is boring, one-sided, or arcane. All this must be accomplished while living and working in a series of hotel rooms, cramped production trucks, and the inevitable airport waiting rooms. It is a challenge to make the productions seamless, and a far greater one to make them look easy. Yet, that is what viewers demand.

10   Many television sports fans are (or regard themselves as) experts regarding the program content—that is, the actual playing of the game, the players, rules, strengths, weaknesses, and strategies of the teams. Armchair coaches all, they can pick apart any zone, always call the right play, and reliably send the pitcher to the showers at the right moment. This is not surprising, given the attention lavished on watching such contests through the years, and it is one of the essential ingredients in the loyal relationship between fans and their chosen favorites.

11   These fans will not be satisfied by a cursory[1] description of the events they are watching, nor with camera shots that miss the key moment, isolate on the wrong player, or omit the most telling replay angle. Their patience with announcers who restate the obvious, misidentify players, talk too much, or commit the unpardonable sin of appearing to be biased against the team they

---

[1] Brief.

are rooting for is minimal at best. They are sports experts and critics simultaneously. This critical viewing skill is also applied by viewers of entertainment television. Loyal viewers of soap opera serials or situation comedies can be depended on to understand the story line and characters well enough to notice any deviation or mistake in the content.

12   What is more surprising, however, is the emerging understanding that many sports viewers have become, often without conscious effort, or even awareness, critical experts on the process of making sports television. They understand the underlying mechanics of getting an event on the air, as well as the unstated intentions of the production team in illustrating and describing the event to fit the demands of art and commerce. They have, essentially, learned the idiom[2] of television sports—its techniques, pacing, formating and rhythms—from watching so much of it.

13   There are very few viewers who can explain their understanding in technical terms, but they certainly know when to expect certain program elements, including replays, slow-motion, promotional announcements, commercials, and even sequences of shots. They seem cognizant of and comfortable with the cadence and pace of each production, and they are sufficiently perceptive not only to differentiate between superior production values and the relatively mundane, but actually to critique those they find lacking. In no other television format must the producers and directors anticipate, and essentially compete with, the audience's own practiced directorial instincts.

14   For example, consider the relatively slow, short, and simple sequence that begins when a batter approaches the batter's box: he digs in (while the announcers discuss him), faces the pitcher, gets his statistics flashed on the screen (from a third base camera with a lefty, first base for righties), looks over the players in the field and their relationship to any baserunners, receives a stare from the pitcher, whose back is then turned to the audience by a centerfield camera which sets the catcher, umpire, and batter in perspective; the pitching begins, followed by commentary, shots of coaches, fielders, and dugouts, replays, crowd shots, and a repeat of the whole sequence for each pitch and for each batter. The longer the turn at bat, the closer the camera moves in, increasing the tension and the sense of human drama. When a ball is finally put into play, a whole other sequence is released, gushing forth fast edits, fleeting glances at speeding targets, and the blossoming of wide, encompassing shots.

15   It all has a wonderful, soothing, and familiar rhythm, one which conveys a sense of time and place, so that the viewer can say, "Ah, yes, this is baseball, not football or basketball, and it feels right." Each sport has its own analogous "feel" and timing. Each contains whole series of sequences which act not only as descriptive illustrations of the game at hand but also offer the experienced viewer subtle clues into the mindset of the show's producer and director, as they weave together the story line. Consider the quarterback breaking the huddle to

---

[2] Jargon; specialized vocabulary.

survey the defense, or the basketball player at the foul line, or the golfer over a putt. We may think of each as a single image, but in reality they are composites of numerous sights, sounds, and actions. Audiences have learned how to watch, and what to watch for, and woe unto the director or producer who misses a step in this intricate dance.

16   Sports viewers expect still more from a production. They want to experience a different view of the game than is garnered by ticket-buying customers at the ball park, and that view had better be more detailed, more comprehensive, more illuminating, and more dramatic. It also has to live up to, or exceed, the home viewers' sense of their own expertise, so that it shows them things they couldn't have seen, or wouldn't have noticed, by themselves: exquisite details, microscopic closeups, unusual angles, realistic sounds; in-depth information and unique commentary, interviews with participants; technical analysis, non-stop action, perfect sightlines under any playing conditions; endless replays, isolations, and slow-mo shots without missing a play, and of course, suitable opportunities to head for the refrigerator or bathroom thrown in for good measure.

17   Oddly, the viewing public often seems to rely on these production techniques to validate what they have just seen with their own eyes. They want to watch the replays again and again, as if suspending disbelief through the use of videotape. This trend has spawned an interesting phenomenon at the ball parks, to which many of these same fans now bring their own television sets to watch on TV what they have just seen, live, right in front of them. Many stadia and athletic facilities have now installed giant replay screens, so the paying customers won't be at a disadvantage relative to those who stayed home to watch from the living room couch. They are further reassured that watching at the stadium will be comparable to watching at home—a progressive reversal of logic no one would have believed a few short years ago. It is now almost instinctual to look for a replay in sports stadia of any quality, and many spectators feel a real sense of loss, should none be available. And throughout the land, the prevalence of portable videotape cameras assures that even Little League is recorded for replay, analysis, and critique.

REACTING

1. Do you agree with David Klatell and Norman Marcus that TV sports are great entertainment?
2. Which sports are most enhanced by television coverage? Which ones fare worst? Explain your answers.

CONNECTING

1. Turn to p. 182 and read Maya Angelou's "Joe Louis." Would Angelou agree with Klatell and Marcus's ideas about why we like to watch sports on television?

2. Turn to p. 185 and see if Jay Coakley's comments in "Media, Sports, and Gender" on television sports programs have changed your reaction to Klatell and Marcus's article.

LEARNING ABOUT WRITING FROM READING

This article shows a very effective way of setting up a convincing rebuttal. The authors describe one view of television sports programs and their fans in paragraph 1—a negative view—and then proceed to knock it down, or at least modify it, by offering a positive viewpoint.

This contrasting pattern is effective in persuading an audience because it allows the opposite side some airtime (or page space). Klatell and Marcus allow readers who are opposed to sports on television to be satisfied that their objections have at least been noted.

There is one pitfall to avoid when using rebuttal: the so-called straw man effect. Don't set up an easy target just so that you can have the effortless pleasure of shooting it down. The opposing viewpoint must be solid and real in order for this persuasive strategy to work well.

MAYA ANGELOU

Joe Louis

Maya Angelou, poet and author of several books, describes a scene from her childhood: the day Joe Louis became heavyweight champion of the world.

BEFORE YOU READ

1. What do you know about Joe Louis? Do you consider him a hero?
2. What draws people to the sport of boxing?

1 The last inch of space was filled, yet people continued to wedge themselves along the walls of the Store. Uncle Willie had turned the radio up to its last notch so that youngsters on the porch wouldn't miss a word. Women sat on kitchen chairs, dining-room chairs, stools and upturned wooden boxes. Small children and babies perched on every lap available and men leaned on the shelves or on each other.

2 The apprehensive mood was shot through with shafts of gaiety, as a black sky is streaked with lightning.

3 "I ain't worried 'bout this fight. Joe's gonna whip that cracker like it's open season."

4 "He gone whip him till that white boy call him Momma."

5 At last the talking was finished and the string-along songs about razor blades were over and the fight began.

6 "A quick jab to the head." In the Store the crowd grunted. "A left to the head and a right and another left." One of the listeners cackled like a hen and was quieted.

7 "They're in a clench, Louis is trying to fight his way out."

8 Some bitter comedian on the porch said, "That white man don't mind hugging that niggah now, I betcha."

9 "The referee is moving in to break them up, but Louis finally pushed the contender away and it's an uppercut to the chin. The contender is hanging on, now he's backing away. Louis catches him with a short left to the jaw."

10 A tide of murmuring assent poured out the doors and into the yard.

11 "Another left and another left. Louis is saving that mighty right . . ." The mutter in the Store had grown into a baby roar and it was pierced by the clang of a bell and the announcer's "That's the bell for round three, ladies and gentlemen."

12 As I pushed my way into the Store I wondered if the announcer gave any thought to the fact that he was addressing as "ladies and gentlemen" all the Negroes around the world who sat sweating and praying, glued to their "master's voice."

13 There were only a few calls for R. C. Colas, Dr. Peppers, and Hire's root beer. The real festivities would begin after the fight. Then even the old Christian ladies who taught their children and tried themselves to practice turning the other cheek would buy soft drinks, and if the Brown Bomber's victory was a particularly bloody one they would order peanut patties and Baby Ruths also.

14 Bailey and I lay the coins on top of the cash register. Uncle Willie didn't allow us to ring up sales during a fight. It was too noisy and might shake up the atmosphere. When the gong rang for the next round we pushed through the near-sacred quiet to the herd of children outside.

15 "He's got Louis against the ropes and now it's a left to the body and a right to the ribs. Another right to the body, it looks like it was low . . . Yes, ladies and gentlemen, the referee is signaling but the contender keeps raining the blows on Louis. It's another to the body, and it looks like Louis is going down."

16 My race groaned. It was our people falling. It was another lynching, yet another Black man hanging on a tree. One more woman ambushed and raped. A Black boy whipped and maimed. It was hounds on the trail of a man running through slimy swamps. It was a white woman slapping her maid for being forgetful.

17 The men in the Store stood away from the walls and at attention. Women greedily clutched the babes on their laps while on the porch the shufflings and smiles, flirtings and pinching of a few minutes before were gone. This might be the end of the world. If Joe lost we were back in slavery and beyond help. It would all be true, the accusations that we were lower types of human beings. Only a little higher than the apes. True that we were stupid and ugly and lazy and dirty and, unlucky and worst of all, that God Himself hated us and ordained us to be hewers of wood and drawers of water, forever and ever, world without end.

18 We didn't breathe. We didn't hope. We waited.

19 "He's off the ropes, ladies and gentlemen. He's moving towards the center of the ring." There was no time to be relieved. The worst might still happen.

20 "And now it looks like Joe is mad. He's caught Carnera with a left hook to the head and a right to the head. It's a left jab to the body and another left to the head. There's a left cross and a right to the head. The contender's right eye is bleeding and he can't seem to keep his block up. Louis is penetrating every block. The referee is moving in, but Louis sends a left to the body and it's the uppercut to the chin and the contender is dropping. He's on the canvas, ladies and gentlemen."

21 Babies slid to the floor as women stood up and men leaned toward the radio.

22 "Here's the referee. He's counting. One, two, three, four, five, six, seven . . . Is the contender trying to get up again?"

23 All the men in the store shouted, "NO."

24 "—eight, nine, ten." There were a few sounds from the audience, but they seemed to be holding themselves in against tremendous pressure.

25 "The fight is all over, ladies and gentlemen. Let's get the microphone over to the referee . . . Here he is. He's got the Brown Bomber's hand, he's holding it up . . . Here he is . . ."

26 Then the voice, husky and familiar, came to wash over us—"The winnah, and still heavyweight champeen of the world . . . Joe Louis."

27 Champion of the world. A Black boy. Some Black mother's son. He was the strongest man in the world. People drank Coca-Colas like ambrosia[1] and ate candy bars like Christmas. Some of the men went behind the Store and poured white lightning in their soft-drink bottles, and a few of the bigger boys followed them. Those who were not chased away came back blowing their breath in front of themselves like proud smokers.

28 It would take an hour or more before the people would leave the Store and head for home. Those who lived too far had made arrangements to stay in town. It wouldn't do for a Black man and his family to be caught on a lonely country road on a night when Joe Louis had proved that we were the strongest people in the world.

REACTING

1. What's your reaction to Maya Angelou's last paragraph?
2. Does her description remind you of a time when you listened to or watched an important sports event? What are the similarities and differences?

CONNECTING

1. Compare Angelou's view of the importance of boxing with José Torres's view ("Let's Stop Glorifying Bullies," p. 169) of the same sport.

---

[1] The food of the gods.

2. Both Angelou and William Rhoden ("Strong in the Blood," p. 165) show that sports are important in American culture. Compare their ideas about why this is so.

LEARNING ABOUT WRITING FROM READING

This excerpt comes from an autobiographical novel. Look at how Angelou handles direct speech, both from the radio announcer and among the listeners in the store. Her method should be familiar from your own reading of novels.

Punctuation of conversation or direct speech is relatively simple, if you follow a model.

1. Introductory phrases, such as "he said," "they said," and the like, are followed by a comma, or, more rarely, with a dash.
2. What is actually said goes within quotation marks.
3. The first word inside the quotation marks is capitalized, with rare exceptions made for dramatic effect.
4. At the end of the direct speech, the period comes before the quotation marks.
5. Each time the speaker changes, the change is indicated by a new paragraph.

Here is an example from Angelou's article (paragraphs 22–26):

> "Here's the referee. He's counting. One, two, three, four, five, six, seven . . . Is the contender trying to get up again?"
>
> All the men in the store shouted, "NO."
>
> "—eight, nine, ten." There were a few sounds from the audience, but they seemed to be holding themselves in against tremendous pressure.
>
> "The fight is all over, ladies and gentlemen. Let's get the microphone over to the referee . . . Here he is. He's got the Brown Bomber's hand, he's holding it up . . . Here he is . . ."
>
> Then the voice, husky and familiar, came to wash over us—
> "The winnah, and still heavyweight champeen of the world . . . Joe Louis."

Jay J. Coakley

Media, Sports and Gender

Jay J. Coakley, writer of textbooks on sports and society, examines the role of the sports media in shaping our views of men and women in modern American culture.

BEFORE YOU READ

1. What ideas about gender roles of men and women do you get from sports coverage on television or from the sports pages in newspapers?
2. Do you watch women's sports on television?

1   The mass media have the potential to change ideas about masculinity and femininity in society. In some cases this has happened, but the net result of the media influence in North American sport has been to reproduce and perpetuate traditional definitions of gender—even when those definitions are seen as outdated and restrictive by many people. According to Sabo and Runfola (1980), the media presentations of sport have been produced to emphasize ideals of male dominance and aggressiveness that have been rejected by many people. Furthermore, these presentations have focused almost exclusively on commercial sports like football, baseball, ice hockey, basketball, and automobile racing, which confine women to the sidelines as cheerleaders, spectators, and advertising images—a situation that does not accurately reflect the changing lives of North American women.

2   In the 1970s one of the most obvious characteristics of the mass media in North America was poor coverage of women's sports. Seldom did women athletes receive more than 5% of the total coverage given to sport in newspapers, magazines, radio, and television; and books and movies about women in sport were practically nonexistent. When coverage was given, it usually focused on sport activities that fit comfortably with traditional images of women. Petite gymnasts and figure skaters were always favorite subjects, along with a few golfers and tennis players, especially the ones who wore designer clothes, styled hair, and attractive smiles. This type of coverage—characterized by the underrepresentation and distortion of women in sport—was not so extreme in the 1980s, but it did not disappear, even though the media attention given to women became more frequent and representative. This change was not a result of the social consciences of those who control the media; instead, it was a response to the significant changes in women's sport participation since the mid-1970s. A brief look at coverage patterns in newspapers, magazines, and television will show how things have changed and why more changes are needed in the future.

3   **Newspapers.** Newspapers have seldom covered women's sports in a consistent fashion. Before the 1980s stories about women athletes were rare. They were usually confined to the back pages of the sports section, and they contained little of the detailed information that was a standard feature in stories about men's sports. For example, in 1979 when Grete Waitz set a world record in a 10,000 meter race in New York, the story was carried on page 9 of the Sunday *New York Times* sports section. The headline read "Grete Waitz Sets Record in Park Run," which would lead most readers to assume that the accomplishment was not very noteworthy, and that it was probably a story about someone who had a good run in a race at an annual company picnic. Interestingly, no male

athletes covered in any of the stories in the first 8 pages of the sports section had set any comparable records (Boutilier and SanGiovanni, 1983).

4   Studies of the sports pages of newspapers have found that women get less than 15% of the space devoted to sport coverage, and the coverage given to women is less likely to include photographs and in-depth reporting than the coverage given to men (Bryant, 1980; Lenskyj, 1988; Woolard, 1983). In big city newspapers, where the emphasis is usually on the national coverage of commercial sports, women get even less space and fewer pictures than they get in papers serving smaller communities. Local newspapers in some smaller cities and towns have been quicker to give attention to girls and women. Since 1980 many of them have started to give representative coverage to girls in youth sports and to women's teams in the local high schools. And in some university towns where the women's intercollegiate teams have good records, there is reasonable coverage. However, coverage is rarely equal. A weak men's intercollegiate football or basketball team almost always receives better coverage than the strongest of the women's teams.

5   Much of this unequal coverage is associated with (1) the standardized formats used by newspaper sport sections, (2) the traditional work routines of sports reporters at newspapers, and (3) the lack of women reporters covering sports (Theberge and Cronk, 1986). For example, information about men's sports has traditionally been defined as news, while women's sports are more often seen as special-interest events. Furthermore, there is simply more standardized information available on men's sports events. It comes over the wire services, and it is supplied by sports information directors and others hired to generate publicity for men's teams and male athletes. The work assignments given to reporters are based on an extended definition of this approach to the news. Sportswriters automatically cover men's sports as part of their beat, and when they have additional time, they generally choose to cover what they know and feel comfortable writing about. Since close to 100% of the sports reporters are men, their work routines are geared to covering men's events. Women reporters are scarce because many women are not interested in work routines organized by men to cover men's events, and because many male sports editors evaluate women applicants for jobs in terms of criteria[1] reflecting the way men have traditionally reported on sports. Therefore, these editors often conclude that if a woman applicant isn't just like them and the other male reporters, she is unqualified.

6   Changes in the future will occur if more people are put in charge of generating publicity for women's sports, if male sportswriters become more familiar with women's sports and more comfortable covering them, and if more women are hired as sports reporters. Some changes have occurred, but they have been slow, and there is still plenty of room for improvement.

7   **Magazines.** Women's magazines have never given a high priority to the coverage of women's sports. When articles on sport-related topics have appeared, the emphasis has traditionally been on topics such as beauty, fashion, travel,

---

[1] Standards of judgment.

and sex discrimination. In other words, the coverage of sport has been merged with traditional images of women so that readers will not be threatened or discouraged from consuming the fashion and beauty products advertised in the magazines. This type of an approach has even been adopted by *Women's Sports and Fitness* magazine. Since magazines make their profits on advertising, and since advertising rates are based on circulation figures, the editors at *Women's Sports and Fitness* decided in 1979 to emphasize the fact that "there is no conflict between femininity and athletics" and that "beauty and sports are not mutually exclusive." Their decision was clearly based on economic considerations. They knew that another magazine, *The Sportswoman,* tried to cover women as serious athletes instead of members of "the fairer sex" and was forced to stop publication in 1977 for economic reasons. Magazines have always had a difficult time being successful without matching coverage and editorial policies with traditional values.

8   This point was clearly made in a study by sociologist Dan Hilliard (1984). Hilliard did a content analysis of 115 popular magazine articles written about male and female tennis players during the period from June 1979 to September 1983. His goal was to see if the coverage of top-ranked men and women players was the same. He picked tennis because it was one of only two commercial sports in which men and women compete on a similar tour throughout the year (golf being the other). His initial finding was that male players received more magazine coverage than female players "even though female tennis players . . . receive more media attention than any other group of female athletes." In mixed tournaments the male players received top billing in nearly all the coverage, and the men-only tournaments received more coverage than the women-only tournaments. In fact, the four top-ranked male players during the time period of the study received more combined coverage than the eight top-ranked female players.

9   When Hilliard dug into the articles, he found they often tended to focus on the character flaws of the athletes. This was true for both the men and women. However, there was a crucial difference in the kinds of flaws connected with each of the sexes. The male players were flawed because they exaggerated traditional masculine characteristics: they were "too determined, too aggressive, too independent, obsessed with perfection, too stoic, too concerned with maintaining their privacy and their individuality." The female players were flawed because they were too "feminine": they were "too emotional, too dependent, [and] unfulfilled by their personal achievements in the absence of meaningful . . . relationships [with men]." The character weaknesses of the men were connected with their quest for success and perfection; the weaknesses of the women were connected with their failure to achieve success and perfection. In the articles about the men, the status of athlete always took priority over other roles, such as father, husband, and so on; in articles about the women, the status of female took priority over the status of athlete.

10 Hilliard explains these differences in the following manner:

11 [In the case of the women] it is of great economic interest to Avon and Virginia Slims that the athletes participating in the events they sponsor be perceived as feminine by the potential buyers of their products. It is

also to the players' benefit to be perceived as feminine because their personal endorsement incomes will be adversely affected if they are not. Thus, the athletes and the journalists, as participants in an ongoing commercial athletic system, may enter into an unspoken complicity to present an image that emphasizes underlying femininity. Sponsors of male events have no analogous[2] concerns. The players are already perceived as being consistent with the traditional masculine image; their standard of play alone is sufficient to attract crowds, and indeed their on-court histrionics probably attract additional public attention.

12   *Sports Illustrated,* the most widely circulated sports magazine in the world, runs into the same economic issues, and its editors have generally responded in the same fashion (Reid and Soley, 1979). For example, during the first 25 years of the magazine's existence, women appeared in only 115 of the 1,250 *Sports Illustrated* cover photos—and 60 of those women were not even athletes. Coverage of women in feature articles during those same years was disproportionately low, and it generally concentrated on women in traditionally acceptable sports like golf, tennis, figure skating, and gymnastics (Zang, 1976). These articles always contained descriptions of the athletes that focused on dimensions of appearance and attractiveness and had nothing to do with the women's athletic accomplishments (Corrigan, 1972). Boutilier and SanGiovanni (1983) did an analysis of the photos *Sports Illustrated* used in its Silver Anniversary Edition (Aug. 13, 1979) to sum up its 25 years of sports coverage and found the following:

13
- Only 14 women were pictured in the 119 photos.
- No women were pictured in 14 of the 25 years covered (including 1974, 1975, and 1979).
- Men were pictured in 15 different sports, women in only 8.
- In 58% of the pictures of women, the women were shown in passive, nonathletic poses, while only 44% of the men were pictured in such a manner.

14   A 1987 study sponsored by the Women's Sports Foundation suggests that changes in *Sports Illustrated*'s coverage of women during the 1980s were not very encouraging. An analysis of issues published between April 1986 and April 1987 showed that less than 10% of all articles were devoted to women, and 33% of the articles about women also contained significant coverage of men. When the coverage of men was included in the articles, about 60% of the photos centered attention on the men or on scenery rather than the women.

15   Consistent with this tendency to ignore the depth and diversity of participation among women, *Sports Illustrated* still publishes its annual swimsuit issue, in which women are featured as beach decorations rather than athletes. The issue is used to advertise subscriptions and to boost revenues. The fact that the 1989 twenty-fifth anniversary issue accounted for $30 million in revenue means that it will be quite some time before the editorial policy on the coverage of women

---

[2] Similar or parallel.

will be changed. In the face of such potential profits, efforts to push for more serious coverage of women in sports are unlikely to produce dramatic change.

16 **Television.** In 1974 Jan Felshin made the following statement about the television coverage of women in sport:

17 > The analyses that have been done suggest that women do not receive one percent of the sport coverage. The kind of attention that women in sport do receive is frequently in the context of news of the "dog bites man" variety. Apart from minimal coverage of women in the Olympic Games . . . the only programming of actual women's events has been a few scattered tournaments in golf and tennis. There has been some special attention to gymnastics and figure skating, but it is almost impossible to watch an entire competition involving women on television and almost impossible to avoid watching one involving men.

18 Felshin made this statement the year after Billie Jean King had to play a tennis match against Bobby Riggs, a 55-year-old retired tennis pro, to get nationwide television coverage. In the following year, the only regular television coverage of women athletes was in the made-for-television "trash sport" called *The Superstars*. Then, in the late 1970s, some people at a few major corporations with either cigarettes or beauty products to sell decided there were enough well-educated, gainfully employed women in the United States to use women's sports as an advertising tool. They sponsored regular coverage of women in golf and tennis. However, involvement in basketball, volleyball, track and field, and softball was ignored. In fact, a professional women's basketball league and a sex integrated professional volleyball league both went broke in the early 1980s for lack of sponsorship and television coverage.

19 The U.S. television coverage of women athletes in the 1984 and 1988 Olympic Games (both winter and summer) was much greater than it had been in past games. Part of the reason for this was that women made up a larger proportion of the viewing audience than ever before. In fact, during the 1988 Winter Games in Calgary women accounted for well over half the U.S. viewing audience during all but 3 of the 94.5 hours of television coverage; even during the 3-hour broadcast of the United States versus USSR hockey game, the gender breakdown was 50–50. The specific coverage of women, however, still tended to emphasize sports in which grace and beauty were dominant or in which there were women athletes who reinforced traditional definitions of gender. The media attention paid to Florence Joyner in the Summer Games was certainly deserved for her accomplishments in the 100- and 200-meter sprints, but the facts that she ran in full make-up, had an interest in turning running clothes into fashion statements, and was constantly in the company of her husband-coach made her a particularly attractive personality for television coverage.

20 Even though coverage tends to reinforce traditional definitions of gender, it is possible that the exceptions to this tendency signal what may lie in the future. For example, there seems to be a willingness among some cable television

channels to cover women's sports that have been given little attention in the past. This was illustrated during the 1988–89 college basketball season in the United States, when over 100 women's games were televised, mostly on cable. Major networks are often slow to make changes, but cable channels are sometimes willing to do new things to attract subscribers and viewers.

References

Boutilier, M.A., and L. SanGiovanni. 1983. The sporting woman. Human Kinetics Publishers, Champaign, Ill.
Bryant, J. 1980. A two-year selective investigation of the female in sports as reported in the paper media. ARENA Review 4(2):32–44.
Corrigan, M. 1972. Societal acceptance of the female athlete as seen through the analysis of content of a sports magazine. Unpublished paper (cited in Boutilier and SanGiovanni, 1983).
Felshin, J. 1974. The social view. In E. Gerber et al., eds. The American woman in sport. Addison-Wesley, Reading, Mass.
Hilliard, D. 1984. Media images of male and female professional athletes: An interpretive analysis of magazine articles. Sociol. Sport J. 1(3):251–262.
Lenskyj, H. 1988. Women, sport and physical activity: Research and bibliography. Minister of State, Fitness and Amateur Sports, Ottawa.
Reid, L.N., and L. C. Soley. 1979. Sports Illustrated's coverage of women in sports. Journalism Q. 56(4):861–863.
Woolard, H.F. 1983. A content analysis of women's and girls' sports articles in selected newspapers. Master's thesis, University of Iowa, Iowa City.
Zang, K.M. 1976. An analysis of selected aspects of the treatment of sports as reflected in the content of Sports Illustrated, from the inception of the magazine. Master's thesis, East Stroudsburg State College, East Stroudsburg, PA.

REACTING

1. What information most surprised you in Jay Coakley's article? Explain your answer.
2. Coakley's survey is of media coverage in the 1970s and 1980s. Do you think the picture has changed since then? Why?

CONNECTING

1. How might David Klatell and Norman Marcus ("What We Are Watching," p. 177) respond to Coakley's article?
2. Would Coakley claim that William Rhoden's article on football in Valdosta, Ga. ("Strong in the Blood," p. 165) is part of the problem? Why or why not?

LEARNING ABOUT WRITING FROM READING

Coakley's article summarizes information from research studies over a period of several years. It demonstrates some useful points about condensing a lot of information and citing its sources correctly. Here's an example (paragraph 12):

> *Sports Illustrated,* the most widely circulated sports magazine in the world, runs into the same economic issues, and its editors have generally responded in the same fashion (Reid and Soley, 1979). For example, during the first 25 years of the magazine's existence, women appeared in only 115 of the 1,250 *Sports Illustrated* cover photos—and 60 of those women were not even athletes. Coverage of women in feature articles during those same years was disproportionately low, and it generally concentrated on women in traditionally acceptable sports like golf, tennis, figure skating, and gymnastics (Zang, 1976).

Points to note: Coakley uses APA (American Psychological Association) style in citing references. Author and year of publication appear in parentheses after the summarized information. Remember that summaries and paraphrases of other people's information—not just direct quotations—must be fully documented. The author's name is separated from the year by a comma; the period concluding the sentence is placed after the parentheses. Full bibliographical data appear at the end of the article, for readers to follow up on if they wish.

WRITING ASSIGNMENTS

ASSIGNMENT I
WHAT ARE PEOPLE MISSING OUT ON IF THEY AREN'T INTERESTED IN SPORTS?

Coming Up with Ideas and a Focus

This open-ended question could lead in several directions, as you will quickly find once you start listing all the things that people who do like sports might consider in connection with them: teamwork, exercise, friendship, entertainment, physical challenge, for example. So focus on only a few things that people are missing out on if they are not involved in sports.

Organizing Your Ideas

Probably the simplest way of seeing this paper is as a statement about what people miss by ignoring sports, backed up with supporting illustrations and examples. For example, if you want to say that people miss out on excitement if they don't watch or play a sport, prove your point by narrating an exciting sports event or by describing a crowd of fans in a stadium—or even in your dorm room in front of the television set. (For help with statement-support papers, see pp. 305 and 365.)

Audience

This assignment is an opportunity to persuade an audience of skeptics—people who are fairly sure that they are not missing out on anything at all by ignoring the world of sports. (They may even feel superior about it.) Keeping this kind of audience in mind may help you to find the right scenes and the telling details that will win this group over to your side.

ASSIGNMENT II
EXPLAIN THE GAME OF FOOTBALL TO A REPORTER FROM THE PLANET MARS.

Coming Up with Ideas and a Focus

As you begin work on this paper, start by listing the different parts of the game itself and its immediate context. What positions and players are involved? What other people besides players are important? Where is the game played? Questions like these will help to remind you of some of the things you'd like to tell your Martian reader. You can't cover everything about football in a single paper, though, so you'll need to decide what's most important. Do you want to focus on the players on the field, the positions they fill, the fans, the stadium, or even the televised coverage of the game?

Organizing Your Ideas

There are more choices to be made here. You might tell (or narrate) the story of the game itself, moving chronologically from the kickoff to the final whistle. Or you could describe different elements of the game in some other order, such as most to least interesting plays. Describing the game as experienced by one of the players is another suggestion. (For help with narrative papers, see p. 366.)

Audience

The assignment itself tells you who your audience is. The reporter from Mars is the kind of uninformed listener who forces us to be specific and to explain carefully things we might otherwise skim over without thought. You may be surprised at what you will discover about a topic that you thought you already knew very well, when your purpose is to explain a familiar part of American culture to someone who is eager to learn but lacks the information we take for granted.

ASSIGNMENT III
WRITE AN ANALYSIS OF TV SPORTS COVERAGE.

Coming Up with Ideas and a Focus

This assignment gives you many choices—too many! You will first need to generate some ideas and then decide which ones to focus on. You might begin by asking yourself questions like: Do different games get different kinds of coverage?

Who sponsors particular sporting events, or advertises during them? What do commentators discuss besides the game itself? Are male and female athletes presented or discussed differently? How are fans, coaches, and referees presented on television? Come up with your own questions and decide which question or questions interest you most. Then focus on TV coverage that will help you answer your questions. (For help with analysis, see Chapter 12.)

Organizing Your Ideas

These three steps suggest one way to organize your ideas: (1) present the focusing questions that guided your TV viewing research; (2) present your data (the information you gathered from television); (3) summarize your findings and say what conclusions you draw from them. If you want to get your readers' interest by previewing your results in the first paragraph, go ahead. You don't have to wait until the last paragraph to share your conclusions.

Audience

Depending on what you find and conclude, you might want to write directly to a television station, with the purpose of explaining your findings and saying why you are pleased, or concerned and see a need for change. Or your audience might be your own classmates, whom you wish to inform about the significance of some aspects of TV sports coverage that they take for granted.

ASSIGNMENT IV
CHOOSE A SPORT AND EXPLAIN WHAT IT TELLS US ABOUT OUR CULTURE'S VALUES.

Coming Up with Ideas and a Focus

Try beginning work on this paper with a list of American sports, brainstorming about the values they suggest. As you work toward finding a focus, you might choose to show what a particular sport tells us about several of our culture's values—success, competition, money, teamwork, individual achievement. Or you might decide to show in more detail how a sport tells us about one value on its own, for example, violence. You will need to decide, too, if you are going to focus on the sport alone and/or on fans' reactions to it.

Organizing Your Ideas

You may want to try writing this paper as a series of examples that illustrate and support a general statement about the sport and its connection with our culture's values. (For help with statement-support papers, see pp. 305 and 365.)

Audience

Try writing your paper for people who love the sport you have chosen, just for its own sake. They may be unwilling to believe that the game they love has any hidden messages. You will need to persuade them that their beloved football, hockey, or tennis is even more important than they thought: it tells them things they need to know about the culture they live in.

Chapter 6

Poverty and Wealth

KEY QUESTIONS

What are Americans' attitudes about poverty and wealth?

What role do the media play in presenting and solving the problem of poverty?

Give me your tired, your poor,
Your huddled masses yearning to breathe free,
The wretched refuse of your teeming shore,
Send these, the homeless, tempest-tossed to me;
I lift my lamp beside the golden door.
—Emma Lazarus, *The New Colossus*

It is easier for a camel to go through the eye of a needle, than for a rich man to enter the kingdom of God.
—Gospel According to St. Matthew, 19:24

If the world were a global village of 100 people, 70 of them would be unable to read, one would have a college education, over 50 would be suffering from malnutrition, and over 80 would live in what we call substandard housing.

If the world were a global village of 100 residents, 6 of them would be Americans. These 6 would have half the village's income, and the other 94 would exist on the other half. How would the wealthy 6 live "in peace" with their neighbors? They would be driven to arm themselves against the other 94, perhaps even to spend, as we do, more per person on military defense than the total income of the others.
—Neil Q. Hamilton

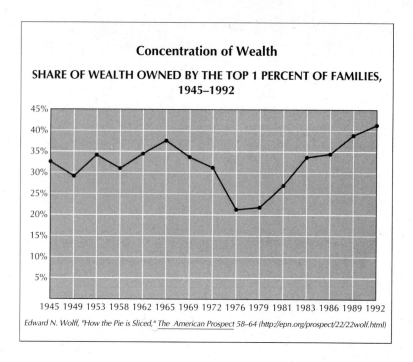

Concentration of Wealth

SHARE OF WEALTH OWNED BY THE TOP 1 PERCENT OF FAMILIES, 1945–1992

Edward N. Wolff, "How the Pie is Sliced," *The American Prospect* 58–64 (http://epn.org/prospect/22/22wolf.html)

Introduction

Would you rather be rich or poor? That question will get a fast answer from most of us. But "How do you feel about the rich and the poor?" may take some soul-searching. In a country where the work ethic, individual responsibility, and money are stressed, attitudes about those who have money and those who don't are highly charged. In this chapter you can investigate your own attitudes toward wealth and poverty, where you got those attitudes, and how the media have contributed to them.

Many of us know something about poverty firsthand. Applying for food stamps, worrying about medical bills and the rent check, getting a third and final demand for payment of the electric bill, having to drop out of school—all these are personal angles on the more general problem whose extreme is the hungry and homeless woman in the subway station or the man under cardboard in the local park. Even those of us who have never worried about food and shelter have probably felt poor in comparison with someone else because we could not have expensive sneakers, a house in the country, a luxury car, or an Ivy League education.

Whatever our experiences, we have probably absorbed some of our attitudes about poverty and wealth from the dominant views in our culture. Jo Goodwin Parker, in "What Is Poverty?" tells the reader flat-out what it feels like to be poor. When Katherine van Wormer contrasts Norwegian and American societies in "A Society Without Poverty," she finds very different cultural attitudes about poverty that result in very different treatments of the poor. And

Frances Moore Lappé and Joseph Collins, in "There's Simply Not Enough Food," suggest that often Americans' attitudes are not based on knowledge of the facts about hunger, at home or abroad.

Some of our attitudes and impressions about poverty may be formed by the television or movie screen or the newspaper or magazine page. This chapter's readings take a look at how the mass media deal, or fail to deal, with poverty, in America and elsewhere. In "Hunger in Africa," for example, Jane Hunter and Steve Askin comment on the way that newspapers and television in the United States have inadequately covered the problem of African hunger, at least in comparison with other media in the West. In "Freedom of Speech for the Wealthy," Jerry Mander looks at how money affects what is on television and what messages are presented. Should the media be doing more to expose and reduce the gap between the haves and the have-nots? Carol Bradley Shirley says yes in "Where Have You Been?" and sketches in the role she thinks the mass media need to play.

As you read, consider how well the media help us to work out answers to inevitable questions: Why is there poverty in such a wealthy country? What changes in attitude and policy do Americans need to make to have a healthy and fair society?

Starting Out: Finding Out What You Already Know

1. Freewrite about a time when you felt poor (or rich) in comparison with someone else.
2. List what comes to mind when someone says "poor people in America."
3. List what comes to mind when someone says "poor people in Africa."
4. Discuss your feelings about a television program or film touching on poverty in the United States.
5. Think about and list your own reasons for the existence of poverty in the United States.

Learning More Through Observation: Taking a Look Around You and Talking to People

1. Pick one of the media (a television news broadcast or a newspaper) and monitor for five days how poverty issues are covered. Compare your results with those of others in your class and see what you can conclude about how much and how well poverty is reported.
2. List the signs of poverty and the signs of wealth in your community. When you compare your list of "signs" with those of your classmates, what patterns or similarities do you notice?
3. Interview someone about poverty in America. Here are some possible questions: How do you feel about the problem? What have your own experiences been? What are the causes of poverty? What are the solutions?

4. List as many films as you can that deal with poverty in the United States, then list the ones that deal with wealth and affluence in some way. Which list is longer? What contrasts do you see?

Questioning: Deciding What Else You Would Like to Know

List five questions that you still have about poverty and wealth in the United States.

Jo Goodwin Parker

What Is Poverty?

Jo Goodwin Parker recounts her own experiences of poverty.

BEFORE YOU READ

1. Answer the title question.
2. How do you think it feels to be poor?

1   You ask me what is poverty? Listen to me. Here I am, dirty, smelly, and with no "proper" underwear on and with the stench of my rotting teeth near you. I will tell you. Listen to me. Listen without pity. I cannot use your pity. Listen with understanding. Put yourself in my dirty, worn out, ill-fitting shoes, and hear me.

2   Poverty is getting up every morning from a dirt- and illness-stained mattress. The sheets have long since been used for diapers. Poverty is living in a smell that never leaves. This is a smell of urine, sour milk, and spoiling food sometimes joined with the strong smell of long-cooked onions. Onions are cheap. If you have smelled this smell, you did not know how it came. It is the smell of the outdoor privy. It is the smell of young children who cannot walk the long dark way in the night. It is the smell of the mattresses where years of "accidents" have happened. It is the smell of the milk which has gone sour because the refrigerator long has not worked, and it costs money to get it fixed. It is the smell of rotting garbage. I could bury it, but where is the shovel? Shovels cost money.

3   Poverty is being tired. I have always been tired. They told me at the hospital when the last baby came that I had chronic anemia caused from poor diet, a bad case of worms, and that I needed a corrective operation. I listened politely—the poor are always polite. The poor always listen. They don't say that there is no money for iron pills, or better food, or worm medicine. The idea of an operation is frightening and costs so much that, if I had dared, I would have laughed. Who takes care of my children? Recovery from an operation takes a

long time. I have three children. When I left them with "Granny" the last time I had a job, I came home to find the baby covered with fly specks, and a diaper that had not been changed since I left. When the dried diaper came off, bits of my baby's flesh came with it. My other child was playing with a sharp bit of broken glass, and my oldest was playing alone at the edge of a lake. I made twenty-two dollars a week, and a good nursery school costs twenty dollars a week for three children. I quit my job.

4   Poverty is dirt. You can say in your clean clothes coming from your clean house, "Anybody can be clean." Let me explain about housekeeping with no money. For breakfast I give my children grits with no oleo or cornbread without eggs and oleo. This does not use up many dishes. What dishes there are, I wash in cold water and with no soap. Even the cheapest soap has to be saved for the baby's diapers. Look at my hands, so cracked and red. Once I saved for two months to buy a jar of Vaseline for my hands and the baby's diaper rash. When I had saved enough, I went to buy it and the price had gone up two cents. The baby and I suffered on. I have to decide every day if I can bear to put my cracked sore hands into the cold water and strong soap. But you ask, why not hot water? Fuel costs money. If you have a wood fire it costs money. If you burn electricity, it costs money. Hot water is a luxury. I do not have luxuries. I know you will be surprised when I tell you how young I am. I look so much older. My back has been bent over the wash tubs every day for so long, I cannot remember when I ever did anything else. Every night I wash every stitch my school age child has on and just hope her clothes will be dry by morning.

5   Poverty is staying up all night on cold nights to watch the fire knowing one spark on the newspaper covering the walls means your sleeping child dies in flames. In summer poverty is watching gnats and flies devour your baby's tears when he cries. The screens are torn and you pay so little rent you know they will never be fixed. Poverty means insects in your food, in your nose, in your eyes, and crawling over you when you sleep. Poverty is hoping it never rains because diapers won't dry when it rains and soon you are using newspapers. Poverty is seeing your children forever with runny noses. Paper handkerchiefs cost money and all your rags you need for other things. Even more costly are antihistamines. Poverty is cooking without food and cleaning without soap.

6   Poverty is asking for help. Have you ever had to ask for help, knowing your children will suffer unless you get it? Think about asking for a loan from a relative, if this is the only way you can imagine asking for help. I will tell you how it feels. You find out where the office is that you are supposed to visit. You circle that block four or five times. Thinking of your children, you go in. Everyone is very busy. Finally, someone comes out and you tell her that you need help. That never is the person you need to see. You go see another person, and after spilling the whole shame of your poverty all over the desk between you, you find that this isn't the right office after all—you must repeat the whole process, and it never is any easier at the next place.

7   You have asked for help, and after all it has a cost. You are again told to wait. You are told why, but you don't really hear because of the red cloud of shame and the rising cloud of despair.

8 Poverty is remembering. It is remembering quitting school in junior high because "nice" children had been so cruel about my clothes and my smell. The attendance officer came. My mother told him I was pregnant. I wasn't, but she thought that I could get a job and help out. I had jobs off and on, but never long enough to learn anything. Mostly I remember being married. I was so young then. I am still young. For a time, we had all the things you have. There was a little house in another town, with hot water and everything. Then my husband lost his job. There was unemployment insurance for a while and what few jobs I could get. Soon, all our nice things were repossessed and we moved back here. I was pregnant then. This house didn't look so bad when we first moved in. Every week it gets worse. Nothing is ever fixed. We now had no money. There were a few odd jobs for my husband, but everything went for food then, as it does now. I don't know how we lived through three years and three babies, but we did. I'll tell you something, after the last baby I destroyed my marriage. It had been a good one, but could you keep on bringing children in this dirt? Did you ever think how much it costs for any kind of birth control? I knew my husband was leaving the day he left, but there were no goodbys between us. I hope he has been able to climb out of this mess somewhere. He never could hope with us to drag him down.

9 That's when I asked for help. When I got it, you know how much it was? It was, and is, seventy-eight dollars a month for the four of us; that is all I ever can get. Now you know why there is no soap, no needles and thread, no hot water, no aspirin, no worm medicine, no hand cream, no shampoo. None of these things forever and ever and ever. So that you can see clearly, I pay twenty dollars a month rent, and most of the rest goes for food. For grits and cornmeal, and rice and milk and beans. I try my best to use only the minimum electricity. If I use more, there is that much less for food.

10 Poverty is looking into a black future. Your children won't play with my boys. They will turn to other boys who steal to get what they want. I can already see them behind the bars of their prison instead of behind the bars of my poverty. Or they will turn to the freedom of alcohol or drugs, and find themselves enslaved. And my daughter? At best, there is for her a life like mine.

11 But you say to me, there are schools. Yes, there are schools. My children have no extra books, no magazines, no extra pencils, or crayons, or paper and most important of all, they do not have health. They have worms, they have infections, they have pink-eye all summer. They do not sleep well on the floor, or with me in my one bed. They do not suffer from hunger, my seventy-eight dollars keeps us alive, but they do suffer from malnutrition. Oh yes, I do remember what I was taught about health in school. It doesn't do much good. In some places there is a surplus commodities program. Not here. The county said it cost too much. There is a school lunch program. But I have two children who will already be damaged by the time they get to school.

12 But, you say to me, there are health clinics. Yes, there are health clinics and they are in the towns. I live out here eight miles from town. I can walk that far (even if it is sixteen miles both ways), but can my little children? My neighbor will take me when he goes; but he expects to get paid, *one way or another*. I bet

you know my neighbor. He is that large man who spends his time at the gas station, the barbershop, and the corner store complaining about the government spending money on the immoral mothers of illegitimate children.

13   Poverty is an acid that drips on pride until all pride is worn away. Poverty is a chisel that chips on honor until honor is worn away. Some of you say that you would do *something* in my situation, and maybe you would, for the first week or the first month, but for year after year after year?

14   Even the poor can dream. A dream of a time when there is money. Money for the right kinds of food, for worm medicine, for iron pills, for toothbrushes, for hand cream, for a hammer and nails and a bit of screening, for a shovel, for a bit of paint, for some sheeting, for needles and thread. Money to pay *in money* for a trip to town. And, oh, money for hot water and money for soap. A dream of when asking for help does not eat away the last bit of pride. When the office you visit is as nice as the offices of other governmental agencies, when there are enough workers to help you quickly, when workers do not quit in defeat and despair. When you have to tell your story to only one person, and that person can send you for other help and you don't have to prove your poverty over and over and over again.

15   I have come out of my despair to tell you this. Remember I did not come from another place or another time. Others like me are all around you. Look at us with an angry heart, anger that will help you help me. Anger that will let you tell of me. The poor are always silent. Can you be silent too?

REACTING

1. If you were actually talking with Jo Goodwin Parker, what would you say to her?
2. How does the writer want you to react? Describe how the "tone of voice" of the paper makes you feel. (See the discussion below in "Learning about Writing from Reading.")

CONNECTING

1. What are the causes of Parker's poverty, from what you can infer from this article? Are they particular to her, or are they general causes of poverty?
2. Turn to p. 217 and read Katherine van Wormer's "A Society Without Poverty." What might van Wormer say about Parker's essay?

LEARNING ABOUT WRITING FROM READING

Notice how Parker talks to the reader. You may want to experiment with a style that is just as informal, direct, and emotional. Parker imagines the reader to be a middle-class person who is ignorant and prejudiced about the poor, and, from the very start of the essay, she challenges her reader to listen:

> You ask me what is poverty? Listen to me. Here I am, dirty, smelly.... I will tell you. Listen to me. Listen without pity.... Put yourself in my dirty, worn out, ill-fitting shoes, and hear me.

Here the directness of Parker's conversational style makes the essay powerful. Try this sometime: picture yourself addressing someone and write down what you would say in response to that person's questions and reactions.

FRANCES MOORE LAPPÉ AND JOSEPH COLLINS

There's Simply Not Enough Food

The authors, both active in the Institute for Food and Policy Study, examine a common response to the problem of world hunger.

BEFORE YOU READ

1. Read the myth which is the first paragraph of this essay. Do you agree with it? Why or why not?
2. Why do you think some Americans suffer from malnutrition and hunger?

1   **MYTH:** With food-producing resources in so much of the world stretched to the limit, there's simply not enough food to go around. Unfortunately, some people have to go hungry.

2   **OUR RESPONSE:** The world today produces enough grain alone to provide every human being on the planet with 3,600 calories a day.[1] That's enough to make most people fat! And this estimate does not even count the many other commonly eaten foods—vegetables, beans, nuts, root crops, fruits, grass-fed meats, and fish.[2]

3   *Abundance, not scarcity, best describes the supply of food in the world today.* Rarely has the world seen such a glut of food looking for buyers.[3] Increases in food production during the past 25 years have outstripped the world's unprecedented population growth by about 16 percent.[4] Indeed, mountains of unsold grain on world markets have pushed prices downward over the past three decades.[5]

4   All well and good for the global picture, you might be thinking, but doesn't such a broad stroke tell us little? Aren't people starving because of food shortages where most hungry people live—in Africa, Asia, and Latin America?

5   Hunger in the face of ample food is all the more shocking in the third world. In every region except Africa, gains in food production since 1950 have kept ahead of population growth.[6] During the 1970s, only 12 percent of the world's population lived in countries where food production per person was falling.[7]

6 One hypothetical question best highlights how misleading it is to think of food shortages in the third world as the root cause of hunger: how much of the food now available within third world countries would it take to make up for the total food lacking in the diets of each country's chronically* hungry people?

7 According to the World Bank, the answer is but a tiny percentage.[8] In India, home of over a third of the world's hungry people,[9] the reallocation of a mere 5.6 percent of current food production would wipe out hunger, making an active life possible for everyone.[10] For Indonesia, with the second greatest number of undernourished people in the world, only 2 percent of the country's food supply would make the difference. And in Africa, 7.8 percent of the food supply of Tanzania and 2.5 percent of that of both Senegal and Sudan could meet the needs of the hungry.

8 This is, we underline, a hypothetical† exercise. As the World Bank itself cautions, even though enough food exists, the poor are not able to purchase it.

9 Thus, even most "hungry countries" have enough food for all their people right now. This finding turns out to be true using official statistics even though experts warn us that newly modernizing societies invariably underestimate farm production—just as a century ago at least a third of the U.S. wheat crop went uncounted. Moreover, many nations can't realize their full food production potential because of the gross inefficiencies caused by inequitable ownership of resources. We will discuss this in chapters 4 and 6.

10 Finally, many of the countries in which hunger is rampant export much more in agricultural goods than they import. It is the industrial countries, not the third world countries, that import more than two-thirds of all food and farm commodities in world trade. Imports by the 30 lowest-income countries, on the other hand, account for only 6 percent of all international commerce in food and farm commodities.

11 Looking more closely at some of the world's hunger-ravaged countries and regions confirms that scarcity is clearly not the cause of hunger.

12 **Africa.** Bombarded by images of barren landscapes in Sub-Saharan Africa, many of us are surprised to learn that the region is a net exporter of agricultural commodities.

13 Despite widening hunger, food exports from the Horn of Africa—Ethiopia, Kenya, Somalia, the Sudan, Tanzania, and Uganda—were worth nearly $1 billion more in 1983 than the food imported. When all agricultural commodities are counted in, the difference rises to $1.5 billion.

14 The Sahelian countries of West Africa are known for recurrent famines, but in most years they export more agricultural products than they import. Even during the drought years 1970 to 1974, the value of the region's agricultural exports—$1.25 billion—was three times greater than the value of grain imported, and such figures don't take into account unreported exports. Reports

---

*Continuing over a long period.

† Imaginary, rather than actual.

from two of the Sahelian countries, Niger and Burkina Faso (formerly Upper Volta), estimate that traders smuggle out as much as half the grain produced to sell elsewhere to customers able to pay more.

15   While television coverage has awakened the world to hunger in the Horn of Africa and the Sahel, some of Africa's worst hunger is rarely covered. In South Africa, some 50,000 black children starve to death every year; 136 die every day. Yet South Africa is a net exporter of agricultural products, even exporting corn, the basic staple of black families.

16   Despite the productive capacity suggested by Africa's agricultural exports, by the mid-1980s food production per person had been declining for more than a decade and as much as a quarter of the continent's grain consumption was reportedly coming from imports. With so much of Africa's food production undercounted—especially the food poor women grow for their own families—a truly accurate assessment of the problem is impossible. But repeated reports about Africa's failing agriculture and growing dependence on imports have led many to assume that simply too many people are pressing against too meager resources. Africa's food crisis is real—but how true is this assumption?

17   Many longtime observers of Africa's agricultural development tell us that the real reasons for Africa's food problems are no mystery. Africa's food potential has been distorted and thwarted.*

18   Colonizers and, subsequently, national and international agencies, have discredited peasant producers' often sophisticated knowledge of ecologically† appropriate farming systems. Promoting "modern," often imported, and ecologically destructive technologies, they have cut Africa's food producers out from economic decisions most affecting their very survival.

19   Public resources, including research and agricultural credit, have been channeled to export crops to the virtual exclusion of peasant-produced food crops such as millet, sorghum, and root crops. In the 1980s, pressure to export to pay interest on foreign debt only reinforced this imbalance.

20   While Africa's principal food producers are women, decisions over land use and credit have been made the domain of men.

21   Governments beholden to urban classes demanding cheap food have paid peasants so poorly for their crops that they have often had little incentive to produce for the market.

22   Aid policies unaccountable to African peasant producers and pastoralists have generally bypassed their needs in favor of expensive, large-scale projects. Africa receives less aid for agriculture than any other continent, and of the $14 billion pouring into the eight Sahelian nations in the decade ending 1984, less than 5 percent went to rainfed agriculture, although it accounts for 95 percent of grain production. What funds did go to farming went overwhelmingly to the irrigated systems of the richer farmers.

---

* Prevented.
† Concerning the link between people and their environment.

23 African governments—like most in the third world—allocate, on average, less than 10 percent of their budgets to agriculture, in contrast to a much larger share going to the military and police.

24 Many governments have also overvalued their currencies, making imported food artificially cheap and undercutting local producers of millet, sorghum, and cassava. Urban tastes then increasingly shift to imported grain, particularly wheat, which few countries in Africa can grow economically. Twenty years ago, only a small minority of urban dwellers in Sub-Saharan Africa ate wheat. Today bread is a staple for many urbanites, and wheat products account for over a third of all the region's grain imports. U.S. food aid and advertising by multinational corporations ("He'll be smart. He'll go far. He'll eat bread.") have played their part in molding African tastes to what the industrial countries have to sell.

25 Thus beneath the "scarcity diagnosis" of Africa's food situation lie many human-made and therefore reversible causes. Even Africa's high birth rates are not independent variables but are determined by social realities that shape people's reproductive choices.

Notes

1. Calculated from Food and Agriculture Organization, *FAO Production Yearbook 1984*, vol. 38 (Rome: FAO, 1985). Over 40 percent of the world's grain supply is now fed to livestock. Most of the land and other resources now used to produce feed grain could be used to grow grain and other foods for human consumption. Feed grains are grown because better-off consumers prefer livestock products, making feed grains more profitable than food grains. According to the FAO, the recommended energy allowance for a U.S. "reference man" in his 20s weighing 155 lbs. and not very active is 2,700 calories/day and for a U.S. "reference woman" weighing 127 lbs. is 2,000 calories/day. Calories adequate to cover energy needs are generally sufficient to meet protein needs, except for people (especially young children) subsisting on low-protein roots, tubers, and plantains.

2. According to one estimate, if all foods are considered together, enough is available to provide at least five pounds of food per person a day. See Douglas La Roche, "Feeding the World: The North and South of It," *Plowshare* 6, no. 2(1981):11. Root crops are second in importance after grains in the third world (communication from Uwe Kracht, senior economist, World Food Council, 5 May 1986).

3. Barbara Insel, "A World Awash in Grain," *Foreign Affairs* (Spring 1985): 892–911. See also Peter F. Drucker, "The Changing World Economy," *Foreign Affairs* (Spring 1986).

4. Calculated from *FAO Production Yearbook* 1966, 1974, 1984.

5. This refers to prices adjusted for inflation. World Bank, *Poverty and Hunger: Issues and Options for Food Security in Developing Countries* (Washington, D.C.: World Bank, 1986), 14.
6. *FAO Production Yearbook* 1966, 1974, 1984, table 10.
7. Food and Agriculture Organization, *UN Socio-economic Indicators Relating to the Agricultural Sector and Rural Development* (Rome: FAO, 1984), table 27.
8. World Bank, *Poverty and Hunger.* For these estimates, the World Bank used a nutritional standard adequate for an active working life. Even these low percentages are reduced by three-quarters if a lower nutritional standard—a diet adequate to prevent stunted growth and serious health risks—is used.
9. In *Poverty and Hunger,* the World Bank estimates the number of hungry people to be 730 million using a caloric standard necessary to sustain an active life. The FAO, using a nutritional standard lower than that used by the World Bank, estimated that 201 million people in India are undernourished out of a total 435 million hungry people in the third world. See FAO, *Dimensions of Needs* (Rome: FAO, 1982), Part III. Other studies estimate the number of chronically hungry people in India closer to 300 million; see, for instance, U.S. Department of Agriculture, *Agricultural Outlook* (December 1985).
10. World Bank, *Poverty and Hunger,* 20.

REACTING

1. Do the authors convince you that the myth is false? Why?
2. This article is full of statistical evidence. What statistics do you find most persuasive? Least persuasive? Why?

CONNECTING

1. How might Frances Lappé and Joseph Collins answer the question: Why is there poverty in a wealthy country like America?
2. Turn to p. 224 and read Carol Bradley Shirley's "Where Have You Been?" Would Shirley be likely to disagree with this article? Why?

LEARNING ABOUT WRITING FROM READING

There are many ways writers try to persuade: by appealing to readers' emotions, their reason, their sense of justice. Here the appeal is to reason—our minds—and the authors use facts, numbers, and statistics to convince us. Furthermore, they tell us where these numbers come from, as these paragraphs (7 and 8) illustrate:

> According to the World Bank, the answer is but a tiny percentage.[8]
> In India, home of over a third of the world's hungry people,[9] the

reallocation of a mere 5.6 percent of current food production would wipe out hunger, making an active life possible for everyone.[10] For Indonesia, with the second greatest number of undernourished people in the world, only 2 percent of the country's food supply would make the difference. And in Africa, 7.8 percent of the food supply of Tanzania and 2.5 percent of that of both Senegal and Sudan could meet the needs of the hungry.

This is, we underline, a hypothetical exercise. As the World Bank itself cautions, even though enough food exists, the poor are not able to purchase it.

The numbers and the references cited cannot by themselves prove the authors' argument; but they suggest careful research and they can be checked for accuracy. In fact, the authors' documentation is so extensive that we have included only the first ten endnotes here.

JERRY MANDER

Freedom of Speech for the Wealthy

Jerry Mander, author of several books and articles on media topics, examines how money influences the messages we hear on television.

BEFORE YOU READ

1. Are there any restrictions on freedom of speech in the United States?
2. If all you knew about the United States were from watching television, what would you think about wealth and poverty in American culture?

1   We think of television as a democratic medium, since we all get to watch it in our homes. But if it is "democratic" on the receiving end, it is surely not that on the sending end.

2   According to *Advertising Age*, about 75 percent of commercial network television time is paid for by the 100 largest corporations in the country. Many people do not react to this statistic as being important. But consider that there are presently 450,000 corporations in the United States, and some 250 million people, representing extremely diverse[1] viewpoints about lifestyle, politics, and personal and national priorities. Only 100 corporations get to decide what will appear on television and what will not. These corporations do not overtly

---

[1] Varied.

announce their refusal to finance programs that contain views disconsonant[2] with their own; their control is far more subtle. It works in the minds of television producers who, when thinking about what programs to produce, have to mitigate[3] their desires by their need to sell the programs to corporate backers. An effective censorship results.

3   While a small number of corporations pay for 75 percent of commercial broadcast time, and thereby dominate that medium, they now also pay for more than 50 percent of public television. During the Reagan years, federal support for noncommercial television was virtually eliminated,[4] leaving a void that public television filled by appealing to corporations. As corporate influence has grown in public TV, so has the quality and length of the corporate commercial tags before and after the shows they sponsor. Whereas public television once featured such messages as "This program has been brought to you through a grant by Exxon," now we see the Exxon logo, followed by an added advertising phrase or two and an audio slogan.

4   The reason why only the largest corporations in the world dominate the broadcast signals is obvious: They are the only ones who can afford it. According to the present structure of network TV, a half-minute of prime time sells for about $200,000 to $300,000; during events such as the Super Bowl, the price is more like $700,000. Very few medium-sized corporations or businesses, and even fewer individuals, could pay $200,000 for a single message broadcast to the world.

5   If you and your friends decided that you had a very important statement to make about an issue—let's say the cutting down of old-growth redwoods in the Pacific Northwest—and if you were very fortunate (and rich), perhaps you could manage to raise sufficient money to actually place your message on the airwaves—*once*. Meanwhile, the multinational corporation doing the logging could buy the spot that appears before yours, and the one immediately after, and then three more later in the evening, and then five more tomorrow and the next day and the day after, and so on throughout the month. Some corporations have advertising budgets ranging from 100 million to over one billion dollars per year. Television is effectively a "private medium," for their use only.

6   That television is a private system in the hands of the largest corporations is difficult for most Americans to grasp. This is because we believe that freedom of speech is an inalienable[5] right that we all enjoy equally. Nothing could be further from the truth. As A. J. Liebling said, "Freedom of the press is available only to those who own one." Similarly, freedom of speech is more available to some than to others, namely, to the people who can purchase it on national television. This leads to certain kinds of information dominating the airwaves.

---

[2] Out of harmony.
[3] Modify.
[4] Removed, wiped out.
[5] Permanent.

7   The 100 largest corporations manufacture drugs, chemicals, cosmetics, packaged-processed foods, cars, and oil, and are involved in other extractive industries. But whether you are viewing a commercial for aspirin, cars, or cosmetics, the message is exactly the same. *All* advertising is saying this: Whether you buy this commodity or that one, satisfaction in life comes from commodities.

8   So we have the most pervasive and powerful communications medium in history, and it is totally financed by people with identical views of how life should be lived. They express this view unabashedly.[6] Which brings us to the most shocking statistic: *The average American who watches five hours of television per day sees approximately 21,000 commercials per year.* That's 21,000 repetitions of essentially identical messages about life, aggressively placed into viewers' minds, all saying, *Buy something—do it now!*

9   So an entire nation of people is sitting night after night in their rooms, in a passive condition, receiving information from faraway places in the form of imagery placed in their brains, repeated 21,000 times per year, telling them how to live their lives. If the instrument responsible for this activity weren't TV, our familiar companion, then you, like the Andromeda scientists, would probably call it a system of mass brainwashing and political control, and would be damned worried about it.

REACTING

1. "About 75 percent of commercial network television time is paid for by the 100 largest corporations in the country." Is this a serious problem? Why or why not?
2. Would you agree that television serves the wealthy best?

CONNECTING

1. According to Jerry Mander, the dominant message of television, whatever the particular content of a show, is *"Buy something—do it now!"* How might another author in this chapter react to that idea? Explain your answer.
2. Turn to p. 224 and read Carol Bradley Shirley's "Where Have You Been?" What would Mander be likely to say to her about the role the media play in solving the poverty problem?

LEARNING ABOUT WRITING FROM READING

It isn't easy to give statistical information—numbers—and have your reader absorb their importance. Mander does a good job of making numbers meaningful by:

---

[6] Without shame.

1. Spending time on one set of statistics
2. Explaining their significance
3. Telling the reader directly that the numbers are important
4. Only asking the reader to think about one point at a time.

> According to *Advertising Age,* about 75 percent of commercial network television time is paid for by the 100 largest corporations in the country. Many people do not react to this statistic as being important. But consider that there are presently 450,000 corporations in the United States, and some 250 million people, representing extremely diverse viewpoints about lifestyle, politics, and personal and national priorities. Only 100 corporations get to decide what will appear on television and what will not.

Without these statistics, clearly communicated, the rest of the argument would not be as well supported or as convincing.

JANE HUNTER AND STEVE ASKIN

Hunger in Africa: A Story Untold Until Too Late

Journalists Jane Hunter and Steve Askin analyze and evaluate media coverage of hunger and poverty in some African countries.

BEFORE YOU READ

1. Based on the title, sum up what you expect the authors to talk about.
2. What responsibility do you feel for people in other countries who are suffering from hunger?

1   It could have been the greatest rescue story in history: Millions of lives were at risk from war-induced food crises in six African nations; thanks to newly strengthened early-warning systems, virtually all could be saved with speedy deliveries of aid.

2   That was the story UN and private aid agencies began to tell in October 1990, when they issued urgent appeals for aid to prevent an even greater tragedy than the famine that ravaged much of Africa in 1984 and 1985.

3   Alarms sounded louder in December, when a senior official of the U.S. Agency for International Development told Congress that "tens of thousands" of

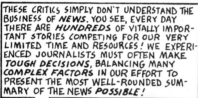

famine victims were beyond help because aid had not been delivered fast enough. By January 1991, six of the world's leading aid agencies were warning that "about 20 million people in Africa will face starvation this winter unless food aid is provided immediately." Most were in the civil war-torn nations in the Horn of Africa—Ethiopia, Somalia and Sudan. Millions of people were also at risk in civil war-racked Liberia and in two southern African nations—Angola and Mozambique—torn apart by the violence of externally backed rebel movements.

4   These timely aid appeals were made possible by one of the great humanitarian advances of 20th century technology: the development and expansion of monitoring systems designed to predict crop failures and trigger aid deliveries before food shortage turns into famine.

5   British and other European newspapers headlined these appeals for aid. Associated Press, Reuters, and other news agencies carried details to the editors' desks in U.S. newsrooms and TV studios. Yet most of this country's mass media—as the *Wall Street Journal* noted months later in a March 22 report on the non-coverage of African famine—ignored the continent's needs.

6. With a few praiseworthy exceptions, the U.S. press paid more attention to the lives of animals—featuring safari stories on elephants, rhinos and other endangered species—than the specter of death from starvation haunting millions of human beings in Africa.

7. The U.S. public's generosity helped save millions of African lives in the mid-1980s after TV broadcast dramatic footage of starving Ethiopian children. But this time, Americans weren't given a chance to hear the cries for help . . . until it was too late for many of the victims.

8. Not until April and May did the networks and major dailies give significant space to African famine, and then usually as a sidebar: the "other emergency" taxing the resources of humanitarian agencies already stretched to the limit by natural and unnatural disasters in Iraq, Bangladesh, the USSR and Costa Rica.

9. As late as May 4, the *New York Times* found it appropriate to give less than 1.75 inches to the UN World Food Program's urgent appeal for aid to 1 million refugees in southeastern Ethiopia who were already on half-rations and would run out of food entirely within two weeks. Compare this with that week's issue of *The Economist,* a conservative British magazine not known for mawkish sentimentalism, which contained 21 inches of copy on African famine, accompanied by a two-column photo.

10. Only on May 25 did the crisis in the Horn of Africa make it to the most prestigious spot in U.S. print journalism: the upper right hand corner of the *New York Times* front page. And this story, filed by Clifford Krauss from Addis Ababa, Ethiopia's capital, contained no mention of the fact that at least 5 million Ethiopians needed massive and immediate aid to save them from famine. Instead it reported a rescue mission affecting 16,000 Ethiopians: "Israelis Begin Airlift of Ethiopia's Jews."

11. Some reporters found space for a brief mention of the nation's broader crisis. The *Washington Post*'s Jennifer Parmlee, for example, sensitively wove the famine into her airlift story of the same day, reporting, "The timing of the airlift at a period of profound crisis in Ethiopia and the potential for mass starvation as a famine threatens 5 million to 6 million people here caused many in the international aid community to question the huge diversion of resources."

12. The week after the airlift to Israel, however, neither the *Times* nor the *Post* covered a Congressional hearing where U.S. officials and private aid workers described an unfolding human tragedy of immense proportions. One witness who had just returned from Ethiopia, Sharon Pauling from the aid advocacy[1] group Bread for the World, warned that the famine "promises to be worse than any in living memory." She said that "hundreds of thousands of people, including a minimum of 300,000 people in Sudan, will likely die no matter what we do. Whether that number will double or triple will depend on what actions are taken by the United States and others in the international community in the next few weeks."

---

[1] Support.

Silence Kills

13   The modern world *never* experiences food shortages, only food maldistribution. Mountains of surplus grain pile up in the United States, in Europe and in agriculturally productive Third World nations from Argentina to Zimbabwe, while people starve in countries too poor to import grain.

14   When crops fail or wars disrupt food production, as happened this year, there is almost always enough time to prevent famine by bringing surplus food from other nations. As the Aga Khan's Independent Commission on International Humanitarian Issues reported after the famine of 1984–85: "The circumstances which lead to famine actually build up quite slowly." Starvation can occur only if food-rich nations ignore impending disasters in remote and forgotten corners of the world.

15   In such a world, editors make life-and-death decisions when they decide how to cover famine and famine warnings. It is therefore vital to understand why most newspapers and TV news operations failed to report the early warnings that could have evoked a compassionate public response and thus prevented much of this year's famine suffering.

16   Was it simply that there were too many more interesting and important stories to cover in Eastern Europe and the Persian Gulf? Or had editors decided that readers and viewers suffered from "compassion fatigue," as the *Wall Street Journal* called it, and didn't want to read or view stories about Africans in need? Or was the non-coverage partly reflective, as Michael Hiltzik of the *Los Angeles Times* (3/8/91) ventured, of the lack of a vigorous U.S. domestic constituency for Africa?

17   Or are other factors at work—like racism? The "little [Kurdish] kids who look just like the kids you see at home—blue-eyed blonds and redheads with freckles" seized the attention of CBS reporter Leslie Stahl, as she sought to explain in an April 28 60 Minutes segment why the Kurdish refugees attracted so much American compassion. "These people are not Arabs. They have their roots in Europe. They are as distinct a people as the Italians or the Russians." Class too struck the unblushing Stahl as significant: "The women here used to enjoy the luxury of washing machines. Now they wash their clothes and their dishes in the muddy stream that runs through the camp."

18   "If these were white Europeans dying, or even Latin Americans," coverage would be far more intense, Bill Ayres, executive director of World Hunger Year, told *EXTRA!* Asked to comment, *New York Times* deputy foreign editor Michael Kaufman maintained that the story of hunger in Africa must compete with other stories for the paper's space and resources. But he acknowledged that—in deciding which stories to cover most intensely—"we are probably more Eurocentric than not."

19   Yet it would be inadequate to blame the paucity of African coverage solely on race and class prejudice. Several journalists interviewed by *EXTRA!* expressed skepticism[2] about projections of famine, suggesting that aid agencies

---

[2] Disbelief; suspicion about the truth of a statement.

were overstating the case to attract donations. One reporter, who asked not to be quoted, referred to the current African food situation as a "so-called famine."

20 "Projections don't inspire coverage," Kaufman of the *New York Times* said, adding that "people whose agenda is to save the world" are mistaken to assume "that we're their ally." When asked if the *Times* would increase its coverage if the projections turned into actual Africans dying by the millions, Kaufman replied, "That becomes news." In mid-May, National Public Radio senior foreign editor Cadi Simon said that NPR was still assessing the situation, receiving briefings from relief specialists.

21 Of course, projections *do* inspire coverage on subjects that editors consider genuinely important: Reflect for a moment on the reporting of debates about the likely timetable for recovery from a recession or the projected size of next year's U.S. budget deficit. Are projections that 6 million Ethiopians or 10 million Sudanese may die in the next few months somehow less newsworthy? At minimum, shouldn't reporters be sent to investigate? That's not easy, said Simon at NPR and Kaufman of the *Times*, because of the difficulty of obtaining visas to the worst-afflicted countries.

22 Neither visa problems nor ambiguous[3] projections stopped PBS's MacNeil/Lehrer Newshour, which was months ahead of network television and most newspapers in its dogged, continuing coverage of African hunger. In November 1990, soon after UN agencies issued their first dire famine warnings, MacNeil/Lehrer broadcast footage from a Sudanese refugee camp in Ethiopia where, according to reporter Kwame Holman, "every day for the past six months Sudanese refugees in the Ethiopian camp of Utang died of hunger or the diseases caused by it." This was followed by a heated on-air debate between Sudan's ambassador to Washington, who denied the existence of famine, and an aid expert who denounced the Sudanese government for dropping bombs on famine relief camps.

Incomplete Reporting

23 Even after they noticed an African famine, most of the U.S. press remained unable or unwilling to examine its fundamental causes. Our media have generally failed, for example, to link the famine in Angola, where UN officials estimate that 2 million people face starvation, to the dislocation, minefields and disruption of transport links caused by the contra-style war that the CIA actively sponsored and funded until the end of May.

24 Even the more sophisticated U.S. analyses on the causes of famine—such as Jane Perlez's May 12 *New York Times* "Week In Review" analysis, "African Dilemma: Food Aid May Prolong War and Famine"—dance around the questions of political responsibility. As Perlez rightly states: "It is clearly no coincidence that the countries most menaced by famine this season are those that have

---

[3] Uncertain.

been mired in long civil wars. . . . Humanitarian policies of donating millions of tons of food to warring governments and rebels have helped prop up combatants who care little for the civilians they purport to represent."

25   Her words are vague and indecisive in comparison with a sharp and appropriately harsh piece co-authored the same week by London *Financial Times* Africa editor Michael Holman and correspondent Julian Ozanne in Nairobi: "Dictatorships and uncaring rebel groups, blinded by pride and a lust for power, have prepared the ground for the crisis . . . but outsiders also share the blame for the human catastrophe. Inadequate aid, frustration at a continent where disaster seems never-ending, and putting political considerations above humanitarian obligations have all compounded the crisis. U.S. patronage of corrupt and authoritarian regimes such as Liberia and Somalia has been matched by Soviet support for Ethiopia, while Angola suffered under the attention of both superpowers."

26   The blame for inadequate coverage does not lie primarily with the few reporters covering Africa for the U.S. mass media, but with editors, publishers and news directors who make Africa their lowest priority.

27   Each of Britain's "serious" dailies has a full-time Africa editor, backed up by correspondents or stringers in major capitals across the continent. Holman and Ozanne can credibly reach strong conclusions because they draw on their own reporting and that of other *Financial Times* correspondents who have been regularly covering the African famine on an almost daily basis for six months. The *New York Times*, by comparison, has no Africa editor, and divides responsibility for covering the 50 black-led nations of Africa between just two foreign correspondents.

28   British reporting on Africa is far from perfect, shaped as it has been by the malign[4] influence of colonial racism and post-colonial[5] preoccupation with British economic interests. Yet, whatever the reasons, African peoples and nations are visible in the British press. For the average American newspaper reader and TV viewer, the continent's 500 million people and 50 nations—spread across an area more than three times the size of the U.S.—are almost invisible.

Africa Reporting Through the Years

In its Dec. 4, 1964 issue, *Time* magazine reported on an uprising in what is now Zaire's Shaba province. "The rebels were, after all," the magazine said, "only a rabble of dazed ignorant savages."

When Shaba exploded again in 1978, Walter Cronkite opened the 6:30 P.M. feed of the CBS evening news for May 19 with these words:

---

[4] Evil.

[5] After the end of colonial rule.

> "Good evening. The worst fears in the rebel invasion of Zaire's Shaba province reportedly have been realized. Rebels being routed from the mining town of Kolwezi are reported to have killed a number of Europeans."
>
> (By the 7:00 feed, the lead had been rewritten to avoid the suggestion that white deaths were the worst possible development in a war whose casualties were overwhelmingly black.)
>
> More than a decade later, the U.S. media are all but silent on Zaire. Even the killings of between 60 and 150 Zaire university students by government troops in May 1990—reported widely in the European press and prompting a Belgian cutoff of aid and loans—went almost unnoticed.
>
> One television producer, who doesn't want to be named, suggests that the killings of the Zaire students failed to capture media attention for a familiar reason—the general negative image of the continent. If African despots kill their own citizens, the producer said, it isn't news, because the attitude is, "Well, what do you expect?"
>
> From "Capturing the Continent: U.S. Media Coverage of Africa." Africa News. 6/18/90.

REACTING

1. Do you share Jane Hunter and Steve Askin's concern that hunger in Africa is not fully reported by the U.S. media? List examples that seemed like strong or weak evidence to you.

2. What explanation do you give for the limited coverage of famine in Africa?

CONNECTING

1. How might Frances Moore Lappé and Joseph Collins ("There's Simply Not Enough Food," p. 202) comment on this article? Explain your answer.

2. Compare TV/newspaper coverage of hunger in Africa with coverage of domestic poverty and hunger in America. What conclusions do you come to?

LEARNING ABOUT WRITING FROM READING

This article shows how effectively writers can pile up examples as support for a main idea, or thesis. Hunter and Askin, in fact, have two sets of examples to back up their main statement that the media in the United States have not adequately covered hunger in Africa: one set comes from the U.S. media, and the other from the press in the United Kingdom. Thus they build up a comparison-and-contrast pattern: the British press has done well, but the American media, with a few exceptions, have failed. Alone, the examples of what the U.S. media haven't done are support for their opinion. But their argument is further strengthened by the comparison showing how another country's press has managed quite well, even under difficult circumstances.

KATHERINE VAN WORMER

A Society Without Poverty

Katherine van Wormer, an associate professor of social work at the University of Northern Iowa in Cedar Falls, tells us about her visit to Norway and what she learned about poverty and social policies there.

BEFORE YOU READ

1. Do you think that people cause their own poverty?
2. Is the government responsible for those living on very low incomes? To what extent?

1   Yes, there is another way.

2   I went to Norway to teach American methods of alcoholism treatment and to learn of life in a welfare state. My stay of almost two years informed me in the way that firsthand experience informs—rudely, indelibly.[1] My family and I have experienced the Norwegian community—the schools, social services, the health care system. And I have come to see how each dimension is connected to every other dimension of the cultural whole. In the high quality of life in Norway is the key to the larger pattern.

3   To the American visitor, the lack of poverty is striking, even puzzling. The outsider is inclined to see what *is* in terms of what is not: the southerner noting, for instance, the complete absence of palm trees. The Norwegian, meanwhile, is aware neither of the lack of poverty nor the absence of palm trees.

4   To understand the lack of poverty, you have to first understand poverty. And I am speaking of poverty in a rich society, there being no need to explain poverty in the absence of resources. The sociologists of the 1960s conceived of the existence of poverty in a prosperous society as functional for the total community. What were the social functions of poverty? (For a literature review, see Blau, 1988.) Poverty or the threat of poverty provided a steady pool of compliant[2] workers; poverty provided jobs for bureaucrats who were to ameliorate the poverty; the poverty of some provided for a natural division of classes. The existence of poverty in America is consistent with teachings of the Protestant ethic and the survival-of-the-fittest mentality.

5   Whereas Americans think individually, Norwegians tend to think collectively. Whereas Americans value competition, Norwegians value cooperation. The thesis of this article is that poverty persists in the United States because our values say it will persist. It does not persist in Norway because the society

---

[1] In a way that cannot be erased.
[2] Willing.

chooses not to tolerate it. This article examines the general economic conditions in Norway and views them against the Norwegian cultural context—values of egalitarianism[3] and the collective will, trust in the social system, and above all a tradition of kindness to the weaker members of society. Implications for the United States and for American social workers are drawn.

Norwegian Economy

6   Norway is a socialist country in terms of social policy but a capitalist nation in terms of the ownership of business. Because of Norwegian control of North Sea oil industries, a great deal of wealth is available to the nation. This fact helps compensate for the poor agricultural conditions—rocky, mountainous land and a short growing season.

7   Personal income taxes in Norway are among the highest in the world. The higher the income, the higher the percentage of taxes paid. The value-added tax is a sales tax of 20 percent on virtually all items sold. Consequently, food and services are extremely expensive in Norway.

8   Income differences across occupational groups are relatively slight. Virtually no group of employees earns more than twice the average earnings of all employees (Selbyg, 1987). The equalization of income is a reality in Norway.

Poverty

9   Official estimates put the percentage of people living in poverty at 16.0 percent in the United States and 4.8 percent in Norway (Zimbalist, 1988). In fact, these figures were based on relative income in each country. My personal impression is that the gap between poverty in the United States and Norway is much higher than the numbers indicate. Even in my work with alcoholics, I did not come across one truly impoverished person. When an individual gets into economic trouble, the state provides help. Statistics on poverty thus do not portray the reality in a cradle-to-grave, highly protective society.

10 Kohlert's (1989) description of the universalism philosophy in welfare is pertinent to Norway. Universalism views those in need as no different from other people. Benefits-for-all programs can effectively prevent the occurrence of poverty in the first place. Such programs as redistribution of wealth, guaranteed income, and children's allowance schemes are examples. Theoretically, benefits from the state are rights, not privileges, and schools teach children that they have earned them. No one will go homeless, hungry, or sick (Henriksen, 1988).

11 Norway's family policy provides a universal tax-free child allowance for all children younger than 16. Single mothers or fathers receive double the allowance for each child. Older children are eligible for educational stipends.[4] Actually, the amount of the family allowance, about $100 per child, is far below

---

[3] Belief in equality.

[4] Grants of money.

the cost of caring for a child and needs to be increased considerably to keep up with inflation. Elderly people are guaranteed a basic pension. In short, considerable sums are filtered through the tax and social systems to those who need assistance. The result is a society in which there are few truly rich or poor individuals.

Homelessness and Housing

12 Homelessness is simply not a problem in Norway as it is in some other countries. The government subsidizes low-cost housing so that adequate housing is available to everyone. If a person loses a home through inability to pay the rent, for instance, the social office will assist that person in finding other suitable housing. Housing and income are provided for refugees when they arrive. Like Sweden (Zimbalist, 1988), Norway has no deteriorated housing anywhere. Buildings are well-maintained and warmly heated. In many homes, flowers, visible through well-lighted windows, give a cheerful impression in all the neighborhoods.

Health Care

13 A recent feature article in the leading Oslo paper carried the headline "Norway Teaches USA on Health Services for Children" (1990). The medical professor interviewed in the article described an international conference attended in Washington, D.C. According to Professor Lie, "America totally lacks official health care for children. . . . In infant mortality and death of children due to violence and accidents, the USA is far ahead of Europe and Canada. Twenty-five percent of American children live in poverty" [author's translation] (p. 11).

14 The public health service and the hospitals are the responsibility of the government. A hospital stay is free, and medicine and primary health care cost minor sums. Mothers or fathers of newborn infants receive extended paid leaves of absence.

15 Present health policies give Norwegians one of the longest life expectancy rates in the world. Access to excellent health care is not available only to a certain class of citizens but to all members of society. In contrast to the United States, which has the best technology in health care in the world but lags behind other developed countries in coverage, care in Norway is readily available to all.

Norwegian Culture

16 Two countries of great natural resources and highly industrious people move in different directions. Why? The persistence of poverty in the United States and the elimination of poverty in the Nordic countries reflect the cultural values of the two respective countries. In the United States there are many opportunities, but the cost of failure is high; in Norway there is great security, but the cost of security is high.

17 Three dominant cultural orientations of Norwegians may provide clues to the economic structure: (1) egalitarianism and the collective ideal, (2) trust in

the social system, and (3) kindness toward the weak and vulnerable. These cultural orientations are consistent with those observed by Stevens (1989).

Egalitarianism and the Collective Ideal

18 The link between these dual concepts is in the tendency toward unity that is evidenced in all areas of Norwegian life. The stress on egalitarianism is exemplified in the organization of schools. Competition is largely absent. Children do not receive grades until they are 13, and then only rarely. Homework is minimal, and there are no special classes according to achievement level. Sports are noncompetitive as well; there are no school teams. There are no class officers. Teachers are addressed by their first names until the gymnasium, or high school. Norms favor belonging to the group and not rising above the group (Stevens, 1989).

19 Group conformity experiments by Milgram (1977) objectify the phenomenon[5] of the collective ideal. A cultural comparative study of conformity to group norms in Norway and France indicated that the pull toward conformity, even to obvious judgmental fallacies,[6] was significantly stronger among the Norwegians than among the French. In addition, although Norwegians accepted criticism impassively, the French subjects made pointed retaliatory responses.

20 "Do not stand out from the crowd" is the unwritten cultural norm. In my work in alcoholism treatment, the group was used to positive and compelling effect. Clients who were full of denial and minimization of their problems on day 1 seemed to all have undergone some sort of strange transformation by day 28. Never have I observed such consistent turnover of arguments and beliefs in treatment groups in the United States. Trust in the group is exceedingly strong in Norway (Ekstrom, 1988). The group in America is powerful, but in Norway it is more powerful still.

21 Woe to the group member in Norway who even mentioned connections with wealth or power! Indeed, the only insults uttered in the treatment groups were related either to lying or to bragging. "You are not one of us. You feel superior to the rest of the group" is a hard-hitting complaint.

22 This verbal enforcement of egalitarianism is reified in the tax system, which demands a heavy toll from those with high incomes, as well as in wage distribution. The disparity[7] in wages among occupational groups is slight (Selbyg, 1987). As they do in the United States, however, capitalists earning money from investments have available to them the usual loopholes that effectively preserve their control of the nation's wealth. The elimination of poverty does not always carry with it the elimination of great wealth. Every system is full of contradictions.

---

[5] Notable characteristic.
[6] Errors.
[7] Difference.

Trust in the Social System

23 Security is provided by the social system. Economic security is available to all, even to malingerers. Extended sick leave provides 100 percent of their pay to people suffering from such intangible[8] conditions as back pain and nervousness from stress. Money is provided by the employer for the first two weeks, then by the government thereafter.

24 Social workers have a great deal of authority within the social system, especially in regard to child welfare and public welfare. (For a critical analysis, see van Wormer, 1990.) Professionally trained practitioners work with families in need; they arrange for people in economic difficulty to receive allotments from the state. Because the stigma attached to receiving aid is absent or very slight, no stigma attaches to working at the "social office."

25 Trust in the system that is for the most part not corrupt and that provides help when needed is logical. A latent effect of the tendency to turn to the state for help is reflected in the small minority of elderly people who live with their families or in nursing homes. Most often they live in easily accessible apartment buildings, where they receive extensive home help and health care. The emphasis on independence, however, is often at the price of loneliness. The very system that takes care of sick and elderly people appears to reduce the responsibility of the family proportionately.

Kindness Toward the Weak and Vulnerable

26 Even the dogs do not bite in Norway; they rarely even bark. Owners of disobedient dogs speak quietly to them. These remarkable animals ride the trains with their owners and often accompany them to work. This illustrates one aspect of Norwegian life that is consistent with other aspects—kindness and nonaggression.

27 The kindness toward children in Norway is evidenced in law and social custom. Laws forbid corporal punishment against children by teachers and by parents. These laws are widely accepted and vigorously enforced. Norwegian visitors to the Anglo-American countries often remark on the shocking display of violence against children they encountered there. Americans, in contrast, often remark that children in Norway are babied and pampered. Indeed they are! Very large babies are pushed around in baby carriages and continue to take the bottle as long as they wish. They do not start school before age seven and are not taught to read before then.

28 Norway is not a punitive society. By international standards, criminals receive remarkably light sentences. The treatment of children, poor people, and even criminals is all of a pattern, and this pattern is characterized by individual and systematic kindness to people of all sorts.

---

[8] Cannot be touched or seen.

Implications for U.S. Social Policy

29 To grasp the meaning of poverty or its absence is to grasp the sense of cultural style. The poverty that exists so ubiquitously in America, North or South, and the poverty that is prevented in a country like Norway mirrors the larger system. To understand a living system, it is necessary to look at a constellation of factors, not in and of themselves, but in their relationships and in their contexts (Bateson, 1984). To know one living system in its uniqueness is to learn of another in terms of the contrast.

30 Change will come in the United States when the values begin to change and emulate those in Norway. Generally, the laws in a society are consistent with traditional or current values. Hoefer (1988) used the example of Sweden's shift in politics and social welfare policies to illustrate the theory of changes in personal values (postmaterialism) as related to structural change.

31 To change the social system with reference to poverty in the United States, the country will need to change its values. For instance, both the collective good and individual protections will have to be emphasized above individual growth. Leaders in both the public and private sectors will have to articulate this consciousness. Coverage in the mass media will help. Once a collective sense of urgency is established (such as a demand for national health care), the mobilization of forces to carry out the prerequisite tasks will follow. I emphasize the word "urgency" because a passive belief system will not suffice. The equivalent of wartime fervor,[9] however, would breed rapid mobilization and concomitant change.

32 Recently, U.S. national leaders talked of a "kinder, gentler society." Also, some action has been taken to shift from counterproductive defense spending to a reform of public welfare spending. Social workers, individually and as a profession, are speaking out for a reprioritizing[10] of interests (Day, 1989). The consensus of social workers seems to be that they must work toward policy change (Hartman, 1989). They must also work toward achieving value change. But whether these diverse "voices in the wilderness" will lead to institutionalization of the efforts will depend on the national sense of urgency and the belief that something can be done.

33 Meanwhile, Norway is an example of the possible. The solution is simple and described by Selbyg (1987) as follows: "Norway is a welfare state, a country where extensive systems of social care and social insurance make most residents who find themselves in a difficult economic situation legally entitled to aid from the government" (p. 72). Instead of the work ethic, a helping ethic prevails. This ethic is not an individualistic, Band-Aid approach but rather a universal, preventive one, a policy consistent with a value system based on care and absolute security. Norway has found another way and, in my opinion, a far better way.

---

[9] Passion; enthusiasm.
[10] Putting in a new order of importance.

References

Bateson, M. C. (1984). *With a daughter's eye: A memoir of Margaret Mead and Gregory Bateson.* New York: William Morrow.

Blau, J. (1988). On the uses of homelessness: A literature review. *Catalyst, 6*(2), 5–27.

Day, P. (1989). The new poor in America: Isolationism in an international political community. *Social Work, 34,* 227–232.

Ekstrom, J. (1988, July–August). *Cross cultural adaptation of drug and alcohol educational program.* Paper presented to the 35th International Congress on Alcoholism and Drug Dependency, Oslo, Norway.

Hartman, A. (1989). Homelessness: Public issue and private trouble [Editorial]. *Social Work, 34,* 483–484.

Henriksen, J. F. (1988). On being retired in Norway: Is the welfare state living up to expectations? *Norseman, 6,* 8–10.

Hoefer, R. (1988). Postmaterialism at work in social welfare policy: The Swedish case. *Social Service Review, 62,* 383–395.

Kohlert, N. (1989). Welfare reform: A historic consensus. *Social Work, 34,* 303–306.

Milgram, S. (1977). Nationality and conformity. In S. Milgram et al. (Eds.), *The individual in a social world: Essays and experiments* (pp. 159–173). Reading, MA: Addison-Wesley Press.

Norge laerer USA on helsetjeneste for barn. [Norway teaches USA about health services for children.] (1990, March 28). *Aftenposten,* p. 11.

Selbyg, A. (1987). *Norway Today.* Oslo: Norwegian University Press.

Stevens, R. (1989). Cultural values and Norwegian health services: Dominant themes and recurring dilemmas. *Scandinavian Studies, 61*(2–3), 199–212.

van Wormer, K. (1990). The hidden juvenile justice system in Norway: A journey back in time. *Federal Probation, 54*(1), 57–61.

Zimbalist, S. (1988). Winning the war on poverty: The Swedish strategy. *Social Work, 33,* 46–49.

REACTING

1. Would you like the United States to adopt the Norwegian model for dealing with poverty?

2. Through this article, Katherine van Wormer characterizes values and attitudes in the United States about poverty. Do you agree with her description? Why or why not?

CONNECTING

1. Pretend you are Jo Goodwin Parker ("What Is Poverty?" p. 198) reading this article. What is your response to Norway's approaches to the problems of poverty?

2. What common ground do Frances Moore Lappé and Joseph Collins ("There's Simply Not Enough Food," p. 202) have with the ideas here?

LEARNING ABOUT WRITING FROM READING

Van Wormer's article shows how a clear structure can make for easy reading. Throughout her article, van Wormer uses headings to alert readers to her main topics. And when she discusses Norwegian culture in the middle of her article (paragraph 17), she highlights three dominant traits by numbering them, by listing them, and by giving each one a separate heading in her subsequent discussion:

> Three dominant cultural orientations of Norwegians may provide clues to the economic structure: (1) egalitarianism and the collective ideal, (2) trust in the social system, and (3) kindness toward the weak and vulnerable.

This kind of outline helps the reader with comprehension and note taking. Although no one considers the outline to be the finest literary style, many are grateful for the easy reading it can provide.

CAROL BRADLEY SHIRLEY

Where Have You Been?

Carol Bradley Shirley, assistant editor of the Westside section of the Los Angeles Times, *brings insights and perspectives from that experience to this article on news coverage of inner-city areas.*

BEFORE YOU READ

1. Why do you think people rioted in Los Angeles after the Rodney King decision?
2. Do you think that the media cover events that are important in your community?

1   After the recent days of rage in South Central Los Angeles, journalists sifted through the rubble in search of the cause and they all came up with the same answer: racism. Not just black against white, but especially African-American against Korean-American.

2   I have no doubt that is what the reporters and editors believe. But I don't buy it. This was the powerless lashing out at the powerful. And the press is the voice of the powerful.

3   South Central Los Angeles has long been the kind of place that holds little interest for the powerful. It has been neglected for decades,[1] not only by the

---

[1] Ten-year periods.

government, but by the press. A perfect example of that is right here at the *Los Angeles Times*. The paper has community sections that cover the suburbs of Los Angeles County, Orange County—even Ventura County—but not a single page devoted to the center city. So what? you say.

4   Let's say you live in Santa Monica and someone wants to put a liquor store on your block. You don't want a liquor store on your block. You and some neighbors get together and make a couple of signs. You go to the city council. The Westside section of the *Times* is right there to report how you feel, and to let people know about the plans for the liquor store. Others read about it and join your little group. Soon your voice grows loud and is amplified by the coverage of the *Times*. Next thing you know, the council decides that a hearing is in order. You may not get your way, but you get a hearing.

5   If you live in South Los Angeles, as I do, you are on your own. Hundreds of people would have to show up at a council meeting before anyone in the press would take notice of your unhappiness with the plans for the liquor store. Another one goes up and there's not much you can do about it. And then another and another. Sooner or later, you give up. Anyone, it seems, can do anything he wants in the place where you live.

6   The kinds of businesses that have proliferated in South Los Angeles sap the strength of the area. Small liquor stores provide a powerful drug, but no jobs. The area is littered with places to spend money, but no place to earn it.

7   The city government and the press, the supposed public watchdogs, have stood by in silence. Sure, the press steps in when there is a riot or a shooting. Many a Pulitzer has been won by covering the woes of the inner city. But no one is there day to day to cover the issues that are standard in the coverage of any white middle-class area. While zoning and planning may not be a reporter's dream subjects, they provide the infrastructure of a community. When residents lose control of the infrastructure, they lose control of the community.

8   The newspapers say there are valid economic reasons for ignoring South Los Angeles and other areas like it. The industry calls it "bad demographics."[2] The people who live in these areas are not the kind of people advertisers want to reach. So advertisers and newspapers have a de facto pact to not serve a certain portion of the population, leaving it open to exploitation[3] from business and indifference by government. Some might call it institutional racism.

9   Don't get me wrong. I don't believe that there is some plot against the people of South Los Angeles in which the press is involved. What I do believe is that the press is so much a part of the establishment, so much a part of the inside, that it can no longer recognize what is before it. In the old days, reporters and editors were outsiders. We knew what was happening on the street because we came from the street, and we spoke for the disenfranchised.[4]

---

[2] Population statistics.
[3] Making use of people.
[4] People without a voice or a vote.

10   Today we wear three-piece suits and carry briefcases and drive in from the suburbs. We are attorneys with computers. Much of our reporting is done from our desks and our sources all belong to the club of power. Few of us belong to a minority group and fewer still come from the inner city. Those minority group members who have managed to break in have had to learn to conform to a white male standard of behavior to get along. Those who dare to challenge the prevailing perceptions are ignored or disbelieved and labeled "problems."

11   Although most people in my neighborhood had a horror story to tell about their treatment at the hands of the LAPD long before Rodney King, the papers ignored the issue of police brutality. If it didn't happen to the editors driving in from the suburbs then it didn't happen. No one in my neighborhood was surprised at the brutality of the videotape, but almost everyone in the newsroom expressed shock. Where had they been? Obviously not in South Central.

12   During the riots, we were all over South Los Angeles. We were doing what we do best: covering crisis. But the reason most of the reporters were out there was because it was a journalistic opportunity of a lifetime, not because their city was burning. To many who live in the area, it was just another form of exploitation. "Just doing my job" doesn't protect journalists anymore because people have begun to ask why the media weren't doing their job all along. What happens to South Los Angeles now depends a great deal on where the media will be now that all the fires are out.

13   *(In late June the* Times *announced plans for a Central City section.)*

REACTING

1. Do you agree that the media tend to ignore issues in low-income communities? What evidence would you give to support your view?
2. What changes does Carol Bradley Shirley recommend for better media coverage of low-income inner-city communities? If you were an editor, would you make those changes? What others would you make?

CONNECTING

1. Jerry Mander ("Freedom of Speech for the Wealthy," p. 207) also suggests that the media do not represent the poor well. What differences are there between the reasons and evidence that he and Shirley give?
2. What reasons might Jane Hunter and Steve Askin ("Hunger in Africa," p. 210) give for the lack of media coverage that Shirley describes?

LEARNING ABOUT WRITING FROM READING

You have a feeling as you read this article that Shirley is a real person. She chooses, even though she is a journalist, to write this article in the first person and in an informal style that suggests she is talking to you. What effect does this style have on your reading? To find out, you might want to rewrite paragraphs

2–5 in a more formal, third-person style, avoiding "I" and "you." What's lost or gained by the change in style?

WRITING ASSIGNMENTS

ASSIGNMENT I
WHAT MESSAGES DO THE MEDIA SEND ABOUT THE IMPORTANCE OF WEALTH? CHOOSE ONE OF THE MEDIA—AN ADVERTISEMENT, TV PROGRAM, SONG LYRIC—AND ANALYZE ITS MESSAGE ABOUT WEALTH.

Coming Up with Ideas and a Focus

It's clear you need to choose one example. If nothing immediately comes to mind, look at the day's TV listings or flip through a magazine for ideas. Once you've made a choice, use the chapter on analysis (p. 331) to come up with questions that will give you ideas about what parts of the example to emphasize in your discussion.

Organizing Your Ideas

You might organize your paper by telling the story of your research: why a particular subject drew your attention, what you discovered when you studied its parts, and what final conclusion you reached. Usually, it's helpful to the reader if early on in your paper you include a brief preview of your purpose and your findings. This preview will help keep the audience on track as they follow the stages of your research.

Audience

You might try addressing your classmates. Then, when all papers have been shared, there can be discussion of the way your ideas on media messages about wealth differed from one another. If you imagine your own argument about media messages competing with all the others in the class, you may be encouraged to sharpen your analysis and be even more persuasive about the validity of your findings.

ASSIGNMENT II
READ A CURRENT ISSUE OF A WEEKLY NEWSMAGAZINE. WHAT DOES IT TELL YOU ABOUT POVERTY IN THE UNITED STATES TODAY?

Coming Up with Ideas and a Focus

As you begin work on this paper, browse the newsstands and library shelves for likely publications. You will get most of your ideas from analyzing the magazine, keeping in mind the assignment's question as your focus: What does this magazine tell me about poverty in the United States? Note not only details about articles and editorials but also titles, images, pictures, and other design elements that seem significant. (For help with analysis, see p. 331.)

Organizing Your Ideas

This paper will involve a lot of description. It might be organized successfully within a statement-support outline, where you make a statement about what the magazine tells you about poverty in the United States and support it with a carefully selected description of the magazine's contents. (For help with statement-support papers, see pp. 305 and 365.)

Audience

Try writing this paper to inform an audience of high school students about the significance of a magazine they may often see but rarely think deeply about. If they haven't considered close analysis of a popular magazine, your paper would be a first step on that road.

ASSIGNMENT III
IF YOU COULD DO ONE THING TO SOLVE THE PROBLEM OF POVERTY IN THE UNITED STATES, WHAT WOULD IT BE?

Coming Up with Ideas and a Focus

Begin by brainstorming and freewriting about as many solutions to this huge problem as you can think of. Consider even apparently wild and crazy possibilities, at least to begin with. To find a focus, you will have to expand on just one of these. What will it be? What do you think has the most chance of working? Imagine that you have the power, just for a day, of making a real difference.

Organizing Your Ideas

A problem-solving model might provide a useful outline here. Simply present the problem briefly and then offer your solution in as much detail as assignment length allows.

Audience

Your choice of audience depends to a large extent on the solution you have in mind. If your purpose is to get the solution directly carried out, consider writing your paper as a letter to a senator or representative, or as a proposal to an employment commission or a local housing organization, for example. Direct the paper to any person or group that might have the power to use your ideas, if only you are persuasive enough!

ASSIGNMENT IV
WHY IS THERE SO MUCH POVERTY IN A COUNTRY AS WEALTHY AS THE UNITED STATES?

Coming Up with Ideas and a Focus

This is too big a question for one essay, so try to focus on one or two reasons that can be explored in detail. To begin, though, generate as long a list of reasons as you can, including even outlandish and off-beat ideas. Are people poor because they were born that way? Because they like being poor? Because there's a government conspiracy to keep a certain percentage of the population under the poverty level? Now make your choice from your list and go from there.

Organizing Your Ideas

When we answer the question "Why?" we usually begin with the word "because." So you might see your organizational pattern as a cause-and-effect outline: What are the causes of poverty in the United States today?

In what order will you present your causes? You might move from the least important to the most important cause, or deal with the main reasons and then address, in a brief final paragraph, some other possibilities for consideration.

Audience

This paper will work well if addressed to almost any group of people with a genuine interest in solving social problems but without expert knowledge. Your paper might aim to persuade them that poverty has causes that we can identify and perhaps even eliminate.

Chapter 7

Violence

KEY QUESTIONS

Why is America so violent?

How are we affected by violence portrayed in the media?

• •

In 1992, handguns killed 60 people in Japan, 33 in Great Britain, 97 in Switzerland, 128 in Canada, 36 in Sweden, 13 in Australia and 13,220 in the United States.
HANDGUN CONTROL, INC

Budget per episode of <u>Miami Vice</u>: $1,500,000; <u>annual</u> budget of the (real) Miami Vice Squad: $1,161,741.
THE HARPER'S INDEX BOOK.

The prison population doubled in the 80's. Over 100 prisons are being built at a cost of $70 billion. After war, prisons are the number one industry in America, permeating our economy and having little effect on crime.
WAR RESISTER'S LEAGUE, The Fortress Economy,
A.C. LICHTENSTEIN AND M.A. KRON AS REVIEWED IN "NONVIOLENT ACTIVIST"

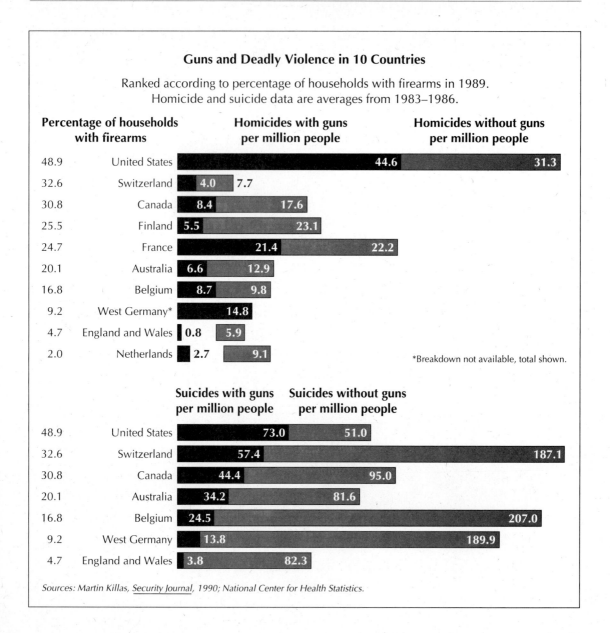

Introduction

Violence. On the screen it's excitement and thrills; but in real life it's fear and pain. Why are America's streets and homes violent, and what impact do the media have on our culture's level of violence and our willingness to accept it?

Consider the first question. Why do we have such a violent society? For all kinds of crimes, the United States ranks high. The number of people in U.S. prisons is among the highest in the world. Most of us, however, don't have to look at statistics to know that fear of theft and of physical violence is part of many Americans' lives.

Investigating violence in our culture might begin with a look at the topics in other chapters. For example, how is violence linked with gender roles, work, sports, and poverty? Does violence become more understandable when we see it as part of a culture's definition of maleness? Joan Meier's article, "Battered Justice," suggests that female and male gender roles play a part in the way that domestic violence is handled in our culture.

What other possible causes of violence are there? Perhaps violence is part of American culture's intense interest in sports, which often involve, if not actual violence, then achievement by physical strength and skill rather than by words and reason. Or, to take another angle, does poverty, or any other social disadvantage, breed an anger that finds release only in violent action? Some social critics and analysts maintain that violence always exists in an unjust society, that is, one with extremes of wealth and poverty. Mike Males's article "Public Enemy Number One?" follows this same line of reasoning.

Our culture's emphasis on competitive individualism and success might be another cause of violence. Outside observers of the United States often note how much the individual is stressed over the community: we take care of ourselves and we make ourselves. We are not bound to a community. Such an interest in individual success might make us more willing to strike out for ourselves—even in a criminal way.

Some say the cause is our gun laws, or lack of them. But that still leaves the question, "Why haven't we tightened our gun laws?" Jean Prokopow's article, "Get to the Root of Violence: Militarism," gives one possible answer: that our "militaristic" culture encourages us to accept, or even glorify, killing.

Many people claim that the media encourage violence. In videos, television, movies, and the lyrics and sounds of heavy metal, hard rock and the top forty, violence is dominant. Does this media violence stir up violence in our society, or does it just depict what is already out there? Do viewers distinguish between media violence and the real thing? Stephen King believes that horror in print or on the screen gives us a safe way to release the violence in our natures. Not everyone agrees that the media are blameless, though. Eugene Methvin, in "TV Violence: The Shocking New Evidence," cites experiments that show even our irritability is heightened by watching violence on television. In "On Rap, Symbolism and Fear," Jon Pareles cautions us to consider rap carefully and question whether all or any rappers promote violence.

In exploring the question "Why are we so violent?" you will certainly be considering how violence in the media affects us. But you may question whether the root cause of violence is to be found there, in other aspects of our complex culture, or in our own natures and personalities.

Starting Out: Finding Out What You Already Know

1. Write two quick paragraphs trying to answer the two key questions for this chapter: "Why is America so violent?" and "How are we affected by media violence?"
2. Freewrite for ten minutes about how your own life has been affected by violence.
3. Write about why you enjoy (or don't enjoy) horror films or action-packed police dramas. What's the attraction or revulsion?
4. Freewrite about an occasion when you were violent or when you stopped yourself from being as violent as you wanted to be.
5. Why do you think the United States has a much higher murder rate than that of other industrialized nations?

Learning More Through Observation: Taking a Look Around You and Talking to People

1. List five television shows or movies that are violent in some way. You might choose "Matlock," "Cops," or "Star Trek," or any of the James Bond movies, *Texas Chain Saw Massacre*, or even *Bambi*! Describe the kinds of violence that occur. How different are these movies and television shows from one another?
2. Think of the most violent real-life event you can remember. Describe it. Tell how the media reported it or might have reported it. (The answers to the last two questions may be almost identical.) Was it also a criminal act?
3. Interview someone 30 years or so older than you are to find out his or her views on violence in our culture.
4. Why do people get angry? Why does anger sometimes lead to violence?
5. Interview people your own age about times when they feel on the edge of violent action.

Questioning: Deciding What Else You Would Like to Know

List five questions that you still have about violence in American culture.

Mike Males

Public Enemy Number One?

Mike Males, freelance writer and psychology student, argues that the media do not play a major role in causing our culture's violence.

BEFORE YOU READ

1. How responsible is violence on television for real-life violence?
2. What makes people violent?

1. Forget about poverty, racism, child abuse, domestic violence, rape. America, from Michael Medved to *Mother Jones,* has discovered the real cause of our country's rising violence: television mayhem,[1] Guns N' Roses, Ice-T and Freddy Krueger.

2. No need for family support policies, justice system reforms or grappling with such distressing issues as poverty and sexual violence against the young. Today's top social policy priorities, it seems, are TV lockout gizmos, voluntary restraint, program labeling and (since everyone agrees these strategies won't work) congressionally supervised censorship. Just when earnest national soul-searching over the epidemic violence of contemporary America seemed unavoidable, that traditional scapegoat[2]—media depravity—is topping the ratings again.

3. What caused four youths to go on a "reign of terror" of beating, burning and killing in a New York City park in August 1954? Why, declared U.S. Sen. Robert Hendrickson, chair of the Juvenile Delinquency Subcommittee, the ringleader was found to have a "horror comic" on his person—proof of the "dangers inherent in the multimillion copy spate of lurid comic books that are placed upon the newsstands each month."

4. And what caused four youths to go on a brutal "wilding" spree, nearly killing a jogger in a New York City park in May 1989? Why, Tipper Gore wrote in *Newsweek,* the leader was humming the rap ditty "Wild Thing" after his arrest. Enough said.

5. Today, media violence scapegoating is not just the crusade of censorious conservatives and priggish preachers, but also of those of progressive stripe—from Sen. Paul Simon (D-IL) and Rep. Edward Markey (D-MA) to *Mother Jones* and columnist Ellen Goodman. "The average American child," Goodman writes, "sees 8,000 murders and 10,000 acts of violence on television before he or she is out of grammar school." Goodman, like most pundits, expends far more outrage on the sins of TV and rock 'n' roll than on the rapes and violent abuses millions of American children experience before they are out of grammar school.

6. The campaign is particularly craven in its efforts to confine the debate to TV's effects on children and adolescents even though the research claims that adults are similarly affected. But no politician wants to tell voters they can't see *Terminator II* because it might incite grownups to mayhem.

---

[1] Chaos, disorder.

[2] Someone taking the blame for others' wrongdoing.

7   Popular perceptions aside, the most convincing research, found in massive, multi-national correlational studies of thousands of people, suggests that, at most, media violence accounts for 1 to 5 percent of all violence in society. For example, a 1984 study led by media-violence expert Rowell Huesmann of 1,500 youth in the U.S., Finland, Poland and Australia, found that the amount of media violence watched is associated with about 5 percent of the violence in children, as rated by peers. Other correlational studies[3] have found similarly small effects.

8   But the biggest question media-violence critics can't answer is the most fundamental one: is it the *cause*, or simply one of the many *symptoms*, of this unquestionably brutal age? The best evidence does not exonerate[4] celluloid[5] savagery (who could?) but shows that it is a small, derivative influence compared to the real-life violence, both domestic and official, that our children face growing up in '80s and '90s America.

9   When it comes to the genuine causes of youth violence, it's hard to dismiss the 51 percent increase in youth poverty since 1973, 1 million rapes and a like number of violently injurious offenses inflicted upon the young every year, a juvenile justice system bent on retribution against poor and minority youth, and the abysmal neglect of the needs of young families. The Carter-Reagan-Bush eras added 4 million youths to the poverty rolls. The last 20 years have brought a record decline in youth well-being.

10   Despite claims that media violence is the best-researched social phenomenon in history, social sciences indexes show many times more studies of the effects of rape, violence and poverty on the young. Unlike the indirect methods of most media studies (questionnaires, interviews, peer ratings and laboratory vignettes),[6] child abuse research includes the records of real-life criminals and their backgrounds. Unlike the media studies, the findings of this avalanche of research are consistent: child poverty, abuse and neglect underlie every major social problem the nation faces.

11   And, unlike the small correlations or temporary laboratory effects found in media research, abuse-violence studies produce powerful results: "Eighty-four percent of prison inmates were abused as children," the research agency Childhelp USA reports in a 1993 summary of major findings. Separate studies by the Minnesota State Prison, the Massachusetts Correctional Institute and the Massachusetts Treatment Center for Sexually Dangerous Persons (to cite a few) find histories of childhood abuse and neglect in 60 to 90 percent of the violent inmates studied—including virtually all death row prisoners. The most

---

[3] Research projects that try to connect (or relate, in this case) real violence with violence watched in the media.

[4] To free from blame.

[5] The synthetic material from which movies are made.

[6] Quick sketch of a scene or event.

conservative study, that by the National Institute of Justice, indicates that some half-million criminally violent offenses each year are the result of offenders being abused as children.

12. Two million American children are violently injured, sexually abused or neglected every year by adults whose age averages 32 years, according to the Denver-based American Humane Association. One million children and teenagers are raped every year, according to the 1992 federally funded *Rape in America* study of 4,000 women, which has been roundly ignored by the same media outlets that never seem short of space to berate violent rap lyrics.

13. Sensational articles in *Mother Jones* ("Proof That TV Makes Kids Violent"), *Newsweek* ("The Importance of Being Nasty") and *U.S. News and World Report* ("Fighting TV Violence") devoted pages to blaming music and media for violence—yet all three ignored this study of the rape of millions of America's children. CNN devoted less than a minute to the study; *Time* magazine gave it only three paragraphs.

14. In yet another relevant report, the California Department of Justice tabulated 1,600 murders in 1992 for which offenders' and victims' ages are known. It showed that half of all teenage murder victims, six out of seven children killed, and 80 percent of all adult murder victims were slain by adults over age 20, not by "kids." But don't expect any cover stories on "Poverty and Adult Violence: The Real Causes of Violent Youth," or "Grownups: Wild in the Homes." Politicians and pundits know who not to pick on.

15. Ron Harris' powerful August 1993 series in the *Los Angeles Times*—one of the few exceptions to the media myopia on youth violence—details the history of a decade of legal barbarism against youth in the Reagan and Bush years—which juvenile justice experts now link to the late '80s juvenile crime explosion. The inflammatory, punishment-oriented attitudes of these years led to a 50 percent increase in the number of youths behind bars. Youth typically serve sentences 60 percent longer than adults convicted for the same crimes. Today, two-thirds of all incarcerated youth are black, Latino, or Native American, up from less than half before 1985.

16. Ten years of a costly "get tough" approach to deter youth violence concluded with the highest rate of crime in the nation's history. Teenage violence, which had been declining from 1970 through 1983, doubled from 1983 through 1991. It is not surprising that the defenders of these policies should be casting around for a handy excuse for this policy disaster. TV violence is perfect for their purposes.

17. This is the sort of escapism liberals should be exposing. But too many shrink from frankly declaring that today's mushrooming violence is the predictable consequence of two decades of assault, economic and judicial, against the young. Now, increasingly, they point at Jason, 2 Live Crew, and *Henry: Portrait of a Serial Killer*.

18. The insistence by such liberal columnists as Goodman and Coleman McCarthy that the evidence linking media violence to youth violence is on par

with that linking smoking to lung cancer represents a fundamental misunderstanding of the difference between biological and psychological research. Psychology is not, despite its pretensions, a science. Research designs using human subjects are vulnerable to a bewildering array[7] of confusing factors, many not even clear to researchers. The most serious (but by no means only) weakness is the tendency by even the most conscientious researchers to influence subjects to produce the desired results. Thus the findings of psychological studies must be swallowed with large grains of salt.

19   Consider a few embarrassing problems with media violence research. First, many studies (particularly those done under more realistic "field conditions") show no increase in violence following exposure to violent media. In fact, a significant number of studies show no effect, or even decreased aggression. Even media-violence critic Huesmann has written that depriving children of violent shows may actually increase their violence.

20   Second, the definitions of just what constitutes media "violence," let alone what kind produces aggression in viewers, are frustratingly vague. Respected researchers J. Singer and D. Singer found in a comprehensive 1986 study that "later aggressive behavior was predicted by earlier heavy viewing of public television's fast-paced *Sesame Street*." The Parent's Music Resource Center heartily endorsed the band U2 as "healthy and inspiring" for youth to listen to—yet U2's song "Pistol Weighing Heavy" was cited in psychiatric testimony as a key inspiration for the 1989 killing of actress Rebecca Schaeffer.

21   Third, if, as media critics claim, media violence is the, or even just a, prime cause of youth violence, we might expect to see similar rates of violence among all those exposed to similar amounts of violence in the media, regardless of race, gender, region, economic status, or other demographic[8] differences. Yet this is far from the case.

22   Consider the issue of race. Surveys show that while black and white families have access to similar commercial television coverage, white families are much more likely to subscribe to violent cable channels. Yet murder arrests among black youth are now 12 times higher than among white, non-Hispanic youth, and increasing rapidly. Are blacks genetically more susceptible to television violence than whites? Or could there be other reasons for this pattern—perhaps the 45 percent poverty rates and 60 percent unemployment rates among black teenagers?

23   And consider also the issue of gender. Girls watch as much violent TV as boys. Yet female adolescents show remarkably low and stable rates of violence. Over the last decade or so, murders by female teens (180 in 1983, 171 in 1991) stayed roughly the same, while murders by boys skyrocketed (1,476 in 1983, 3,435 in 1991). How do the media-blamers explain that?

---

[7] Impressive collection or display.

[8] Related to a particular population.

24   Finally, consider the issue of locale. Kids see the same amount of violent TV all over, but many rural states show no increases in violence, while in Los Angeles, to take one example, homicide rates have skyrocketed.

25   The more media research claims are subjected to close scrutiny, the more their contradictions emerge. It can be shown that violent people do indeed patronize more violent media, just as it can be shown that urban gang members wear baggy clothes. But no one argues that baggy clothes cause violence. The coexistence of media and real-life violence suffers from a confusion of cause and effect: is an affinity for violent media the result of abuse, poverty and anger, or is it a prime cause of the more violent behaviors that just happen to accompany those social conditions? In a 1991 study of teenage boys who listen to violent music, the University of Chicago's Jeffrey Arnett argues that "[r]ather than being the cause of recklessness and despair among adolescents, heavy metal music is a reflection of these [behaviors]."

26   The clamor over TV violence might be harmless were it not for the fact that media and legislative attention are rare, irreplaceable resources. Every minute devoted to thrashing over issues like violence in the media is one lost to addressing the accumulating,[9] critical social problems that are much more crucial contributors to violence in the real world. In this regard, the media-violence crusade offers distressing evidence of the profound decline of liberalism as America's social conscience, and the rising appeal (even among progressives)[10] of simplistic Reaganesque answers to problems that Reaganism multiplied many times over.

27   Virtually alone among progressives, columnist Carl T. Rowan has expressed outrage over the misplaced energies of those who have embraced the media crusade and its "escapism from the truth about what makes children (and their parents and grandparents) so violent." Writes Rowan: "I'm appalled that liberal Democrats . . . are spreading the nonsensical notion that Americans will, to some meaningful degree, stop beating, raping and murdering each other if we just censor what is on the tube or big screen. . . . The politicians won't, or can't deal with the real-life social problems that promote violence in America . . . so they try to make TV programs and movies the scapegoats! How pathetic!"

28   Without question, media-violence critics are genuinely concerned about today's pandemic violence. As such, it should alarm them greatly to see policymakers and the public so preoccupied with an easy-to-castigate[11] media culprit linked by their research to, at most, a small part of the nation's violence—while the urgent social problems devastating a generation continue to lack even a semblance of redress[12].

---

[9] Piling up, increasing.

[10] Liberals in politics.

[11] Punish.

[12] Correction, remedy.

Hollywood Shuffles

The campaign against television violence has had a bracing side effect: suddenly, Hollywood is gun-control crazy. The effect of having to acknowledge that television violence has any social consequences has perked up every producer's interest in far larger sources of violence in the society—such as guns. Maybe they'll eventually notice poverty and racism as well.

Still, just because television violence isn't the only cause of violence in the real world, we shouldn't claim that it doesn't matter at all. True, social science research on violence and television has all the flaws common to social science: lack of control groups, difficulty in sorting out independent variables, influencing the subject. That's why social scientists refuse to depend on one study to refute another. Instead, they look for trends and similar kinds of results.

After decades of research and hundreds of studies, there is a general consensus that watching violence on television is correlated—even accounting for other social variables like poverty—with increased aggressive behavior, fearfulness and depression. Yes, such correlations are affected by other powerful social factors, such as gender. But that doesn't mean they don't exist.

The data on violence and TV comes under fierce scrutiny by an industry eager to conduct its business with no strings attached. But you have to wonder about the intellectual honesty of those TV executives who claim that their shows have no impact—especially when the sales department is busy drumming up advertising business on the strength of the power of television to persuade and move to action.

Violence has been more thoroughly studied than any other behavior on television. These studies have been funded over the years, in part, by a Congress happy to play on the anxieties of a moralistic public. But the debate over violence may help to force the issue of television's social effects into public discussion—although, as Paul Simon (D-IL) has repeatedly warned the industry, the dangers of setting harmful First Amendment precedents are real.

TV violence, though, may be far less important to society than television's incessant dunning of commercial consciousness, its commodification of emotions, its exploitation of passion and desire. If you think measuring the social impact of violence in a way that the industry will acknowledge is hard, it pales before the challenge of assessing (credibly enough to take policy action) the social impact of TV's emotional exploitations.

—Pat Aufderheide

REACTING

1. What statistics in Mike Males's article seemed most important to you? Why?
2. Do you agree with Males or with Aufderheide's editorial reaction to his article?

CONNECTING

1. Turn to p. 243 and read Jon Pareles's "On Rap, Symbolism and Fear." Make a list of the similarities and differences between Males's and Pareles's articles. Are they basically in agreement? Give reasons for your answer.
2. Turn to p. 249 and read Stephen King's "Why We Crave Horror Movies." What do you think Males's response would be to King's ideas?

LEARNING ABOUT WRITING FROM READING

You often hear, "You can't trust statistics." It is probably truer to say "All statistics must be examined." In his article Males leads the reader through a series of questions about statistics and other kinds of evidence. He puts his own thinking and questioning down on paper for the reader to follow.

When he questions the evidence that the media cause violence, he asks (paragraph 20) how media violence is defined. Then he goes on to ask why violent behavior isn't the same for all races, genders, income levels, and regions if, indeed, the media are the prime cause. In paragraphs 22–24 he explores that question in detail, starting the paragraphs with clear topic sentences:

Consider the issue of race.

And consider also the issue of gender.

Finally, consider the issue of locale.

Analysis of evidence can be complex, but Males guides us clearly, step-by-step, through the maze.

JEAN PROKOPOW

Get to the Root of Violence: Militarism

Jean Prokopow, national vice president of Women's Action for New Directions, examines the role of militarism in creating our violent culture.

BEFORE YOU READ

1. What is "militarism"?
2. The United States has been described both as a militaristic country and as the world's peacekeeping force. Which description seems more accurate? Give reasons.

1   Violence in America. Political candidates call for more police on the streets. Congress debates a major crime bill. The Brady Bill, a modest proposal to require a five-day waiting period before the purchase of a handgun, is now the law. Do these "solutions" eliminate root causes?

2   We know some of the causes: Many prisoners cannot read; most were abused as children; more crime occurs in areas of poverty. These contributing factors seem obvious. But are there other, more subtle ways in which violence is promoted? We in Women's Action for New Directions are digging deeper for less visible components of America's love affair with violence.

3   Militarism is a possibility. The dictionary definition of militarism is: "the principle of maintaining a large military establishment, and a tendency to regard military efficiency as the supreme ideal of the state."

4   The connection is clear within U.S. budget allotments. This fiscal year alone, Congress spent $291 billion on the military, more than 50 percent of all discretionary spending. Bombs and bullets get the bucks, while more than one of five American children live below the poverty level.

5   A less obvious connection is the possibility that military attitudes and behavior rub off on society. What behaviors are necessary to military success? Domination, top-down communication and glorification of violence are mandatory.

6   Militarism assumes that when there is disagreement, one country must prevail[1]. Soldiers are indoctrinated to accept killing, and are taught the necessary skills. When militarism reigns, civilians adopt the belief that differences in opinions, ethnicity or race inevitably require a struggle for dominance. Oppression, and sometimes violence, result.

7   Battlefield success requires unquestioning obedience. But true democracy requires questioning minds and free political discourse. The warrior culture provides the exact opposite of the attitudes necessary for democracy. Militarism justifies secrecy in the name of national security. Recent revelations about nuclear experimentation on uninformed people present glaring evidence of the consequences of such secrecy.

8   Militarism not only promotes violence, it glorifies violence. There always has been violence in literature, but now it is more pervasive than ever, and more graphic. Its assault on the senses is global, and yet the way it is depicted is often desensitizing.[2] Violence has spilled over into the toy industry. During the '80s, sales of violent war toys increased 800 percent, paralleling the huge arms buildup of the same period.

9   Forty-five years of Cold War attitudes and behavior have militarized American society in a way never envisioned by our Founding Fathers. Domination over others is preferred, democratic and open discussion is subordinated[3] to claimed military necessity, and violence is sanctioned as the appropriate and exciting response to conflict.

10   The post-Cold War period demands a lot more than the dismantling of weapons. If we truly want to eradicate violence in America, we must give up our love affair with it.

---

[1] Win.

[2] Having the effect of numbing people to violence.

[3] Made less important.

REACTING

1. Write a letter to the editor either supporting or attacking Jean Prokopow's guest editorial column.
2. Do we, American citizens, really have a "love affair with violence," as the author suggests? Why do you think so?

CONNECTING

1. Do the data in the chart on p. 241 support Prokopow's view that militarism is the root cause of violence in the United States?
2. With a partner, discuss the root causes of violence. One of you take the viewpoint of Mike Males ("Public Enemy Number One?", p. 232) and the other Prokopow's.

LEARNING ABOUT WRITING FROM READING

We hope that your experiences in writing courses will give you the confidence and ability to write letters to the editor and guest editorials. Exchanges of opinion and information are part of a working democracy. Prokopow's guest column is a model of good newspaper communication.

- The headline (chosen by the editor) tells you Propkopow's main point.
- She only develops one idea. This is important for the short, clear style expected by newspaper readers. She argues that although there are other causes of violence, militarism is the root cause and she gives reasons to support that point.
- She keeps her essay to about 500 words, the usual limit for guest columns. The limit for letters to the editor is generally 250 words.

Look at the Letters to the Editor section in a newspaper and see what makes some of the letters more readable than others.

JON PARELES

On Rap, Symbolism and Fear

Jon Pareles, New York Times *music critic, examines common stereotypes about rap music and rappers.*

BEFORE YOU READ

1. Finish this sentence: The kind of people who like rap music are. . . .
2. Is rap music dangerous?

1   Over the last decade rap has become the epicenter¹ of popular music and a significant influence on fashion, visual arts and language. But to much of the American mainstream, rap is an outlaw music that otherwise well-informed people vilify and fear. Rap marks a generation gap. As young people dance to it, some elders pronounce it unlistenable and others are disturbed by its messages. There's a perception gap, too, reinforced by media, both responsible and irresponsible, that reflexively connect rap and violence. The reasons generally have less to do with rap's rhetoric than with larger tensions of race and class.

2   Trouble at the movie "Juice"? Commentators point not just to its crime-story plot, but to its rap soundtrack. (No riots have been reported, however, at "The Addams Family," which has a theme song by Hammer.) People trampled to death at an ineptly² promoted, poorly policed basketball game at City College in New York? Out come the statistics about violence at rap concerts, although the rap celebrities were invited to shoot hoops, not to perform.

3   No one considered it odd when City College revealed it has a standing policy against presenting rap-related events; imagine the reaction if klezmer³ or country music were prohibited. And when, shortly after the City College deaths, three times as many people gathered without arrests or major incidents for a rap concert at Madison Square Garden, at least one television correspondent played up a minor altercation as if it eclipsed the whole show. Television, tabloids and some newspaper columnists tend to present rap as one indivisible, alien morass,⁴ "an increasingly sociopathic⁵ form of pop music," quoth one *Washington Post* contributor.

4   Rap gets plenty of publicity when it turns most offensive. When Ice Cube spews racist demagoguery⁶ on his album "Death Certificate," or when Public Enemy releases a video clip that sets out to honor Martin Luther King Jr. by killing a fictitious senator and governor of Arizona, shows like "Nightline" pay attention.

5   But too many people leap from a handful of lyrics to blanket denunciations. The bulk of rap lyrics, in fact, completely ignore whites, to concentrate on boasting and lately, lectures on black self-help. While rap-haters focus on the racism of Ice Cube and the sex-and-guns fantasies of N.W.A., they tend to ignore the many rappers who plead for an end to violence, and who find a wide audience. Chubb Rock, for instance, had a No. 1 single on Billboard's rap chart with "Treat 'Em Right," which urges fellow rappers to bring "decency" back to

---

¹ Focal point.
² Inefficiently.
³ Jewish musicians once banned in Europe from playing at Christian festivals or even Jewish weddings.
⁴ Swamp.
⁵ Hostile to society.
⁶ Appeals to the masses.

lyrics and tells would-be gang warriors, "Leave the knife and gun in the store and ignore temptation."

6. Hip-hop culture, which also includes dancing, fashion and visual arts, has been widely available for at least 13 years—longer in the right neighborhood. As early as 1974, disk jockeys in the South Bronx were chopping up and recombining music on multiple turntables, and they were soon joined by rhyming rappers. In 1979, the Sugar Hill Gang released "Rapper's Delight," the single that announced the arrival of a new genre. Kurtis Blow took rap further up the pop charts with "The Breaks" in 1980; Blondie's "Rapture," the first white rap hit, followed in 1981.

7. In pop terms, that ought to be ancient history. By the time rock-and-roll was 13 years old, in the mid-1960's only the most lunatic of fringes still denounced the entire genre as a threat to public morals and safety. Rap hasn't had it so easy. There are still some people proclaiming that it's not music, and more who are convinced that rap exists only to incite violence, corrupt children and destroy all that is good and decent.

8. Why hasn't rap's success, with performers ranging from Run-D.M.C. to Hammer to P.M. Dawn, made it just another branch of entertainment, taken for granted? Obviously, rap has become a symbol in a United States obsessed with race.

9. Representative Barney Frank, the Massachusetts Democrat, wrote in *The New York Times* that contemporary political campaigns use crime as "a marker for race." Rap is an even more precise marker; despite the growing number of rappers who are white, female, suburban or all three, rap is still overwhelmingly made by young, black, urban males—a demographic segment that many Americans consider threatening. Hating rap, a purportedly esthetic judgment, can be a synonym for hating and fearing young black men.

10. Yet clear-cut racism is only part of the anti-rap sentiment. As a matter of taste, hip-hop does challenge older pop esthetics. Unless a rap song lifts a whole melodic hook from an older song, as Hammer does, it's likely to be atonal or tuneless, building its catchiness on a slogan, a rhythm or a sound effect—closer to non-Western music than to Tin Pan Alley. In that, however, it is part of a larger trend in popular music; other styles like speed-metal and industrial rock also downplay melody in favor of rhythm, texture and impact. To listeners weaned on the jolting jump-cuts and assertive self-promotion of television and the electronic soundscape of video games, rap sounds familiar. If it annoys parents, all the better.

11. Rap is also foreground music, abrasive and insistent, perfect for blasting from a club sound system or a portable boom box or a car stereo; people who use Bach or Bon Jovi as congenial background music are irritated by the noise. But opera also shrieks for attention, and it doesn't trigger the kind of self-righteous response that rap does.

12. Some reactions against rap involve historic friction among races and classes. In "Popular Musics of the Non-Western World" (Oxford University

Press, 1988), Peter Manuel writes that new kinds of music usually arise from "an unassimilated,[7] disenfranchised, impoverished, socially marginalized class." Styles as far flung as Greek rebetika, Jamaican reggae, Argentine tango and American jazz have all trickled up from outcast or gangster netherworlds, eventually to be embraced by middle and upper classes (some seeking vicarious thrills) while drawing widespread denunciations on the way up. In that, hip-hop is true to form.

13   But when suburbia embraced hip-hop during the 1980's, the alarmist reactions only increased. For one thing rap remains defiantly unassimilated, profane[8] and disdainful[9] of middle-class proprieties. In the mainstream American imagination, blacks have historically been considered the Other, the opposite of the mainstream's genteel self-image. That mysterious, imagined Other is considered uncivilized, sex-crazed, irrational, angry.

14   Hip-hop, many commentators have inveighed, is intended solely to spur violence, race hatred and general lawlessness. Not so coincidentally, that's what those commentators fear from an urban black population whose prospects deteriorated steadily through the 1980's.

15   It's not hard to detect signs of a guilty conscience projected onto the Other. Rap often sounds like a young black man shouting; what else would he be shouting about, thinks a listener who can't understand all the words, but how angry he is at people like me? And how he's going to hurt us?

16   Rap is not so single-minded. Hundreds of thousands of words have been rapped on recordings in the last decade, on innumerable subjects: Egyptology, sex, sneakers, gang vendettas, the recession. Chuck D. of Public Enemy has compared rap to a black cable-news network, but rap also has something in common with citizens'-band radio and computer bulletin boards. Rap mixes public messages and private references, distress calls and jokes, information and fiction, retorts and pontifications. Sensationalism and images of violence appear, along with occasional glints of racism.

17   Rappers, of course, are not philosopher-kings. Like rock musicians, many rappers are immature or stupid or wildly egotistical, and they don't always hang out with the nicest people. Some rappers use criminal records as proof of authenticity, as Leadbelly did in the 1930's. And some, recognizing that outlaw images sell, set out to shock and titillate, claiming the same artistic license as the makers of, say, "A Nightmare on Elm Street." If young black men are to be stereotyped, their raps suggest, then they'll exaggerate the stereotype as far as it will go.

18   To be "hard"—to please a hypothetical "street" audience that will only accept the most brutal scenarios—too many rappers confuse manliness with misogyny and homophobia. Gangster rap, rap's equivalent of action-adventure films, offers frightening messages in abundance, for those who want to find them.

---

[7] Left out; rejected.

[8] Unholy.

[9] Scornful.

19   Many political rappers are followers of the Rev. Louis Farrakhan's Nation of Islam, whose message of black self-reliance has been widely criticized for invoking anti-white and anti-Semitic racism. Farrakhan-ite rappers tend to be more circumspect, saying "devils" instead of "white devils" and usually condemning the system rather than the race of the people who run it. Lately, Public Enemy and other rappers have denounced self-destructive elements among blacks—drug dealers, gangsters, alcoholics—as much as they've attacked outsiders. But Public Enemy gets far more attention for its blunders, like the video clip for "By the Time I Get to Arizona," which ignores Martin Luther King Jr.'s philosophy and chooses revenge (and machismo) over persuasion.

20   Even at its rare racist extremes, rap simply picks up demagogic ideas that have long been heard on ghetto streets, allowing them to be monitored—and answered—and reminding a wider public that racism can cut two ways. Sensible or virulent, rap also continues to be a voice of the disenfranchised; unlike David Duke, no rapper has yet been a serious contender for public office.

21   David Samuels, writing in *The New Republic* (Nov. 11), contended that gangster raps and racist raps (which he conflates with all of rap) foster a "voyeurism and tolerance of racism in which black and white are both complicit," particularly when whites treat gangster raps as a window into ghetto life. But only a naïve listener would fail to distinguish between tall tales and reportage.

22   As a business, hip-hop has problems akin to early jazz and early rock-and-roll: a mixture of honest and fly-by-night entrepreneurs, some of whom exploit both performers and fans. And yes, rap audiences, with some members from poor, crime-wracked communities, can include troublemakers. But the vast majority of concert goers are happy to see metal detectors and extensive security, and rappers on stage invariably urge audiences to stay peaceful. The sensationalist image of rappers inciting slavering hordes to acts of mayhem has no basis in reality.

23   Rap's internal troubles reflect the poverty, violence, lack of education, frustration and rage of the ghetto. Yet in the end, rap is not a way of exporting those troubles, but a way of transcending them.

24   People who can't afford musical instruments or lessons—and who aren't getting much music education in the wake of school budget cuts—have made their own music with turntables, changing the passive act of playing records into the active creation of new songs. People who might be proving their toughness in street fights are, instead, proving themselves with elaborate boasts and taunts, trading physical threat for verbal dexterity.[10] Rap has also provided new, legitimate avenues for entrepreneurs and technicians—it testifies to the spirit of free enterprise.

25   It's time to recognize what rap is: a huge, varied symbolic realm, too big to be stereotyped. There are smart rappers and idiotic ones, positive forces and nasty ones, rappers who want to teach and rappers who want to pander

---

[10] Skill.

and rappers who just want to make people laugh. Until rap is treated as something other than a terrifying monolith,[11] people within hip-hop may well be justified in thinking that, to the outside world, they all look alike.

REACTING

1. Did Jon Pareles's article change your view of rap music? Explain.
2. Write a letter to the editor responding to what Pareles says about rap.

CONNECTING

1. Turn to p. 249 and read Stephen King's "Why We Crave Horror Movies." What might King's response to Pareles be?
2. How do you think Pareles would answer the chapter's key question: "Why is America so violent?"?

LEARNING ABOUT WRITING FROM READING

Pareles knows that examples catch our interest and make points in a way that the reader is likely to remember. He gives three examples of prejudice against rap at the beginning. He develops them by staying with them long enough for the examples to make several key points and by using them to compare media responses to rap concerts and other public events:

> Trouble at the movie "Juice?" Commentators point not just to its crime-story plot, but to its rap soundtrack. (No riots have been reported, however, at "The Addams Family," which has a theme song by Hammer.) People trampled to death at an ineptly promoted, poorly policed basketball game at City College in New York? Out come the statistics about violence at rap concerts, although the rap celebrities were invited to shoot hoops, not to perform.
>
> No one considered it odd when City College revealed it has a standing policy against presenting rap-related events; imagine the reaction if klezmer or country music were prohibited. And when, shortly after the City College deaths, three times as many people gathered without arrests or major incidents for a rap concert at Madison Square Garden, at least one television correspondent played up a minor altercation as if it eclipsed the whole show.

These concrete examples are a good start. Now the reader also has to ask if they are persuasive.

---

[11] Single entity.

STEPHEN KING

Why We Crave Horror Movies

Stephen King, author of many horror novels, tries to answer the question suggested by his article's title.

BEFORE YOU READ

1. Why do you crave (or avoid) horror movies? List your reasons.
2. If you have heard of Stephen King or have read any of his books, try to guess what he is going to say about why we desire horror movies.

1   I think that we're all mentally ill; those of us outside the asylums only hide it a little better—and maybe not all that much better, after all. We've all known people who talk to themselves, people who sometimes squinch[1] their faces into horrible grimaces when they believe no one is watching, people who have some hysterical fear—of snakes, the dark, the tight place, the long drop . . . and, of course, those final worms and grubs that are waiting so patiently underground.

2   When we pay our four or five bucks and seat ourselves at tenth-row center in a theater showing a horror movie, we are daring the nightmare.

3   Why? Some of the reasons are simple and obvious. To show that we can, that we are not afraid, that we can ride this roller coaster. Which is not to say that a really good horror movie may not surprise a scream out of us at some point, the way we may scream when the roller coaster twists through a complete 360 or plows through a lake at the bottom of the drop. And horror movies, like roller coasters, have always been the special province of the young; by the time one turns 40 to 50, one's appetite for double twists or 360-degree loops may be considerably depleted[2].

4   We also go to re-establish our feelings of essential normality; the horror movie is innately[3] conservative[4], even reactionary. Freda Jackson as the horrible melting woman in *Die, Monster, Die!* confirms for us that no matter how far we may be removed from the beauty of a Robert Redford or a Diana Ross, we are still light-years from true ugliness.

5   And we go to have fun.

6   Ah, but this is where the ground starts to slope away, isn't it? Because this is a very peculiar sort of fun, indeed. The fun comes from seeing others menaced—sometimes killed. One critic has suggested that if pro football has become

---

[1] Squeeze and pinch.
[2] Reduced.
[3] Intrinsically; essentially.
[4] Traditional; not radical or revolutionary.

the voyeur's version of combat, then the horror film has become the modern version of the public lynching.

7   It is true that the mythic, "fairy-tale" horror film intends to take away the shades of gray . . . it urges us to put away our more civilized and adult penchant for analysis and to become children again, seeing things in pure blacks and whites. It may be that horror movies provide psychic relief on this level because this invitation to lapse into simplicity, irrationality[5] and even outright madness is extended so rarely. We are told we may allow our emotions a free rein . . . or no rein at all.

8   If we are all insane, then sanity becomes a matter of degree. If your insanity leads you to carve up women like Jack the Ripper or the Cleveland Torso Murderer, we clap you away in the funny farm (but neither of those two amateur-night surgeons was ever caught, heh-heh-heh); if, on the other hand, your insanity leads you only to talk to yourself when you're under stress or to pick your nose on your morning bus, then you are left alone to go about your business . . . though it is doubtful that you will ever be invited to the best parties.

9   The potential lyncher is in almost all of us (excluding saints, past and present; but then, most saints have been crazy in their own ways), and every now and then, he has to be let loose to scream and roll around in the grass. Our emotions and our fears form their own body, and we recognize that it demands its own exercise to maintain proper muscle tone. Certain of these emotional muscles are accepted—even exalted—in civilized society; they are, of course, the emotions that tend to maintain the status quo of civilization itself. Love, friendship, loyalty, kindness—these are all the emotions that we applaud, emotions that have been immortalized[6] in the couplets of Hallmark cards and in the verses (I don't dare call it poetry) of Leonard Nimoy.

10   When we exhibit these emotions, society showers us with positive reinforcement; we learn this even before we get out of diapers. When, as children, we hug our rotten little puke of a sister and give her a kiss, all the aunts and uncles smile and twit and cry, "Isn't he the sweetest little thing?" Such coveted treats as chocolate-covered graham crackers often follow. But if we deliberately slam the rotten little puke of a sister's fingers in the door, sanctions follow—angry remonstrance from parents, aunts and uncles; instead of a chocolate-covered graham cracker, a spanking.

11   But anticivilization emotions don't go away, and they demand periodic exercise. We have such "sick" jokes as, "What's the difference between a truckload of bowling balls and a truckload of dead babies?" (You can't unload a truckload of bowling balls with a pitchfork . . . a joke, by the way, that I heard originally from a ten-year-old). Such a joke may surprise a laugh or a grin out of us even as we recoil, a possibility that confirms the thesis: If we share a

---

[5] Lack of reason.
[6] Enabled to live forever.

brotherhood of man, then we also share an insanity of man. None of which is intended as a defense of either the sick joke or insanity but merely as an explanation of why the best horror films, like the best fairy tales, manage to be reactionary, anarchistic, and revolutionary all at the same time.

12   The mythic horror movie, like the sick joke, has a dirty job to do. It deliberately appeals to all that is worst in us. It is morbidity[7] unchained, our most base instincts let free, our nastiest fantasies realized . . . and it all happens, fittingly enough, in the dark. For those reasons, good liberals often shy away from horror films. For myself, I like to see the most aggressive of them—*Dawn of the Dead*, for instance—as lifting a trap door in the civilized forebrain and throwing a basket of raw meat to the hungry alligators swimming around in that subterranean river beneath.

13   Why bother? Because it keeps them from getting out, man. It keeps them down there and me up here. It was Lennon and McCartney who said that all you need is love, and I would agree with that.

14   As long as you keep the gators fed.

REACTING

1. Were you surprised by any of Stephen King's reasons for our love of horror films? What other reasons would you add, or give in place of King's?
2. Is King right that horror movies do us some good?

CONNECTING

1. Turn to p. 252 and read Eugene Methvin's "TV Violence: The Shocking New Evidence." What would Methvin say about King's idea that we love horror films because our "insane" side needs to be satisfied safely? Write a dialogue of their conversation.
2. If Mike Males ("Public Enemy Number One?" p. 234) read King's article, what would he say to King?

LEARNING ABOUT WRITING FROM READING

Notice how King uses the basic statement-and-support pattern to organize his argument in an entertaining and convincing way. He doesn't just give one reason why we crave horror movies, and this strengthens his argument. Something so complex as people's attraction to horror is likely to have more than one reason. His essay is a list of reasons, but the order is important. Why does he put "we need to keep the gators fed" last?

---

[7] Obsession with disease and death.

EUGENE H. METHVIN

TV Violence: The Shocking New Evidence

Eugene Methvin, senior editor at Reader's Digest, *examines some research data on the impact of TV violence on viewers.*

BEFORE YOU READ

1. Study the title for a moment. What is Methvin's position on TV violence probably going to be? Make a guess, then check to see if you are right.
2. How do you think children are affected by violence on television? Are the effects different for adults?

1 San Diego: A high-school honor student watches a lurid ABC-TV fictionalization of the 1890s Lizzie Borden ax murder case; then chops his own parents and sister to death and leaves his brother a quadriplegic.

2 Denver: *The Deer Hunter* is telecast and a 17-year-old kills himself with a revolver, acting out the movie's climactic game of Russian roulette. He is the 25th viewer in two years to kill himself that way after watching the drama on TV.

3 Decatur, Ill: A 12-year-old overdoses on sleeping pills after her mother forbids her to date a 16-year-old-boy. "What gave you the idea of suicide?" an investigating psychiatrist asks. The answer: A little girl tried it on a TV show, was quickly revived and welcomed back by her parents with open arms.

4 Ten years ago, after studying massive research on the subject, the U.S. Surgeon General, Jesse L. Steinfeld, declared, "The causal relationship between televised violence and antisocial behavior is sufficient to warrant[1] immediate remedial action." Called before Congress, the presidents of the three networks solemnly agreed.

5 Yet the University of Pennsylvania's Annenberg School of Communications, which for 14 years has charted mayhem in network programming, reports that violent acts continue at about six per prime-time hour and in four out of every five programs. The weekend children's programs are even worse.

6 Last May the National Institute of Mental Health (NIMH) issued a report summarizing over 2500 studies done in the last decade on television's influence on behavior. Evidence from the studies—with more than 100,000 subjects in dozens of nations—is so "overwhelming," the NIMH found, that there is a consensus in the research community "that violence on television does lead to aggressive behavior."

---

[1] Justify.

7   Television ranks behind only sleep and work as a consumer of our time. In fact, according to the 1982 Nielsen Report on Television, the average American family keeps its set on for 49 1/2 hours each week. The typical youngster graduating from high school will have spent almost twice as much time in front of the tube as he has in the classroom—the staggering equivalent[2] of ten years of 40-hour weeks. He will have witnessed some 150,000 violent episodes, including an estimated 25,000 deaths.

8   Despite the mayhem,[3] the viewer sees little pain or suffering, a false picture that influences young and old. At a Capitol Hill hearing on TV violence, a dismayed Rep. Billy Tauzin complained to network executives that his three-year-old son had poked his fist through a glass door—an imitation of a TV cartoon character—and almost bled to death. In New Rochelle, N.Y., a killer who re-enacted a TV bludgeon murder told police of his surprise when his victim did not die with the first crunch of his baseball bat, as on the tube, but instead threw up a hand in defense and groaned and cried piteously.

9   The effect of all this? Research points toward these conclusions:

10 **1. TV violence produces lasting and serious harm.** University of Illinois psychology professor Leonard Eron and colleagues compared the television diets and level of aggressive behavior of 184 boys at age eight and again at 18. His report: "The more violent the programs watched in childhood, the more combative the young adults became. We found their behavior studded with antisocial[4] acts, from theft and vandalism to assault with a deadly weapon. The children appeared to learn aggressive habits that persisted for at least ten years."

11 **2. Those "action" cartoons on children's programs are decidedly damaging.** Stanford University psychologist Albert Bandura found cartoon violence as potent as real-life models in increasing violence among youngsters. A University of Kansas researcher reported that Saturday-morning cartoons markedly decreased imaginative play and hiked aggression among 66 preschoolers. In a year-long study of 200 preschoolers, Yale University Drs. Jerome L. and Dorothy Singer found that playground depredations like fighting and kicking were far greater among steady action-cartoon viewers.

12 Indeed, the Saturday morning "kid vid" ghetto is the most violent time in TV. It bathes the prime audience of youngsters from 3 to 13 years old with 25 violent acts per hour, much of it in a poisonous brew of violent programs and aggressive commercials designed to sell such products as breakfast cereals

---

[2] Equal measure.
[3] Chaos.
[4] Against society.

and action toys. According to one study, these commercials have a rate of violence about three times that of the programs themselves.

13   **3. TV erodes[5] inhibitions.[6]**   With a $290,000 grant from CBS, British psychologist William A. Belson studied the television diets and subsequent behavior of 1565 London boys ages 12 to 17. He found cartoon, slapstick or science-fiction violence less harmful at this age; but realistic fictional violence, violence in close personal relationships, and violence "in a good cause" were deadly poison. Heavy viewers were 47 percent more likely to commit acts such as knifing during a school fight, burning another with a cigarette, slashing car tires, burglary and attempted rape. To Belson's surprise, the TV exposure did not seem to change the boys' opinions toward violence but rather seemed to crumble whatever constraints family, church or school had built up. "It is almost as if the boys then tend to let go whatever violent tendencies are in them. It just seems to explode in spontaneous[7] ways."

14   **4. The sheer quantity of TV watching by youngsters increases hurtful behavior and poor academic performance.**   "When the TV set is on, it freezes everybody," says Cornell University psychologist Urie Bronfenbrenner. "Everything that used to go on between people—the games, the arguments, the emotional scenes out of which personality and ability develop—is stopped. When you turn on the TV, you turn off the process of making human beings human."

15   Studies in the United States, Canada, Israel, Australia and Europe show that the amount of TV watched, regardless of program content, is a critical variable that contributes heavily to children's later aggressive attitudes and behavior. Dozens of other studies indicate that TV impairs the children's verbal skills and creativeness.

What Parents Can Do

16   First of all, they can help by realizing that their own TV viewing affects the quality of family life. Until recently most adults worried that violent programming might be harmful to children, but assumed they could gorge[8] themselves with impunity[9] on whatever programs caught their fancy. Not so . . .

17   In one study, U.C.L.A. researchers Roderic Gorney and David Loye divided 183 husbands, ages 20 to 70, into five comparable groups. The groups were assigned 21 hours of varied TV fare at home during a single week, and each

---

[5] Wears away.
[6] Restraints, controls on behavior.
[7] Unplanned.
[8] Eat greedily.
[9] Without fear of punishment.

man kept a diary of his "moods." Wives, without knowing which TV diet the husbands watched, recorded "hurtful" and "helpful" behaviors. The result: husbands who watched violent programming recorded a significantly higher level of aggressive moods. Furthermore, their wives noted about 35-percent more daily incidents of hurtful behavior than did wives whose husbands watched "prosocial" programming.

18 "The important lesson of our experiment is that adults, by their own programming choices, may actually *reduce* aggressive moods and hurtful behavior," says Gorney. "In a home the climate generated by parental moods and conduct is surely as crucial as what children see on TV in determining the family's mental health."

19 Further, parents can curtail the total time children watch television. Investigators find that parents are consistently unaware of how long their children are watching, and underestimate how much violence they see and how much it disturbs them. Experts agree that three hours a day should be an absolute maximum for subteen children and far less than that of action drama, cartoons and other violence-packed programming. Advises syndicated columnist Ann Landers: "Be firm. You wouldn't allow your child to eat garbage, would you? Why, then, let him put it in his head?"

20 Parents can avoid using TV as a baby-sitter, and they can watch with their children—making certain that incidents of violence or sex never go without comment. Parents can encourage children to identify and watch programs of educational and social value. They should not hesitate to change channels or turn off the set. As an aid, Yale University's Family Television Research and Consultation Center has produced a carefully tested program for parents and teachers of children ranging from nursery to junior high: *Getting the Most Out of TV*, published at $7.95 by Scott, Foresman & Co., 1900 East Lake Ave., Glenview, Ill. 60025.

What Everyone Can Do

21 In legal theory, "the airwaves belong to the people," and the nation's 1067 television stations enjoy their federally awarded monopoly only in return for programming "in the public interest." In general, the government cannot deny any corporation the right to advertise on any program it chooses. But the viewer has a right to declare that he is not going to help pay for those programs by buying the advertised products.

22 Both the American Medical Association and the National PTA have urged their members to bring public pressure against advertisers on high-violence programs. The National Coalition on Television Violence (NCTV), formed by psychiatrists, pediatricians and educators, carefully grades network prime-time and weekend children's programs. Each quarter it publishes lists of the companies and products that sponsor the most mayhem, and also companies that allot the largest portion of their television budgets to violent programming. (The

NCTV's address: P.O. Box 2157, Champaign, Ill. 61820.) It promotes legislative action and urges school, church and parent groups to publish its lists and to complain to advertisers.

23   Some companies need little prompting. Kodak has always shunned violent programming and consistently ranks low in NCTV monitoring lists. Kraft, Inc., also has a long-standing policy against programming that depicts excessive violence. Other companies that rate well with NCTV include Hallmark Cards, Schering-Plough and Campbell Soup.

24   Too much TV watching—and violent programming in general—can indeed be harmful to viewers' health. Says NCTV's chairman, Dr. Thomas Radecki, a psychiatry professor at Southern Illinois University, "Each of us bears a responsibility in stopping this ubiquitous[10] teacher of rage and hate. Each of us must live in the world it is destroying."

REACTING

1. Does your own experience support Eugene Methvin's conclusions about the effect TV violence has on us?
2. Do you agree that TV violence affects adults as well as children? Give reasons for your answer.

CONNECTING

1. Turn to p. 257 and read Joan Meier's "Battered Justice." How might a conversation between Methvin and Meier go? Would Meier be able to use Methvin's material to expand or deepen her own argument?
2. How would Methvin answer the question: "Why are we so violent?"

LEARNING ABOUT WRITING FROM READING

Notice Methvin's beginning. He uses brief stories, or anecdotes, to grab your attention in the opening paragraphs. Paragraph 1 gives us an example:

> San Diego: A high-school honor student watches a lurid ABC-TV fictionalization of the 1890s Lizzie Borden ax murder case, then chops his own parents and sister to death and leaves his brother a quadriplegic.

These opening stories are also tiny versions of Methvin's argument that violence on television is a kind of fantasy that viewers act out—but with very real results.

---

[10] Present everywhere.

Joan Meier

Battered Justice

Joan Meier, writing for the Washington Monthly, *analyzes police and judicial responses to cases of domestic violence.*

BEFORE YOU READ

1. Look at the title and then the subheads in the article. If you put the subheads together, relating them to the title, what kind of story do they tell?
2. How should cases of domestic violence be handled, by the police and by neighbors?

1   Last August in Somerville, Massachusetts, Pamela Nigro-Dunn was coming home from work and got off the bus at the stop where her mother met her each day. A man drove up and insisted Nigro-Dunn get into his car. When she and her mother resisted, he threw mace into her mother's face. Then he shot Pamela, who was five months pregnant, in the abdomen and dragged her into the car. Her body was found in a garbage dump nine hours later. She had been shot, strangled, and stabbed. The murderer was arrested three months later in Florida. He was her husband.

2   Roughly 1,350 women were killed by their spouses, ex-spouses, or boyfriends in 1985. They were the victims of the most extreme form of wife battering but represent only a fraction of those who have suffered from what appears to be an epidemic of violence within marriages. National surveys have suggested that as many as one out of four married couples endure at least one act of serious violence during their marriage.

3   This domestic violence is one-sided: 85–95 percent of assault victims and two-thirds of domestic murder victims are women. And it usually is not an isolated event, but part of a pattern of escalating violence. Where there has been murder, there has usually been a history of beating. Consequently, many killings were predictable and could have been stopped. In most cases, the victims had brought their abusers' earlier assaults to the attention of the police, prosecutors, or courts. Pamela Nigro-Dunn had been to court four times trying to stop her husband's attacks before she was murdered. She received a restraining order, but the judge refused to give her police protection. Similarly, the murder of Leedonyell Williams in Washington, D.C., this past summer was committed the day after charges against her attacker were dropped. One Minneapolis study found that in 85 percent of spousal murder cases there had been prior contact with the police; in 50 percent they had been called at least five times in the preceding two years.

4. Many people are aware that wife-beating is a problem. But few are aware of the shocking way that violence is ignored by the criminal justice system. When called for help, police rarely make arrests. When they do, prosecutors rarely bring charges. And when cases are brought to court, judges too often have the attitude of Paul Heffernan, the Massachusetts judge who was sitting on the bench when Pamela Nigro-Dunn requested help.

5. In the first affidavit Pamela filed, just six weeks after her wedding, she stated, "I'm a prisoner in my apartment. He locks me in and takes the phone cord out. He choked me and threatened to kill me if I try to leave. He made me work only where he works.... My life is in danger so long as he is around."

6. Pamela asked Heffernan to order Paul Dunn out of the apartment, but the judge refused and then asked her, "Did he demonstrate this type of behavior before you married him?" presumably reasoning that, if the husband had hit her before they were married, she was not entitled to police protection if she was beaten—however badly—after she was married. Pamela moved out.

7. Five days later, she returned to court to obtain a police escort so she could return to the apartment for her clothes. "I don't think it's the role of this Court to decide down to each piece of underwear who owns what," Heffernan said. "This is pretty trivial.... This court has a lot more serious matters to contend with. We're doing a terrible disservice[1] to the taxpayers here." Heffernan then turned to her husband and said, "You want to gnaw on her and she on you fine, but let's not do it at the taxpayers' expense."

8. Pamela moved in with her parents, but after pressure from Paul to return home and promises that he'd reform, she reconciled with him for several weeks. The abuse resumed. She didn't go back to court to seek further protection. Why would she? She moved back to her parents', and her mother began accompanying her to and from the bus stop because they had seen Paul circling in his car. Shortly thereafter he murdered her.

9. It is appalling that so many women suffer as Pamela did at the hands of their spouses. But it is perhaps even more appalling that so many are further abused by the criminal justice system. Although in recent years several cities have moved toward reform, domestic violence remains at best a low priority. There are many reasons for the reluctance of police, prosecutors, and judges to handle these cases, but at the root is the belief that wife-beating is simply not criminal behavior.

Police who won't arrest

10. The passivity of the police in dealing with domestic assaults was made clear in a landmark case in New York City in 1976. Twelve battered wives sued the city police department and family court for failing to arrest and prosecute men who attacked their wives—simply because the victim and assailant were married.

---

[1] Injury.

The out-of-court settlement required the police department to change its policies and was hailed as a turning point in the country's police and court treatment of domestic violence cases.

11   But in the four years I have represented battered women in Chicago and Washington, D.C., it has become clear that little has changed since the New York case. Catherine Klein, who has worked with about five hundred battered women over the past five years, cannot recall a single arrest that happened without her intervention. Early last year, for example, the D.C. police were called by nurses at a hospital where Dawn Ronan,* who was five months pregnant, had gone for treatment after being kicked in the back by Jimmy Smith, her boyfriend and the father of her child. The police refused to arrest Jimmy because they hadn't seen the assault. "It's a domestic problem. We really don't get involved," they explained to the nurse. . . .

12   Why don't police arrest these abusers? Some states have historically prohibited arrests on misdemeanor[2]—though not felony—charges unless the police have witnessed the crime. Many states, however, have changed the law so police can make misdemeanor arrests in domestic violence cases without having seen the assault if there is sufficient evidence of probable cause. In D.C., police concede they have always been authorized to make arrests for misdemeanors they didn't witness. They simply don't—sometimes not even when they can see blood streaming down a woman's face.

13   The legal excuses often give way to the real reasons for not arresting. "They always said they couldn't do anything because he was my husband," recalls Jean Cook, whose husband had, on various occasions, thrown a brick through her window, broken a beer bottle over her head, threatened to kill her, and lurked with a gun around the shelter where she was staying. Barbara Nelson was advised by a supportive police officer to tell the dispatcher there was "a man with a knife" when she called for help, rather than say "my husband has a knife." Last January, another D.C. woman was on the floor being kicked by her boyfriend when the police arrived. The police told the man that if the couple had lived together at least six months, making them common law husband and wife, they couldn't do anything. The police then asked how long the two had lived together. The man said six months; she denies they had ever lived together. The police left. Yet another recent D.C. victim, who had been held hostage all of one night and hit repeatedly in the head with a hammer, was told by the police, "he'd have to kill you or damn near kill you" for them to take any action.

14   The hands-off approach that still operates in most police departments gained theoretical justification in the early seventies when social work alternatives to punishment were popular for a number of offenses, including drug use and prostitution. In 1970, Morton Bard, a clinical psychologist, set up a demonstration project to teach police special counseling skills for intervening in

---

* Some of the victims' names have been changed.

[2] Minor crime.

family disputes. Even though the project did not show a reduction in violence, it was hailed as a success. Other well-intended psychologists followed suit. By 1977, a national survey of the larger police departments found that more than 70 percent had implemented[3] some kind of family crisis intervention[4] training program.

15 At best, such policies help the victim. Police should usually be applauded for their efforts to be more humane, but it is curious, given their occupational bias toward punishing offenders, that they eagerly embrace a soft approach toward domestic violence. Unfortunately, experts in domestic violence now agree that mediation as a substitute for arrest is the wrong answer when there is violence.

16 D.C. police officers typically say they are reluctant to arrest wife-beaters because these "fights"—a term reflecting a belief that spousal violence is minor and mutual—"are much more dangerous for police." They also reason that, as one said, "when people are in a relationship, I assume she could leave and avoid the man if she wanted to."

17 Both reasons contain a kernel of truth. That police fear domestic violence cases is understandable, although it contrasts strikingly with their notion that such cases are trivial and not very dangerous for the women. When police respond to a domestic call, tempers are usually still hot, and often get hotter at the sight of a cop. One 1983 study by the D.C. Metropolitan Police Department stated that "nationally, more police officers were injured while responding to disturbance calls than in any other type of call for service." But recent FBI Uniform Crime Reports show that police fears are overstated and that a domestic call is one of the least likely of all calls to lead to assaults on officers or to their deaths. Similarly, Don Pfouts, a detective with the Baltimore City Police Department who has been reviewing his department's records, confirms that domestic calls are "not that dangerous.". . .

Prosecutors who won't prosecute

18 The most understandable reason police give for their reluctance to arrest is their belief that such cases are not likely to be prosecuted. When Michael Anthony Scott broke into the Washington, D.C., apartment of Leedonyell Williams, his former girlfriend and the mother of his two children, he held a gun to her head and sat waiting at the dining room table for her mother to come home. When she arrived, he said, he would shoot both of them and himself. Eventually he got restless and left, taking his two-year-old son and warning Leedonyell not to tell anyone what had happened or he would kill the baby.

19 But Leedonyell did tell the police. Because there was a bench warrant out on him already for failure to appear in a traffic case, they arrested Scott. The prosecutor's office decided to drop Leedonyell's charges. The reason? One prosecutor later explained, "It appeared to be a domestic dispute over child

---

[3] Put into practice.

[4] Interference.

custody." The next day Scott shot and killed Leedonyell on the stairs of her apartment. After hearing of the murder, another prosecutor said, "It's just one of those horrible, bizarre things. . . . You deal with a thousand of these kinds of cases and 999 of them turn out as you expect them to: just a domestic problem."

20   Prosecutors in many jurisdictions are known to avoid prosecuting domestic cases. In some offices special "cooling off" periods are imposed in the expectation that the woman will change her mind. In the rare case where a prosecutor presses charges, it is almost always as a misdemeanor rather than a felony, regardless of the severity of the assault.

21   Standards for when to prosecute are, if anything, more vague and discretionary than police standards for arrest. When pressed for his reasons for dropping the charges in the Williams case, Joseph DiGenova, the U.S. attorney for the District of Columbia, said he was "satisfied that everything was done properly," and that the decision had been "handled according to guidelines." As to what those guidelines called for, he would say only "a host of factors" such as the arresting officer's "impressions" and prosecutors' "experience."

22   Most prosecutors will admit that they view domestic assaults very differently. They frequently mention that such cases are hard to win. Since domestic assaults usually occur behind closed doors, there are rarely witnesses and when there are, they are usually children. Still, prosecutors often refuse to take a case even when evidence of physical abuse is strong. Denise Wiktor, a D.C. attorney, recalls on one occasion presenting a U.S. attorney with bloody clothes, two eyewitnesses, and three affidavits as corroborating evidence. The attorney still refused to prosecute, citing "insufficient evidence."

23   Prosecutors most often attribute the failure to prosecute to the woman's ambivalence[5] about pressing her complaint. "These are very, very difficult decisions to make because of the regularity with which the complainant refuses to go forward," DiGenova told *The Washington Post*. In some studies, as many as 80 percent of complaints were dropped by the complainant before prosecution. Even battered women advocates agree that this ambivalence can be a problem. If a woman does drop charges, prosecutors frequently treat a second complaint as "crying wolf" and refuse to process it.

24   Why do the victims drop charges? Some women blame themselves, believing the batterers when they say they had it coming. "It'll never happen again, it was my fault," is a common refrain heard by Vicky Vossen, an assistant district attorney in Manhattan. Frequently a batterer goes through a period of contrition after an attack, pleading with the woman to stay and promising never to hurt her again. If she cares for the man at all, it is difficult to reject his pleas and promises, and particularly difficult to send him to jail.

25   More importantly, women drop charges for the same reason they don't leave their abusers; fear. It is not uncommon for abusers to sit in the courtroom and intimidate a woman into dropping the charges. Vernon Nelson, while in

---

[5] Mixed feelings.

court, told his wife that if she got him ordered out of the house, he would burn it down. Barbara Nelson withdrew her request.

Judges who won't convict

26   Prosecutors' attitudes are shaped in part by those of the judges before whom they appear. In August 1983, I was an advocate in Chicago for a battered woman who wanted her abuser prosecuted for assault and an order of protection issued barring him from harassing her again. On the day of the trial the defendant agreed to one year of court-supervised counseling and a one-year order of protection. The agreement had to be approved by the judge to be enforceable. Approval of out-of-court settlements is usually little more than a formality. But not in this case.

27   State's Attorney Michael Balksus: We would like to stress the seriousness of the crime to the defendant, and make sure that he is well aware that under the Order of Protection he cannot threaten or harass the complainant or have any sort of physical contact with her in any unlawful manner . . . .

28   Judge William Wood: This is a husband and wife situation?

29   Balksus: That is correct.

30   Wood: I assume they are not living together?

31   Public defender: They are living in the same house.

32   Advocate for Complainant, Joan Meier: Your honor, may I interrupt to fill in some details? The complaining witness has filed for divorce. They are living in the house together, not happily. He has threatened to kill her several times, particularly if she brings him into court. And that is why we would like a warning about threats. We do not want him threatening to kill her.

33   Wood: If people live together, how do you control human behavior?

34   Meier: It is a problem.

35   Wood: It certainly is a problem. Now if she's going to live with him for whatever reasons and then is going to ask the Court to tell him not to hit me [sic] this is ridiculous and stupid.

36   Meier: She would be happy to ask the Court for him to leave, but she understands there is an agreement being made. There is something short of that that could resolve the situation.

37   Wood: I'm going to give him supervision as long as they are living together. I'm not going to enter any order like this. This is just my view. And I see you have a surprised look, but I think it is ridiculous to have people living together and then you're going to have the court say, don't do this.

38   Meier: Your Honor—

39   Wood: And I would say go to divorce court; this is a criminal court.

40   Meier: Your Honor—

41   Wood: This is a criminal court, do you understand? Go to divorce court. Let them put an injunction against him. Let them look into the domestic matters. But I'm not going to take up time with this.

42   Meier: The law permits you to and suggests that you should.

43   Wood: Okay, and after having heard it and considered everything this is my considered judgment: one year social service supervision, August 23. That's it; and take that back with you.

44   Clerk: Order of Protection?

45   Wood: Order of Protection is denied.

46   The tragic irony of this case was that Pat White wanted nothing more than to have her husband out of the house. She had not requested that much relief for fear the judge might refuse, making her husband think he had license to beat her. Judge Wood's view is not unique. According to Assistant D.A. Vicky Vossen, several judges in Manhattan frequently refuse to grant orders of protection when the parties have been seeing each other.

47   This refusal to treat violence as criminal as long as the woman is still in contact with the man is a strange way to apply the law. Nowhere is it written that behavior can be criminal only if the victim has done everything possible to avoid her attacker. We do not let a savage mugger go because his victim unwisely walked down a dark alley late at night. We do not expect someone who is attacked by a burglar in his own home to crawl out the back window. Yet violence against a woman in her own home is not considered a crime because she stays in the house.

48   Judge Wood's suggestion that the case be dealt with in domestic relations court is also ironic in light of the refrain frequently heard by battered women from civil court judges, such as the Somerville, Massachusetts, district court judge, who said, "Hey, sister, if things are that tough, file a criminal complaint."

49   Judges sometimes claim that they dislike domestic assault cases because orders of protection, central to most domestic violence cases in both civil and criminal courts, are ineffective. Francis G. Poitrast, the chief justice of the Somerville juvenile court, told *The Boston Globe* that judges are frustrated with "abuse cases" because the orders are just "an empty shell. Its only enforcement is in the event of a violation." But judges rarely express reluctance to convict a repeat burglar merely because jail does not deter recidivists[6] from resuming their crimes.

50   Simply put, many judges are hostile to these cases, and, it appears, to the victims. According to Eileen McNamara, author of the *Globe* series that broke the Pamela Nigro-Dunn story, Judge Heffernan's behavior was not an isolated or extreme example. Presiding Judge Henry Tempone is even worse than Heffernan, she says. For example, he told one woman, "You don't look beat up to me." She was wearing a full-length coat. He also told the *Globe* that he believed that most women seeking orders of protection were lying. Judges' attitudes towards these cases may be symptomatic of a larger problem. Investigations in New York, New Jersey, and Rhode Island, and other states have found widespread patterns of judicial insensitivity to women, including stereotyping, treatment of women as property, as well as a tendency to "blame the victim" in domestic violence cases. Nor is the problem limited to male

---

[6] Repeat offenders.

judges. Although some women judges are among the best on domestic violence issues, others are known for their impatience and hostility.

51   Unfortunately, the judiciary is for the most part invulnerable to reform, as strong peer review and discipline is rare, and judges, particularly those with life tenure, are effectively accountable to no one. The problem is worse in domestic violence cases, since the one avenue that serves as a modest constraint, appeal, is rarely taken. The prosecution cannot appeal an acquittal of an abuser in a criminal case. Although appeal is possible for protection orders, in most cases it is simply impractical. Petitioners often need emergency relief, making a time consuming appeal of little use. And since most petitioners have no attorney, they don't know how to file an appeal anyway.

52   The failure of judicial self-regulation was particularly evident in the case of one judge in Massachusetts who was found in the course of divorce proceedings to have severely beaten his wife at least three times. Yet he continued to preside over domestic violence cases for two more years before retiring with an unblemished record.

Violence is violence

53   Slowly, things are changing. When Jean Cook now says, "I didn't give up all my rights when I got married," she has the support of at least two federal courts. In ruling that the Torrington police department violated Tracy Thurman's civil rights, the federal district court firmly stated that a "man is not allowed to physically abuse or endanger a woman merely because he is her husband" and it held that the police cannot avoid making arrests "simply because the assaulter and his victim are married to each other." The jury awarded Thurman $2.3 million. Suits like Thurman's have been brought against police departments in numerous other cities and states, including New York, San Francisco, Los Angeles, Dallas, Tennessee, Pennsylvania, Alaska, and Ohio. All have been won or settled on terms favorable to the plaintiffs, and have required police to stop discriminating against married women or girlfriends who ask for help. Other police departments, including D.C.'s, are beginning to adopt policies that favor arrests or require that domestic violence cases be treated no differently from other assault cases. When Denver recently adopted a pro-arrest policy, arrests jumped 60 percent one year and 46 percent the next.

54   Recently, the Attorney General's Task Force on Domestic Violence, the Bureau of Justice Statistics, and the National Institute of Justice produced reports urging that domestic violence be treated as a serious crime. Justice Department funding, although far lower than in the past, now supports eight demonstration projects to develop new policies and procedures for police and prosecutors.

55   A firm criminal justice response works. After Duluth, Minnesota, instituted a mandatory arrest program, 70 of a group of 86 women reported at the end of two years that the combined assistance of police, courts, and shelters was helpful in ending their abusers' violence. According to Dr. Anne Ganley, a psychologist and counselor for batterers, "Perpetrators tend to minimize and deny the violence and place the blame on others." Therefore, she says, it is crucial that

batterers be held responsible for their violence. As one former abuser said in the National Institute of Justice report: "It was such an extreme experience having actually been arrested and dealt with rather harshly . . . that I sought help." Advocates frequently comment that even the slightest acknowledgment from an official that women do not deserve to be beaten can give victims an enormous boost of strength and energy to take action to end the abuse. Even if the couple stays together, outside disapproval can make both aware that the man does not have "the right to beat" the woman. Barbara Nelson's husband, who was finally arrested and jailed after ten years of violence now says, "There's nothing I want to do enough to go back there. . . . You don't have to be afraid of me; it's not worth it to go back."

56   If the message is clear, the actual punishment is less important. A study of the Minneapolis Police Department by the Police Foundation concluded that when the officer "advised" the suspect and did not lock him up, violence recurred within the next six months in 37 percent of the cases; when the suspect was arrested, even if he wasn't prosecuted later, violence recurred in only 19 percent of the cases. In Jean Cook's case, a mere warning letter from her attorney to her abuser brought a sudden halt to seven months of almost daily harassment.

57   Even if the evidence weren't as clear as it is that criminal justice intervention reduces domestic violence, it would still be called for. Society punishes behavior it finds morally opprobrious. The refusal of the police and courts to insist that domestic violence is a crime allows people to go on believing it's not so bad. It's time to teach a different set of lessons.

REACTING

1. What were your immediate feelings on reading "Battered Justice"?
2. Would you agree with Joan Meier that far too much domestic violence is overlooked by police and courts? Give some anecdotes and statistics to back up your opinion.

CONNECTING

1. Would Eugene Methvin ("TV Violence: The Shocking New Evidence," p. 252) or Jean Prokopow ("Get to the Root of Violence: Militarism," p. 241) have explanations for domestic violence beyond those offered by Meier?
2. Turn to the chapter on gender roles and read Herb Goldberg's "In Harness: The Male Condition" (p. 138). What might Goldberg say about causes of domestic violence?

LEARNING ABOUT WRITING FROM READING

Meier tries to persuade us by giving some vivid and terrible stories of domestic violence. They are powerful and hard to ignore. An argument based on these as evidence is off to a good start, as long as the reader is convinced that the accounts are true in themselves and representative of the situation as a whole. Otherwise, the author may be accused of biased selection of the most sensational examples.

Meier helps her case by beginning the article with some statistics which indicate that domestic violence, particularly against women, is indeed a widespread cultural problem. Her later anecdotes are then seen against this background of supporting documentation. Here are her opening figures, all occurring in the second and third paragraphs:

> Roughly 1,350 women were killed by their spouses, ex-spouses, or boyfriends in 1985.
>
> 85–95 percent of assault victims and two-thirds of domestic murder victims are women.
>
> One Minneapolis study found that in 85 percent of spousal murder cases there had been prior contact with the police; in 50 percent they had been called at least five times in the preceding two years.

These numbers add power to the stories that follow.

WRITING ASSIGNMENTS

ASSIGNMENT 1
WHY IS AMERICA SO VIOLENT?

Coming Up with Ideas and a Focus

This is such a broad question, that trying to answer it completely will lead to disaster. Begin by talking or freewriting about different kinds of violence. Then, after listing as many reasons as you can to explain the violence, find a focus by deciding which of these reasons are most important. You can then just acknowledge in your introduction in some quick way that you know you are addressing only part of the question.

Organizing Your Ideas

Try organizing your ideas within a cause-and-effect pattern. By giving reasons for America's violent culture, you are essentially saying what the causes of that violence are. (For help with cause-and-effect papers, see pp. 310 and 368.)

Audience

You might try writing this paper for an audience of interested foreigners: people who are curious about American culture but puzzled by some of its characteristics. Imagining an audience of outsiders will encourage you to give full explanations and may also suggest useful cross-cultural comparisons.

ASSIGNMENT II
EXPLAIN WHY YOU WOULD OR WOULD NOT LET A CHILD OF YOURS WATCH A TV SHOW THAT YOU CONSIDER VIOLENT. (SAY HOW OLD THE CHILD IS.)

Coming Up with Ideas and a Focus

One way to begin your thinking is to list as many examples as you can of TV shows that usually contain violence of some kind. Specific cartoon shows, police dramas, sitcoms, and local news shows might be on your list. Then try brainstorming about the likely effect of these shows on, for example, a ten-year-old child. To find a focus, you will need to pick a single show and develop your ideas about its likely effects, perhaps pick the one that is most disturbing or the one that seems most harmless, even with its violent content. You might even find a show where its violent content might be considered positive.

Organizing Your Ideas

This assignment might work well within a cause-and-effect pattern. By establishing the effects of a certain show's violence on children, you will be able to say why you would or would not allow your child to watch. (For help with cause-and-effect papers, see pp. 310 and 368.)

Audience

If other members of your class are addressing this issue, try directing your paper to them, with the purpose of persuading them that your reasons for saying yes or no to this particular TV show are sound. Then pool your responses to see if there is any general agreement about what people mean by "violent" TV and about their reasons for limiting children's viewing.

ASSIGNMENT III
WHY ARE YOU, OR PEOPLE YOU KNOW, DRAWN TO HORROR AND VIOLENCE ON THE SCREEN?

Coming Up with Ideas and a Focus

This assignment asks the question "Why?", and you will need to respond with a reason or list of reasons. Before you can get to your reasons, though, it might help to generate a list of movies or television shows you have seen, with notes on what they were like to see and hear. Then try freewriting about your reactions to them. You don't need to cover all angles on this topic, because that will spread you so thin that you won't be able to say much that is new or interesting about any of them. Find a focus by choosing the reasons that seem most important.

Organizing Your Ideas

In some form or other, you will probably want to try out a statement-support pattern. A scratch outline would include a list of main reasons for liking the movie or television show. Try to think also about the best order of presentation for those reasons. (For help with statement-support papers, see pp. 305 and 365.)

Audience

Choose an audience that is almost certain to disagree with you. Accept the challenge of persuading them that you are right.

ASSIGNMENT IV
COMPARE AND CONTRAST MEDIA VIOLENCE WITH REAL-LIFE VIOLENCE.

Report a violent incident you were involved in or which you witnessed. Then tell the same episode as it might have been treated on a specific movie or television program. Be sure to name the movie or program whose style you are using.

Coming Up with Ideas and a Focus

To write this paper, you will need to recall one or more of your own experiences, with lots of details of scenes and feelings. Then you can find a focus by selecting one event. Generating a list of media violence styles—police dramas, cartoons, war stories, thriller and horror—may help you to match the real event with a media presentation.

Organizing Your Ideas

The organization of your ideas is suggested by the assignment itself: comparison and contrast. You might first show real violence, then media violence. You will need to open your paper with some kind of brief guiding statement about the purpose and results of your comparison. (For help with comparison-contrast papers, see pp. 310 and 367.)

Audience

Who would get the most out of a paper that shows the differences and similarities between real-life violence and media violence? Perhaps junior high or middle school students. These age groups may need to know that television and the movies aren't always accurate guides to reality. Or they may want your recommendation for a film or TV show that does present violence realistically and meaningfully.

Chapter 8

The Environment

KEY QUESTIONS

How are our environmental problems rooted in our cultural values and attitudes?

What role do the media play in presenting and solving environmental problems?

• •

Rather than bore us with the ups and downs of the stock market every night, why don't newscasts tell us the day's smog levels in our major cities?
—MARK HERTSGAARD, *ROLLING STONE*, NOVEMBER 16, 1989

The energy saved from re-cycling one glass bottle will light a 100-watt bulb for four hours.
—*EARTHWATCH*, 1990

Each American now uses as much electricity as 200 people in China.
—*THE NEW YORK TIMES*, APRIL 22, 1990

Introduction

Do you know where your old aluminum cans and newspapers are today? You probably do, in fact, because how you dispose of these items may now be regulated by law. Even where no law is involved, environmental issues seem to be staying on many people's minds. People who had never thought twice about buying disposable diapers are refusing to do so now. Television programs and magazines and newspapers may be encouraging them not to waste the earth's resources—or are they? That is one question we explore in this chapter.

"Environmental issues" is a catchall phrase for a host of problems that go way beyond the need for recycling aluminum cans: the holes in the ozone layer, huge landfills, mountainous heaps of trash, deteriorating air quality, shrinking rain forests, concrete jungles covering woodlands, and aging nuclear power stations and nuclear weapons stockpiles. Even this very incomplete list raises fundamental questions about how we should live and what kind of energy we should use. These are global concerns, but certainly America's as well, for our country contributes heavily to world pollution.

This is an ironic twist to the last five hundred years of America's history. What early European settlers in North America saw—inaccurately—was a vast unclaimed wilderness and a promise of abundant riches, just waiting to be possessed. Around the world, America—the New World—became an image of nature, savage or innocent. In this chapter, Annie Dillard's "Seeing" shows how innocence can survive in the simple but intense relationship Dillard cultivates with the natural world.

But the history of the new country—paralleling the history of technology and industrialization—has drastically changed most Americans' relationships with nature. Some of this chapter's readings indicate this change. Now, because of the rapid growth of video technology, Richard Louv can ask in all seriousness, "Are Today's Kids Detached from Nature?" whereas Amory Lovins suggests that some technology can in fact play a major role in helping us lessen pollution and waste in "Technology Is the Answer (But What Was the Question?)."

The early European settlers came into conflict with Native Americans over the value and meaning of the land they sought to settle and own. The Blackfeet Chief's short speech, "Our Land Is More Valuable Than Your Money," illustrates how their values differed. More than a century later, Jerry Mander, in "TV's Capture of the Mind," discusses the Hopi Indians' distress over the destruction of their land by a mining company in pursuit of its own values. Mander also suggests that television coverage didn't help the Hopis' cause. Can the media in fact help us to understand and solve the threats to our global environment? Do the media distort the environmental crisis? Susan McDonald gives one point of view in "The Media and Misinformation."

From old newspapers and aluminum cans to town planning and nuclear waste, the problem we call "environmental" is large and complicated. This chapter invites you to explore some environmental issues and to consider how, or if, the mass media help us to understand and solve them.

Starting Out: Finding Out What You Already Know

1. Who or what first made you aware that "the environment" was in trouble?
2. What is your own role in solving environmental problems? Indeed, do you see a role for yourself at all?
3. If you have lived in another country for any length of time, talk or write about the level of concern there about environmental issues.
4. List as many environmental problems as occur to you.
5. What will it take to solve our environmental problems? List three solutions.

Learning More Through Observation: Taking a Look Around You and Talking to People

1. List any recent television programs or movies that deal with environmental issues. Choose one and freewrite about it, focusing on the images presented and any solutions offered.
2. Interview someone older than you to find out what that person thinks about depletion of the ozone layer, increased urbanization, landfills and hazardous waste sites, or some other environmental problem.
3. Do you think that people who live in different areas of the United States feel differently about environmental problems? Why or why not?
4. Interview some grade-schoolers to find out how much time they spend playing outside and how much time they spend watching television. Compare your results with those of others in your class and see what conclusions you can reach.
5. Look around at school or work and jot down the things that happen (or don't happen) because people are unaware of environmental problems. Do a comparison in class to see which items were on everyone's list. Brainstorm about why those changes aren't made.

Questioning: Deciding What Else You Would Like to Know

List five questions that you still have about environmental problems in the United States.

Richard Louv

Are Today's Kids Detached from Nature?

Richard Louv, author of the book Childhood's Future, *looks at the effects that television and video games are having on children's lives.*

BEFORE YOU READ

1. How would you answer the title question?
2. After reading the first paragraph, what answer do you expect from the author of the article?

1   Last spring a friend and I went for a walk through the neighborhoods surrounding Swarthmore Pennsylvania. We passed through a wooded area and crossed a little creek, stepping across large, flat stones. The trees in this damp countryside were still budding. I asked my friend if his son ever came down to these woods. "No, never," he said. "He's just not interested. He's interested in baseball and organized sports. I don't know if any of his friends come down here either."

2   I though about this on the way home, wondering how much of people's adult relationship with nature has something to do with their childhood fantasies. As a child, I brought cowboys and Indians and Davey Crockett and war to the woods. They were pre-packaged fantasies, and often violent, but most of them did bring human beings to nature, and served as doorways into unpackaged mysteries. Sometimes, at age eight or nine or ten, I would be in the woods alone with my BB gun, intent on shooting something, and I would end up sitting beneath a tree or next to the creek, touching my finger to my tongue and wetting my nostrils so that I might be able to smell better, listening, breathing, watching for the small critters to re-emerge, the frogs' eyes to pop up once again above the water. How many children of the 1950s and before became environmentalists or otherwise deeply concerned with the fate of nature in this way? Walking silently with my friend, I wondered how the current generation of children will relate to nature in the future: What fantasies will they bring to it: what doorways will it open for them?

3   I had spent the last two years traveling the country, talking with and listening to parents, children, and, on occasion, experts.

4   What emerged from these conversations was often stunning, sometimes terrifying, and ultimately hopeful. Parents and children described a physical environment that no longer makes sense—a divorce from nature, sprawling cities with no centers and few natural meeting places, residential areas that can barely be called neighborhoods—an environment that no longer nurtures children, and that drives family life deeper into itself.

5   The relationship between children and nature today is a puzzling one. On one hand, children's sophistication about global environmental issues is very high—and intensely felt. On the other hand, they have much less physical and unstructured contact with nature than my generation did.

6   In the early 1980s, an advertisement began to appear in national magazines, depicting[1] a little boy silhouetted against a cabin window, tapping at a computer terminal. Beyond the glass, trees could be seen, and a sailboat moved lazily across a pond. In Southern California, Girl Scouts can now attend a "High-Tech

---
[1] Showing a picture of.

Computer Whiz" camp—with $50,000 worth of terminals and software. Could it be that computers are viewed as more important to a child's life than access to nature?

7   With the steady disappearance of farmland and woods and streams and fields adjacent to housing, the increasing programming of children's time, and the evolving high-tech fantasies and obsessions of the nation's culture, nature—for children and adults—is becoming something to wear, to watch, to consume. We sport Irresistible Sea Otter T-shirts and view "natural mood" videos (electronic images of streams flowing, to relax and distract us), while the forests are cut, the sea is despoiled, and hilltops are decapitated to make room for more malls.

8   Parents speak often, and sometimes defensively, of this strange divorce between children and the outdoors. At a parent meeting in San Diego a woman said, "It's all this *watching*. We've become a more sedentary[2] society as a whole. I see ads for toys, VCRs, videos: all these machines that kids just sit there and watch. When I was a kid growing up in Detroit, we were always outdoors. The kids who were indoors were always the odd ones. We didn't have any wide-open spaces, but we were outdoors on the streets, in the vacant lots, playing baseball, hopscotch. We were out there playing even after we got older."

9   I would have suspected, before my interviews in Kansas, that children there would still be playing in the woods and along the streams. But the middle-class parents of Overland Park, a Kansas City suburb, viewed such activities as a vanishing part of childhood.

10   "The only time the kids associate with nature is when it's a science project," said one mother. "They had an assignment in the seventh grade—every morning at a certain time they had to go away from the house, somewhere they could be alone with nature and write things down. And that's the only time that they really would venture off on their own to do something like that—because it was an assignment."

11   "No, they're not interested," another mother said. "When the kids go skiing down a beautiful mountain on a perfect, quiet day, they've got their headphones on. They can't enjoy hearing nature and being out there alone. They can't make their own entertainment. They have to bring something with them."

12   She added, "Of course, we discourage them from going in the woods alone. But we're trying as a family to encourage our kids to love nature. We take them camping, we try to get them to go on bike rides and walks. We even pitch the tent in the basement in the winter when it's too cold to pack or go outside."

13   One of the mothers was perplexed. "I don't really know what you mean," she said. "I think that my girls enjoy a full moon, a pretty sunset, and flowers. They enjoy the trees when they turn. That sort of thing. I don't know what else you mean."

14   I clarified the question: What I meant was being *engaged* with nature—free, with time to connect with it, time to bring some fantasies to nature.

---

[2] Inactive.

15 "What you're talking about is something that's totally different today," said Jack, who was raised in a farming community. "Where I grew up, no matter which direction you went, you were outdoors—it was a plowed field or woods or streets. You couldn't walk a quarter mile without getting into something like that. We're not like that here. Overland Park is a metropolitan area now. The kids don't see that type of thing around here as much. They see houses being built."

16 The group was quiet for a moment. I was incredulous[3] at this description of the use of the surrounding countryside in Overland Park. Yes, much of the farmland and woods were being graded and built upon, yet one could see the woods from the windows of the house in which we were sitting. They were still there. Something other than a lack of access was keeping their children away from nature.

17 "Our kids and the neighborhood kids rush into the house, and they head straight for the video games," said one of the fathers in Overland Park. "It's almost like the house with the most kids in it is the house with the best Nintendo cartridges." Another mother added, "We can't get some of our kids' friends to come to our house because we only have kids to play with."

18 All these screens in children's lives can reverse the very polarity of childhood reality. One fourth-grader told me, "I like to play indoors better 'cause that's where all the electrical outlets are."

19 When I asked the gifted students, third- to sixth-graders, in the class at San Diego's Dewey Elementary—children who spoke at length of their relationship to computers—how many would rather be outside with nature instead of working on their computers, 12 of the 40 raised their hands. One pragmatic girl said that it all depended on the weather. "It's kind of a toss-up. But a computer will always be there as opposed to the good weather."

20 While children do seem to be spending less time physically in natural surroundings, they also seem to worry more about the disappearance of nature—in a global sense—than my generation did. At Kenwood Elementary in Miami, most of the fourth-graders in one class said that they would rather play in their house or on the street. I asked them if they thought that kids would play in the woods or in the fields in the future. One boy, who had said earlier that his ambition was to be an astronaut, offered: "Maybe, but not if the city keeps making these new ventures, making new buildings and tearing down all the wilderness."

21 I shifted the subject: You kids are going to be in charge of the environment in the future. What do you think could be done?

22 "If I was in charge, in one part you would have city and the other part of it would be forest, and you couldn't pollute it and if you do, you would get punished. You could live in the forest too, but you wouldn't be allowed to pollute."

23 "If people pull down nature, if they pull down all the trees to put up buildings, how are they going to make their living if they can't use the trees to build their furniture?"

24 These comments, it seemed to me, expressed some surprisingly sophisticated environmental concepts. As a boy, I was intimate with the fields and the

---

[3] Unbelieving.

woods behind my house, and protective of them. Yet, unlike these children, I had no sense of any ecological degradation beyond my small natural universe. Children today may be less intimately involved with nature than many of us were, but they exhibit far more global environmental awareness. Ironically, the electronic world that disrupts intimacy with nature has also been used to communicate nature's distress to these children.

25   One of my journey's last Midwestern stops was at Southwood Elementary in Raytown, Missouri, near Kansas City. This had been my elementary school. As the teachers herded the children in from several classrooms, second through fifth grade, I unpacked my tape recorder and glanced at the ridge of blue-green elms moving slowly in the spring breeze. How often I had dreamed of those trees...

26   I turned to the children and felt suddenly that they might have been friends from my own childhood. There were fewer slogans on the T-shirts than I remembered seeing in other schools. Many of the girls in this class wore cotton print dresses. Perhaps this sense of continuity had to do with the geography of Raytown, which still exists on the edge of farmland and woods. Developers apparently lost their interest in it and moved west, on to Johnson County and Overland Park. Whatever the reason, the school and these children seemed suspended in time.

27   I began by telling them that I had gone to this school, that I had lived on Ralston Street, that there had been a big woods behind my house, and that the woods were all gone now, replaced by a housing tract—in which some of these children might now live.

28   I told them I wanted to know how kids felt about nature. I asked: How many kids here spend a lot of time in woods and fields? Almost all of them raised their hands. I was astonished. This was the opposite of the response in every other classroom that I had visited around the country.

29   "Let me ask you a specific question," I said. "When you go out into the woods and fields, what are the fantasies—the images—in your mind? What do you think about, who do you pretend to be?"

30   The answers came quickly. Many of them were connected to science.

31   "I'm some famous mad scientist out looking for some frogs or something to stick in a new chemical to make the world explode or something."

32   "I feel like I'm a scientist and I'm looking for cures for diseases. And like I'm finding some secret passages."

33   "What I imagine whenever I go in the woods and go look for stuff is I'm one of the world's great explorers and I'm exploring something else. I'm trying to look for something."

34   The fantasies these children took into the woods are more indirect than mine were. Rather than being associated with the cowboys, Indians, and frontiersmen of my boyhood, these fantasies were more likely to involve technology, space, and—particularly for the girls in this class—family issues.

35   "Well, when I'm in the woods, I play like it's just a home. I just go back to the woods and with all the trees gathered together, and some of the trees split, it sort of looks like a home."

36 One fifth-grader was wearing a plain print dress and an intensely serious expression. She later told me that she wanted to be a poet when she grew up. She said, "When I'm in the woods, I feel like I'm in my mother's shoes."

37 In addition to the sense of freedom and fantasy, access to nature also gives children a sense of privacy, a place separate from the adult world, *older* than the adult world:

38 "Whenever I'm out in the woods, it feels like that's where I should go, like it's your home, and you can do anything you want to because there's not anyone bothering you. You have the woods to yourself."

39 The young poet said, "For me it's completely different there. It's more peaceful and it's like you're free when you go out there, it's your own time. When you go back in the woods, it's like if your brain's empty, you got everything back there. Sometimes, I go there when I'm mad and then just with the peacefulness I'm better. I can walk back and be happy and my mom doesn't even know why."

40 I asked them how their parents felt about their being in the woods. Several of the kids said their parents didn't want them going out there because of fear of strangers.

41 "My parents are always worrying about me. I don't know why. And I'll just go and usually I don't tell 'em where I'm going so that makes 'em mad so usually I go without them knowing 'cause I just want to go freely. I'll sit behind the tree or something, or lay in the field with all the rabbits."

42 Finally, I asked if any of them had had a favorite woods or favorite field replaced by a housing development.

43 "We had a field," said a boy. "They were going to tear it down, so we had this meeting, and we sat in this real tall grass where nobody could see us and we all discussed what we were going to do. We said we wouldn't let 'em. We moved our hideout to right on the edge of the field where they started to build and we started just sittin' there and sayin' to them that this was ours but they just said, 'Sorry kids, we already planned this out to make houses here so you're going to have to find someplace else.' That made us really mad."

44 It touched me deeply that these children still felt the way about the woods that I had, that this part of childhood was not lost for them, and that for others, perhaps, it was only misplaced.

45 Listening to them, I remembered how, from third to sixth grade. I had pulled out hundreds of survey stakes—the wooden stakes with the bright orange flags attached to them. I knew what they were for. The year we moved out of that neighborhood, the woods were torn down and a new housing development went up.

46 I asked if any of them had ever pulled out a survey stake. More than 20 of them raised their hands. Enthusiastically. And I laughed.

47 I told the kids it was almost time to leave and began to ask another question, but one red-haired girl, who had not yet talked, began to wave her hand frantically.

48 "Behind Ralston Street!" she exclaimed. "There's still some woods back there!"

49 No, it was all torn down. I was sure of it.

50 "But some of it *is* still there, and there's a park back there. It's *your* woods!"

51 After the class, I found myself driving toward Ralston. I was sure that the kids and I were talking about different places. But, still, I drove back to my old neighborhood and looked for the woods.

52 The kids were right. There was a little park. But where most of my woods had been, now there were houses. According to a hand-made sign, the little park was called Cap Garvin Park. I got out of the rental car and walked the length of it. It was just a long field, located at the extreme end of where the woods had been. A few trees remained near the end of the field.

53 As I passed under one tree, I remembered walking in the snow there with my father, now dead. He had his old army coat on, and was holding an air pistol. We were looking for rabbits, and I saw a trail of ungraceful tracks across the snow through the trees.

54 Now this part of the field was covered with dandelions. In the branches of one of the old trees were the remnants of a treehouse built a long time ago.

55 The end of the park was marked off with barbed wire. Beyond the wire were more woods, as the schoolkids had said. I could barely see the old farmhouse hidden in the trees and brush. When I was a boy, an old horse had grazed near a swamp in those woods: I had to stand on a fence to mount him, and I'd ride wherever he chose to go.

56 From the fence on, the woods were dark and thick. Maybe the swamp was still down below where the dam had been broken out, where at dusk I had seen, in one of those blinding flashes, a great heron lift up on the air, lift up above the old barn, which stared with vacant windows out across the swamp.

57 No doubt the horse was gone, but maybe the swamp and the barn were still there. Maybe sometimes a great heron sailed through the sky. Maybe that part of childhood still existed. If I had been a kid, I would have crossed the barbed wire and gone down there.

58 It was good to know that the best part of my childhood was still safe. I turned and walked back to the car, and as I passed the little sign, I thought: Here's to you, Cap Garvin, whoever you are.

REACTING

1. Do you agree with Richard Louv about children's relationship with nature? Why or why not?
2. Was your childhood different from those described in Louv's article?

CONNECTING

1. How does Louv's article help you to answer one of this chapter's key questions: "How are our environmental problems rooted in our culture's values and attitudes?"

2. In the eighteenth and nineteenth centuries, attitudes and values in American culture were shaped by the sense of an endless source of open land—the frontier. Is technology our new frontier?

LEARNING ABOUT WRITING FROM READING

Louv begins his essay with a brief story, or anecdote, from his own life. In paragraph 2, he tells us about his own childhood experience of nature, and uses the story as a springboard for his main point: that today's children, unlike him, will not have that close connection with woods and trees. The "bridge" between the anecdote and his main idea is underlined:

> I would end up sitting beneath a tree or next to the creek, touching my finger to my tongue and wetting my nostrils so that I might be able to smell better, listening, breathing, watching for the small critters to re-emerge, the frogs' eyes to pop up once again above the water. <u>How many children of the 1950s and before became environmentalists or otherwise deeply concerned with the fate of nature in this way? . . . I wondered how the current generation of children will relate to nature in the future.</u>

Using brief stories like this to lead into main points or main ideas is an interesting way to draw readers into your concerns.

JERRY MANDER

TV's Capture of the Mind

Jerry Mander, writer on media topics, especially television, analyzes and evaluates television's portrayal of a Hopi land dispute.

BEFORE YOU READ

1. Can television "capture the mind"? How? Give examples.
2. How would you convey your love of nature and the land on television?

1 I was once asked to give advice on publicity to some traditional Hopi elders, who were fighting a strip mine on their reservation at Black Mesa, Arizona. Black Mesa was sacred ground to the traditional Hopis. To rip it open and remove its contents was a violation of the Hopis' most ancient religious tenets.

2 The problem at Black Mesa was typical of what has happened on many American Indian reservations. The traditional Hopis had always refused to deal with the Bureau of Indian Affairs, which functions as overlord on all

reservations, and so they had been pushed aside. In their stead, the Bureau had created a tribal council composed mainly of Indians who no longer lived on the reservation. The tribal council members were not really even Hopis anymore; they were Mormons. Most had moved to Salt Lake City, had businesses there and returned to the reservation only for their council meetings. They agreed with the BIA that their job was to sell off Indian resources and land at the best possible price, thereby helping Indian people turn into Americans more quickly. The sale of strip-mine rights to a coal company was part of this process.

3   The traditional "government" that had preceded the tribal council was not really a government at all. It was a kind of informal grouping of religious leaders from the dozens of independent clans that together formed the Hopis. They did not sit in a hierarchical[1] arrangement over the rest of the Hopis; they functioned more as teachers or as guides to their religious conceptions.

4   The religion itself was based on what we would now think of as ecological laws of balance. The land was alive, the source of life. To rip it up and ship away its contents was so outrageous as to be unthinkable. To the Mormon-American Hopis, however, strip mines were indeed thinkable.

5   Eventually the traditionals realized that while they were ignoring the BIA and the tribal council, the land was being destroyed and the religion with it. The elders decided to fight. To fight they needed to learn white legal systems, white tactics and white means of manipulating the media. To learn these, they had to restructure their minds and conceptions. And so, to fight the enemy, the traditional Hopis began the process of self-destroying what remained of their own Indian-ness.

6   At some point television news discovered the struggle. Network crews were flown out from Hollywood. They shot images of the deserts, images of the 50-foot cranes, images of the older men and women standing picturesquely near their kivas.[2] Following the network news guidelines for "good television," they sought a "balanced report." They interviewed members of the Bureau of Indian Affairs, members of the tribal council and representatives of the coal company, all of whom discussed the issues in terms of contracts, rights, jobs and energy.

7   These opinions were juxtaposed with shots of some of the elderly Hopis, standing in the desert, speaking of the Great Spirit being represented in all things.

8   The news people added some footage of Hopi sacred dances and some images of the Hopis' most spiritual place, the kiva. The elders limited how far the reporters could go into their religion. It is against the Hopi religion for ceremonies and "power objects" to be photographed. The elders felt that to photograph these things "steals their aura." They also felt that exposing their ceremonies to people who have not been trained to understand them—a process that takes Hopi apprentices many years—would undermine the meaning of the ceremonies.

---

[1] Arranged according to increasing power.
[2] Underground rooms.

9   A week later, I watched the report on television. It got four minutes on the evening news. It was an earnest report. The reporters revealed that their sympathies lay with the traditionals, but they had created—as they had no choice but to do—a formula story: Progress vs. Tradition. Forty million Americans obtained their first, and perhaps only, views of the Hopi people in the form of images of cranes juxtaposed with Indians in suits and ties, responsible government officials concerned about jobs, and a lot of old savage-looking types in funny clothes, talking about a religion that says that to dig up the land is dangerous for the survival of every creature on the planet. These 40 million people also saw a white, modishly dressed TV newsman explain the crosscurrents in the struggle and plaintively ask whether something of an earlier culture couldn't be permitted to remain. "From Black Mesa, Arizona, this is John Doe reporting." This was followed by a commercial for Pacific Gas and Electric on the growing energy crisis and the need to tap all energy resources. The next story on the news was about a bank robbery.

10 I turned off the television set and wondered what effect this story had had on viewers. Did it help the Hopis? Would any good come from it?

11 It was certain that the old people had not come through as well as the businessmen, the government officials and the reporter's objective, practical analysis. The old people just seemed tragic and a little silly, if poignant.[3] They were attempting to convey something subtle, complex, foreign and ancient through a medium that didn't seem able to handle any of those things, one that is better suited to objective data, conflict and fast, packaged information.

12 I wondered, if I had been shooting that story myself for the evening news, could I have done a better job of it? Would I have been able to explain to white America that to care about what was going on down there they would have to care about the Hopi perception of reality, the Hopi mind and its integration with natural forces? Viewers would have to care about the landscape, the spaces, the time, the wind, the color, the feel of the land and the sacred places and things. How could I have conveyed something through the medium so that anyone would have cared, when everyone was sitting at home in darkened living rooms, watching television? It was time travel that needed to be conveyed. How could I have carried a viewer from home through time and space to another reality that can only make sense if experienced directly? I decided that my report would have been no better than this Hollywood crew's had been. In fact, theirs was probably as good as could have been done within the limits of the medium. But in the end, the Hopis were hurt, not helped. Their struggle was revealed, perhaps, but they themselves were further fixed into the model of artifact.[4] The medium could not be stretched to encompass[5] their message.

13 On the other hand, what if I had four minutes, or even one minute, to convey the essence of a product? A car? A stereo set? A vacuum cleaner? Could I

---

[3] Sad, touching.

[4] Something manufactured; an object.

[5] Include.

accomplish that efficiently? I certainly could. A product is a lot easier to get across on television than a desert or a cultural mind-set. Understanding Indian ways enough to care about them requires understanding a variety of dimensions[6] of nuance[7] and philosophy.

14 You don't need any of that to understand a product. If you are attempting to convey the essence of a product, you do not have problems of subtlety, detail, time and space, historical context or organic form. Products are inherently communicable on television because of their static quality, their sharp, clear, highly visible lines, and because they carry no informational meaning beyond what they themselves are. They contain no life at all and are therefore not capable of dimension. Nothing works better in telecommunication than images of products. Might television itself have no higher purpose?

REACTING

1. Do you agree with Jerry Mander's statement that television is better suited to conveying the characteristics of a product rather than nature itself or a culture? Why or why not?
2. What is the best program about nature you have seen on television? Describe it and suggest what Mander might say about it.

CONNECTING

1. Mander focuses on some Hopi attitudes toward the land. What other articles in this section may cause you to reconsider your own feelings about the earth we inhabit?
2. What ways can you find to connect this article to Richard Louv's "Are Today's Kids Detached from Nature?" (p. 271)?

LEARNING ABOUT WRITING FROM READING

Part of Mander's article uses concrete and specific language to give a quick description of the television news report that resulted from the journalists' visit to the Hopi reservation at Black Mesa, a description of "four minutes on the evening news":

> Forty million Americans obtained their first, and perhaps only, views of the Hopi people in the form of images of cranes juxtaposed with Indians in suits and ties, responsible government officials concerned about jobs, and a lot of old savage-looking types in funny clothes, talking about a religion that says that to dig up the land is dangerous for the survival of every creature on

---

[6] Levels or layers.

[7] Shade of meaning or expression.

the planet. These 40 million people also saw a white, modishly dressed TV newsman explain the crosscurrents in the struggle and plaintively ask whether something of an earlier culture couldn't be permitted to remain. "From Black Mesa, Arizona, this is John Doe reporting." This was followed by a commercial for Pacific Gas and Electric on the growing energy crisis and the need to tap all energy resources. The next story on the news was about a bank robbery.

When you are trying to describe a television show or news footage to your readers, you might use this paragraph as a model. Mander gives plenty of specific sight-and-sound details to help re-create the news report for readers who didn't see it for themselves.

BLACKFEET CHIEF

Our Land Is More Valuable Than Your Money

This speech was recorded in a nineteenth-century Treaty Council.

BEFORE YOU READ

1. Given what you know of American history, what would you expect a Native American in the 1800s to say about land and land use?
2. How do you react to a "No Trespassing" sign on open land or woods?

1   Our land is more valuable than your money. It will last forever. It will not perish by the flames of fire. As long as the sun shines and the waters flow, this land will be here to give life to men and animals; therefore, we cannot sell this land. It was put here by the Great Spirit and we cannot sell it because it does not belong to us. You can count your money and burn it within the nod of a buffalo's head, but only the Great Spirit can count the grains of grasses on these plains. As a present to you, we will give you anything you can take with you, but the land, never.

REACTING

1. Freewrite on your feelings about this short speech.
2. Do you think private ownership of land is good and necessary? Why or why not?

CONNECTING

1. What is the difference between owning land and using land?
2. How does this speech help you to answer the key question: "How are our environmental problems rooted in our cultural values and attitudes?"?

LEARNING ABOUT WRITING FROM READING

This short piece forms a useful example of a style that employs three basic sentence structures: *simple, complex,* and *compound.*

The opening sentences are simple declarative ones: "Our land is more valuable than your money. It will last forever. It will not perish by the flames of fire." Short sentences can be powerful in their effect.

Three of the Chief's sentences are longer. One is a compound sentence, joined by "and"; and two are complex sentences, joined by "therefore" or "but."

Think about varying your own sentence structure in this way. Blackfeet Chief uses only seven sentences, but he has three different *types* of sentences. In writing, as in speech, variety of sentence structure is one way to keep your audience's interest and to communicate different kinds of relationships between ideas.

ANNIE DILLARD

Seeing

Annie Dillard, naturalist and writer, lived by herself in the woods to duplicate an experiment that Henry David Thoreau had conducted in the 1840s and recorded in his book, Walden.

BEFORE YOU READ

1. Freewrite about a nature experience of your own.
2. Find out something about Henry David Thoreau as a nature writer. (He is mentioned by Dillard in paragraph 3.)

1   When I was six or seven years old, growing up in Pittsburgh, I used to take a precious penny of my own and hide it for someone else to find. It was a curious compulsion; sadly, I've never been seized by it since. For some reason I always "hid" the penny along the same stretch of sidewalk up the street. I would cradle it at the roots of a sycamore, say, or in a hole left by a chipped-off piece of sidewalk. Then I would take a piece of chalk, and, starting at either end of the block, draw huge arrows leading up to the penny from both directions. After I learned to write I labeled the arrows: SURPRISE AHEAD or MONEY

THIS WAY. I was greatly excited, during all this arrow-drawing, at the thought of the first lucky passer-by who would receive in this way, regardless of merit, a free gift from the universe. But I never lurked about. I would go straight home and not give the matter another thought, until, some months later, I would be gripped again by the impulse to hide another penny.

2   It is still the first week in January, and I've got great plans. I've been thinking about seeing. There are lots of things to see, unwrapped gifts and free surprises. The world is fairly studded and strewn with pennies cast broadside from a generous hand. But—and this is the point—who gets excited by a mere penny? If you follow one arrow, if you crouch motionless on a bank to watch a tremulous[1] ripple thrill on the water and are rewarded by the sight of a muskrat kit paddling from its den, will you count that sight a chip of copper only, and go your rueful way? It is dire poverty indeed when a man is so malnourished and fatigued that he won't stoop to pick up a penny. But if you cultivate a healthy poverty and simplicity, so that finding a penny will literally make your day, then, since the world is in fact planted in pennies, you have with your poverty bought a lifetime of days. It is that simple. What you see is what you get.

3   I used to be able to see flying insects in the air. I'd look ahead and see, not the row of hemlocks across the road, but the air in front of it. My eyes would focus along that column of air, picking out flying insects. But I lost interest, I guess, for I dropped the habit. Now I can see birds. Probably some people can look at the grass at their feet and discover all the crawling creatures. I would like to know grasses and sedges—and care. Then my least journey into the world would be a field trip, a series of happy recognitions. Thoreau, in an expansive[2] mood, exulted, "What a rich book might be made about buds, including, perhaps, sprouts!" It would be nice to think so. I cherish mental images I have of three perfectly happy people. One collects stones. Another—an Englishman, say—watches clouds. The third lives on a coast and collects drops of seawater which he examines microscopically and mounts. But I don't see what the specialist sees, and so I cut myself off, not only from the total picture, but from the various forms of happiness.

4   Unfortunately, nature is very much a now-you-see-it, now-you-don't affair. A fish flashes, then dissolves in the water before my eyes like so much salt. Deer apparently ascend bodily into heaven; the brightest oriole fades into leaves. These disappearances stun me into stillness and concentration; they say of nature that it conceals with a grand nonchalance, and they say of vision that it is a deliberate gift, the revelation[3] of a dancer who for my eyes only flings away her seven veils. For nature does reveal as well as conceal: now-you-don't-see-it, now-you-do. For a week last September migrating red-winged blackbirds were feeding heavily down by the creek at the back of the house. One day I went out to investigate the racket; I walked up to a tree, an Osage orange, and a hundred

---

[1] Trembling, shaking.

[2] Exuberant, optimistic.

[3] Uncovering, manifestation.

birds flew away. They simply materialized out of the tree. I saw a tree, then a whisk of color, then a tree again. I walked closer and another hundred blackbirds took flight. Not a branch, not a twig budged: the birds were apparently weightless as well as invisible. Or, it was as if the leaves of the Osage orange had been freed from a spell in the form of red-winged blackbirds; they flew from the tree, caught my eye in the sky, and vanished. When I looked again at the tree the leaves had reassembled as if nothing had happened. Finally I walked directly to the trunk of the tree and a final hundred, the real diehards, appeared, spread, and vanished. How could so many hide in the tree without my seeing them? The Osage orange, unruffled, looked just as it had looked from the house, when three hundred red-winged blackbirds cried from its crown. I looked downstream where they flew, and they were gone. Searching, I couldn't spot one. I wandered downstream to force them to play their hand, but they'd crossed the creek and scattered. One show to a customer. These appearances catch at my throat: they are the free gifts, the bright coppers at the roots of trees.

REACTING

1. What does Annie Dillard value in her experience of the natural world? Is it what you value?
2. If you are a city dweller, can you respond to your urban environment in the same way that Dillard responds to nature?

CONNECTING

1. Compare Dillard's views of nature with those of Richard Louv ("Are Today's Kids Detached from Nature?" p. 271). Why do these two writers think that experiencing the natural world is so important for us?
2. Would most Americans agree with the feelings expressed here about nature? Support your view.

LEARNING ABOUT WRITING FROM READING

Annie Dillard's essay contains some useful examples of semicolon use. Semicolons can be used (like periods) to separate independent clauses. The difference between semicolons and periods, though, is that the period is a very sharp divider and separator of ideas; the semicolon leaves the gate open and asks the reader to connect the two independent clauses in some way. Here are some examples of Dillard's semicolon use:

> These disappearances stun me into stillness and concentration; they say of nature that it conceals with a grand nonchalance, and they say of vision that it is a deliberate gift, the revelation of a dancer who for my eyes only flings away her seven veils.

and

> Or, it was as if the leaves of the Osage orange had been freed from a spell in the form of red-winged blackbirds; they flew from the tree, caught my eye in the sky, and vanished.

and

> These appearances catch at my throat; they are the free gifts, the bright coppers at the roots of trees.

Points to note about semicolon use:

1. You can use a semicolon where you would use a period. A semicolon separates two independent clauses, or ideas, that can stand on their own.
2. A semicolon indicates more of a connection between ideas than a period would.
3. Don't use a comma instead of a semicolon, or you will create a comma splice.

AMORY B. LOVINS

Technology Is the Answer (But What Was the Question?)

Amory B. Lovins, physicist and energy consultant, looks at how better use of technology can reduce our energy and environmental problems.

BEFORE YOU READ

1. List five solutions to environmental problems.
2. List images or ideas that come to mind when you hear the phrase *energy conservation*.

1   The answers you get depend on the questions you ask. But sometimes it seems so important to resolve a crisis that we forget to ask what problem we're trying to solve.

2   It is fashionable to suppose that we're running out of energy and that the solution is obviously to get lots more of it. But asking how to get more energy begs the questions of how much we need. That depends not on how much we used in the past but on what we want to do in the future and how much energy it will take to do those things.

3   How much energy it takes to make steel, run a sewing machine, or keep ourselves comfortable in our house depends on how cleverly we use energy, and the more it costs, the smarter we seem to get. It is now cheaper, for example, to

double the efficiency of most industrial electric motor drive systems than to fuel existing power plants to make electricity. *(Just this one saving can more than replace the entire U.S. nuclear power program.)* We know how to make lights five times as efficient as those presently in use and how to make household appliances that give us the same work as now, using one-fifth as much energy (saving money in the process).

4 Ten automakers have made good-sized, peppy, safe prototype cars averaging 29–59 kilometers per liter (62–138 miles per gallon). We know today how to make new buildings and many old ones so heat-tight (but still well ventilated) that they need essentially no energy to maintain comfort year-round, even in severe climates. (In fact, I live in one.)

5 These energy-saving measures are uniformly cheaper than going out and getting more energy. Detailed studies in more than a dozen countries have shown that supplying energy services in the cheapest way—by wringing more work from the energy we already have—would let us increase our standard of living while using several times less total energy (and electricity) than we do now. Those savings cost less than finding new domestic oil or operating existing power plants.

6 However, the old view of the energy problem included a worse mistake than forgetting to ask how much energy we needed: It sought more energy, in any form, from any source, at any price—as if all kinds of energy were alike. This is like saying, "All kinds of food are alike; we're running short of potatoes and turnips and cheese, but that's okay, we can substitute sirloin steak and oysters Rockefeller."

7 Some of us have to be more discriminating than that. Just as there are different kinds of food, so there are many different forms of energy, whose different prices and qualities suit them to different uses. . . . There is, after all, no demand for energy as such; nobody wants raw kilowatt-hours or barrels of sticky black goo. People instead want energy services: comfort, light, mobility, hot showers, cold beverages, and the ability to bake bread and make cement. We ought therefore to start at that end of the energy problem and ask, "What tasks do we want energy for, and what amount, type, and source of energy will do each task most cheaply?"

8 Electricity is a particularly high-quality, expensive form of energy. An average kilowatt-hour delivered in the United States in 1992 was priced at about 7¢, equivalent to buying the heat content of oil costing $116 per barrel—about six times the average world price in 1992. The average cost of electricity from nuclear plants (including fuel and operating expenses) beginning operation in 1988 was 13.5¢ per kilowatt-hour, equivalent on a heat basis to buying oil at about $216 per barrel.

9 Such costly energy might be worthwhile if it were used only for the premium[1] tasks that require it, such as light, motors, electronics, and smelters. But those special uses, only 8% of all delivered U.S. energy needs, are already met

---

[1] Most important.

twice over by today's power stations. Two-fifths of our electricity is already spilling over into uneconomic, low-grade uses such as water heating, space heating, and air conditioning; yet no matter how efficiently we use electricity (even with heat pumps), we can never get our money's worth on these applications.

10   Thus, *supplying more electricity is irrelevant to the energy problem we have*. Even though electricity accounts for almost all of the federal energy research and development budget and for at least half of national energy investment, it is the wrong kind of energy to meet our needs economically. Arguing about what kind of new power station to build—coal, nuclear, solar—is like shopping for the best buy in antique Chippendale chairs to burn in your stove or brandy to put in your car's gas tank. *It is the wrong question.*

11   Indeed, *any kind of new power station is so uneconomical that if you have just built one, you will save the country money by writing it off and never operating it.* Why? Because its additional electricity can be used only for low-temperature heating and cooling (the premium "electricity-specific" uses being already filled up) and is the most expensive way of supplying those services. Saving electricity is much cheaper than making it.

12   The real question is, What is the cheapest way to do low-temperature heating and cooling? The answer is weather-stripping, insulation, heat exchangers, greenhouses, superwindows (which have as much insulating value as the outside wall of a typical house), window shades and overhangs, trees, and so on. These measures generally cost about half a penny per kilowatt-hour; the running costs alone for a new nuclear plant will be nearly 4¢ per kilowatt-hour, so it's cheaper not to run it. In fact, under the crazy U.S. tax laws, the extra saving from not having to pay the plant's future subsidies is probably so big that by shutting the plant down society can also recover the capital cost of having built it!

13   If we want more electricity, we should get it from the cheapest sources first. In approximate order of increasing price, these include:

14   • Converting to efficient lighting equipment. This would save the United States electricity equal to the output of 120 large power plants plus $30 billion a year in fuel and maintenance costs.

15   • Using more efficient motors to save half the energy used by motor systems. This would save electricity equal to the output of another 150 large power plants and repay the cost in about a year.

16   • Eliminating pure waste of electricity, such as lighting empty offices at headache level. Each kilowatt-hour saved can be resold without having to generate it anew.

17   • Displacing with good architecture, and with passive and some active solar techniques, the electricity now used for water heating and space heating and cooling. Some U.S. utilities now give low- or zero-interest weatherization loans, which you need not start repaying for ten years or until you sell your house—because it saves the utility millions of dollars to have available the electricity you don't use instead of building new power plants. Most utilities also offer rebates for buying efficient appliances.

18. • Making appliances, smelters, and the like cost-effectively efficient.

19. Just these five measures can quadruple U.S. electrical efficiency, making it possible to run today's economy, with no changes in lifestyles, using no power plants, whether old or new and whether fueled with oil, gas, coal, or uranium. We would need only the present hydroelectric[2] capacity, readily available small-scale hydroelectric projects, and a modest amount of wind power. If we still wanted more electricity, the next cheapest sources would include:

20. • Industrial cogeneration, combined heat-and-power plants, low-temperature heat engines run by industrial waste heat or by solar ponds, filling empty turbine bays and upgrading equipment in existing big dams, modern wind machines or small-scale hydroelectric turbines in good sites, steam-injected natural gas turbines, and perhaps recent developments in solar cells with waste heat recovery.

21. It is only after we had clearly exhausted all these cheaper opportunities that we would even consider:

22. • Building a new central power station of any kind—the slowest and costliest known way to get more electricity (or to save oil).

23. To emphasize the importance of starting with energy end uses rather than energy sources, consider a sad little story from France, involving a "spaghetti chart" (or energy flowchart)—a device energy planners often use to show how energy flows from primary sources via conversion processes to final forms and uses. In the mid-1970s energy conservation planners in the French government started, wisely, on the right-hand side of the spaghetti chart. They found that their biggest need for energy was to heat buildings; and that even with good heat pumps, electricity would be the most costly way to do this. So they had a fight with their nationalized[3] utility; they won, and electric heating was supposed to be discouraged or even phased out because it was so wasteful of money and fuel.

24. Meanwhile, down the street, the energy supply planners (who were far more numerous and influential in the French government) were starting on the left-hand side of the spaghetti chart. They said: "Look at all that nasty imported oil coming into our country! We must replace that oil. Oil is energy. . . . We need some other source of energy. Voilà![4] Reactors can give us energy; we'll build nuclear reactors all over the country." But they paid little attention to who would use that extra energy and no attention to relative prices.

---

[2] Electricity produced by waterpower.
[3] Owned and run by the government.
[4] There you have it; there it is.

25   Thus the two sides of the French energy establishment went on with their respective solutions to two different, indeed contradictory, French energy problems: *more energy of any kind* versus *the right kind to do each task in the most inexpensive way*. It was only in 1979 that these conflicting perceptions collided. The supply side planners suddenly realized that the only thing they would be able to sell all that nuclear electricity for would be electric heating, which they had just agreed not to do.

26   Every industrial country is in this embarrassing position (especially if we include as "heating" air conditioning, which just means heating the outdoors instead of the indoors). Which end of the spaghetti chart we start on, or *what we think the energy problem is*, is not an academic abstraction: *It determines what we buy*. It is the fundamental source of disagreement about energy policy.

27   People starting on the left side of the spaghetti chart think the problem boils down to whether to build coal or nuclear power stations (or both). People starting on the right realize that *no* kind of new power station can be an economic way to meet the needs for using electricity to provide low- and high-temperature heat and for the vehicular liquid fuels that are 92% of our energy problem.

28   So if we want to provide our energy services at a price we can afford, let's get straight what question our technologies are supposed to answer. Before we argue about the meatballs, let's untangle the strands of spaghetti, see where they're supposed to lead and find out what we really need the energy *for*!

REACTING

1. Does Amory Lovins convince you that technology is the answer? List specific examples of where his evidence convinces or fails to convince you.

2. What solutions to the environmental crisis can you think of that are in conflict with Lovins's solutions?

CONNECTING

1. How do you think that Lovins might answer the key question, "How are our environmental problems rooted in our cultural values and attitudes?"?

2. What are the articles in this chapter that view technology differently than Lovins does? What role do you think technology plays in environmental change?

LEARNING ABOUT WRITING FROM READING

When an article persuades us, it may be, according to Aristotle, by appealing to our emotions, or sense of morality, or logic. In this article Lovins is appealing to our sense of logic. He does not move the reader emotionally with images or stories but asks us to consider rationally, even mathematically, the evidence he presents. Here's an example:

> Electricity is a particularly high-quality, expensive form of energy. An average kilowatt-hour delivered in the United States in 1992 was priced at about 7¢, equivalent to buying the heat content of oil costing $116 per barrel—about six times the average world price in 1992. The average cost of electricity from nuclear plants (including fuel and operating expenses) beginning operation in 1988 was 13.5¢ per kilowatt-hour, equivalent on a heat basis to buying oil at about $216 per barrel.

What are the strengths and weaknesses of Lovins's appeal to his readers' sense of logic? To answer this question, imagine this article making emotional or moral appeals.

SUSAN MCDONALD

The Media and Misinformation

Susan McDonald, an environmental writer and editor in Washington, D.C., analyzes and evaluates press coverage of environmental issues in the early 1990s.

BEFORE YOU READ

1. When you read the newspaper or watch the news on television, how do you decide if you are getting good and fair coverage of an issue or event?
2. Would you call yourself an environmentalist? Give your reasons.

1   In March 1993, when *The New York Times* published a five-part series on the seemingly misguided nature of U.S. environmental policy, the news reverberated through the mainstream media like a children's game of telephone. Other publications picked up the story, adopting its claims, while the story's misleading message took on a life of its own. Reporters facing tight deadlines and limited budgets recycled the news, trusting that the larger newspaper got the facts right. And, as pointed out in an *American Journalism Review* indictment of the series, inaccuracies printed in the series trickled down through smaller publications,

gaining momentum[1] and credibility.[2] By the time the story settled in the ear of the public, it was difficult to know what to believe: Had policy makers and the environmental movement overstated environmental threats? Were chemical contamination, sewage sludge, and ozone depletion no longer dangerous?

2   Answering these questions requires a deeper understanding of the whole story: Whispering in the ear of the mainstream media—and Congress and the public—has been a new set of pro-industry players calling themselves the "wise-use movement." Called counterenvironmentalists, or Multiple Abusers by environmentalists, they have generated a high-profile backlash against long-accepted environmental concerns, attempting to create false distinctions between environmental and economic health.

Rehashing Industry Arguments

3   In the first article of the *Times* series, reporter Keith Schneider claims that much of the environmental legislation of the past 20 years, especially those laws designed to protect the public against toxic waste and chemical hazards, was based on scientific ignorance and public panic. He announces a "new . . . wave of environmentalism sweeping across America" that questions the value of expensive environmental initiatives.

4   Schneider criticizes the high cost of toxic cleanup programs such as Superfund, implying that protection against low levels of chemical toxins and radioactive waste is not necessary or cost-effective. The reporter never mentions that Superfund's high cost often is due to fraud in the implementation of the program, not the cleanup itself. In a written response to the article, Michael Gregory, director of Arizona Toxics Information, places the blame squarely with "the inept and often corrupt management practices of the past twelve years which have encouraged contractor fraud and nearly abandoned the polluter pays principle."

5   While Schneider tries to minimize the notion of health risks from "low-level" doses of toxins, *Rachel's Hazardous Waste News* points out that he fails to mention prominent research such as the 1991 National Academy of Sciences study confirming the incidence of birth defects, miscarriage, heart problems, and neurological impairment among people living near chemical dumps as well as some higher rates of cancer "in residents exposed to compounds found at hazardous waste sites."

6   Schneider's report on a "new view" reiterates long-held industry arguments that certain forms of pollution pose little risk to the public because definitive proof linking pollution with public health effects is lacking. Moreover, they say the cost of cleanup in many cases outweighs risks. There's nothing new about this approach, says Fred Millar, director of Friends of the Earth's Toxic

---

[1] Speed.
[2] Believability.

Chemicals Project. "Ever since the Three Mile Island nuclear accident, we've been encountering risk assessment as a strategy deployed by the representatives of dangerous industries."

7 The problem, he says, is that companies themselves monopolize the "pseudo-scientific" determinations of "acceptable risk." Chemical industries that possess the information about the potential dangers effectively do not have to share this information with the public. The result: "The public bears the burden of proof of risk. It's very difficult to establish scientifically that a molecule from that industrial plant caused my cancer. Most health effects don't manifest themselves until long after exposure to pollution." The chemical companies get the benefit of the doubt, not the people, Millar says.

Unwise Use of Sources

8 It is only later in *The New York Times* series that the roots of this new wave of "environmentalism" become clear. Schneider cites a movement of "homeowners, farmers and others . . . upset by the growing cost of regulations," such as the Endangered Species Act and the Clean Water Act. What he doesn't tell us is that they are largely organized and funded by industry under the name "wise use," a loose coalition[3] of pro-industry groups, many based in the Western states, pushing a corporate agenda under the guise of grassroots activity.

9 The funders of the "movement" include timber, mining, and oil companies. The movement's agenda, detailed in "The Wise Use Agenda," a booklet by Ron Arnold and Alan Gottlieb of the Center for the Defense of Free Enterprise, includes opening the Arctic National Wildlife Refuge to oil and gas drilling, slashing the protections of the Endangered Species Act, opening protected public lands to mining and drilling, opposing automobile fuel efficiency standards, and "disproving" the value of community recycling campaigns.

10 Using grassroots strategies borrowed from the environmental movement—media campaigning, lobbying, and public education—these anti-environment groups have garnered attention for their claims. The result: The media has taken the bait and is fueling the backlash by recycling "wise use" misinformation.

Science versus Deadlines

11 Media coverage since last spring has attacked the full spectrum of well-accepted environmental claims. Articles and opinion pieces in the *Wall Street Journal*, *The New York Times*, the *Washington Post*, the *Arizona Republic*, and other outlets have challenged the threats of global warming, ozone depletion,[4] endangered species, acid rain, dioxin, radon, pesticides, and deforestation while questioning the value of conserving biodiversity[5] and recycling programs.

---

[3] Association.

[4] Reduction.

[5] Varied forms of life.

12   The irony in the coverage is that environmentalists, often accused of propagating[6] shoddy, emotionally-based science, have become increasingly scientific in their approach and employ some of the leading experts in environmental science; at the same time, reporters are rarely scientists themselves nor are they experts in the subject matter they cover. In pursuit of credibility and objectivity, they are forced to rely on "dueling experts" when covering an environmental topic, sometimes falling prey to the scientific theory or crackpot of the month.

Unfair Language

13   The backlash has taken other forms as well. In late 1991, Junior Bridge, a media and communications consultant, studied environmental coverage for Fairness and Accuracy in Reporting. Reviewing more than 800 environmental articles pulled from mainstream U.S. newspapers and magazines, Bridge discovered a disturbing trend. Of attributed quotes published in these articles, more than 50 percent were drawn from government officials—individuals who were identified in the story by name, title, and credentials, such as academic degrees. The second largest group of attributed quotes came from industry, again cited with credentials and described as experts.

14   The lowest number of quotes—less than four percent of the total—came from environmental groups, who were almost always quoted simply as "environmentalists," without reference to a particular organization, individual, or credential.

15   The effect, says Bridge, is subtle yet devastating. Even highly qualified experts quoted from environmental organizations "were nameless, faceless, credential-less," she says. "If they are not given credit for the same credentials as the others are, people are going to think 'environmentalists' are just wild-eyed radicals."

The Real Environmental Response

16   Fortunately, environmental groups and the public are growing wise to the misinformation put forth by the anti-environmental movement and the media outlets that buy into it. "Backlash in the Wild," an August 8 cable documentary produced by the National Audubon Society depicted the struggle on both sides of the land use debate. Said Arthur Kent, the journalist hosting the show, "In the West, the easiest thing to do is to say, 'You're going to lose your job if someone protects that tree over there.' . . . The wise-use people have quite crudely used language to create fear." Previous Audubon programs on logging and overgrazing of Western lands have faced their own backlash hurdles, as two corporate sponsors withdrew funding in the wake of boycotts organized by pro-industry groups, although both sponsors said the boycotts did not influence their decision.

17   At Friends of the Earth, Millar emphasizes a science-*and*-policy oriented approach as the community and environment's best weapon against the

---

[6] Spreading.

backlash. He calls it adversarial expertise. "We need to force companies to pay fees so that the local communities or governments can hire their own scientific experts to analyze the *company's* documents. We also must make sure companies report to the government what they know about environmental risks and what they're doing about it. What we have to do is put the burden on the polluter."

REACTING

1. Have you ever noticed who is consulted in news stories and who is treated like an "expert"? Would you agree with Susan McDonald's points in the section "Unfair Language" that words are used to discredit or endorse sources?
2. Is McDonald going too far when she labels corporate press releases and reports as "misinformation"? Explain the reasons behind your opinion.

CONNECTING

1. How would McDonald answer the question, "What role do the media play in presenting and solving environmental problems?"?
2. Compare the role that Jerry Mander ("TV's Capture of the Mind," p. 278) and McDonald think the media should play.

LEARNING ABOUT WRITING FROM READING

McDonald shows us how language can be used to promote or discredit positions. In a controversy, it is not always easy to find neutral terms for each side. In paragraph 2, McDonald draws attention to the way labels have been used on both sides. She also makes use of them herself:

> Whispering in the ear of the mainstream media—and Congress and the public—has been a new set of pro-industry players calling themselves the "wise-use movement." Called counterenvironmentalists, or Multiple Abusers by environmentalists, they have generated. . . .

You can decide for yourself how fairly McDonald uses labels for groups in the rest of the article, but here she does discuss the problem of labels and notes how different perspectives suggest different labels: environmentalists, multiple abusers, counterenvironmentalists, wise-use movement.

Think of other words you've heard used to describe the opposing positions covered in this article. What ones will you use when you write about the environment? Why?

WRITING ASSIGNMENTS

ASSIGNMENT I
WRITE A PAPER EXPLAINING WHY PEOPLE SOMETIMES CONTINUE TO DO THINGS THAT ARE HARMFUL TO THE ENVIRONMENT.

Coming Up with Ideas and a Focus

You might begin by generating a list of reasons for the things you yourself do that continue to harm the environment. To get more ideas, try interviewing other people about their own attitudes and lifestyles. After reviewing your material, focus on people's reasons for continuing one specific activity: using disposable diapers, commuting alone in their cars, or voting against local or national environmental legislation.

Organizing Your Ideas

Probably the simplest way of seeing this paper is as a statement-support kind of argument. You can make a statement about why people continue to do things that harm the environment and then support it with reasons that can be developed through example and illustration. (For help with statement-support papers, see pp. 305 and 365.)

Audience

Try writing this paper with dedicated environmental activists in mind. Imagine that they are so committed to their cause that they find it hard to understand how people could remain unconcerned. It's your job to convince them why—perhaps so that they may work to change more minds.

ASSIGNMENT II
INTERVIEW SOMEONE ABOUT HER OR HIS SOLUTION TO AN ENVIRONMENTAL PROBLEM.

Coming Up with Ideas and a Focus

Whom will you interview? Locate a good candidate by asking around at your school or workplace or among family members. Read your local paper to find public figures who might be good subjects for this kind of interview. The assignment suggests a central focus: the solution to a specific problem. But you will probably need to design some smaller, follow-up questions under this umbrella question: How much would the solution cost? Is it practical? Will people accept it? What are its drawbacks? And so on.

Organizing Your Ideas

The assignment clearly suggests some kind of interview format. Review the chapter on interviewing (Chapter 13) and then decide which one to choose. You could use the question-and-answer format in which you include your questions and record the interviewee's answers. Or you might want to write up those answers in a statement-support format.

Audience

You might try directing this paper to the readers of a magazine or of your local or campus newspaper. Try to define the typical readers of the publication and then emphasize issues in the interview that will interest them most.

ASSIGNMENT III
EVALUATE A TV NEWS ITEM OR NEWSPAPER REPORT DEALING WITH AN ENVIRONMENTAL ISSUE. FIRST RESEARCH THE PROBLEM, THEN EVALUATE THE TV OR NEWSPAPER TREATMENT FOR FAIRNESS, ACCURACY, AND COMPLETENESS.

Coming Up with Ideas and a Focus

Reading the newspaper or watching television, notebook in hand, is the best way to get ideas for this assignment. Only then can you find a focus by choosing a specific report. Your research will then help you to focus on the second part of the question: figuring out whether the report has been fair, accurate, and complete in its coverage of the issue.

Organizing Your Ideas

The assignment provides one kind of outline for organization: describe the item's coverage and evaluate it for fairness, accuracy, and completeness. You may want to make some kind of evaluative statement early on in your paragraph, to guide your readers as they follow your initial description of the news item.

Audience

Try directing your paper to a group of television network news executives, or to a newspaper editor, as a reasoned critique of their presentation of an important issue. With such an audience in mind, you'll be encouraged to be accurate yourself, because your audience may be defensive and need convincing.

ASSIGNMENT IV
DESCRIBE YOUR OWN EXPERIENCE WITH AN ENVIRONMENTAL PROBLEM.

Coming Up with Ideas and a Focus

What experiences have you had? Before you find a focus for this paper, you might want to recall the past by freewriting about certain events or experiences in your own life. Think about standard environmental problems—landfills, noise, toxic waste, deforestation, industrial emissions, pollution at the beach, fishkills—and focus on your own experience with one of them in particular. How have you personally been affected by it?

Organizing Your Ideas

Your organizational pattern will probably be basically descriptive, as the assignment suggests. But you may also find yourself telling a story as a way of conveying what happened and what you felt. (For help with narrative papers, see pp. 306 and 366.)

Audience

You could try writing this to someone your age who is concerned about the environment, but who lives on the other side of the world. This audience (with little or no knowledge of life in the United States) should encourage you to provide specific details about the nature of the problem and how it has felt to experience it firsthand.

SECTION II

Working on Your Paper: A Guide to Writing

Getting into a Working Mood

We thought of titling this half of the book "How to Write a Paper," but that sounded too authoritative, as if we could give just one set of instructions. What follow are lots of ideas for you to pick and choose from—whether you are editing or organizing, drafting or revising, or trying to come up with ideas.

What generally makes a paper turn out well is your being willing to work at it and having enough time to keep going back to it. Only rarely will your best writing come easily. To give yourself some company, read what other students say about working on their writing.

> *A metaphor [for writing] that I have discovered myself is that writing is like shooting and editing a video. (I'm a communications major.) We have to go out and shoot every possible thing that could be related. We often have to do it quite a few times to get it just right. . . . Sometimes we shoot for hours and only come up with a few minutes worth of usable material. The most frustrating thing is finding out when you get to the editing lab that you don't have enough footage to fill your time allotment. Then you have to go back and redo some things and see where it can be changed. I have found that the processes involved in shooting a video very closely parallel the processes of writing a paper.*
>
> —AMY ROBINSON

> *Revise—the only word that starts to cramp up my right hand. . . . Sometimes I think God himself could not write a paper without needing some revision.*
>
> —MARTIN CHADWICK

> *Revision sometimes comes easy to some people, but to me nothing comes easy. When I take on revision I sometimes feel like I'm taking on the whole world. . . . I can never revise my papers well, but for someone else's I can usually give good advice. That's why I like other people's advice. A person gets bogged down with their own paper and they don't see other views or questions that could be added.*
>
> —ANGIE SYKES

> *Sometimes I have this voice in the back of my head saying that— "You're no good, go ahead and quit!" then another voice says—"but you have so much to say."*
>
> —SHILOH PEARCE

There are more ideas in this half of the book than you can use for any one paper, especially in the "Coming Up with Ideas and a Focus," "Organizing," and "Revising" sections. To avoid trying to do too much, scan the section, then choose one or two ideas in that section to try out for your paper. You can try other ideas on other assignments.

Chapter 9

Coming Up with Ideas

Brainstorming to Find Your Ideas
Freewriting to Find Your Ideas
Using Questions to Turn Up Ideas
Talking Ideas Out
Finding a Focus

Most people, even professional writers, have trouble getting started on their writing. One of the following profiles may describe you.

You have **too much to say.** You feel as if you can never get it all down. You need to find a way to see what all your thoughts are so you can start to look for a focus around which to organize them.

You have **too little to say.** Everything you want to say you can say in one short paragraph. You cringe when you hear that the paper is supposed to be four pages long. You need to play around with ideas so one idea will trigger another.

Your **ideas are buried.** Maybe you're like the writer Joan Didion, who said: "Had I been blessed with even limited access to my own mind there would be no reason to write. I write entirely to find out what I'm thinking, what I'm looking at, what I see and what it means. What I want and what I fear." For you, writing is discovering what you think.

You **can't find a focus.** You have lots of ideas but don't know what your focus—sometimes called main point or thesis statement—should be. If you cover everything you are thinking about, you could write a ten-volume series on the subject.

- Your ideas are **confused.** You may get into a paper and suddenly find that you are not sure what you think. Robert Frost would tell students that confusion was the start of thinking. You need to explore your confusion, which often comes from a positive trait—your ability to see an issue from two sides and to be pulled in two directions.
- You get **stuck on your rough draft.** You've read and reread your draft, and you still don't know how to expand or change it. You need to come up with more ideas or details for a particular section.

No matter what difficulties you have in getting started or focused, take heart. In this section we describe three strategies to help: brainstorming, freewriting, and asking questions. These strategies, which will get you talking or writing about your paper in a quick, stress-free way, can dredge up amazing ideas. Working fast and loose and sloppy is best. Working quickly can help you to concentrate. Being loose and sloppy keeps you from blocking the fine ideas that come from throwing guesses and hunches around.

Brainstorming (listing ideas), freewriting (writing without pause), and asking questions are all good, quick ways to start thinking about your paper. If you do this a day or a week before the paper is due, you engage your subconscious mind on the assignment. So your brain is thinking about the paper and puzzling over trouble spots even as you sleep. Have you ever gone to sleep worrying about a personal problem and then woken up with a new angle to think about or a clearer sense of the problem? You will often find that your subconscious is very bright.

As you probably have already heard, the brain we're aware of is like the tip of an iceberg; nine-tenths is submerged. When you jot ideas down fast, you dig in to see what else is in the vast regions of your brain. So these exercises should get you talking to yourself and finding out what you know.

Jotting ideas down on paper will help you in all stages of the writing process. It helps you:

Get your subconscious brain going on the assignment

Find all the ideas that you have

Organize your ideas by laying them all out in front of you

Find out what you think or feel

Surprise yourself

Revise a paper

I discard much more than I use, sure. I wouldn't call them blocks, though. I suppose it's simply that one is walking into the dark. When you walk in the dark, you touch objects you can't recognize, and you then have to stop and go back and walk around them from another angle.

Arthur Miller, Author of *Death of a Salesman,* Quoted in Donald Murray's *Shoptalk*

Brainstorming to Find Your Ideas

Brainstorming involves making a list of whatever comes into your head. Set aside five or ten minutes for it and try to keep coming up with ideas the whole time. Brainstorming is often used in the corporate world, where managers use flip charts to record ideas. The "rules" they follow are the important thing:

- Just keep listing ideas. Don't worry if it's a good or a bad idea.
- Don't comment on or worry about anyone else's idea.

Later, you can go back over the list and pick through it. With brainstorming, anything goes. Someone else's or your own "dumb" idea may trigger a brilliant one. So put that vital part of your brain that censors and edits "on hold" for a few minutes, and write down anything and everything that comes to mind.

Here is the result of one writer's brainstorming about a topic that is discussed in the chapter on violence.

Why Is America So Violent?

lots of violence
on television
on the streets too
people have guns
and see them being used
gun laws
criminals use them
drugs
always has been outlaw country
wild frontier
every man for himself
cars are violent
machinery is violent
school can be
competitive beating someone out
sports we like to watch that are violent
Romans did too
lions at the Coliseum
man has always been violent
look at wars
may be women, too
are all countries equally violent
if they aren't then why not
Americans more violent
frontier—wild cowboy wild Indian
individual
anger
lots of poverty
lots of people not having
not having jobs, cars, things, Air Jordans
not having
having guns

After five or ten minutes of brainstorming, you will have a list like this. This writer came up with lots of ideas—which is good in itself. Just seeing the list may help the writer zero in on one idea and investigate and develop it. Maybe the writer will do a paper showing the links or chain reaction among all these ideas, or maybe focus on television and show how one program works to reinforce some of these ideas. In any case, some of what's in the writer's brain is down on paper, and she or he is able to look at it and go on from there to focus and organize.

Freewriting to Find Your Ideas

In freewriting, the important rule is: *Don't stop writing.* Give yourself a ten-minute limit to start. And make yourself write without even pausing for the whole ten minutes. Because freewriting works the way brainstorming does—on guesses and hunches and quick reactions—you need to move fast. You still won't be able to record every thought you have, but you want to come as close as you can. Do not worry at all about mistakes or correct sentences or finishing ideas or bad spelling. The best, most useful freewriting can be the messiest and hardest for someone else to understand. You freewrite for yourself.

When you freewrite with a focus, you choose a topic and try to stay with it. If your writing wanders very far from your topic, then you try to pull it back.

Again, the main rule is: *Don't stop writing*—even if you have to write "writing writing writing" to keep your pen moving. Keep writing.

Here's an example of a student's freewriting on a time when she felt poor, one of the questions suggested in Chapter 6, on poverty and wealth:

> Feeling poor, actually I've never been poor when I think about it. Been well off with extra money for padding but we never spent extravagantly or anything. Once my family went to florida in the spring to a resort that was closing down; that was the only time I felt hey we're rich. Yet we are kind of rich, when it came to going to college, there was no question the money was there, but I didn't go out and get all new clothes like they act like everyone does at Mademoiselle. I think I've felt poor a lot though, kind of weak and powerless, the first time I remember was when I was in first or second or third grade. It wasn't first grade I was too young then but I was waiting for the bus and I remember Evelyn Roberts. she was the richest girl in our class and we talked over that a lot, even as second and third graders we talked over alot who had money and who didn't. That morning it was cold and we were waiting for the bus in the sheltered doorway of an apartment building. It's funny I don't remember what led up to it but I remember the pile lining of my hood and being pressed into a crevice of the building that had surfaces like sandpaper and Evelyn's warm breath when she got right up into my face and asked me. Is your family poor? She didn't say it in a mean way at all, but she said it low and confidential, like she wanted to know if we had leprosy or something that should be kept a secret. The funny thing is I can't remember what I answered, but that's the first time I remember feeling poor. It was not a good or powerful feeling.

Here the writer jumps around at the start before focusing on an anecdote, which is exactly what happens in freewriting. She does focus on one incident and remembers it in good detail. Maybe at the end she tries to wrap up too neatly, but you can tell she has started to tap into memories of what "being poor" feels like. Notice all the errors; they were left in to remind you that, in freewriting, errors don't matter.

Using Questions to Turn Up Ideas

Questions are more important than answers.
I'm looking for openings, not closings.
     MADELEINE L'ENGLE, *On Being a Writer*

Asking questions: What better way to learn and to get thinking on paper. Children take us aback with some of their questions: "What makes thunder?" We start to explain about thunder and then realize that we don't really know. Questions can make us think about things we hadn't considered before. Questions get a writer going. In asking yourself questions, you come up with ideas and can revise and invent. Reporters use who, what, where, when, and why? And media analyst Earl Babbie recommends: "Who says what to whom? Why? How? To what effect?" in his book, *The Practice of Social Research*.

But sometimes the question "What questions?" comes up. That takes some inventing on its own. Following are some questions to help you get moving in your writing. We discuss each one in detail.

   What evidence supports this statement?

   What happened?

   What is it like?

   What does this word mean?

   How are two things alike or different?

   What caused this? What are the effects of this?

   What is the problem? How can it be solved?

These questions can be useful for producing ideas when you are starting out, organizing, or revising. Each of these broad questions can be broken down into more specific subquestions, helping you to produce more and more ideas. You won't be able to use all of these questions at once. Work with the one or two questions that best help you to do your assignment.

Question: What Evidence Supports This Statement?

If you intend to give reasons to support a statement or opinion, this is the question you ask. This approach, known as *statement and support,* is the basic framework of many articles and papers, whether the writer consciously planned it that way or not. You make a statement and then tell the reasons for that statement being true or valid. When you use this format for coming up with ideas, you turn the statement into a question and answer it. Because "What evidence supports this statement?" is a very broad question, you'll need to break it down into several smaller, related questions, such as these:

1. What anecdotes/statistics/testimony of experts/facts/examples/moral reasons support this statement?
2. How is this evidence related to the statement?
3. What other support is needed to be convincing?
4. What evidence is there that this statement is not true?

When you come up with a list of answers to these questions, you will have some ideas to work with.

Question: What Happened?

You answer "What happened?" if you are giving the reader an account of an event or series of events. *Narrative* is simply a word for story; it means that you tell what happened. Often in narratives the order is chronological—by the clock—and you tell what happened in the order as it happened. Some writers, though, start a story and then move back into the past—sometimes with flashbacks—so the movement is not always by the clock or calendar. Because telling what happens could go on forever, any narrative is selective; it begins at a certain point, ends at another, and selects what to report on in between. Here are some questions that will help you answer the larger question, "What happened?"

1. What was happening before the events?
2. Who did it happen to?
3. Why did it happen?
4. What did it feel like when it happened?
5. What sights, sounds/conversations, smells were part of the event?
6. Where and when did it happen?
7. In what order? (What happened next?)
8. What were the consequences of its happening?
9. What was most important?

> **Example:**
>
> Here's a student writing about the time his apartment was robbed. He's got a topic and wants to find out what's in it. Note that he freewrites answers to the questions above, although he doesn't handle them one by one:
>
> *In New York, you always feel like you could get robbed especially when you take the subway. You can feel where your wallet is every minute. My roommates and I were careful though and spent a hundred dollars having*

another lock put in. Then this guy showed up at our apartment bringing a pizza we hadn't ordered. It could have been a mistake but it put us on alert even more. We didn't go down to the laundry without double locking. We had friends with triple locks. Then it happened I got home one day and the door was slightly opened. I called. No one answered. This was an eerie feeling. And then I saw the empty spaces where the TV and CD had been. I had that creepy feeling of someone having been in my place. I almost expected to be mugged from behind like you see on <u>McAllister</u>. I've seen someone mugged in their apartment 50 times this year on TV. So I slowly checked the apartment out til I was sure no one was there. I felt better, but that creepy subway feeling didn't go away.

What happened next?

Then it was time for damage control. What other holes and empty spaces were there going to be. The drawers had been gone through, but frankly we don't have a lot around to resell. A piggy bank my roommates girlfriend had given him was smashed and on the bed. He didn't think there was more than two dollars in that. I had left my watch and camera in my room on my chair. The fact I'm a slob saved me. There they were under my favorite T shirt and some other stuff.

My roommates wouldn't be coming back for a while but it looked like we had sustained minor damages. I called the police. I guess I expected flashing blue light out on the street. The guy on the phone sounded real tired; I had to repeat half the stuff twice and he said they'd send some detectives over.

By then I didn't have to be told it wouldn't be Sunday. I would have waited for my roommates to come but there was no CD and no TV so I went upstairs and waited for them at my buddies. I left a note on the door.

When they came back, I could see the shock and a bit of fear too. But with all of us there together it quickly heated up to anger. We'd been ripped off. They looked around it was just the CD and TV and a broken piggy bank.

Why did it happen?

The door was marked so it was pretty clear that the last one out had forgotten the double lock. Gary felt lousy about that, especially because he never forgets stuff like that. We tried slipping a Visa card through when the door was shut, and it sure was easy. Hey, we told Gary you didn't steal it, but we all felt lousy because we didn't have insurance.

What was most important?

The police came and they could have been off a TV comedy show. One of them picked up the piggy bank and the other one had to tell him to check it for fingerprints. Actually maybe he only did that because we had made a

> *big point of not having touched it. They looked around and we talked a little about crime. It was pretty clear when they left that we would never see our stuff again. I wouldn't want their job. Now on TV the whole thing would have been a lot more exciting. The thieves would have had a very deep reason for wanting our TV—stolen jewels in it or something—and Sherlock would have unraveled the whole thing or some dude would have at least crashed through the door shooting to solve the case. This was just part of the uneasy routine of the city—a minor business transaction—faceless. Thank God.*

As you can see, this student launched into a kind of focused freewrite that pretty much answers the subquestions listed earlier, though not in the same order. His "freewriting" exercise looks more like a rough draft, in fact.

With an unfamiliar topic, though, you may not feel able to launch into this kind of writing. Imagine, for example, that you have to write a report about a robbery that didn't happen to you. You may find it helpful to take each smaller question separately, much as a reporter on a newspaper would, in order to explore all aspects of the topic.

Question: What Is It Like?

The question "What is it like?" will help you come up with ideas when your paper is focused on describing something to the reader. When you use this description format to get ideas down on paper, you are asking yourself to think about and explain to someone what a person, place, or thing is like. To come up with ideas, try these subquestions:

1. What does it look/feel/taste/sound or smell like?
2. What goes on there?
3. What images suggest what the person or place or thing is like?
4. What conversations or remarks are said?
5. What is done there, or what does this person typically do?
6. What does this person typically say?
7. What are typical gestures?
8. How do people feel when they are around this person or place or thing?

Question: What Does This Word Mean?

If your paper is defining and exploring the meaning of words, then this is the question you are answering for the reader. What do you do when you define something? You tell what it means. That sounds simple or obvious, but defining clarifies your thinking. Forget the times you've gone to the dictionary and found nothing new or found an entry that sent you in circles (like "revision—

the act of revising"). But sometimes it is surprising how many avenues of thinking will open up to you when you ask the simple question, "What does this mean?" about your subject. Here are some questions that will help expand your thinking as you try to find out what a word means:

1. What are other ways of saying this word, or synonyms for this word?
2. What is the opposite of this word?
3. What associations do I have with this word?
4. How has this word or phrase changed in meaning?
5. What examples or images can I give of this word?

Example:

Say you are starting the chapter on poverty and just want to get yourself thinking about what poverty is. Here's what using the definition question might produce. This one was done by a class exploring what they meant by "poverty."
What do we mean when we talk about poverty?

- "I don't have as much as someone else even though I am well off. My car is a Prelude, but my roommate has a Mercedes."
- "it is hard to get ahead. You can go to school, but you have no extra advantages—trips, books, leisure time for reading."
- poverty could be starvation—not being able to stay alive.
- poverty could be having so much less than other people that you are different, alone, or at least isolated. Like standing out at school because of the clothes you wear or not having a car to go places.
- poverty could be in your mind. You could be rich but lonely, mean, miserable. That could be a kind of poverty too.
- poverty could be something you don't notice. Like kids who have enough to eat but wear ragged clothes. They don't know that or care. Is that poverty if you don't know you're poor?
- poverty line. There's something like the government draws and they say below that you are poor. But you can be below it and still not get government aid.
- you're on welfare—That's poverty.

This list shows that a lot of ideas can be floating around in our heads when we think about "poverty." It suggests different focuses for papers on poverty. It also shows the importance of defining exactly what we mean when we talk about poverty with others. They may mean feeling poor in a new Prelude next to a Mercedes. We may mean starving to death.

Question: How Are Two Things Alike or Different?

This question asks you to compare and contrast, as we do all the time in our daily lives when we want to learn. For example, you may not feel on top of things in Spanish class if you sit next to someone with a photographic memory. But if you compare yourself with someone in the back row who never does the assignment, you may feel pretty sharp.

When starting a paper, write out answers to these questions to see what ideas you come up with:

1. How do the two things appear, the same or different?
2. Does one have the same kinds of articles and features as the other?
3. Do they function in the same way?

Questions: What Caused This? What Are the Effects of This?

If you are explaining in your paper the causes or effects of something, then you will need to answer these questions for both the reader and yourself. When you ask questions about cause and effect, you are looking at a chain reaction. How does one event or person or thing change another? What caused something to happen? What are the results of its happening? Following are some questions that can help you explore these larger issues:

On Causes

1. What are all the possible causes of something?
2. Are there deep-rooted causes of this?
3. What are the minor, less important causes?
4. What are the most important causes?
5. What are the most recent causes?
6. Was there one cause that started this off?
7. What are the hidden causes?
8. What are the obvious causes?

On Effects

1. What are all the possible effects?
2. What are the short- and long-term effects?
3. What are the good and bad aspects of each effect?
4. What could have prevented this from happening or from having these effects?
5. What would make sure that this always happens?

Questions: What Is the Problem?
How Can It Be Solved?

These are the two questions you ask yourself when writing a paper that describes a problem or its solution. This format asks you to take an active approach to your topic, looking at why something is a problem and what can be done about it. Some topics lend themselves immediately to this approach. Poverty and violence, for example, are recognized as problems immediately, and you can start thinking about what causes them and possible solutions. But other topics may surprise you with the way they fall into a problem-solving format. Asking the following subquestions will help you pursue the broader questions "What is the problem?" and "How can it be solved?"

1. What is the problem?
2. Why is it a problem?
3. What caused it?
4. What are the effects of this problem?
5. What should our goals be in solving this problem?
6. How can people be persuaded to care about this problem?
7. What are possible solutions?
8. What are the advantages of each solution?
9. What are the disadvantages of each solution?
10. How likely is each solution to work?
11. How much will each solution cost?
12. Which solution is best?
13. Would this solution create other problems?
14. How will life be different if this problem is solved?

Talking Ideas Out

Sometimes you get your best ideas just talking to another person. You start to talk and you hear yourself say something that is new or surprising or suddenly makes your thinking clear. Some people do much better talking their way to new ideas because talking relaxes them or makes them feel like taking risks or helps them to concentrate. With talk, there is nothing to erase. You just go on and forget what doesn't help you.

In this section we'll look at different ways to talk your ideas out to someone. All of these suggestions could also be done with a group or in writing, but here we'll discuss them as if you were working with a single partner, who plays one of the following roles:

The listener. Have the other person just listen to the ideas that you come up with; your partner won't be commenting at all. Just brainstorm or talk to find out what you have to say. Then do the same for your listener. Just listen to ideas—without commenting.

The recording secretary. Have your partner listen to and write down your ideas as you talk. It isn't necessary to get everything down; he or she should make a list or pause every so often to orally sum up the point you are making. When you do this for your partner or she does it for you, you may be surprised at the difference between what is written and what you think was said. Sometimes ideas become clearer just from noticing that difference.

The echo. This is a lot like playing the role of the recording secretary, only this time you repeat back what you heard the person say. You can wait until your partner has talked for a few minutes, or you can pause every minute and tell what you heard him say. This repetition can be surprising and useful, even if the summary is not quite right. And it won't always be; it is not that easy to sum up what another person said. But getting your ideas clear to someone else is a way to get them clear to yourself.

The questioner. This time, you and your partner play the role of questioner for each other. Your questions should focus on asking what your partner means rather than on doubting or raising objections. As you listen to your partner, think of all the questions you can, like "Do you mean? . . ." "Can you give me an example of? . . ." "What do you mean by? . . ." "Can you tell me more about? . . ." This questioning may help each of you to expand on ideas and to find new angles. If the person is describing, the questioner can help the describer expand on details and fill in the picture. All too often we assume people can see what's in our minds as we write; but they can't unless we fully describe what is there.

The objector. The objector type of listening and reacting is hard for some people and all too easy for others. The objector has to think of doubts and objections to the ideas the other person is presenting: "What's wrong?" "What's not believable?" "What's too sweeping a generalization?" "Where's the evidence?" These are the questions the objector has in her mind as she listens. Hearing your ideas doubted or challenged can give you more ideas and help you to question and expand on your ideas.

The yes-man. The "yes-man" listener helps you to expand your thinking by telling you what's right with it and why someone else would agree with it. Maybe the yes-man even gives you examples and proof to back up the points you are making. Playing the role of a yes-man can be productive, and it's fun to talk to someone who you know is going to support and agree with you.

The reactor. This time the person who is listening doesn't assume a role. She just tells you what she's thinking and feeling while listening to your ideas.

This running account of what "goes through your listener's mind" is what Peter Elbow called giving someone a movie of your mind.

The conversation partner. Think of this as a tennis match in words. You say something and the other person replies to what you have said. You reply back, and on it goes, like a rally in tennis. The dialogue has an agreed upon subject, but how it goes is determined by the two people. They can go back and forth supporting and agreeing with each other or disagreeing and trying to score a point.

All of the roles and exercises have the same thing in common: They are ways for you to work out your ideas informally, without worrying about how right or solid they are, and to use other people's reactions to spur your thinking and memory and curiosity. Because they are just invention exercises, you need to remember to keep loose and free, so that you will feel like exploring new ideas.

Finding a Focus

Narrowing your topic, developing your thesis, getting your angle—these are ways writers and teachers go about finding a focus. Seldom is our writing interesting if we try to cover a huge topic in a short paper. So, after you get all your ideas down on paper by brainstorming, freewriting, or using questions, look over what you've written and see what you can use for the focus, or topic, of your paper.

The following chart illustrates the difference between a book-length subject and a paper-length focus.

Violence in America

SUBJECT (book-length project)

Homicide

TOPIC (chapter-length project)

Handgun Laws and Homicide Rates

FOCUS (paper-length project)

The sooner you can find your focus, the easier your paper will be to draft. Plus, if you are doing research, having a focus will save you from spending time researching topics or even subjects you aren't going to write about.

Chapter 10

Keeping a Journal

Why Keep a Journal?
The Personal Journal
The Media Journal

Why Keep a Journal?

Keep a journal? How will that help me on my paper that's due next week? If that's your reaction, you are probably right. Keeping a journal is not likely to help you with next week's paper. But it will help you come up with ideas over the long haul. Every time you write in your journal you are storing away ideas, mulling ideas over; and when you do that, ideas start to multiply and change. It is because journals are storehouses of ideas that writers, scholars, researchers, politicians, and investigators find them so valuable.

F. Scott Fitzgerald, who wrote *The Great Gatsby,* kept notebooks and files filled with material that he could later use in his stories and novels. Here's a sample:

"Call me Mickey Mouse," she said suddenly.
"Why?"
"I don't know—it was fun when you called me Mickey Mouse."

or

"I didn't do it," he said using the scented I.

or

"Prowling the rattlers"—robbing freight cars.

Parts of these notes were published as *The Crack-Up* after Fitzgerald's death. But what was important to Fitzgerald was that keeping a notebook kept him observing, endlessly, and what he saw and thought didn't get lost.

Whether you write in a notebook everyday or a few times every week, you're doing invention exercises. You're exploring what you think without having to worry about other people's reactions. You can flip through your journal to see what ideas are there; but the actual writing will help you to sharpen your thinking.

Keeping a journal requires that you follow a routine that doesn't have to take more than ten minutes every time you write and maybe less than an hour a week. But you do need to write regularly.

Persons who only dream of becoming writers spend their time dreaming of becoming writers. Those who really intend to become writers keep a journal and work the mind.

—Ken Macrorie, *Telling Writing*

Seven Reasons to Keep a Journal

1. Your journal will be a storehouse of ideas for you. (We've already talked about this one.)
2. You will be improving your writing without even thinking about it. Writing every day works in the same way that swimming laps does for a swimmer. You just keep doing it, and things get smoother.
3. Journals can help you work through any problems and worries you may have. Perhaps just writing about something makes what the problem is or what to do clearer.
4. To increase your learning and involvement, try keeping a journal for one of your courses; some teachers require journals because they feel that the kind of mulling over of ideas and questions that goes on in a journal is the heart of learning.
5. Journals can be record books that help you to be a sharp and accurate observer. Later on in this chapter we will look at some formats for keeping a media journal.
6. Writers, like Henry David Thoreau, keep a journal to record experiences. In Thoreau's case it was the experience of living two miles from town in a shack so he could experience nature and life fully. His journal became *Walden*, now, 150 years later, considered a great American classic. Other writers, too, have had a journal turned into a published book and masterpiece.
7. One final reason: even if your journal doesn't get published, it will probably be fascinating for you and your grandchildren to read later.

The Personal Journal

What is a personal journal? A quick answer would be: anything you want, but make it specific and detailed.

1. Try to get down an important detail or the image that will bring back the whole to you. A journal is not going to be valuable to anyone if it is a dreary recital of your day, like *Diary of a Cat* (see below). Ken Macrorie suggests that the best test of a journal is if it will still interest you in 20 years. So write down now exactly what your boss said or why, and how it made you feel when your child was upset, or what your boyfriend or girlfriend did that made you angry, or what the tree looked like outside your window.

2. Try to stay with one topic. *Diary of a Cat* has little detail because it tries to cover whole days. Covering too much and a lack of interesting detail often go together. Let something that is on your mind choose you. Then write about it.

3. Keep writing regularly, even when a topic doesn't come to you. If a journal is going to be your own, then you will need to find your own topics. But at the start, it may help to keep a list of possible ideas in the front of your journal. If you find yourself sitting and staring at a blank page, flip to the front, pick a topic, and write on it.

Record a dream.

Describe your earliest memory.

Write how you feel about your name.

Do a sketch in words of something you see.

Pick one word and write about it—everything you can possibly think of to say.

Talk about a movie you saw or a song you like.

Write about what's going on in the news and how you feel about it.

Describe yourself as you think someone else sees you.

This list could go on. You can also get ideas just as good by asking everyone in your class to suggest one idea for writing. Keep a list of classmates' suggestions.

The Media Journal

A media journal is a record of observation about media programs, as for example, news television coverage of an issue. You can use simple forms like those here, suggested by Kathleen Bell in *Developing Arguments*. Choose one and use it repeatedly for a month, and then look over all your observations and see what you notice. There is nothing elaborate about these forms, so you could easily come up with your own. In this type of journal, as well as in a personal journal, the more specific and concrete you can be the better.

Television News: _____

Date: _____

Top Story: _____

Comments: _____

_____

_____

_____

_____

Keeping a Journal

Television Show: _____

Date: _____

Reason for Watching: _____

Comments: _____

_____

_____

_____

_____

_____

_____

_____

Rock Music Song: _____

Artist: _____

Date: _____

Comments: _____

_____

_____

_____

_____

_____

_____

_____

Chapter 11

Making the Most of Your Reading

What Is Reading?
A Quick Course in Reading
Demonstration of a Reading

Very often, avid readers are excellent writers. They seem to have lots of ideas and to write with ease. It's logical, isn't it? When you read a lot, you are unconsciously picking up information, reacting to it, and shaping your own ideas. Something else is also going on unconsciously: you are studying writing styles and learning new ways of phrasing and organizing.

In fact, this book is organized to make the most of the learning that goes on while you read. That's why we put questions and essays before the writing assignments, so that before you *write* about "American culture and the media," you have a chance to *think* and *read* about it.

If you have trouble coming up with ideas for an assignment, it may be because of the way you are reading or because of what you think reading is.

What Is Reading?

Take a few seconds to ask yourself what reading is and come up with an answer.

If your answer is something like "Translating letters on a page into words and then understanding those words," then you've gotten the tip of the iceberg only. Reading is not merely passing your eyes over the letters and understanding what the words or sentences mean. Reading means you also react to what you read and see how it fits with what you thought before.

Reading is

- Understanding
- Interpreting
- Reacting
- Learning
- Bringing new ideas into your thinking

Why do you need to think about all that? Because many times, when class discussion or a quiz or a test comes along, you realize that you haven't done the reading at all—at least, not in the way the teacher seems to expect. Except for those enviable few with photographic memories, most of us forget a lot of what we read right away if we don't study it. And the point of reading, in any case, is not merely to take in information but to react to it and so, perhaps, reshape our own thinking.

Jot down what you typically do when you are given an essay to read. Then compare your sequence with the sequence recommended in the next section. Be honest. Don't write down what you "should" do. Did your notes look something like this?

Open book.

Check length of assignment.

Check clock.

Read assignment.

Close book.

If they did, then you are not alone. But you still need a very quick course in reading.

A Quick Course in Reading

Step One: Guess What's Coming

To understand what you are reading, you need to make predictions or guesses about what is coming. Why? Because you will, without thinking, start to remember what you know on the subject and get involved. You will also be able to read more quickly and feel more confident about the material because you can see what's coming.

Before you start, look over the reading and make some guesses about what the article will tell you.

a. Look at the title. What does it suggest about the author's focus and point of view?

b. Read the first and last paragraphs. Refine your original guess.

c. Read any headings

Step Two: Question

Use your guess to ask some questions about what you are going to read.

Take a minute to think of a question or two that you want answered when you read this article. You will be thinking up new questions as you go along. Turn the title into a question. If the title is "In Harness: The Male Condition," ask, "In what way(s) are men in harness?" or "Why are men in harness?" or "What does the phrase 'in harness' actually mean?"

Why force yourself to ask questions in this self-conscious way? Odd as it may seem, it does help you to concentrate and to take in information. It gives you motivation. Think about it. Do you remember better when information is part of a lecture or when it is part of an answer to a question you have asked?

Step Three: Read—With a Pencil in Hand

As you read, mark any places that are unclear. Teachers are usually grateful if you raise questions about the reading or can be specific about what was confusing in the reading.

Make notes in the margin as you read, marking main points or questions that you have. Underlining the text is one of the easiest ways of noting passages or points. It is a quick way to highlight material. Just don't let it be too easy and start highlighting everything.

Step Four: Review

When you review, you put what you've read into your own words and in your own form. Generally, the method of reviewing that takes the most effort helps you remember the best. The following are suggestions for review:

UNDERLINE/HIGHLIGHT

Read over what you have highlighted, or save highlighting for a second reading and use it as a way to review. Sometimes readers highlight too much; it is awfully easy to glide that marker across the page. Highlight only key points, so you focus your attention while reading or reviewing on the main ideas.

MARGINAL NOTES

Review the notes you have made or rewrite them as marginal notes during a second reading as a way to review.

SUMMING UP

After you've read something, pause and ask yourself what it was about. It is especially good to do this for long passages. It will help you to remember as well as concentrate and thus reduce time wasted drifting off track.

ONE-SENTENCE SUMMARY

To help you get a good grip on the author's ideas, write a one-sentence summary. Limiting yourself to one sentence will force you to decide what is essential.

OUTLINING

Outlining helps you to understand and remember by forcing you to organize the main ideas. If you see relationships, you will remember better. Here is some quick proof.

Which letters are easier for you to remember?
(a) Mississippi   (b) X edd edd eqqe   (c) idgkkikgiigd?

All three contain only four different letters. Certainly (a) is the easiest to remember, because meaning and relationship are clear. Example (b) has no meaning, but you can see a pattern or relationship there which will help memory. Example (c) has neither meaning nor pattern, so it is harder to remember than the other two.

An outline makes you put ideas down in some kind of pattern and makes you decide which are main ideas and which are supporting details; both processes help you to remember.

Step Five: React—Make What You Read Your Own

You're not done yet. Many students (but few really good ones) think that as soon as they've read and taken notes, their work is done. Not true. You haven't "read" something until you have "made it your own" by reacting to it.

You can just think about what you have read, but when most of us do that, we risk drifting off on another train of thought. Often, writing can help us to remember the most. Here are some ways to write about what you've read:

LETTERS

You may have noticed that you do your easiest and most convincing writing in letters to friends. Write to a friend about the article you have read, and don't worry about a teacher's careful eye falling on it.

LISTS AND FREEWRITES

- *Write about any questions and doubts* you have about what was said in the article. Remembering that most teachers love questions from students sparked by their readings, come in with your list to the next class, and use it.
- *Freewrite on any connections* you can make between this author and others or between this article and your own experience.

- *Discuss the implications of this article.* If, for example, you agree with an author who claims that AIDS testing should be mandatory and universal, what other actions might follow as a result of that decision?
- *Explore your feelings.* What parts angered you? What appealed to you? What interested you in any way, for whatever reason? Then go on to figure out why you felt that way.

REVERSE ROLES

Try predicting the discussion questions that your teacher will ask about the reading, and write out quick, informal answers to them. This is called "psyching the teacher out." Some students will think of it as fooling the teacher, but it does require excellent analysis and thinking.

Demonstration of a Reading

Now read the article "TV Insults Men, Too," below, using the five steps just discussed. Do each step and then compare what you thought or wrote with the responses given here. Remember, the examples are not *the* answers but only good possible responses. Especially when you come to Step Five: React, there is no reason for your response to be at all the same.

TV Insults Men, Too
Bernard R. Goldberg

It was front page news and it made the TV networks. A mother from Michigan singlehandedly convinces some of America's biggest advertisers to cancel their sponsorship of the Fox Broadcasting Company's "Married...With Children" because, as she put it, the show blatantly exploits women and the family.

The program is about a blue collar family in which the husband is a chauvinist pig and his wife is—excuse the expression—a bimbo.

[margin note: main idea. you can insult men not women]

These are the late 1980's, and making fun of people because of their gender—on TV no less, in front of millions of people—is déclassé. Unless, of course, the gender we're ridiculing is the male gender. Then it's O.K.

[margin note: example Roseanne]

Take "Roseanne." (Please!) It's the season's biggest new hit show, which happens to be about another blue collar family. In this one, the wife calls her husband and kids names.

"Roseanne" is Roseanne Barr who has made a career saying such cute things as: "You may marry the man of your dreams, ladies, but 15 years later you are married to a reclining chair that burps." Or to her TV show son: "You're not stupid. You're just clumsy like your daddy."

The producer of "Roseanne" does not mince words either: "Men are slime. They say they're going to do 50 percent of the work around the house, but they never do."

I will tell you that the producer is a man, which does not lessen the ugliness of the remark. But because his target is men, it becomes acceptable. No one, to my knowledge, is pulling commercials from "Roseanne."

In matters of gender discrimination, it has become part of the accepted orthodoxy—of many feminists and a lot of the media anyway—that only women have the right to complain. Men have no such right. Which helps explain why there have been so many commercials ridiculing men—and getting away with it.

[margin: example — cereal ad]

In the past year or so, I have seen a breakfast cereal commercial showing a husband and wife playing tennis. She is perky and he is jerky.

She is a regular Martina Navratilova of the suburbs and he is virtually dead (because he wasn't smart enough to eat the right cereal).

She doesn't miss a shot. He lets the ball hit him in the head. If he were black, his name would be Stepin Fetchitt.

[margin: example — razor ad]

I have seen a commercial for razor blades that shows a woman in an evening gown smacking a man in a tuxedo across the face, suggesting, I suppose, that the male face takes enough punishment to deserve a nice, smooth shave. If he hit her (an absolutely inconceivable notion, if a sponsor is trying to sell a woman something) he would be a batterer.

[margin: examples — airline ad, "Charlie ad"]

I have seen an airline commercial showing two reporters from competing newspapers. She's strong and smart. He's a nerd. He says to her: I read your story this morning; you scooped me again. She replies to him: I didn't know you could read.

I have seen a magazine ad for perfume showing a business woman patting a businessman's behind as they walk down the street. Ms. Magazine, the journal of American feminism, ran the ad. The publisher told me there was nothing sexist about it.

A colleague who writes about advertising and the media says advertisers are afraid to fool around with women's roles. They know, as she puts it, they'll "set off the feminist emergency broadcast system" if they do. So, she concludes, men are fair game.

[margin: survey suggests these examples are typical]

<u>In 1987</u> Fred Hayward, who is one of the pioneers of the men's rights movement (yes, there is a men's rights movement) <u>studied thousands of TV and print ads and concluded: "If there's a sleazy character in an ad, 100 percent of the ones that we found were</u>

male. If there's an incompetent character, 100 percent of them in the ads are male."

double standard in ads

I once interviewed Garrett Epps, a scholar who has written on these matters, who told me: "The female executive who is driven, who is strong, who lives for her work, that's a very positive symbol in our culture now. The male who has the same traits—that guy is a disaster. He harms everybody around him; he's cold; he's unfeeling; he's hurtful."

main idea

<u>The crusading mother from Michigan hit on a legitimate issue. No more cheap shots, she seems to have said. And the advertisers listened. No more cheap shots is what a lot of men are saying also. Too bad nobody is listening to *them*.</u>

Step One: Guess What's Coming

This is how one reader tried to guess what was coming.

> *Let's see . . . the title is "TV Insults Men, Too." Must be about how television insults men. Who else does it insult? First paragraph is about a woman who protested against television insulting women. Last paragraph talks about that woman again, but when men complain about television taking cheap shots at them no one listens. OK, I guess I am going to hear about how television can't insult women, but can insult men.*

Step Two: Question

Again, a sample of the same reader thinking of questions:

> I'll use the title, "TV Insults Men, Too." Then my questions are: Does television insult men? How does it, and why does it?

Step Three: Read

Read the article.

Step Four: Review

a. Try a one-sentence summary. Here's one attempt at a summary of the article:

> *Sponsors are scared of women's, not men's, complaints about their television image, so men get the inept, cruel or sleazy roles nearly all the time.*

b. Marginal notes were already on the article, so it would be hard to add your own. How helpful would these notes be for reviewing?
c. Try an informal outline. Here's one way of doing it:

TV insults men.

Proof: *Insults by women in Roseanne and airline ads;*
Perfume ad.: woman pats man's behind
Razor ad.: cute when man is hit
Hayward survey in 1989—100% of sleazy characters are men

Why?   *Producers are afraid of women*
Women are organized into "feminist emergency broadcast system."

Step Five: React

a. Try listing some doubts you had as you read the article. Here is a list of doubts one reader had:

> *Does all this television image stuff really influence anyone? Do I decide my Dad is a bimbo because I see an inept male in a cereal ad.? How much of this stuff do you have to see before it affects you?*
>
> *Not all men on television fit this category. What about Dan Rather and Bill Cosby? The most respected people on television are probably male. Isn't it always the top dog who gets knocked down anyway? If men have most of the power and status in this country, isn't it funniest to see them made fun of? Isn't comedy allowed to be insulting?*
>
> *Is that survey reliable? Is it really so 100% anti-male? Some men behave like jerks, so shouldn't that be reflected on television?*

b. Try to connect this article to others you have read. Here's one attempt to do that:

Herb Goldberg, "In Harness: The Male Condition" on p. 138 thought men were programmed to be competitive and destructive. What would he say about their looking like bimbos? Maybe that this is just more pressure on men. Be a real male or be completely ridiculed.

Self Test

Come back to this article in two weeks. Just glance at it (for five seconds) and then see how much you remember. You should be pleasantly surprised. If you really read something, it stays with you.

Final Review

Reading is more than just understanding or even remembering what you read. To have read something means to react to it and make it your own. Readers need to

1. Guess what's coming
2. Question
3. Read
4. Review
5. React

Maybe you're reacting to what you have read just now and thinking, "Doesn't all this take a whole lot longer than just opening the book, reading something, and shutting the book?" It all depends on what you mean by reading!

Chapter 12

Analysis: Going Deeper to Come Up with Ideas

What Is Analysis?
Why Analyze the Media?
How to Do Analysis

"Sure, we all watch television—but how many of us really see television?"

What Is Analysis?

As the man in the cartoon suggests, there is a difference between watching television and really seeing, or analyzing, television.

Analyzing means examining the parts of something in order to understand how it works and what it means. When we analyze something, we observe it, study it, and look at it from different angles to see what new conclusions we can come to. Anytime we read a poem carefully over and over, we are analyzing it. If we study the people at the bus stop day after day, taking note of their behavior, we are analyzing. Or if we take apart a rock video to determine how it creates the effect it does, we are analyzing. In analyzing, part of us stands back and consciously observes and questions; we look for unspoken messages about values and attitudes and study how these messages are being sent.

In television news, for example, we're often told we are listening to expert opinions. Suppose we move beyond just listening, though, and analyze what it means to be an expert and who is considered an expert. How often is that person a government official? a man? a woman? a person over fifty? a member of a minority? That's analyzing and it's different than just taking in information.

Good, tough analyzers make good students because analyzing is a skill that you will need throughout college and beyond. Students who think analytically know how to break down the whole into its parts, whether the "whole" is an essay, article, novel, used car deal, television show, shopping mall, or budget. They don't just passively absorb surface appearances, as the cartoon figure suggests; they try to find out what those outward signs actually mean. They ask questions. For example, a good analyst—in a variety of classroom and real-life situations—might ask the following questions:

> Why did the novelist choose to have a small child as a narrator?
>
> Why is this car dealership offering this car at such a low price?
>
> Why does this type of story end the nightly television news?
>
> What will the impact of this purchase be on my budget for the rest of the year?
>
> How else could this movie have ended?
>
> Why is this shopping mall arranged this way, with the two big department stores at the ends?

Being active and analyzing is less relaxing than just watching, but it can be even more interesting. Our senses are taking in stimuli all the time; it's when we stand back and observe and analyze those stimuli that we come up with ideas. When we analyze what's going on around us, we also start to gain some control over its influence on us.

The unexamined life is not worth living.
—SOCRATES

Why Analyze the Media?

The media give us complex, unspoken messages about the values and attitudes in our culture, messages that come from the ways images and sounds are presented rather than the actual words we read or hear. This means that, along with the surface level, there is a deeper level to most of what goes on in communication. In many advertisements, for instance, the unspoken content is the most important part of the message—at least from the seller's point of view.

In every TV show, advertisement, magazine, or movie, there may be characters, a story line, a theme, and a message. But many other things are also going on. Take, for example, a Marlboro cigarette ad. The only words are "Marlboro" on the cigarette package and, of course, the Surgeon General's warning. Yet the advertisement communicates much more than the name and the warning. The picture of the cowboy on a horse charging down a hill in front of a red sunset tells you to associate the cigarette brand with wide open spaces, with freedom, with the American frontier, with energy, with nature, with virility, with being a real man. These associations become the unspoken message that is the real purpose of the advertisement. If it were not, the cigarette makers would hardly spend hundreds of thousands of dollars on an advertisement when most of the words are a warning not to use the product.

Why bother to analyze the Marlboro ad? One answer might be that people considering buying any product should know what they are really getting in exchange for their money. And some sociologists would say that, in this case, they are buying the American culture's idea about what it means to be an American man. Final thought: Why do women (as well as men) buy this brand of cigarette? More analysis is needed to find out.

So when you do more than just watch television or glance at a magazine ad, when you analyze what you are seeing (or hearing), you can get a lot of insight into the media and ideas for papers.

How to Do Analysis

Analyzing is something that we do, to some extent, unconsciously all day long. But for a more thorough and complete analysis, we need to work through the following stages:

Find a subject to analyze.

Collect information.

Come to conclusions from the information.

Finding a Subject

Turning an Impression into a Theory

Start with a hunch or impression that you have and turn it into a theory that you can test. For example, Bernard Goldberg, who wrote "TV Insults Men,

Too," started with his own reaction to his TV viewing—that television was putting men down. That was his impression, and he turned it into a theory: television puts men down more than it does women. He tested his theory by counting the number of times men play the fools on screen compared to women. For his results, see page 325.

Here are some examples of impressions that might become theories to test. Perhaps you notice the way a particular singer's music videos convey a very aggressive image; or that a particular local TV network covers all abortion issues with a very liberal slant; or perhaps you're sitting in a college lecture and notice that fewer men than women seem to be taking notes. All of these first impressions or feelings could become theories—and these theories could be tested with some basic research.

For instance, you could try to define more clearly what you mean by the singer's "aggressive image" and then see how often it occurs; you could define "liberal" and note down specific examples of "liberal" abortion coverage; or you could do more observation to see if the women really are doing more note taking than men.

In the following diagram are some questions that can be used for many different subjects to help you decide what is significant in your impressions.

Questions to Ask About a Subject

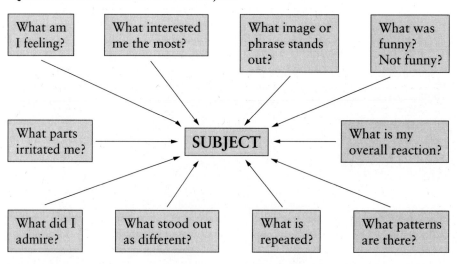

Following an Interest You Already Have

Another way to find a subject is to start with a general topic or a specific work or event that already interests you.

We are all members of groups that are stereotyped (introverts, single mothers, athletes, intellectuals) and tend to notice how those groups are treated by others in real life and in the media. So you can try to find questions that help you analyze how your particular group is treated.

Or you can pick a specific work or event and observe and analyze it in detail, as Arthur Berger does in his analysis of a Revlon ad, "Sex and Symbol in Fashion Advertising." The ad intrigued him so much that he carefully studied all its parts. (See page 336 for his analysis.)

Once you have your subject, or the impression you are testing, you are ready to collect information about it.

Collecting Information

In collecting information, more scientifically known as data, it is crucial that you ask the right questions to get the information you need to support your theory. Sometimes coming up with those questions is easy; sometimes it is the hardest part of your analysis.

The focus you choose may determine the kind of information you want to collect; but here are three ways of collecting information to consider:

Finding examples

Recording details

Keeping a count

Finding Examples

In "TV Insults Men, Too," Bernard Goldberg gives examples that he collected to support his theory that men are made fools of on television in ways that women would never be. Finding examples to support a theory will help you develop any type of paper, not just an analysis. For more on this technique, see the discussion of statement and support on page 365.

Recording Details

If you choose a single work or event for analysis, then you will want to examine it in as much detail as possible. Note all that you see or hear and record all that seems interesting to interpret. To get the details, you need to think of questions that will help you separate out the work's or event's various aspects. How does it compare to other similar things? How does it taste, look, smell, feel, sound? What are its parts? What kinds of effects does it have? These elemental questions help us examine something and know it better.

Arthur Berger does just this when he looks at a Revlon ad and writes about decoding the ad's unspoken messages. He looks at every detail of color and shape in the ad and discusses what we associate with each detail. As you read, consider whether Revlon executives would be likely to agree with Berger about the real message of this ad. Bear in mind that Berger's essay and analysis in general do not prove anything. The issue is whether he has convinced you, the reader, that his theory is reasonable.

Arthur Asa Berger

Sex and Symbol in Fashion Advertising

A number of advertisements for cosmetics and fashion are analyzed in this chapter in order to further our understanding of how they generate "meaning" and what they reflect about society. First we deal with advertisements for a cleanser and moisturizer, and a treatment for the entire body, after which we examine an advertisement for Danskins, and finally one for Calvin Klein separates. Attention is paid to the language used in the advertisements and to the way graphics are employed to generate beliefs and attitudes. Semiological techniques are employed to show how language and graphics function as signifiers that are derived from codes we all learn. It is also suggested that advertisements work by "striking" responsive chords in us, and not just by giving us information.

While reading an issue of *Vogue* recently, I noticed that I was, somehow, taken by a number of the advertisements for fashions and cosmetics. Many of these advertisements contained striking photographs and suggestive (and in some cases rather overt) copy. I found myself absorbed by the advertisements. They had a remarkable power over me—to seize my attention and to stimulate, if only for a moment, fantasies of an erotic nature. It was not only the physical characteristics of the models that affected me; rather it was a kind of gestalt effect. There was the element of graphic design, of color, of light, and a host of other matters that "conspired" to excite me.

"What's going on?" I asked myself. That question led me to consider how magazine advertising works to stimulate desire and sell clothes, cosmetics, and everything else that is connected with beauty (in this case) or any product.

In analyzing an advertisement there are a number of factors that we must consider, such as: the ambience, the design, the use of white space, the significant images and symbols, the use of language, the type faces used, and the item itself (and its role and function in society). We can also consider how the advertisement attempts to "sell" us and what roles it offers us to imitate, as well as examine how social phenomena might be reflected, indirectly. (Here I'm thinking about such things as alienation, boredom, conformism, generational conflict, and so on.) We can use whatever concepts we have at our command from history, psychology, sociology, anthropology, and any other disciplines to help us "dissect" the advertisement. In applying all of the above it is important to keep one cardinal principle in mind: The creators of any advertisement are trying to generate some kind of an effect or emotional response. So we must start with the effect and work backwards. What is the fantasy? And how is it induced?

Selling Magic

I will answer these questions by examining some of the advertisements in the April 1978 issue of *Vogue* magazine. I've selected advertisements that, for some reason, caught my attention for a moment and that I think are interesting and worth examining closely.

Let me start with a double-page advertisement by Revlon for its Formula 2 cleanser and moisturizer. The left-hand page of the advertisement is devoted to an extreme close-up of a woman's face, but the face is rendered by using quarter-inch squares of various colors. We are, in fact, given an optical illusion. If we squint, or place the magazine fifteen feet away from us, the squares merge together and form a face. But at arm's length, the face is somewhat distorted and out of focus. It is also larger than life in size. From there we move over to the right-hand page, which has a great deal of white space and is formally designed, approximating axial balance. Generally speaking, large amounts of white space and axial balance (and formality) are associated with quality and "class" in most people's minds.

The copy of the ad stresses science and technology as opposed to nature. We find the following suggestive words and phrases in the advertisement:

Revlon Research Group

skincare system

natural electricity

formula

skincare that's simple, scientific

precision tip

beauty technology

hygiene

principle

All of these terms are signifiers for science and technology; we are led to think of scientists in laboratories discovering remarkable things that lead to "the New-Face Hygiene" and "beautiful life for your skin."

Though this is something of a generalization, there seems to be a polar opposition in the public's mind that posits a world divided between culture (and with it science and technology) and nature. Thus the people who created the Revlon advertisement had two possibilities: to stress nature and all that's suggested by it, or to stress culture, in this case, science and technology. They chose the latter course and offered their readers a minicourse in science and technology: *This* principle leads to *those* results.

Ultimately what is being sold here—and what is being sold in most cosmetics ads—is magic, and that is where the large rendering of the woman's face comes in. It is an optical illusion that has two functions: First, it catches our attention because when we look at the face we see that it is really only a huge patchwork of squares. At first glance it seems out of focus and strange. But, if we squint or stare at it, magically it becomes a face, just the same way that Revlon Formula 2's "beauty technology of the future" gives you the gift of "life" (for your skin). Just as the law of closure forces us to complete that which is unfinished, we find ourselves obliged to make sense of the picture, and we visualize the woman's face even more completely than we find it. This act of visualization is what is asked of patrons or purchasers of the product. From the bits and pieces of their old faces they are asked (almost forced) to envision the new faces they will have with Formula 2.

Keeping a Count

A more systematic way of analyzing a subject is the one that sociologists often use—*counting*.

Counting what's there or counting how often something occurs helps you test theories. Does a particular children's cartoon encourage cooperation? You might choose to watch "Batman" one Saturday morning and count the number of times cooperation is used to settle a conflict or get something done and the number of times violence or fighting is used. Do women take notes at public lectures or in class more than men? Is this true? (And if so, what causes this difference in behavior?)

The chart below comes from Earl Babbie's *Practice of Social Research* and shows how counting was used to test how often violent shows have

Sponsor	Men's Product?			Number of Instances of Violence	
	Yes	No	?	Before	After
Grunt Aftershave	✓			6	4
Brute Jock Straps	✓			6	4
Roperot Cigars	✓			4	3
Grunt Aftershave	✓			3	0
Snowflake Toothpaste		✓		3	0
Godliness Cleanser		✓		3	0
Big Thumb Hammers			✓	0	1
Snowflake Toothpaste		✓		1	0
Big Thumb Hammers			✓	1	0
Buttercup Bras		✓		0	0

Source: Adapted from Earl Babbie, *Practice of Social Research*, 3/e, Belmont, CA: Wadsworth, 1983

Example of Recording Sheet for TV Violence

commercials that are directed at men. Setting up the right chart takes lots of thinking and planning. There are more angles to consider than we can go into here, but you will explore them if you take a sociology course. Notice that all advertisers are recorded and rated as producers of men's products. Then the level of violence is established by counting the number of acts of violence in the show.

Coming, Not Jumping, to Conclusions

Does Babbie's kind of analysis of a show's commercials end up proving that men are more violent than women or anything about men's attitudes? Examples, details, and numbers can help you come to a conclusion, even if they don't prove that conclusion. The data are systematically collected, and they can suggest that sponsors believe that men are drawn to violent shows on television or that sponsors want to associate their product with violence to establish its appeal to men. But it is not absolute proof.

Maybe as you were reading some conclusions from the other analyses in this section, your gut reaction was "No way." "Prove it." Analysis and the conclusions that are drawn from it can't be proven the way we can prove that water boils at a certain temperature at certain altitudes. But interpretations, analysis, and conclusions are still very useful. Through thoughtful analysis, you can get the reader to consider your conclusion and to start to question or to be persuaded by the amount and quality of your evidence.

Your argument will end up being most convincing if you suggest conclusions rather than state them as if they were facts and if you are careful that your conclusions don't make generalizations your evidence can't support or justify.

In Earl Babbie's made-up chart, for example, the research shows that men's products are more apt to be advertised on shows with violence than women's products are. So you could suggest to the reader that companies with clearly male products may choose to sponsor shows with violence because violence is considered to be a positive male trait. But you couldn't state as a fact that sponsors choose these shows because they want to encourage male violence or because they think violence is a positive male trait in American culture. Adding qualifying words like "might be," "is a possibility," or "could be" makes a lot of difference in what you are saying and the way you come across to the reader.

Let's use the same example to see what makes unrelated or unsupported conclusions. If you decided that television encourages male violence, that would be an "off-the-wall" conclusion or a response unrelated to the research. It may or may not be true, but the research doesn't prove it or show anything that has much to do with television encouraging violence at all.

If you overgeneralize, you are making an unsupported conclusion—a sweeping statement on the basis of too little evidence. Say you only look at one show with violence and then conclude that men's products are always featured on shows with violence. That would be an overgeneralization.

So what can you say?

You can present your research and let it speak for itself.

You can qualify carefully the conclusions you come to and present them as possibilities.

You can present your conclusion as a temporary one and say that further research is needed to back it up.

Being cautious about conclusions is what respected researchers do.

An intellectual is someone whose mind watches itself.
—ALBERT CAMUS, *Shoptalk.*

Chapter 13

Interviewing: Using Other People's Brains

Preparation
The Interview
After the Interview
Writing Up the Interview

A wonderful way to get ideas and information is by interviewing people. Interviewing may mean a quick phone call or an hour's session. Whatever type of interview you conduct, you will find that people often have information and experiences that you can find nowhere else. In this chapter we'll be looking at what it takes to get a good interview. It's more than just having a conversation. If you prepare for the interview, you will probably be able to get the person you are talking with to do a lot of your thinking and research for you, and you may be well entertained in the process.

Preparing, concentrating, listening with interest, and asking good questions are basically what make for a good interview. The way you record the interview will determine how much you remember.

Preparation

Do Some Basic Research

Get a grounding in your subject before the interview. It would be a shame to waste time when you are interviewing Madonna by asking her to list her hit records. You can go back to the library and do more research, but you can't interview someone all over again. Basically, you've got one shot at it.

Get Your Questions Ready

Write down three to five questions you want to take into the interview with you. More than five, you may be tempted to just go through them, so the person you are talking to will feel like he or she is filling in a form verbally, not sitting back and talking. If you don't take any questions in with you, then you may forget to ask something of major importance. In a lively interview, it is easy to get carried along in one direction. You want to be ready to come back to the questions you intended to ask.

What Sort of Questions Should You Prepare?

Use open-ended questions. Open-ended questions don't have a definite right or wrong answer. Instead of asking, "When is your birthday?" ask, "How do you feel about celebrating birthdays?" Open-ended questions give the person you are interviewing a lot of choices. So when you interview Mick Jagger, don't ask him how old he is; ask him how he feels about aging.

When Studs Terkel wrote *Working,* he got many penetrating interviews by asking two basic open-ended questions about work: What do you do and how do you feel about it? You can read how one interview turned out in "Who Built the Pyramids?" (page 101).

Getting the Interview

We can't tell you how to get an interview with Mick Jagger or Madonna, but most people will be glad to give you interview time. This is especially true if you set up an appointment in advance rather than just dropping in. Here are some steps to remember in setting up your plans:

1. Make your purpose clear when you request an interview.

What do you want to know?

For what audience?

For what purpose?

Is this a paper for your English class that you might publish in your college paper, or are you doing an exposé for "60 Minutes"? Let the person know your purpose, and you establish trust.

2. Be appreciative and show enthusiasm when you request people's time. Most people are very predictable when it comes to what motivates them. You will doom your interview if you start with "My Comp teacher is making us do these interviews." Enough said.

3. To tape, or not to tape? This is a good time to ask if you can tape the interview. Explain that you do not know shorthand (unless you are lucky and this isn't true) and that you want to make sure you quote correctly. Taping will free you from taking detailed notes and interviewing with your head down. But if the tape recorder is going to bother the person talking and make him or her feel like a police suspect, then you will have to do without it and take the best notes you can. Even if you do tape the interview, taking some notes may help

you to concentrate during the interview and record impressions that aren't going to be on the tape.

The Interview

Starting Off Right

Be on time! Begin with a few pleasant or appreciative remarks. Move on by reminding the person you are interviewing what you want to learn about and why.

It may work well to ask some factual questions at the start, just to make sure your basic information is correct. Then the major questions that you prepared should carry you along. Some people are natural talkers and very easy to interview; others have to be coaxed. So some factors in an interview are beyond your control, but you can make the most of an interview even when the person you are interviewing is tightlipped and hard to get reactions from.

Show Your Interest

Showing interest will get almost anyone talking. To a certain degree, let the person direct the interview. Be ready to change the original focus of the interview if the areas the person is getting into seem richer, more interesting than the ones you had anticipated. Interviews are fluid; you're swimming along. It's not like looking up information in a book where the print was fixed long before you got to read it.

Ask Follow-Up Questions

Follow-up questions are any questions that occur to you naturally as the person speaks. These questions are crucial and make or break an interview. You might ask a person to explain a statement in more detail or to take an idea further or to be more specific. Good follow-up questions often call for specific examples or anecdotes. Here are some examples:

> Tell me about your worst experience on the job.
>
> What one thing do you think your employees like best about you?
>
> How did you feel when you became Channel 2's anchorman?
>
> Dan Rather, can you give examples of how news coverage is self-censored?

Ending the Interview

Leave the interview with thanks and with the request that you be able to call if there is a question that comes to mind later.

After the Interview

Within ten minutes after the interview, find a place to sit down and write out all your impressions: what was said, the look of the meeting place, the person's gestures, tone of voice—everything. If you do not do this, and if you do not have a photographic memory, you will forget half of your impressions by the next day.

A week later you will probably only remember 20 to 30 percent of them. (That's the rate at which most of us forget.) Make yourself write down all your impressions, even though you may feel convinced that you will never forget them.

Generally, you don't need to hesitate about calling the person you interviewed if you are confused about anything that was said or if you want to ask another question. Keep it brief and thank the person again.

Writing Up the Interview

Finding Your Angle

Angle is a word reporters use that is similar in meaning to "focus": What original perspective will you organize your write-up around? Finding the angle is important, and your sense of what it is may be very different coming out of the interview than it was going in. That change may be a good sign that you really took in what the person was saying.

Using Quotations and Getting Specifics

If you've bothered to interview someone, by all means let the reader meet him or her too. Whenever you can quote what was said, do so, rather than put it in your own words. Listen to the tape or write down in the interview phrases or thoughts that strike you.

Being Accurate

Accuracy is important. Always put quotations within quotation marks.

Using Examples and Specifics

Use the information you got from all your follow-up questions and put in plenty of specific examples and details. These are more interesting to read than are general statements that anyone could have made.

Choosing a Format

Question and answer. The question-and-answer format is simple, but it puts a lot of demands on the people interviewing and being interviewed to be very interesting. This form is clear-cut and draws attention to what both you and the person being interviewed said.

Monologue. This is the format Studs Terkel uses in "Who Built the Pyramids?" (page 76). The illusion is created here that people were just talking on and on, all by themselves. If you edit well—honestly and smoothly—the monologue can be a very interesting format to read.

"You are there." In this format, the writer is more present, using the first person and giving his or her impressions and reactions as the interview goes along. The reader gets a sense of the writer's own personality, as well as that of the person being interviewed.

Chapter 14

Working the Library

What Is Research?
Finding Sources
Source Notes: Answers to Seven Basic Questions

• •

If you can stay with a thing long enough you can find it, documentation that no one else ever found.
—IRVING STONE, *On Being a Writer*

What Is Research?

Research is just a way to come up with ideas and the information that you want. The word *research* may sound academic, but you do it all the time. For instance, you want to know more about a man or woman you want to go out with or about a movie you might see. What do you do? You ask people their opinions and try to get information that way. And you probably ask more than one person so that you get different points of view and different angles. And you decide which sources you trust.

Your uncle doesn't recommend *Do the Right Thing*, but then you remember that his idea of a racy movie is *Honey, I Shrunk the Kids*. So you turn to another source, your sister, who didn't like *Do the Right Thing* because she only likes movies with happy endings. So you call up your friend Tanya, who says it's the kind of movie she'd see again because it gives you something to think about. You wanted some fast-action entertainment, so you're still not sure, and on it goes.

This is research, and you don't always get an answer quickly, if at all. The essentials are that:

1. You have a question you want answered, and
2. You turn to different people or sources to find their answers, and
3. You make up your mind after you have heard different opinions.

Why do some students say they don't like doing research? Probably because they have memories of a research paper they started without having a question they were really interested in; or they felt they had to pose as experts when they were just ready to get background information together; or they just did not know how to work the library for sources. If you have had trouble with research papers in the past, develop a new attitude by thinking about what research *can be:*

Research can take less than half an hour.

If your goal is to find one fact or statistic that gives punch to your argument or to find an article with an opposing point of view to get you thinking, your research can take less than thirty minutes. You can browse for an idea for a paper. Check out the card or on-line catalog or *Library of Congress Subject Headings* or run your eyes across a section of books—all of these can be sources of ideas for a paper. A quick computer search can get you some abstracts—nice, neat summaries of articles—to give you ideas and facts.

Even research that takes longer can be very satisfying work.

As Ken Macrorie suggests in *Telling Writing*, think of research as a hunt or as detective work or an investigation. To do this, you must start with a question that you really want to know the answer to.

You can find out what is going on in the world. Research in a library can give you a thorough understanding of your topic and surprising—to yourself and others—new information. Most of our information comes from very few sources. Library research is one way for you to look beyond the six o'clock news. There is a lot more going on in the world than what Peter Jennings can tell us in 75-second news summaries. There is no freedom of speech or information if you don't use the library. Democracy really depends on people being able to investigate on their own.

Realize that you are probably very good at research. After all, you have been doing it all your life. Research is just:

Trying to find information *you* want

Getting different points of view

Evaluating your sources

You have all kinds of choices about the sources: people, writers, television shows, movies, radio shows, pamphlets, reference books, magazines, tapes, computer data bases. We've looked at how to interview people (Chapter 13) and how to analyze the media (Chapter 12). Now we'll focus on how to get ideas and locate information in libraries.

Finding Sources

This section presents some basic information about finding the material you need in the library. We'll discuss books, magazines, abstracts, and newspaper articles. There is a lot to know about mining the riches of a library.

Ask the Librarian

There is absolutely no shame in asking a librarian for help. Many of them have advanced degrees that they spent one to five years getting just so they would know how to make full use of a library. Just keep working on learning something new about your library every time you go in. Most librarians love helping people find what they need; if they didn't see their work as detective work, they probably wouldn't be in it. Whether you are looking for books, periodicals, government documents, or videos, librarians will be able to help you get started.

How to Find Books

Use the card catalog or on-line computer listings. Your library will have one or both of these, and they are your guide to what books are in the library and where they are.

You can look up a book by the author, title, or subject.

Books offer extended though not necessarily complete coverage of a topic. They often have references and a bibliography that help your own investigation. The index and table of contents help you to get to information quickly. (You don't have to read the whole book.) *Books don't have* the most up-to-date information, though. Most books take at least a year to print.

How to Find Specific Reference Books

Your library has a separate section for encyclopedias, dictionaries, and books containing facts, statistics, and records. Just ask where this section is and ask for help in using it. Although all reference books are listed in the card catalog or on-line catalog, a librarian knows best what information can be found, and where. Reference books cannot be checked out of the library, so they are always available.

Encyclopedias have lots of information that is organized in alphabetical order, just like dictionaries, and are excellent sources of background information on a subject. *Encyclopedias don't have* an unbiased approach, contrary to what many of us assume. Also, they are not considered an impressive source of reference at the college level because they are seen as just providing necessary background information.

How to Find Articles in Magazines, Journals, and Periodicals

Journals or *periodicals* are just the more academic-sounding names for *magazines*. Current periodicals may be on display in the library; back copies may be bound together in volumes on the shelves or they may be on microfiche or microfilm. Your guide to periodical articles is not the card catalog but volumes called *indexes,* in book forms, or *on-line indexes,* on the computer. These indexes or computer data bases are arranged so that you can find an article by knowing its author, its title, or just the subject you want information about.

Magazines have recent information, and the title is often a quick guide to whether an article contains the information you want. But *magazine articles may or may not* be very thorough or well researched.

How to Find Abstracts

You may never have heard of abstracts. An *abstract* is a summary of an article. Someone else has already done all the work of reading the article and summarizing it for you. Abstracts help you to see whether an article is what you want and worth the time it takes to look it up and read it all.

How to Find Newspaper Articles

So much is written in newspapers that it is not *all* indexed for you to find. However, there are some good newspaper indexes. Here are two of the most frequently used ones:

1. *Newsbank* is a computer system that gives you selected materials from selected newspapers nationwide. *Newsbank* is convenient because the articles themselves are on microfiche right beside the index.
2. *The New York Times Index* is a wonderful source of the articles and reports in our largest national newspaper. You may need to ask the librarian for help the first time you use this index.

Newspapers have very up-to-date information, but they *may not have* carefully researched details, because of the pace reporters work at, or much analysis of events.

How to Find the Right Search Words

In any research, you need to know the right phrases or words that are used. At some time we've all felt caught in a maze when we didn't have the right search word. Say you move, and you need your trash picked up for the first time. You look in the Yellow Pages under trash pick-up and there's nothing, so you try refuse, recycling, sanitation disposal, sanitation retrieval—and nothing. Finally, you find it under garbage collection.

In any language, there are often different terms for the same thing. People who write the Yellow Pages know this and help you out by putting in a cross-reference like "Sanitation Removal, see Garbage Collection." Librarians have ways of helping you find the right search word. Another valuable resource is entitled *Library of Congress Subject Headings.* These books are nothing but lists of possible terms you might use to find information on a subject. Just scanning the alternative terms can give you lots of ideas for subjects and narrower topics.

Computerized indexes often have their own word lists to show you what terms are being used for different subjects. In many programs, the word *or* allows you to link two terms to come up with more articles; *and* or *not* may help you to limit your search so you don't have listed 3,000 different articles to look through. For example, if you are having trouble finding articles on labor unions on television, you could do a computer search with "labor or unions or television," meaning you are interested in articles with any of those terms in the title or body. But if too many articles, or "hits," come up on the screen, you could ask the computer to scan for "labor and unions and television" meaning all three words have to show up in the title or body.

Trusting Your Sources

A note of caution: keep in mind that even statistics—numbers—can reflect bias. Nearly everything that is written reflects the bias of the writers—that is, their point of view or underlying beliefs.

Bias is not always deliberate distortion, in the sense that the author is presenting information to conceal or twist other important facts deliberately. More likely, we are all unconsciously slanted a certain way, just like we all speak with an accent of some sort. A wonderful line by E. B. White sums this up:

> *All writing slants the way a writer leans, and no one is perpendicular, although many are born upright.*
> —E. B. WHITE, QUOTED IN *Telling Writing*, KEN MACRORIE

Some bias is obvious; other times, you simply need to read and research a lot before you can pick up on the different slants each author has. Once you get enough sources together, you will notice differences in points of view and be able to make up your own mind about which source you trust the most.

Source Notes: Answers to Seven Basic Questions

The single most important rule of research is that you must let your reader know where the information you have borrowed comes from. If you remember that and a few other basic points, you will manage documentation quite easily.

1. What Is Documentation?

Documentation is telling your reader where your information comes from and giving credit to your sources. When you document in academic style, it is called a *source note*. There are several ways to document, and you will need to ask each teacher in college what steps to use.

A source note that appears within the text of a research paper is put in parentheses:

> "A Ph.D. is really only a formal certification that a person is capable of independent research" (Harrington 122).

When the reader wants to know more about Harrington and his views, she need only turn to the "Works Cited" page at the end of the paper to find the whole citation. The citations are listed in alphabetical order, by the authors' last names. They give complete information to help the reader trace the source the writer's borrowing is from. A citation looks like this:

> Harrington, Michael. *The Long Distance Runner.* New York: Henry Holt and Co., 1988.

For more detail about how to prepare source notes, consult *The MLA Style Manual.* You can photocopy the sheet on pages 354-5 and carry it around with you to see what information you will need to get from each source for the citation, as well as its format.

2. Why Do You Document Sources?

a. *To give credit to the person who did the work.* Perhaps you are borrowing someone's great way of putting an idea, or statistics, or survey results, or the person's research finds or educated opinion. Whatever it is, you need to repay that person for the work by giving him or her credit. When you do not give credit, it is called plagiarism, and people have flunked papers and courses and lost jobs because of it. *Plagiarism* is presenting someone else's work as your own. It is a form of theft.

b. *To help other researchers along.* Source notes and a "Works Cited" page leave tracks for other investigators to follow. Suppose you are doing research and you come across this statement in a paper:

> There are 66 hours of prime time TV each week, but only 6% of it offers shows with Blacks as leading characters. Yet studies show that Blacks are 13% of the viewing audience at that time (Harris 40).

You're interested, so you turn to the "Works Cited" page and find the citation that tells you everything you need to know to track down the article this information came from.

> Harris, Kathryn. "Money Talks." *Forbes* 28 May 1990: 40–41.

c. *To allow others to evaluate your sources.* This is your way of saying, "Look, my evidence is well supported; check it out." And it lets the reader decide whether that is true.

So if we wanted to evaluate the "Money Talks" article, we would see that it comes from *Forbes* magazine and be able to look it up to see how thorough and fair it is.

These are the three main reasons why you have to note your sources. Noting sources is required of all college work. Don't expect to be told to note your sources; it is assumed that you will.

3. When Do You Document Your Sources?

Now let's consider *when* you note your sources. Try taking the quiz to see if you already know:

Check off when you need to give your sources:

1. _____ When citing someone else's opinion
2. _____ When summarizing someone else's ideas, but not using his or her words
3. _____ When quoting someone else, using his or her exact words
4. _____ When using information you have seen in only one place
5. _____ When mentioning ideas or dates or facts that are generally known and common knowledge
6. _____ When giving statistics
7. _____ When giving the results of someone's research
8. _____ When paraphrasing someone else's ideas without borrowing any words or phrases

If you checked all but number 5 (information that is common knowledge), you are right. Many students are surprised by the results. Nearly everyone knows that when you quote someone and put that person's remarks inside quotation marks, you have to give the source. But not everyone knows that if you put someone else's ideas or statistics or facts in your own words, you still have to give the source.

Borrowing someone's ideas or research results needs to be documented with a source note, just as borrowing their exact wording does.

4. How Do You Handle Quotation, Paraphrase, and Summary?

If you understand the difference between quoting, paraphrasing, and summarizing, then you can handle them correctly and avoid the danger of accidentally plagiarizing. See the example below:

QUOTING

Quoting means that you repeat what the person or writer said word for word, exactly as he or she said it. If you leave out a section of the quote and fill in with ellipses (. . .), you must do it in a way that doesn't change the meaning.

Let's look at an example:

> "*Terminator II is the greatest waste of time of any movie made this decade.*" Ronald Pickwick, *Daily Times*

If you quote it as follows:

> "*Terminator II is the greatest . . . movie made this decade.*" Ronald Pickwick, *Daily Times*

your quotation, with its ellipses, *distorts* the original.

So *quoting* means that you are giving what the speaker or writer said, word for word, and using ellipses in a way that does not distort the content.

Paraphrasing

When you translate what a person has said, phrase by phrase into your own words, that is *paraphrasing*. Here's an example. The first quotation is the original.

> Whereas the Anglo-Saxon model appears to be a system of atomic individuals and high mobility, our model has tended to stress communities of our own, attachment to family and relatives, stability, and roots. Ethnics tend to have a fierce sense of attachment to their homes, having been home-owners for less than three generations: a home is almost fulfillment enough for one man's life. Some groups save arduously in a passion to *own;* others rent. We have most ambivalent feelings about suburban assimilation and mobility. The melting pot is a kind of homogenized soup, and its mores only partly appeal to ethnics: to some, yes, and to others, no.
> (From *The Rise of the Unmeltable Ethnics* by Michael Novak, p. 79.)

Here is the paraphrased version:

> Anglo-Saxons tend to emphasize the individual advancing alone, while ethnic Americans stress family and community and stability. Homes are important—almost a life purpose—for a sense of rootedness because they have always had one. Some save hard to own one—others rent. Ethnic Americans have mixed feelings about melting into suburbia. That kind of mixing in and loss of ethnic identity is only partly welcomed.

Note how the paraphrased version attempts to translate into other words what the author has said. Why paraphrase and not quote? Generally it is better to paraphrase if the information is difficult and your rephrasing makes it easier for the reader to understand.

Summarizing

In *summarizing,* you give the main idea of what is said, and your version is much shorter than the original. Here's one possible summary of the quotation by Michael Novak:

> Unlike Anglo-Americans, Ethnic-Americans favor community and family ties over mobility and individuality. Homes are important although not necessarily homes in that "homogenized soup" that is suburbia.

Note that the summary contains a direct quotation of a phrase the researcher liked especially, "homogenized soup." It is still much shorter than the original, yet it conveys the meaning of the original.

Summaries save time; that's one good reason to do them. Of course, as in paraphrasing or using ellipses in a quotation, *you* are responsible for accurately representing the writer or speaker.

Remember: *Whether it is a quotation, paraphrase, or summary, it needs to be documented.*

5. What Information Do You Need for Source Notes?

You can see from the citations that have appeared so far that you have to tell the exact page that the borrowed material comes from, for example, (Harrington 122). Get in the habit of writing down the page everytime you write down any notes at all. If you don't, you'll have to waste time going back to the library and finding the book or article and the page you borrowed from. Get all the source information you need for the "Works Cited" page when you are taking notes too. Pages 354-5 are meant for you to photocopy and take with you to the library, so you can see what information you need to get.

6. How Do You Show the Reader Where Your Source Begins?

It is not enough to mark the *end* of a passage of borrowed material with a parenthetical reference (Harrington 122). Often you need to show where the borrowing starts. If you are quoting, the quotation marks signal the beginning for the reader, so your start is clear. But if you are summarizing or paraphrasing, the beginning of your borrowing may not be clear at all, and you must show where your borrowing begins.

Consider the following example. It is not clear where the borrowing from Navarro begins:

1 "Poverty is the major cause of poor health disease and death and only
2 46% of the poor are eligible to receive medicare. Soon what little health
3 care the poor do receive will be nonexistent, due to the predicted
4 bankruptcy of the medicare program by the year 2000" (Davis 3171).
5 Health care is being refused everyday throughout this country by
6 hospitals, nursing homes, and private practices to patients they feel
7 are unprofitable. Is this ethical? Is it right to deny these services to
8 another human being? Health is such an unpredictable expense and
9 ironically health care is becoming even more unpredictable. This
10 country has some of the most advanced technological units in
11 hospitals than any throughout the world; more unused beds, more
12 stagnated equipment, and some of the highest average costs for
13 patients. This country is also the only western industrialized nation,
14 besides South Africa, without national health insurance (Navarro 80).

Did Navarro (cited in line 14) say only that the United States and South Africa are the only industrialized nations without national health insurance, or is he responsible for *all* the ideas in between the Davis citation (lines 1–4) and the citation with his name (line 14)?

What the writer needs to do is indicate where the borrowing from each source starts. In your paper, one way to show where your summary or paraphrase of a source starts is to say "so-and-so said" to mark the start, as in the following example:

> . . . This country has some of the most advanced technological units
> in hospitals than any throughout the world; more unused beds, more

stagnated equipment, and some of the highest average costs for patients. <u>As Vincente Navarro points out,</u> this country is also the only Western industrialized nation, besides South Africa, without national health insurance (80).

Notice when you give the author's name or article's title at the beginning of the citation, then you don't need to repeat it in the parentheses. All you need to put there is the page number.

7. What Form Do You Use for Citation?

The following is a summary of MLA forms for doing a variety of citations—from books to the Internet. We suggest you photocopy it, so you will have it with you in the library as a reference for what to write down as you use each source.

MLA Style

BOOK BY A SINGLE AUTHOR

Novak, Michael. *The Rise of the Unmeltable Ethnics: Politics and Culture in the Seventies.* New York: Macmillan, 1971.

BOOK BY A CORPORATE AUTHOR/ORGANIZATION

United Nations Educational, Scientific and Cultural Organization. *Study Abroad.* Paris: UNESCO, 1993.

BOOK WITHOUT AN AUTHOR

Dictionary of Afro-American Slavery. New York: Greenwood Press, 1988.

AN ESSAY IN AN ANTHOLOGY

McIntosh, Peggy. "White Privilege: Unpacking the Invisible Knapsack." *Experiencing Race, Class, and Gender in the United States.* Ed. Virginia Cyrus. Mountain View, CA: Mayfield Publishing Co., 1993. 209–213.

UNSIGNED ARTICLE IN AN ENCYCLOPEDIA OR OTHER REFERENCE BOOK

"Andrew Jackson." *Encyclopaedia Britannica.* 1994 ed.

AN ARTICLE FROM A DAILY NEWSPAPER

Pareles, Jon. "On Rap, Symbolism, and Fear." *The New York Times* 2 Feb. 1992: 2, 1:2.

AN ARTICLE FROM A WEEKLY MAGAZINE

Shaheen, Jack G. "The Media's Image of Arabs." *Newsweek* 29 Feb. 1988: 10.

AN ARTICLE FROM A MONTHLY MAGAZINE

Thomas, Lawrence. "In My Next Life, I'll Be White." *Ebony* Dec. 1990: 84.

TELEVISION SHOW: EPISODE

"The Pilgrimage of Jesse Jackson." *Frontline.* PBS. WUNC, Chapel Hill. 30 Apr. 1996.

RECORDING

Bristol Brothers. *Old Style Acoustic Music from the Mountains.* Dynamic Recording, 1994.

MOVIE

Hoop Dreams. Dir. Steve James. Kartemquin Films, 1994.

PERSONAL INTERVIEW

Myles, Catriona. Personal interview. 31 March 1996.

TELEPHONE INTERVIEW

Andrews, Mary M. Telephone interview. 21 April 1996.

ELECTRONIC SOURCE: NEWSBANK

Perkins, Ken. "Cast in a Similar Role." *Dallas Morning News* 8 Nov. 1992. Newsbank, Film and Television, Dec. 1992, fiche 115, grid F1.

WWW SITES (WORLD WIDE WEB)

Martindale, Linda A. "The Use of Babies: Money and Power Versus Love." *Life on Daytime Dramas.* http://www.amolgh.com (7 Feb. 1996).

Chapter 15

Organizing: Getting Your Ideas Together

What Is Organizing?
Using Focus to Organize Your Paper
Using Audience to Organize Your Paper
Using Purpose to Organize Your Paper
Using Questions to Organize Your Paper

What Is Organizing?

When you see the word *organizing*, images of structured and indented outlines with roman numerals may come to mind. But that's only one way to organize. Organizing your paper doesn't mean fitting your ideas into a mold like the five-paragraph essay you may have learned in high school. Organizing is what makes your paper flow: finding out what your focus is, deciding what you will include and what order you will put it in. Most papers can be organized in several different ways, as long as you let the reader know why and when you are moving on to a new point or idea.

Having an outline of some kind can be helpful as you try to shape your ideas. Whether a full and formal outline that includes all points or a brief "scratch" outline that just covers main points, both styles can help you to come up with ideas and see the overall framework of your paper.

> ## *Suggestions for Discussion and Writing*
>
> 1. How much outlining do you do before you start to write your draft? Compare your methods of working with those of others in your class.
> 2. Does organizing a paper come easily to you, or is it one of the things you struggle with most? Talk with others in your class after you write your response. Compare responses and see if you can figure out why some people organize more easily than others.
> 3. If you don't organize or shape your ideas easily, do you find that coming up with lots of ideas in the first place (invention) is one of your strengths? See what others in your group or class think about this idea—that sometimes people have trouble organizing because they are very good at generating material at the invention stage of composition.
> 4. What ways of organizing your ideas have already worked well for you?

Types of Outlines

There are two basic types of outlines: the full, classic outline and the scratch outline. The *full, classic outline* is for people who prefer to have everything fully mapped out before they begin their first draft. Less important supporting details are indented further from the left-hand margin than details which the writer thinks are more significant. *Full, classic outlines* identify separate ideas by importance, with roman numerals and capital letters marking the longer lines of the most important ideas and shorter lines showing minor or supporting ideas. All points, however minor, are included.

Scratch outlines are for people who like to work from a few points and let their ideas expand as they write. In a *scratch outline,* just the main topics are put down, in order.

> Here are examples of both types of outline for the assignment "Does television promote positive gender roles?"
>
> Thesis: In recent television drama, men and women occupy both traditional and nontraditional gender roles, as career professionals and as family members.
>
> **Full, Classic Outline**
>
> TV Dramas
>
> I. Women
>   A. Roseanne
>   1. housewife and mother
>   2. tough, no-nonsense image

                3. working-class
                4. not slick or dressy looking
            B. Murphy Brown
                1. successful television journalist
                2. one of the boys, career woman
                3. having baby
                4. dressy, executive look
    II. Men
        A. Cliff Huxtable
            1. dad
            2. husband
            3. obstetrician
            4. casual and exec. look
        B. Jean-Luc Picard
            1. career Starfleet officer
            2. wears uniform
            3. tough, in command
            4. soft-hearted, cares about crew's personal lives

Scratch Outline

<u>**Men and Women on Recent Television Drama**</u>

Are they equally independent and powerful, loving, and caring?
   Depends on the drama—

- Roseanne
- Murphy Brown
- Star Trek
- Cosby Show

In the following sections we will discuss ways to organize a paper by focusing on

Focus. What is my main point?

Audience. What does my audience need to hear?

Purpose. Am I trying to inform or persuade or describe an experience?

Questions. What question(s) am I answering?

Remember you will not be able to use all these ideas at once. Browse through them and then select an approach to use for your paper.

Using Focus to Organize Your Paper

Focus: What Is My Main Point?

One way of organizing your ideas is to "nutshell," or sum up your main point and work from there. Try this method if you have a lot of scattered ideas. Make yourself answer in one sentence "What is my paper about?".

You may want to look at the results of your invention exercises (freewriting, listing, etc.), underlining key words or phrases, before making a single statement about what you see as the most important and generally significant ideas so far. By the way, that one-sentence limit is important. It's what forces you to get to *the* main idea. Once you know your focus, you can start to organize the ideas that relate to it.

> ### Example: Moving from Scattered Ideas to a Focus
>
> Let's start with the scattered ideas one student got while freewriting on the assignment "How are athletes portrayed on television?"
>
> What's on TV? Monday night football, the Broncos, John Elway, NCAA basketball championships, regular season, networks and ESPN, this year CBS and Winter Olympics, skating, Kristi Yamaguchi, star players, Duke's Laettner, Gugliotta, the fab five, commentators focus on private lives of key players, some real heroes, not many women's sports, heroes are men, MVPs, interviews and highlights, commentators have favorites, Michael Jordan is the biggest sports star ever, new Jordan ad. with Bugs Bunny in it, when a key player gets injured all losses blamed on absence from team, so even team sports are focused on individuals, Hurley absent from Duke team, critics say it's harder to win.
>
> If you go back and underline ideas that recur, you may see that the most common issue in this invention material is "heroes and stars on TV sports," along with the names of individual players. The nutshell statement might be "TV sports programs focus on individual players rather than on the team and teamwork." You'll have narrowed down and focused on the big question, "How are athletes portrayed on TV?" by examining, selecting, and rejecting some of your own ideas.
>
> ### Moving On to an Outline
>
> Let's say that, for the moment, you're happy with this focus. Then your underlining of repeated ideas or topics may lead you to a kind of outline. To reach your nutshell statement, you had to underline different names of sports stars (in contrast to the team names), as well as names of television

> sports programs. Each underlined phrase might go in your rough outline to provide a separate example to illustrate your nutshell statement.
>
> You could also get at this same outline by asking "Why? What evidence do I have?" after your nutshell statement "TV sports programs focus on individual players as heroes."
>
> Take your focus, that is, your nutshell statement, and ask "What evidence do I have?":
>
> - CBS Olympic coverage e.g., Steffi Graff/Monica Seles conflict
> - Networks and Monday Night football, e.g., John Elway
> - Networks and college basketball, e.g., Laettner and Gugliotta, the fab five of Michigan

Using Audience to Organize Your Paper

Thinking about your readers—your *audience*—is another way to organize your paper. For some writers, picturing real people reacting to their topic gives them the best ideas about what to include and in what order. Below are some questions that will help you answer the broad question "Who am I writing to?"

1. Who is my audience?
2. What background on my topic do they already have?
3. How do they feel about my topic?
4. What questions will they have?
5. What do they need to know?
6. In what order will they want to know it?

Suggestions for Discussion and Writing

1. Have everyone in your group choose the same writing assignment from one of the topic chapters (1–8). Use the audience suggested under the "Audience" head in that assignment. Try the questions "What does the audience need to know? In what order do they need to know it?" to help you to create a rough outline.
2. Compare your outline with those of others in your group. What are the differences and similarities? How do you explain them?

Using Purpose to Organize Your Paper

Our own writing may well have more than one purpose. But to use the exercises and ideas that follow, you need to decide what the main, or dominant, purpose is and work with it.

Your *purpose* is the reason you are writing the particular paper for your audience. Some of the most common purposes for writing include:

Informing your reader about new information

Persuading or convincing your reader to think or act a certain way

Describing an experience or feeling so your readers will be able to understand and share that feeling or experience

In other words, is someone who reads your paper most likely to think:

I learned a lot of new information (*inform*)

I think the author wanted to convince me to think or act a certain way. (*persuade*)

I feel like I understand an experience or feeling the writer has been through. (*describe*)

To see how your purpose can help you organize your paper, consider the examples in the following sections, all of which start with the assignment "What does TV sports coverage tell you about our culture's attitudes toward violence?" Each purpose has its own related questions. Just answering them will help you to organize your ideas and material. In the examples, you'll see how a scratch outline can emerge from the questions connected with each purpose. Notice that although there is one topic for all of these papers, there are three different purposes, which lead to three different scratch outlines, or ways to organize.

Organizing to Inform

If you are trying to *inform* readers, you will need to plan around these three questions:

1. What's my topic?
2. What information is needed? What questions about my topic am I going to answer?
3. In what order?

Example:

The same topic—"What does TV sports coverage tell you about our culture's attitudes toward violence?"—with an *informative* purpose might become a paper that simply describes the different kinds of television sports programs with reference to violent or nonviolent content.

Instead of trying to convince the audience that television sports coverage emphasizes (or de-emphasizes) violence, the writer here wants to present basic information about what is on the screen, so that the reader can judge its significance for him- or herself. Note, again, that a rough outline emerges from answering these questions.

a. Statement to prove
   Most sports on television have violent or physical danger as part of them.
b. Support
   - basketball: not generally violent but some injuries, sometimes very "physical" games
   - ice skating, skiing, gymnastics—not contact sports, very little violence
   - football: battle uniforms and physical plays; people get hurt
   - hockey: battle gear, fights and injuries common on ice
   - motor racing: wrecks, injuries, sometimes even deaths; but no personal violence
   - boxing: a fight in itself, people get hurt
c. Order
   Deal first with violent sports, and then nonviolent ones; deal first with group team sports together and then individual sports.

Organizing to Persuade

If you are writing a persuasive paper, you can make an outline by answering these three questions:

1. What am I trying to prove?
2. What support can I give for this idea? (List your points.)
3. What will be the most convincing order?

Example:

A student with a persuasive purpose will write a paper that tries to *persuade* its audience that television sports programming emphasizes and even celebrates the violence that is part of our general culture.

a. Television sports celebrate violence in some ways
b. Support
   - shots of winning athletes who have been injured being hailed as heroes (Montross goes off court after having stitches—people try to touch him)
   - football—extra television and press coverage of injured players; protective uniforms (like armor?) are highlighted on screen
   - motor racing—people actually get killed; sometimes the race goes on after an accident; dramatic television coverage of blazing wrecks
   - basketball—cameras linger on fights between players and on their facial expressions

- commentators make approving remarks about "rough," "very physical" players and "good college ball" in same breath
- individual and noncontact sports (ice skating, gymnastics) usually not on prime-time television, get less regular coverage

c. Order
most to least violent? most obvious to least obvious?

This writer may decide that everyone will accept the idea that football is a violent game (otherwise, why do they wear pads and helmets?) and so put that idea up-front, leaving the points about commentators' remarks until later, when the audience has started to be convinced.

Organizing to Describe

If your paper will primarily *describe* an experience, then you will in some way be covering the following core questions. Try using them to create an outline.

1. What's important about the experience or person I'm describing?
2. What scenes are important in conveying that experience?
3. What images and details are important in conveying that experience?
4. What's the best order?

Example:

The writer needs to describe an experience that shows her own response to television sports programs, focusing on the issue of violence. She might decide to use a simple chronological order and take the reader through her feelings as she watches a football game from start to finish.

In answering the question "What images and details are important?" the writer comes up with a list that can be cut and rearranged later into a final outline.

a. one evening watching the Broncos
b. list of significant details
- switch on television
- want my team to win, but not very excited at this stage
- by halftime no one's scored, feeling very bored
- go out at halftime to get pizza
- Broncos are down by several points
- Elway's injured in a clash
- he's down, curled up in agony, helmet off
- he's in pain, and I'm angry at the other team

- my friend stops by—I tell him about what's happened
- I get mad at the other team, so does my friend
- they're really physical
- sympathize with the crowd who are furious
- now I *really* want my team to win after that
- feel angry, tense, so does my friend—punch the chair and thump the table
- feel like my Dad, who always stands up and glares at television screen when his team's down or when he's mad at the ref
- we lose, and I feel exhausted and still angry
- my friend thumps the table again and we shrug—
- another loss
- need to decide the Broncos don't matter after all
- hey, I can live without them—

c. Order
Simple, straightforward and chronological.
Since it shows the mood swings well, the writer will probably stick with it.

Using Questions to Organize Your Paper

The same questions that were used in Chapter 9, "Coming Up with Ideas" (see p. 301), can help you develop scratch outlines for your papers. It may be helpful to see each of these questions as an empty outline to be filled in. Try taking your own topic and see if one of the forms below provides you with a useful way of organizing. The following pages give you the empty form and a few filled-in examples of these questions, which we list here again:

What evidence is there that this statement is true? (for the statement-support essay)

What happened? (for a narrative essay)

What is it like? (for a descriptive essay)

How are these things alike or different? (for a comparison-contrast essay)

What caused this? What are the effects of this? (for a cause-effect essay)

What is the problem? How can it be solved? (for a problem-solving essay)

Organizing Question: What Evidence Supports This Statement?

If your paper basically answers this question, try out these ideas for organizing it.

What is the statement, and what evidence supports it?

1. Statement: What are you trying to prove?

---

2. Support: List the examples or reasons or facts that support your idea.

_____
_____
_____
_____
_____

Organizing Question: What Happened?

If your paper is going to describe an event or series of events, this outline may help you organize it.

1. Steps leading up to main event

_____
_____
_____

2. Main event

_____
_____
_____

3. What happens after the main event

_____
_____
_____

Organizing Question: What Is It Like?

"What is it like?" asks you to describe something to the reader. In other words, you ask yourself, "What do I want to describe?" You can plan around these questions:

1. What are the best or most important details and examples for describing this? (List all of them.)

2. How can these details be grouped?

3. What's the best order to present them in?

Organizing Question: How Are These Things Alike or Different?
When you are organizing a comparison-contrast paper, try this outline form and these questions.

1. Why is it interesting to compare these two things?
   _____

2. What are the similarities between these two?

   Subject A   *Subject B*

   _____   _____
   _____   _____
   _____   _____
   _____   _____

3. What are the differences between these two?

   Subject A   *Subject B*

   _____   _____
   _____   _____
   _____   _____
   _____   _____

4. What does the comparison reveal?
   _____

> Here's an example of how these questions can be used to come up with an outline. We used an assignment from Chapter 7, "Violence" on page 268.
>
> **Comparing Media Violence to Real-Life Violence**
> You could come up with a useful scratch outline by looking at each column and deciding what characteristics you want to talk more about. Here's one possibility focusing on how media and real life are different:

> | Television Violence | Real Violence |
> |---|---|
> | exciting | frightening |
> | dramatic | miserable |
> | quick | long psychological aftermath |
> | ends in justice | full justice not possible |
>
> Once you have this outline, you can see how asking yourself questions for each line would develop it. "What's an example?" or "Can you explain why you think that?" are questions that will help you produce a draft.

Organizing Question: What Caused This? What Are the Effects of This?

If your paper is going to explore the causes or effects of something, then this outline form and these questions may help you.

What are the effects (or causes) of _____?

Note: There are many ways to look at causes and effects. You can, to give a few examples, label them as long term and recent, obvious and hidden, bad and good, as well as most and least important.

A. Why are these causes or effects important to know?

_____

_____

Causes | *Effects*

B. List the causes you want to discuss. (hidden, minor, long term, recent, obvious, most important, deepest-rooted) | List the effects you want to discuss. (bad/good, short/long term)

_____

_____

C. What is the best order to present these causes in? Number them.

_____

_____

Organizing Question: What Is the Problem? How Can It Be Solved?

The outline forms and questions here are for a paper that describes and/or looks at possible solutions.

What is the problem? (List all the ways it is a problem.)

_____

How can it be solved?

_____

What is the best solution?

_____

What are the advantages of this solution?

_____

What are any disadvantages to this solution?

_____

> ## Suggestions for Discussion and Writing
>
> Now that you've been thinking about ways to organize, look at the exercises below, which move from making an outline to the work of the next chapter—writing a draft.
>
> 1. In groups, choose one of the suggested assignments from the "Writing Assignments" section at the end of the chapter in Part I you're working on now. Choose a form and use its related questions (as listed earlier here) to arrive at an outline. Compare your outline with those of others in your group, then write down what you conclude about the differences and similarities among the outlines.
>
> 2. Choose one of the outlines that your group came up with and have everyone write a quick draft based on that outline. Read some of the drafts and see what the differences and similarities reveal about the way people use outlines.

This chapter has discussed creating an outline before you do a draft. But outlines can also be useful in revising. If you have a draft that doesn't flow well, try making a scratch outline from it. Make the topic of each paragraph a line in your outline. With your paper stripped down to an outline, you may be able to see what's wrong with the organization and fix it.

Chapter 16

Writing the First Draft

Getting Started
What Is a Draft?
Writing from an Outline

Getting Started

Why is getting out the first draft so hard? For some, of course, it isn't. But many students complain that they waste a lot of time and emotion just getting started. Frustration builds up, and writing, which is seldom easy, seems suddenly much harder. Take a minute now to think about how you go about starting papers.

> *Suggestions for Discussion and Writing*
> Freewrite on, or discuss with your fellow students, the following questions:
> 1. What do you usually do to get going on writing a paper?
> 2. What do you usually do, if anything, to delay starting your paper?
> 3. If writing a paper starts easily for you, what seem to be the reasons for your having an easy time?
> 4. If getting started on a paper is a major problem for you, what do you usually do about it?
> 5. Describe the best and worst experiences you've had in getting reactions to your writing.

Why can getting started on a draft be so hard? We don't know for sure. We can only suggest reasons for you to consider. Read through the following list of possibilities to see if analyzing writer's block can help prevent you from getting one.

> *Don't get it right, get it written.*
> —James Thurber, *Shoptalk*, Donald Murray

Waiting for the Perfect Start

Some people think that if their paper doesn't start perfectly, it will only get worse as it goes along. Other writers want to do so well that they won't go on until they're perfectly happy with their first paragraph. There is nothing right or wrong with either of these ideas, except that very often they seem to block writers' progress, instead of helping. It's true that Hemingway once wrote, "All you have to do is write one true sentence. Write the truest sentence that you know." Getting the first sentence right before you go on was great for Hemingway. You have to decide whether it's good or bad advice for you.

Many writers find that getting the first sentence or paragraph right is something that they do much better after several drafts. As you write your paper, your direction may change and you may need to throw out a wonderful first paragraph that no longer fits.

Advice: If you have trouble with your first paragraph, try skipping the introduction altogether and just start writing. Or just write one dull, ordinary statement about your topic to hold your place, and go from there.

Perfectionism

A rough draft can be *very* rough; this is not the time to worry about being perfect. If you worry too much about the first draft, you may not write at all, or you may waste a lot of time and have nothing to go back to.

Advice: Allow yourself to do an awful first draft. Have your only goal be to write a complete first draft as quickly as possible. Remember what James Michener, author of *Hawaii* and *Centennial*, said:

> I have never thought of myself as a good writer. Anyone who wants reassurance of that should read one of my first drafts. But I'm one of the world's great revisers.

Old Memories

Consider whether old worries about writing are holding you back. Very few of us go through school without some negative experiences in writing papers. You write a paper about the death of your grandfather, and your teacher's only comment is "fragment problem." You slave to put a lot of authoritative information and fact into your research paper, and your teacher accuses you, perhaps rightly, of copying.

So what's the connection between miserable memories and not getting started on a draft? That dread of a bad experience can tell us that if we don't write anything down, then we can't get criticized for it. That strange logic could be holding you back from just getting out a first draft.

Advice: Think about the successes and good experiences you have had in writing. Imagine the perfect audience for your paper. Imagine writing for no one but yourself or for some totally approving reader.

If you want company in your misery, try reading about the troubles professional writers have had when even their next meal depended on their writing.

False Expectations

You see someone get an A or hear others in a computer lab just clicking away rapidly on the keys and then think that writing should be easy for you. But even great writers, who spend hours a day just writing, seldom say it's easy.

*You write with ease to show your breeding
But easy writing's curst hard reading.*
—RICHARD BRINSLEY SHERIDAN, *Clio's Protest*

Easy writing makes hard reading.
—ERNEST HEMINGWAY

Advice: Expect to work hard at writing. In college you will learn ways to write better and more thoughtfully, but don't expect to learn how to write in some quick and easy way.

Procrastination

Procrastination means we put something off until later when we could do it now. Dread, laziness, working eight hours a day *and* going to school *and* raising a family: there are many reasons why we don't get things done on time. Some writers, for whatever reason, procrastinate in the hope that the pressure of a very close deadline will magically get them writing. Although a few probably have turned out a brilliant piece that was started at 3:00 A.M., people who put things off that late usually find themselves in the position of having to hand in a final copy that is, in fact, no more than a rough draft.

Advice: Keep time on your side. Make and stick to a schedule for getting your paper done. Go somewhere where you can think and concentrate on just this paper. Time yourself. Know how long you plan to spend on the draft, and get something done in that time.

Inspiration usually comes during work, rather than before it.
—MADELEINE L'ENGLE, *Shoptalk*, DONALD MURRAY

These are all approaches that make writing harder to get into. Look over this list and think about the way you work as a writer. Just knowing about these common problems may help you to solve any problems you have getting started on a draft.

What Is a Draft?

A draft is simply an early version of your paper, with your ideas written out in sentences, not sketched in as notes or lists or freewriting. That means that you try to include all the ideas you've selected from your freewriting or brainstorming in your draft. It may have only the sketchiest of beginnings and a terrible ending. But you've tried to get the whole thing down on paper.

A rough draft can contain a lot of surface errors. You let others see your rough draft only with the understanding that it is a working copy. Because you are probably going to change whole sections of your draft, you don't need to correct those errors now.

A rough draft will probably be based on the invention exercises that you have done and on your outline, but it is not a freewriting or brainstorming list. You'll select which ideas to include in your draft. Later on, you can go back and add additional marginal comments to go into the second draft.

Writing a rough draft allows you to get some distance from what you have written. You can come back to it, after a break, and see it fresh. While you're away from the draft, your mind will still be working on it subconsciously.

Writing from an Outline

Here's an example where student writer Cheryl Warren uses a scratch outline—printed in the left column with our notes in italics—to get out the first draft. Her assignment was "Describe the true nature of a job that interests you. Find out if your preconceptions are valid by interviewing a person who is doing that job, and consider how the media might have shaped your views about it."

Here's how Cheryl Warren moved from outline to draft in the first half of her paper.

Being a Creeler

by Cheryl Warren

Cheryl's Outline:
What it's like to be a creeler.
What I think . . .

Not being tied to a detailed outline may have helped the writer to get into the lively conversational style she has. She almost seems to have free-associated around her first two main points.

Is her organization clear enough for the reader? Should she have answered the reader's obvious question about what creeling is earlier on, for example?

Cheryl's Outline:
What I learned from the media.

In the second part of her first paragraph (after "As

Being a Creeler is not the job for me. The hours are normal (8 hour shifts), the benefits are OK, and the pay is not all that bad. However; creeling is not the best career choice to choose for a life time job. In fact most people do not chose to be creelers but are forced to. I'm sure you're wondering what a creeler is and what is their job. Therefore, without any further ado a Creeler is a person who works at a textile mill and who participates in making fabric. Actually the creeler ties knots in the fabric while it's running through on a machine.

Paragraph One

As you know textile workers get little to no media exposure. In fact the textile worker (the laborer) doesn't get any media exposure at all. However, the exposure that the textile company gets comes from a "Buy America First" commercial. In the commercial it has a man, a supervisor at a textile plant, who's out of a job. Therefore, *you know, creelers get little to no media coverage"), the writer moves outward from the single main point— media coverage—to include details about absence of media interest in workers contrasted with TV commercials about textile management.*

When Cheryl Warren came to the next section of her paper, she no longer used the kind of minimal outline she had adopted for part one. Because the ideas weren't coming out of her own experience, she worked from a list of interview questions. Here's what her outline for this section might look like:

> *Do you like or dislike your job, and why?*
>
> *Do you like your hours?*
>
> *What benefits does a textile worker receive?*
>
> *Are you fulfilling your talents by being a creeler?*

Cheryl Warren's second paragraph may be too rigidly organized. Would she have been better off writing from her main impressions from the interview, then going back to fill in any gaps later?

he and his family has to move from their home because they can't afford the house payments. Then the announcer comes on and says, "Buy American made products first because it matters." However, that's not telling about the workers. It's telling about the finished product.

Paragraph Two

That is why I interviewed a textile worker. Marilyn Beaufort is a textile worker at Aragontown Mill. Her job title is a creeler and it's a tiresome job, that has no excitement in it. I asked her many questions about her job and her feelings towards it. My first question was, do you like or dislike your job, if so why and if not why not?" Her response was no she doesn't like her job because it was tiresome, her coworkers are lazy and her supervisors are just as lazy and they don't get on the lazy people for being lazy. My second question was, "Do you like your hours?" Her response was yes because she works from 6.30 AM until 2.30 PM. She said that was good because her child is in college and her husband works similar hours. My third question was, "Is your pay satisfying?" Her response was that her pay was decent but she would appreciate a raise. My fourth question was, "What benefits does a textile workers receive?" Her response was mixed. She told me that her insurance was good but she didn't get paid for sick days and if you miss six days from work without a doctor's excuse you could lose your job. My final question was "Are you fulfilling your talents by being a Creeler?" Her response was No. The reason why she wasn't fulfilling her talents is because she was a smart young lady in high school and she had a great job during those years, she was a sectary at A and T. However; she got pregnant during her eleventh grade year and everything changed for her. She dropped out of school and quit her job. Therefore, her talent was typing and not creeling. However, she is surviving working as a creeler; although, she rather be doing something else with her life.

Paragraph Three

In conclusion my views of being a creeler remains the same. No, I do not want to be a Creeler because the job is boring, physically demanding, and it's not fulfilling my talents, which is working with children.

> ## *Suggestions for Discussion and Writing*
> Discuss, or freewrite on the following questions:
> 1. Contrast your responses to the writer's first and second paragraphs. How could that information help the writer revise her paper?
> 2. What do you like best about this draft?
> 3. How could the second paragraph be rewritten?

What is most important is that, with a plan or outline of *some* kind, you can do your first draft. Let your draft sit for a while. Then come back to it later with a fresh eye, and with a brain that, you may find, has been unconsciously working on your paper's problems all along.

Chapter 17

Revising

What Is Revising?
Rethinking Your Paper
    Revising Your Focus
    Revising for Your Audience
    Revising Your Purpose
    Revising Your Organization
    Revising Your Style

What Is Revising?

Revising Is Re-Seeing

"Re-seeing" is literally what the word *revision* means, so to revise a paper you need to look at it afresh in order to rethink it. Revision involves questions like: Have I got to the heart of what I want to say? Have I cut everything that isn't relevant? Have I provided enough support for my points? Have I shaped it in the best way for my audience? Revision is part of giving yourself time away from your paper so that you can come back and see it fresh. If you write a paper in one sitting and immediately look it over, it will be hard to notice the difference between what you meant to say and what you actually put down on paper. Revision is an essential part of writing, not an extra last step you can skip if you run out of time.

Writing is rewriting.
    —Donald Murray

Revising Is Not Editing

It is important to polish your papers and check for spelling, usage, and punctuation errors and problems in style. But that is editing, not revision. Revision happens before editing, and involves reviewing and rethinking what you have said and what you want to say.

For a better idea of how revising and editing are different, look at these questions.

Revision Questions	*Editing Questions*
Should I cut the background material?	How is "separate" spelled?
What would happen if I used a comic tone instead of an outraged one?	Should I cut "of course" in this sentence?
Can the reader follow my transitions?	Do I need a semicolon or a comma there?
What can I do to spark the reader's interest in the beginning?	

Revising Is What You Do When You Care About Your Writing

Revising is not a punishment, as in "You'll have to do this over; it's not satisfactory." If you've had to revise a paper because it "wasn't satisfactory," then it's easy to associate revision with failure. Revising can be hard. But it is the work you do because you want to develop your writing. In revising, you are making your ideas clearer to yourself and to your readers.

Revising Is the Way Professional Writers Approach Their Work

When many writers talk about writing, they are really talking about revising, not the burst of ideas that can come with the first draft. As Toni Morrison says,

> ... the best part of all, the absolutely delicious part, is finishing it and then doing it over. That's the thrill of a lifetime for me; if I can just get done with that first phase and then have infinite time to fix it and change it. I rewrite a lot, over and over again, so that it looks like I never did. I try to make it look like I never touched it, and that takes a lot of time and a lot of sweat. (Toni Morrison, from *Shoptalk*, Donald Murray)

Revising Is Letting Go and Taking Risks

One reason that professional writers make major changes when they revise is confidence. To revise, you have to be willing to try something new, and that is difficult when just getting a draft done is hard enough. Revising can make a mess of your paper. You might even cut it up to reorder it, and the resulting confusion is certainly not as comforting as tinkering with a first draft. But you can always go back to the original copy or to the file you stored on your disk. And your progress as a writer will be faster because you will be taking on new challenges.

Revising Takes Time

Allow yourself at least two blocks of time. First, you'll need to put your paper aside, so you can gain some perspective. And second, you'll need time to revise your paper *at least once*, probably more.

Revising: The Ground Rules

1. *Allow time to leave your draft and come back to it.* You're thinking we've mentioned this too often already, and you're right. But it is so fundamental that we had to slip it in again.
2. *Get reactions from other people, but don't blindly follow them.* See Chapter 18 for a look at the ways you can get and give good criticism. The reactions of others can be very helpful in re-seeing your paper.
3. *Read your paper aloud.* Reading a paper out loud can help you to hear how other people will read it. You'll get ideas for changes that wouldn't occur to you if you reread it silently twenty times.

Suggestions for Discussion and Writing

Think about the way you revise:

1. Write down how you typically change a paper after the first draft. Don't fake it; write down what you actually do or don't do. How different is this from what others in your group or class do?
2. What kinds of questions or reactions most help you to revise?
3. What's your attitude about revising?
4. Try finishing this sentence with a paragraph: "Revising is something I do because . . . ". Compare your paragraph to those written by others in your class.

Rethinking Your Paper from Five Different Angles

- *Focus.* What am I getting at in this paper?
- *Audience.* How will my audience respond to it?
- *Purpose.* How well do I persuade or inform or describe an experience?
- *Organization.* Does the organization work?
- *Style.* Is this written in the best style for my purpose and audience?

You will not be able to use every idea in this chapter on any one paper. Pick one of the five angles and read that section carefully to find one or two ideas that you want to try out. Start with your own best intuition about what your paper most needs work on—focus? audience? purpose? organization? style?

Revising Your Focus: *What Is My Main Point?*

Focus is a good place to start because if you change your focus, it may well alter everything else in the paper.

Identifying Your Focus

Start by trying to identify what your focus is. This is not as easy as it may sound. You need to read your paper over and try to describe your main point. Try to put that description in one spoken or written sentence, perhaps using one of these questions to help you to get at it:

a. If a reader were to sum up this paper in one sentence, what would that sentence be?
b. Is there an image that sums up this paper best?
c. What would be a good title for this paper?
d. What question does this paper answer?
e. What is the main contrast or tension in this paper?

Evaluating Your Focus

Now that you have a description of what your paper is about, see if these questions can help you to rethink what your focus *should* be:

f. Would your paper be less superficial with a narrower focus?
g. Does your description of your focus sound like something you have heard often? (If so, this may mean that you are drifting too close to a cliché and need to question more what your own thoughts and feelings are.)
h. Is your focus too narrow? (Frankly, this is rarely the case, but it might be.)
i. Does the focus answer the assignment?
j. Have you told your readers enough so they can picture any situations, or experiences, or people?
k. If you were going to spend an hour in the library, what information would you want to find to add to your paper?
l. Where do you need to explain more?
m. What parts of this paper can be cut?
n. What parts aren't clearly related to the focus?

You won't use all of these questions, of course, but read through the list, and select a few that seem to echo questions you have in your own mind. Try those out. Write down the answers to them on paper so you can play around with rethinking the focus of your paper. Come up with a revised statement of your focus.

> *Suggestions for Discussion and Writing*
>
> 1. In a group, read each draft aloud. Have everyone suggest at least one possible change in focus for each paper. This could be a statement of how that writer would shift the focus if it were his paper.
> 2. To develop your focus, find sections in your draft that seem thin to other readers. Have them ask you a question, and then freewrite an answer.

Revising for Your Audience: *How Will My Readers Respond to This Paper?*

The ability to picture your readers when you write can be crucial. Take a minute to get in the role of your audience in order to think and feel who they are.

Identifying Your Audience

Here are some questions to help you describe your audience to yourself:

a. Whom do you picture reading this? (Be specific: how old? male or female? with what hobbies or political views or taste in food?)
b. Does the assignment call for a particular audience?
c. Where could your paper be published or read by your audience?
d. What does your audience know and think about your topic?
e. How does the topic affect them personally?

Evaluating Your Audience's Response

Some of these questions may help you to rethink your paper so that it involves your audience more and speaks more directly to them. As you read these questions, write down your response to each one.

f. Does your introduction make clear how the topic relates to your audience?
g. Do you tell the reader early on what your paper is going to cover?
h. Are your transitions from one topic to another clear?
i. Are you using the right style and tone for your audience?
j. What parts of your paper will your reader like best? Why?
k. What parts of the paper will your reader like least? Why?
l. How does your conclusion bring the paper to a close for your reader?
m. What will your readers feel and think after they have read your paper?

> ## Suggestions for Discussion and Writing
>
> You don't need to have identified a problem or a way to improve your paper for this kind of revision. You simply choose a different audience and rewrite the paper for that audience.
>
> *Example:* You were writing for your teacher. Now you write it for the students in the class.
>
> *Example:* You were writing for readers of *Seventeen* magazine in mind. Now you redo what you have written for *Sports Illustrated*.
>
> This kind of rewriting is what professional writers do when one publication refuses their article and they have to adapt it for another. It is great practice and can yield some interesting results that you may use in your final draft. Try to rewrite your draft for a completely different audience.

Revising Your Purpose: *How Well Does This Draft Persuade or Inform or Describe an Experience?*

To use this section to help you revise, you need to think about whether persuade, inform, or describe best describes your purpose.

IF YOU ARE PERSUADING

Identifying Your Purpose—Persuasion

Start by trying to describe how your whole paper works to persuade.

a. What do you want your readers to be convinced of after they have finished reading your paper?

b. What facts or statistics or evidence have you brought to your argument that you think will be new and convincing to your readers?

c. Do you appeal primarily to your readers' heart or brain or morals?

Evaluating How Persuasive Your Draft Is

d. How could your beginning get the readers to sympathize more with your point?

e. Will the ending make a strong impact on your readers?

f. Where in the paper are you missing information needed to support your argument? (Go through and note that, even if you feel you will not be able to do the research to find it.)

g. Read your paper from the point of view of someone who disagrees strongly with it. What will that person say at the end of each paragraph? Can you answer those objections?

h. Are your points arranged in the best possible order?

i. What could be cut because it has nothing to do with your argument?

Suggestions for Discussion and Writing

1. Try rewriting your persuasive paper so that it is informative and suggests no particular point of view.
2. Try rewriting your persuasive paper from the opposite point of view—that of someone who disagrees sharply with your argument. (You may be surprised how doing this can strengthen your original argument.)

IF YOU ARE INFORMING

Identifying Your Purpose—Informative

See if these questions can help you come up with ideas for revising.

a. Describe what your audience will learn.

b. What questions does this draft answer for your audience?

c. Is your personal point of view about your material evident to the reader? (If so, this is not necessarily bad, but you'll want to revise if your goal is to present information neutrally.)

Evaluating How Informative Your Draft Is

d. Could your beginning make the information more interesting or relevant to the reader?

e. Does your conclusion emphasize to the reader the importance of this information?

f. Are you trying to cover too much?

g. Have you explained key terms and concepts?

h. Is your information new or too familiar?

i. Do you need to add more examples and anecdotes to make your material clear and alive to the reader?

Suggestions for Discussion and Writing

1. Try revising your informative paper by telling about only one event to get the same information across.
2. Try writing your paper by taking a strong stand about the information.
3. Rewrite your paper for seventh graders and make sure the information is accessible to them.

If You Are Describing

> Don't say the old lady screamed—bring her on and let her scream.
> (MARK TWAIN, QUOTED IN *Shoptalk*, DONALD MURRAY)

In describing an experience or a person or an object, you need to get enough of what is in your own memory down on paper. You really are researching in your own brain and then selecting details. The challenge is to write down enough of the significant details, remembering that the reader knows nothing about the experience even though it is still vivid in your own head.

What does it mean to give significant, specific details? Compare the differences in these two passages:

A. He was a smartass, and his mouth and smile really bothered me, even the way he talked disgusted me.

B. He wore a smartass, whole-lot-hipper-than-you expression on his face. His mouth is what did it. Pudgy, soft lips with just a hint of blond fuzz above them, pursed into a permanent sneer.
  When he talked, he twisted his mouth so the words slithered out of one corner of his face; like garbage dumped off one end of a cafeteria tray. He pulled a cigarette from a pack in his shirt pocket. Lit it without disturbing the sneer.
  (From John Wideman's *Brothers and Keepers*)

Identifying your purpose—descriptive

a. What do you want to get across?
b. What is the main tension or conflict?
c. What details have you given so that readers can experience
   the setting?
   sights, sounds, smells?
   the way the people talked?
   and gestured or moved?
   or looked?
d. What single image sums up what you are describing?

Evaluating How Vividly You Describe the Experience

e. Do you show readers enough of the experience so that they feel they are experiencing it with you?
f. What additional details are needed so that readers can actually picture and describe in detail the people, the noises and conversation, the smells, sights, feel, and action of what went on?
g. Have you relied on words like "thrilling," "scary," "irritating" to sum up for the reader, instead of letting the reader feel or see or hear what it was like to be thrilled, scared, or irritated?
h. What can be cut?

> ### *Suggestions for Discussion and Writing*
> 1. Try retelling the experience from the point of view of someone else, perhaps one of the other people involved. Select one person involved and do a complete character sketch of him or her.
> 2. Describe the event as someone who is deaf or blind would perceive it.
> 3. Try capturing the experience through dialogue alone.
> 4. Write notes to a film director on how to film the scene.

Revising Your Organization: *Does the Organization Work?*

The order in which you take up points or events in your paper needs to be easy for your reader to follow. There are many possible orders that would work. What's important is that all your points relate to your focus and that you communicate to the reader how you have organized those points.

Here are some questions to help you see your paper's organization. It may not be the same as the outline you were working from.

Identifying Your Organization
a. Go through your paper paragraph by paragraph and write down in a phrase what each paragraph is about. Look at the sequence this list makes. Does the order make sense?

b. Try thinking of your paper in terms of the questions it answers. What question does the whole paper answer? What questions do the paragraphs answer? In what order would these questions probably occur in readers' minds?

Evaluating Your Organization
c. Are points presented in the best possible sequence for your readers?

d. Do you need to show more clearly how each point relates to the preceding and following ones?

e. Is it clear how each point relates to the focus?

f. Where are transitions or connections missing?

> ### *Suggestion for Discussion and Writing*
> Try a different way of organizing. You may like the original better, but you may also come up with some new ideas for your final draft.

Revising Your Style: *Is This the Best Way to Write What I Have to Say?*

Style is difficult to define because it has so many parts. "Discuss the style of the author" is a question that leads many students to talk about content instead. Style and content are not exact opposites, and they always end up overlapping. Here, however, it may be useful to think of them as separate:

> Content is what the writer says.
> Style is how it is said.

All people have style, a way of talking, dressing, moving. They may be saying the same thing, wearing the same kind of clothes, walking in the same direction, but they do it in a different way—in their own style. Do they wear jeans or punk black leather or tweedy suits? Would you call them chic, or frumpy, or bad? Do they stalk or lope, creep or bounce, or glide? There is a lot to a person's style and a lot to a writer's style, more than we will be able to discuss here. But in this section we will look at some aspects of style to consider when you revise.

Style is important. Consciously or unconsciously, readers respond to a writer's style, just as they respond to the ideas or experiences that a writer puts before them.

One way to work on your style over the long haul is to read. As you read, you unconsciously absorb the style of the writer. This won't turn you into a clone, but it will suggest some choices and examples to use when you are writing yourself. Read anything and everything, and slowly you will begin to notice differences in style. In the past, writing has been taught by having students read great authors and imitate their styles. Take the best from this approach and read as much as you can.

Revising for Formality

How formal, or casual, does your writing need to be? Do you want to sound very polite, ceremonial, and respectful, or do you want to sound like you are talking to family and friends? Do you want your readers to feel that you know them well or that you've hardly met one another? The answers to these questions will help you decide what words and phrases to use in a particular situation for a particular audience.

For instance,

> Mr. and Mrs. John Bernsford Tipton request the pleasure of your company at dinner on . . .

is much more formal than

> Come on over and have supper with Johnny and me.

Identifying Your Level of Formality

a. Look at a draft that you are working on and try to characterize its level of formality. Does it sound like you are talking to someone you know personally? Does the draft contain slang?

b. How would you rank it on the following scale?

Very formal ──── Academic ──── Standard ──── Informal ──── Slang

(Classroom talk) (Family talk)

Evaluating Your Level of Formality

c. Are there inconsistencies in the draft, places where you suddenly become more or less formal without any apparent reason?
d. What relationship do you have or do you want with your audience? Is the level of formality of the draft right for that relationship?
e. Consider the nature of your subject. Is the level of formality of your draft appropriate for your subject?

Suggestions for Discussion and Writing

1. Try playing around with levels of formality. Take the phrases listed below and try to move them along a scale from very formal to least formal or slang.
   a. to enjoy a meal
   b. to have a good time
   c. to drink too much
   d. to do well on a test
   e. police officer
2. Revise a paragraph of your paper so that it is much more formal or casual than it already is.

Revising for Tone

Tone is the attitude, or emotion, you want to communicate? How different can tone be? Compare the two examples below:

> I'm tired of the constant carping about demonic rock lyrics—malicious fantasies about what they might mean when spelled on the diagonal or what they will do to prenatal infants when heard upside down.

> It is time to take a close look at the criticism made of rock lyrics to determine if the lyrics can possibly have the harmful influences some critics claim.

What mood, attitude, or emotion is conveyed in these two examples? In other words, what is their *tone*? The first one is annoyed, even angry; in the second example, the writer sounds calm, thoughtful. Is the calmer one better? Not necessarily. The question is, Which tone works better in a particular situation?

Writers, like people, do not always consciously decide to convey a mood, but it is there in what is written. You need to look back at your written draft and see if its tone is what you want.

Identifying Your Tone

    a. When you read your paper, what tone or mood do you sense?

    b. Ask other people to tell you what tone they find in the draft.

    c. What is your feeling about your subject?

Evaluating Your Tone

    d. Does the tone convey your feelings about the subject?

    e. Is the tone consistent throughout, or are there spots where it suddenly changes?

    f. Is there a tone that would have a better effect on the audience?

Suggestions for Discussion and Writing

1. Take a sentence or paragraph from one of your drafts and change the tone. Try writing it so the writer sounds
   a. calm and detached
   b. angry
   c. full of enthusiasm
2. Identify the tone of a paper that you have already completed; then have three people read it and describe the tone. Are there any differences? How would you explain them?

Revising for Voice

Voice is a hard quality to define. When writers use the term, *voice* means the personality of the writer that you sense in the writing. It's the image the reader gets of the writer. Look at the paragraphs below.

> We spend a bit more than 1 percent of our gross national product on sports. My total comes to at least $61 billion compared with $4.9 trillion GNP in 1988. I feel sure that this is the right order of magnitude, because on my odyssey I discovered someone had preceded me. *Sports Inc.*, a recently deceased magazine, and the WEFA Group, a consulting firm, did an estimate. They did some things differently, but the conclusion was similar.

There are some fascinating trends. Golf is up, tennis down. Betting is booming. Have we lost our sense of proportion? Our sports spending roughly equals the total GNP of Yugoslavia or Algeria. Is this wretched excess? Some would say so. Not me. People pay for what they want. The resulting pleasures are immense. It's only a penny on the dollar. Where else can you get so much enjoyment and excitement for so little? (Robert J. Samuelson, "The American Sports Mania," *Newsweek,* September 4, 1989)

I have noticed that this fear of Black men goes way beyond the pale of rationality: I was recently walking down a supermarket aisle with two hand-baskets full of groceries, one in each hand. A White woman saw me and rushed for her pocketbook, which she had left in her cart. I would have had to put my own groceries down in order to take her pocketbook. No doubt she thought to herself: "He won't fool me with that old 'basket-in-each-hand' trick." (Laurence Thomas, "In My Next Life I'll Be White," *Ebony,* December 1990)

If when you are reading an article, you can picture a particular person writing it and what that person is like, then you are aware of the writer's voice. If this quality sounds a bit mysterious, perhaps it is, but writing without voice is flat and impersonal. Writing with it—even in the third person—is more engaging because the personality of the writer is evident. In the passages above, Samuelson's voice suggests someone who is a no-nonsense, enthusiastic sports lover who may be leaning forward while he tells you sports is worth every penny. Laurence Thomas's amused, ironic humor suggests someone who feels anger and pain but controls those feelings with humor. Talking to you, he might lean back, but look you straight in the eye.

It's my tone of voice. It's the writer's presence in the story. (Jessica Anderson, Simpson's Contemporary Quotations)

How do you revise your paper so that the reader senses your voice in it? It's harder to give advice about that. You can look for words or ideas that sound too familiar, like something you have already heard. Clichés will certainly block voice. But voice is something that a writer develops; it comes when he or she is engaged in the writing. It isn't just a professional quality because you may have read writing of a second grader that was full of his personality and spirit—his own *voice*.

Below are some questions that may help you to think about voice and to revise for it.

Identifying Your Voice

a. What do you think a reader would be able to sense about you from the way you have written your draft? Focus on the way you have written your ideas, not on what readers would know about your ideas.

b. What ideas or phrases in your draft sound like clichés—expressions that you have heard others use over and over?

Evaluating Your Voice

c. Does your voice come through?

Suggestions for Discussion and Writing

1. Look back over the readings in this text that you have enjoyed the most. Does the voice of the writer come through? Could you describe the writer's personality based on the way she or he wrote the article?
2. Put together three of your papers and ask two other people in your class to read all of them. Ask them how they would describe the writer's voice. (Do the same for their papers.) What do you make of the results?
3. If you find that your voice doesn't come through on your draft, try imagining a different audience. It might be an enthusiastic friend. Try rewriting a section of your paper with that audience in your mind. Do you think now that your own voice comes through more strongly?
4. Look at the two passages on the preceding page by Samuelson and Thomas. Underline words or phrases that suggest each writer's personality. Try to describe the picture you have of the author. Does your description match other people's?

Revising Sentence Style

The way a writer puts sentences together matters. It matters because if it's not right, readers notice. The readers may feel that they are on a wheel that is backing up after every turn. Readers would rather feel that they are on a wheel that is rolling forward. Good sentence style is like that. A reader is unaware of it. Except that the reader feels the pleasure of rolling easily along. That's the mark of good sentence style. Readers notice this. They say the writing flows.

Perhaps you noticed that that paragraph made for rocky reading. Now try it again, when sentences are combined and repeated phrases are cut:

The way a writer puts sentences together matters. Readers notice when it's not right and feel they are on a wheel that is backing up after every turn instead of rolling forward. Often the mark of good sentence style is that the reader is unaware of individual sentences but feels the pleasure of reading easily along. When readers notice this quality, they say the writing flows.

How Can You Improve Your Sentence Style?

1. Combine short, choppy sentences. If you notice that a word or phrase at the end of one sentence repeats at the beginning of the next one, you should probably combine the two sentences. If you start several sentences with the same words or phrase, often they would be better combined. Try combining the sentences below.

> a. *Avalon* is an interesting movie. The movie is about a family from Western Europe. They come to America in the early twentieth century. Over the years the bonds that held the family together weaken. The family bonds weaken because money-making pursuits pull them apart. TV pulls them apart, too. TV takes over at dinner time. They go to visit the old grandfather in a nursing home. The TV is on when they visit. The children are drawn to it and not the grandfather's talk.
>
> b. Terrell Webb is a senior here. He started working on the college radio station as a freshman. He had a two-hour program. The program was mostly heavy metal. Terrell said heavy metal was his least favorite music then, but he has gotten to like it. He definitely liked having his own show. He is director at the station now.

Now look for choppy sentences in your own writing by listening to yourself or someone else read your paper aloud.

2. Use short, simple sentences when you want to make a point emphatically. Here is an example:

> Make no mistake about it. Life was indeed different before the car, before radio, before television; all these inventions strengthened the youth culture. Technology does change culture.

3. Use repetition if you want to create a pattern or to emphasize a word. Who can forget Martin Luther King Jr.'s "I Have a Dream" speech with the repeating phrases *I have a dream* and *Let freedom ring* bringing power to its ending?

Look how Philip Berrigan uses repetition to hammer his point about the need for change in America:

> Does America exist? Which America? The America that spent $2.5 trillion on war and war preparations in the past forty years? The America of 26,000 nuclear warheads; the America of the first-strike policy? The America that intervenes illegally in El Salvador, Lebanon, Nicaragua, Grenada; the America that manipulates Israel as a proxy;
> ... the America that spies on its citizens, eroding civil liberties? (Philip Berrigan, "Does America Still Exist?" *Harper's,* March 1984)

Repetition draws attention to your words, so make sure that, when you use it, your words can survive that kind of scrutiny.

Identifying Your Sentence Style
   a. How many of your sentences are similar in type and length?
   b. What is the typical sentence type and length?
   c. What phrases or words repeat in the next sentence?

Evaluating Your Sentence Style
   d. Look again at any phrases and words that you find repeating in the next sentence. Is the repetition serving a purpose? If not, how can you combine sentences to get rid of the repetition?
   e. Look at the short sentences. How many short sentences are in a paragraph? Which ones contain statements that you want to emphasize over the rest of the paragraph? Try combining the other sentences.
   f. Read over pages 419–427 on punctuating sentences. Look at the way you have linked complete thoughts together. What changes could you make so that your writing rolled along more smoothly?

Suggestions for Discussion and Writing

1. Look back over your papers and check for the following:
   - How often do you use different kinds of sentences?
   - Are your sentences all roughly the same length?
   - Underline words or phrases that repeat and see if combining sentences will eliminate the repetition.
   - Do your shortest sentences contain the points you want to emphasize?

2. Work with two other people and select a paragraph from each person's paper to work on. With everyone working on that paper together, see how you can improve sentence style by combining sentences and by using short sentences to isolate and emphasize important points.

3. Look at a paragraph from a reading that you enjoyed in this book. How long and varied are the sentences? What do you notice about the different ways that the writer begins sentences? Are you in any way aware of particular sentences as you read? Can you sum up what you could learn from this writer about sentence style?

Revising Word Choice

Le bon mot is a phrase the French use to describe the satisfaction of finding just the right word (literally, it means "the good word"). For anyone interested in writing, juggling choices about which word to use is part of the work and the fun. One of the advantages of writing over talking is that we can reconsider our words. There is no formula for finding the right word, but there are some general guidelines.

1. Being specific. "Be specific." "Be concrete." These are the phrases that generally appear in the margins of student papers. It's rare that a teacher writes, "Try to be more general" or "Can you make this more abstract?" Being specific means that you write using particular examples rather than general categories.

Specific	*Abstract/General*
You write: We need to redo the income tax system and have a flat tax with no exceptions.	*Rather than*: We need fair taxes.
He whispered French vocabulary seductively in my ear and sent me a yellow rose after our study date.	He's romantic.
She's got a blue 1980 Chevette with a missing rear window and two bumper stickers: "I'd rather be shopping" and "Support Jesse Helms."	She's got a method of transportation.
My pregnant half-Siamese, half-alley cat named Sheeba who sleeps on my head.	My cat.

Readers can generalize from the specific examples you give them, but there is no way for readers on their own to come up with the concrete or more specific information you actually have in your mind. If you tell readers your work is demanding, they can nod their heads in general sympathy, but they can't picture what it is like to work the midnight shift at Pizza Hut during final exams when you have three term papers to do—unless you give them those details.

Identifying Specific Language

a. Is the language you use most often general and abstract?
b. Underline detailed and specific examples.

Evaluating Your Word Choice

c. Where do you need to be more specific and concrete? Sometimes this is hard to see because we carry those specific details in our head. You may want to ask one or two classmates to tell you when *they* need those details.

> ### *Suggestions for Discussion or Writing*
>
> 1. In the second column write down more concrete or specific versions of the items in the first column.
>
> | *General/Abstract* | *Specific/Concrete* |
> |---|---|
> | middle-class values | |
> | nice | |
> | glamorous | |
> | evil | |
> | values | |
> | food | |
> | game show | |
> | soap opera | |
> | rap music | |
> | poverty | |
> | courage | |
>
> 2. Scan a paragraph of your paper for words that are too vague and general and substitute more specific words and details. Then trade paragraphs with another student and tell each other your reactions to the changes.

2. Avoid clichés.

Writers, especially, spill out stereotypes and overturn clichés.
    —Doris Betts, *The Independent Weekly*,
           March 25, 1992

  Try to keep your writing free of clichés of all kinds—those words or phrases that are worn out, however expressive they once were, because we have seen or heard them too often.
  Here are some samples:

low self-esteem	That seems to describe everyone who isn't an Olympic winner. Try to pin down why this person lacks confidence and what he has done or said that suggests this.
won't tolerate aggression	How won't this person/state tolerate aggression? What will she do in response?
"I'm comfortable with that."	What is the person's reaction? Agreement?

"She was always there for me."   What does it mean to this writer to be "there for me"? Did she listen to her? Help her with her homework? Shoplift with her? Lie for her?

a caring person   What has he done specifically? Baked some cookies? Given you good advice? What advice? Given in what manner?

Avoid jargon. Many clichés are related to jargon. Plain talk usually works better, particularly if your audience are nonspecialists. Here are examples:

Jargon	*Direct*
proximity to the decision-making process	in on the decision
Americans need to defend their energy independence	Americans must stop relying on Kuwait's oil
single-family dwelling unit	house
health-care professionals	doctors and nurses
interpersonal relationship skills	friendliness
nuclear family unit	mom, dad, and two kids

Write simply. From the authors of *Elements of Style*, E. B. White and William Strunk, comes this good advice:

Never use a multi-syllable word, when a shorter one will do.

Identifying Clichés and Jargon

a. Which words or phrases in your draft please you? Underline those.

b. Which words or phrases are clichés or jargon? Underline those with a wavy line.

c. Are there places where your language could be simpler and more direct without sacrificing subtleties or meaning? Try making those changes.

Suggestions for Discussion and Writing

1. Keep a list of the clichés you hear in the next twenty-four hours.
2. Look over your papers and see if you can find any clichés.
3. Make a list of jargon terms that people use. Can you generalize about why people slip into jargon?

Revising for Cuts

"Less is more" said the architect Ludwig Mies Van Der Rohe, who liked to build houses with a minimum of interior walls, enclosing only the bathrooms and leaving the rest open space. "Less is more" can also apply to writing style. Cutting needless words and phrases makes your writing move along more smoothly. Readers become more engaged because their energy is not being wasted on extra words.

How do you know if something is essential or if it should be cut? That's not easy to see in your own work. As in gardening, you don't want to pull out the flowers, just the weeds. Again, we can only offer general guidelines to think about:

1. Some phrases should almost always be cut because they state the obvious, simply act as filler, or may even confuse the reader. Here are some examples:

   needless to say

   I think

   I feel

   sort of

   kind of

   obviously

   very

   really

   just

2. Concrete details should usually stay.
3. A summary or repetition of what has already been said can usually be cut, unless it concludes a long and complex discussion that may need the added emphasis and clarity. Have confidence that your readers will be paying attention, and don't repeat just for that reader who may doze off on you.

Identifying Cuts You Need to Make

a. Go through your draft and underline all words, phrases, and sentences that you consider absolutely essential. (How much of your draft is underlined?)

Evaluating Your Cuts

b. Go through your draft and see how much you can cut without changing the reader's comprehension or enjoyment. (Check what you have cut. Think three times about cutting concrete details.)

c. Have you cut too much? Remember, surgery is risky work; you just want to cut the dead wood.

Suggestions for Discussion and Writing

1. Try revising these examples to see what cutting can do for style.

   a. She is not the typical sort of cheerleader.

   b. I think that newspapers have a different kind of readership than some people feel they did forty years ago.

   c. One of the most annoying things I can think of is mosquitoes that hang around my ears whining; nothing annoys me more than that.

2. The following passage based on George Orwell's "A Hanging," should be cut at least by half. Try making the cuts, then compare your version to the original (in the box on page 398).

   I remember this especially devastating experience I had in Burma. It was really depressing and made me think about how awful human beings can be to each other. It has been raining for days, I mean a lot! Here was another sodden morning of rains. Ugh! The whole area inside the jail and around it was really creepy. A really sickly light, kind of like yellow tinfoil it seemed to me, was slanting over the very high walls into this depressing jail yard. These people and I, we were waiting outside the cells of the condemned persons. These cells were a row of things like sheds. The sheds were really small. They had double bars, like really small animal cages. Each cell measured about ten feet by about ten feet and nothing was in them. They were quite bare within except for a few things like a plank bed and a pot of drinking water. In some of these cells there were people who were really quiet and depressed, brown-skinned silent men. They were squatting just about next to the inner bars. It was chilly from the rain so they had their blankets draped around them to keep them warm and keep the chill of the rain off. The sad thing was that these men were condemned. We all knew that they would be hanged within a short time, like within the next week or two. I think I will always remember this scene as one of the most dreary experiences of my life. I will never forget it.

3. Read the brief and wonderful book *The Craft of Revision* by Donald Murray, a writer, journalist, and teacher who finds writing a struggle he enjoys. His book takes you through his own revisions, his ideas for revising and the pains and pleasures of writing.

Revising Beginnings and Endings

Revising is a good time to focus on the way you begin and end your paper. Usually you write a good beginning when you have a sense of your whole paper and are in the process of re-seeing it. And usually the best ending gets written after you have been thinking about your paper for a while.

> Below is the original opening to the story George Orwell wrote about working for the British government in Burma in the 1920s. How would you describe the difference in effect from the one above?
>
> *It was in Burma, a sodden morning of the rains. A sickly light, like yellow tinfoil, was slanting over the high walls into the jail yard. We were waiting outside the condemned cells, a row of sheds fronted with double bars, like small animal cages. Each cell measured about ten feet by ten and was quite bare within except for a plank bed and a pot for drinking water. In some of them brown, silent men were squatting at the inner bars, with their blankets draped round them. These were the condemned men, due to be hanged within the next week or two.*

Beginnings

Think about what *you* expect as you start reading someone else's writing. Unconsciously you probably ask questions:

   What is this paper about?

   What does this paper have to do with me?

   Am I interested in this subject?

Readers need to know what any paper is about and why it will interest them. If you address those points when you write your own introduction, you'll be on the right track.

Many students have mastered the *clear* beginning—one that tells the reader what the paper is about. But not all students know how to do an *interesting* start—one that intrigues readers and makes them feel the paper connects to their lives. People who earn their living writing pay a lot of attention to grabbing the reader's attention from the very first sentence. They realize that they have to get the reader's attention right away or they won't get it at all.

Maybe because students know their teacher will have to read papers all the way through, some start with "This paper is about...." Think about when you browse through a magazine. You won't find any articles that start "This article is about...." What usually gets you to read an article? What works in the first paragraph to get you to read on?

Endings

A reader may remember—or forget—your paper largely by its ending. A satisfying ending should do more than just summarize what you have already said. Readers don't need a summary unless your content is so difficult that they need to hear it one more time to understand it.

An ending should give the reader a sense of completion and suggest the importance of what has been covered. It is all right to cover new material in a conclusion, just so long as it connects with or extends what you have been discussing. In a conclusion, you can end with a question that still needs to be pursued. Professional researchers do this. They know it's likely that more research will be done on the subject in the future. You may want to emphasize your main point with a story or image that will leave a strong impression in a reader's mind. If you're arguing to persuade the reader, try to end with a powerful anecdote or quotation or piece of evidence. Nothing hurts an argument more than to fade out in the end.

To give a satisfying sense of completion, try referring back to an opening question or anecdote. For example, if you start a paper with a story about how television has positively affected family life, you could return to that same anecdote at the end of the paper and talk about how family life would be different without television. This gives both you, the writer, and your readers the satisfying sense that a circle has closed.

Suggestions for Beginnings and Endings

Here are some ideas to choose from: eight ways to begin and end papers that go beyond simple statements of purpose or summary.

1. Tell an anecdote. This is a quick scene or story that dramatizes your point vividly for readers so that they feel involved with a real-life situation and people.

Beginning with an anecdote can be a good way to grab your readers' attention. Ending with an anecdote can pull your ideas together for readers and give an emotional impact.

2. Use a quotation. If someone else has said something well, it can focus attention and give authority to your paper to start or end with that quotation—especially if it says a lot in very few words. For example, the following quotation might be a good way to begin a paper on the power of business interests behind television programming:

> Television's first mission is not to inform. It is not even to entertain.
> It is to move goods, and round up viewers for the main event—the commercials. (Ron Powers)

3. Give statistics. Giving a quick dose of the reality of a problem with statistics (one set, not an endless stream of numbers) can get readers to take your point seriously. If you end your paper with an important statistic, it may convey to the reader that the particular point you have been talking about is true on a large scale.

4. Ask a question. If the question is a thoughtful one and is followed up, this can be a natural way to engage a reader's mind. Most readers won't block the automatic response of trying to answer a question. And your question can lead readers into the focus of your paper.

Ending with a question can also be a good way of summing up and asking the reader to consider all that you have written. For example, at the end of a paper on the "I Love Lucy" show in which you have speculated about the popularity of that show, asking a question like "Why is this show the most popular ever on TV?" could work well. It wouldn't suggest that you haven't given good reasons in your paper. Rather, it asks readers to think further and come up with their own ideas about an ultimately mysterious subject.

5. *Make a strong statement.* Powerful or colorful language can convey to readers that the writer is intensely involved in the subject and that the readers will be too when they read on. A strong statement can also bring a paper to an emphatic end. "Men are what television tells them they are" or "Macho maniacs are manufactured in the mass media" could both be strong openings to papers as long as the writers support these bold claims.

6. *Start a conversation with the reader.* Talking directly to readers at the start may make them want to join you. One student started out with "Examine with me, if you will, . . ." and others in the class agreed that this formal yet conversational approach was inviting.

If you start a paper this way, it may also be a good way to close by addressing the reader again at the ending.

7. *Make a comparison.* Poets make comparisons all the time, and it can work in a factual paper too—whether the comparison is a real one or imaginative. "Sportscasting is like ski jumping" is an offbeat start that might puzzle readers enough to get them to stay with you. "Canada's government functions more democratically than America's" is a comparison that might infuriate or intrigue readers into greater interest. As an ending, the comparison can provide an image or a factual reference that emphasizes your focus—in a new and interesting way.

8. *State the subject.* Every newspaper article that reports on an event begins with a summary of the important facts: who, what, when, where, how. And there are other times when it works well to get right down to business with your audience and tell them what you are going to do in your paper. Restating the subject and purpose of your paper can be an effective and businesslike ending as well, especially if your subject is complex and needs summing up.

Identifying the Beginning and Ending of Your Paper

a. What does your first paragraph tell the reader about the topic? About why they need to read your paper?

b. How do you end the paper?
c. Does your ending contain any new ideas?

Evaluating Your Beginning and Ending
d. Is your topic and direction clear from your first paragraph?
e. Does it convince readers that they need or will want to read your paper?
f. How will your beginning affect the reader?
g. How will your ending affect the reader?
h. Does your ending relate back to your beginning?
i. How does your ending bring your whole paper together?

Suggestions for Discussion and Writing

1. In groups, using a paper that someone in the group wrote, try out different introductions for the paper. Come up with one example for each of the eight types of beginnings. Decide which ones work best, keeping your audience in mind, and be prepared to give reasons why.

2. Have everyone read through one paper in the group so that everyone is familiar with it. Then try to use the eight ideas to improve the ending. Discuss how each ending changes the effect the whole paper has on the reader.

3. Have everyone in the group take out a finished paper or draft in progress. Read the opening paragraph and have the group talk about what they expect the paper to be about based on that paragraph. Then discuss whether the first paragraph makes you *want* to read on. Be honest. If group members agree that the opening is not clear or interesting, work together to try and revise it. Don't just stick with what's safe. Experiment with various beginnings. Remember, you are just revising and making suggestions, not carving in stone.

4. Read a draft or paper from everyone in the group all the way through so you can consider the concluding paragraph. How satisfying is each ending? Get beyond "it's O.K.; it's fine," and see if you can come up with a better ending for each paper.

5. Look through several of your favorite magazines and read just the first paragraph of the articles. Find one that appeals to you and makes you want to read on. Bring it to class and analyze with others how it works. Are all reactions to it like yours? Why not?

Chapter 18

Getting and Giving Good Criticism

What Is Criticism?
Four Ways to React to a Paper
Some Critics at Work
Writing Conferences

One of the best ways to get ideas for revising is to have other people read our papers and react to them. Their questions, encouragement, suggestions, and reactions can help us to see our papers in ways we never would have managed on our own.

• •

O would that God the gift
would give us, to see
ourselves as others see us.
—ROBERT BURNS

Readers can tell us a lot through their reactions, but the writer alone must finally decide what revisions to make. And successful revision also depends on how well we ask for criticism and how well we take it when we get it.

What Is Criticism?

Criticism is analysis, reaction, evaluation, and response, both good and bad. A critical review of a movie, for instance, can describe the plot, tell us about the characters, and praise the direction and the acting, as well as tell us how the critic responded to it. All these things are part of criticism.

GOOD CRITICISM CAN HELP YOU SEE AND HEAR.

A critic can be eyes and ears for you. After all, revising is hard because we have trouble seeing our own writing to begin with. We merge what we felt or meant to say with what we actually got down on the paper. So it is literally hard to "see what we've written."

GOOD CRITICISM IS A LABOR-SAVING DEVICE.

This means that someone else steps in and helps you on your paper. Your paper gets the benefit not only of your brains and ideas but also of someone else's. It is easier to edit and revise someone else's writing because you didn't write it. You see *only* what's on the paper, and not what you then think or hope is there.

You may still not like the sound of the word *criticism,* but professional writers rely on it. They expect an editor to help them out with an article or novel. The novelist Thomas Wolfe (*Look Homeward Angel*) arrived at his editor's, Maxwell Perkins's, house with literally a trunkload of pages that Perkins cut and arranged into a novel and—yes—criticized. An exceptional case, of course! Just remember, though, that writers EXPECT criticism from their editors.

GOOD CRITICISM TELLS YOU HOW OTHERS REACT TO YOUR WRITING.

A few critiques don't tell you about every reader's feelings, but they are a start and can help you to see your writing from the reader's point of view. This perspective alone can help you make changes.

BUT ONLY *YOU* CAN DECIDE WHAT IS RIGHT FOR YOUR PAPER.

Criticism isn't the law. You should listen to criticism, but remember that you are free to reject it. YOU have to decide whether the criticism you're getting is valuable to you.

What Other Students Say About Criticism

When some students were asked about other students criticizing their papers, sometimes called *peer review,* two comments came up very frequently:

1. "Getting this criticism was the single step which helped me most in getting my paper written."
2. "The problem with the criticism I got was not that it was too harsh, but that it wasn't 'critical' enough. My partner didn't seem interested enough to tell me things to improve my paper."

Here's what students said was the worst kind of reaction they could get after a critique session:

- Silence
- "It's OK"
- Indifference
- Attention to errors only
- Nasty or snide comments
- Undemanding comments

Here's what they said were the most helpful reactions:

- Honest responses
- Ideas for changes
- Commitment to helping
- Specific suggestions
- Specific questions
- Encouragement and praise
- Detailed comments

Suggestions for Discussion and Writing

Try freewriting about your experiences with criticism, whether from teachers or students. Talk with your class about what experiences they have had. What was helpful? What wasn't?

Four Ways to React to a Paper

Some people are such good critics that they can intuitively help almost anyone with their writing. Most of us are not that good; we need the writer's help. This section should help you to ask for the kind of criticism that will benefit you most. Before you tell your reader what kind of criticism you'd like, make sure to give him or her the answer to three basic questions:

1. What's the assignment?
2. What stage is this paper in?
3. Who is the audience?

Let your critic know whether this is a first freewriting on your topic or a fifth draft of a paper that you consider nearly finished.

We all learn differently, so we don't all benefit from the same kind of criticism. Also, at different stages in our writing, one kind of criticism may be more valuable than another.

Describing the Paper

Sometimes, in day-to-day life, people can help us enormously just by describing how we are acting, or mirroring back to us what we are saying. ("If you could only see yourself . . .") In criticism, describing can work this way. The critic is helping you to see your own work as he or she sees it.

Questions to help a critic describe
- What is the focus?
- How is it organized?
- How are the ideas developed?
- Who is the audience?
- How does the writer feel about the subject?
- How does the writer feel about the audience?
- What is the language like?
- How does the beginning interest the reader?
- How does it end?

Advantages and Disadvantages of Criticizing by Describing

Advantages: This method helps to eliminate any defensive reactions we might have. You are not told, "Your focus is not clear." Instead, you are given a description of a focus, and if it doesn't fit your idea of your main point at all, you can figure out . . . "My focus wasn't clear." Describing can be best for helping us see what we have written.

Disadvantages: Most of us are so used to making judgments, or at least to giving advice, that we need some practice and concentration to simply describe: to tell what we see without commenting on it.

Giving a Reader's Reaction

In reader reaction, critics tell writers what thoughts went through their minds as they read the paper. They might give a stream-of-consciousness account, or they could list the questions and doubts that surfaced as they read.

Questions to help a critic give a reader reaction
- What was your overall impression of the paper?
- What questions came into your mind as you read the paper?
- What went through your mind as you read the paper? Do this paragraph by paragraph in detail.
- What effect did the beginning and ending have on you?

- How did the style of writing affect you?
- Where did you want to know more?
- Where did you doubt what the writer was saying?
- Where were you confused?

Advantages and Disadvantages of Reader Reaction

Advantages: Like descriptive criticism, reader reaction can help you to see your paper more clearly. You keep your reader in mind as you write. This kind of criticism lets you know best what it was like for someone to read your paper.

Disadvantages: You need to consider whether the reader's reaction was irrelevant or too personal. You may get reactions that are difficult to turn into revision ideas.

Evaluating the Paper

Some writers learn best when an evaluation is made: when readers tell them what is good and what is weak in their papers. The key here is to ask for reasons. Evaluations are worth a lot more when we understand why something is good or bad.

Questions to help a critic evaluate
- How strong is the introduction?
- How effective is the ending?
- How well does the organization work?
- Are the ideas fully developed?
- What was most interesting about this paper?
- Is the paper clearly focused?
- Is the writing especially strong or vivid?
- Is the writing confusing or dull or clichéd?
- What are the strongest and weakest points in the paper?
- What grade would you assign to this paper, and why?

Advantages and Disadvantages of Evaluation

Advantages: This kind of criticism is likely to focus on what needs to be changed and what can stay as it is.

Disadvantages: We can get defensive about evaluation. And if an evaluation doesn't include reasons, it probably won't be much help. Evaluations can be both wrong and discouraging.

Giving Advice

With advice as criticism, you get specific ideas for change rather than merely indications of where change is needed.

Questions to help a critic advise
- What is the most important advice you have?
- What sections are strong and should not be changed?
- What advice do you have about _____? (Fill in any aspect of the paper you consider important or a problem.)

Advantages and Disadvantages of Advice

Advantages: This advice is definitely aimed at helping you revise your paper.
Disadvantages: Make sure you understand why this advice is being given. It may be tempting to take bad advice just because it is direct, clear, and different.

Note: Many students think corrections are the heart of criticism. But correcting errors of grammar and spelling belongs under editing, the *final* step. When you're still rethinking your ideas, it's too soon to correct errors. Remember, you're likely to rewrite many of your sentences as you revise.

Some Critics at Work

Here we present illustrations of each type of criticism—description, reader reaction, evaluation, and advice. Each sample is responding to the same student's essay written in response to the assignment below:

Assignment: "Does playing with war toys make children more prone to use and tolerate violence?"
Audience: Readers of a college newspaper
Stage: A second draft

STUDENT'S PAPER: "IS THE CHILD VIOLENT?"—MONROE PATTERSON

As you can see in the projects, and mostly in the poor areas the children are in gangs, drug running or just hanging on the block. You can believe that most of them have guns or have handled a gun. When they leave the streets they go inside and watch the good guys shoot up the bad guys. A childs' life is built around this because this happens every day. What does the child grows up believing; it's all right to kill?

On the other hand in the rich neighborhood the kids are not exposed to the violence on the street but they are violent with their aggression. They compete with each other to get the highest grade. They would do anything to be number one in their class and that aggression can lead to violence.

The parents have alot to do with their children being so violent. They should let the child now what is going on in the world but at the same time let them know that they disapprove of violent behavior. The child would get their aggression out but they will know that it's wrong. If the child grows up thinking the world is a bowl of cherries, will he make it? The child have to have some violent instinct to make it in this violent oriented society.

The US is a violent country. Each generation contributes to the violence because they let their children follow in everybody's footsteps who are violent. They see the US competing to be number one and they make as much nuclear weapons as possible to be more violent. Thing like that make you ask yourself is it worth trying to change. Could I make it trying to change the world. I couldn't tell you the answer, but I can say it's worth trying.

What I'm saying is that, you can grow up in the streets or grow up pushing each other back, so you can get ahead, but the majority of the children is violent because of the values of the US. It starts out with war toys, then the cartoons are violent, and finally they get into the extra violent movies. A large part of their lives they are exposed to violence and being violent.

Then you expect them to change even when the world will chew you up and spit you out if you let your guard down for a second? You have to be realistic.

Now let's look at what each of the different types of criticism would offer the writer. The critical comments here are not the only possible ones or even the best ones; impressions and comments will vary with each critic. You may be surprised how casually some of these comments are written. The informality is okay; in fact, sometimes it's best. Just writing as if you were talking to the writer and letting your thoughts spill out can be very useful.

Describing the Paper

Let's start by supposing the writer has asked for a description of the paper. Here are some questions that might be asked and how one critic answered them.

What is the main point?

Your main point seems to be that there are many paths to violent behavior and also different types of violent behavior. But I'm not sure.

How is this paper organized?

Let me give you an informal, paragraph-by-paragraph outline.

Paragraph 1.	You talk about street violence and its effects on kids.
Paragraph 2.	You tell the reader that competitiveness is a kind of violence in rich kids.
Paragraph 3.	I'm not sure. You say that parents are influential AND that we may need to be violent.
Paragraph 4.	You say that the US is violent and ask if it can be changed.
Paragraph 5.	You end by saying that our culture is so violent that it isn't just war toys alone that train kids for violence. Then you say it's so violent and kids need to be ready for violence.

What style or tone does the writer use toward the audience?

I'd say you feel intensely about this subject because your style is direct and honest. Your audience seems to be people our age. You're not trying to impress anyone with fancy vocabulary. Your tone is intense, almost angry. You get right into each point without wasting time.

Reader Reaction

Here's how a reader might respond to this paper using a set of basic questions as guidelines. Definitely, no two reader-reaction critiques will be alike. This one is an example of someone responding without trying to summarize what's in the paper or to evaluate in any way. The critic is just telling the writer some of the impressions and feelings he had as he read the paper.

WHAT WAS YOUR OVERALL REACTION TO WHAT YOU READ?

I was confused but always interested because you seem to care a lot about what you were saying—enough to even show anger. I thought, this guy is telling it straight and he knows something. He knows about rich kids and project kids. I think I see how your ideas connect, but I couldn't say for sure.

WHAT WAS YOUR REACTION TO THE BEGINNING?

You jump right in and don't waste any time, so I thought, this guy is not going to be boring. But I was asking myself where you were going or how your paper answered the question. How does it? I felt like you were talking to me and you were in a hurry to have me understand.

WHAT WAS YOUR REACTION TO THE ENDING?

"Chew you up and spit you out." That phrase stays with me. I like it. The way you put things makes me feel how tough it all is, a vicious circle. But I'm not sure that I'd agree we are trapped in it. I wonder if we need guns and cartoons and all. Do they really train us like soldiers for this violence? See what I'm saying? You halfway sound like you think they do. By the way, I like the way you started that last paragraph "What I'm saying is . . ." Somehow that helped keep my attention. I see now how this ties in with the question, but I wish I'd seen it earlier.

WHAT QUESTIONS DID YOU HAVE AS YOU READ?

Paragraph by paragraph:

- Paragraph 1. What does this have to do with the question? What is your point here?
- Paragraph 2. How does competition lead to violence or do you mean other kinds?
- Paragraph 3. Are you opposed to war toys or not? I can't really tell.
- Paragraph 4. Why are you so convinced that there is no way out? Is America that violent? Maybe you're right.
- Paragraph 5. So what are you saying here? War toys teach us to be violent, but they also train us to protect ourselves?

Evaluation

For this kind of criticism, you think in terms of what's good, what's bad, what's strong or vivid, and what seems weak or clichéd. Now is the time to make judgments and to back them up with reasons or specific examples. Otherwise, they might not be much use to the writer.

WHAT IS YOUR OVERALL EVALUATION?

The best points are your voice and your ideas. I like the way you talk to the reader, and your idea about rich kids' and poorer kids' different types of violence was new to me. Also the pace is good here.

Your weak points are that it's hard to follow this from paragraph to paragraph. You make the reader work hard to figure out how your writing connects to the question. That doesn't happen until the very end. Sometimes you seem to contradict yourself. There are a lot of errors. Focus, I'd say, is the main problem. What is your main point?

Advice

Here is a sample of straightforward, unadulterated advice given in response to some set questions.

WHAT THREE REVISIONS DO YOU THINK WOULD IMPROVE THE PAPER THE MOST?

1. Focus on the question.
2. Decide what your main point is: what you REALLY feel about war toys. Make that clear at the start.
3. Let the reader have some idea how this paper is going to be organized. How does one paragraph fit with another? Where is the whole thing going?
4. Sorry to add a fourth, but don't forget to work on errors at the end.

WHAT SHOULDN'T BE CHANGED

1. Don't lose the pace of this and don't change the style, the way you talk to the reader as if you were having a real conversation. That part's great.
2. Don't drop out any of your ideas about how different people grow up with different attitudes to violence and how we are violent as a country in many ways.

WHAT SECTIONS ARE BEST WRITTEN?

Your last paragraph. It came across clearly and strongly.

Note: Now think of this paper again as a rough draft. There would be little point in making a lot of corrections now because the writer needs to think his position on war toys through some more and rewrite the paper. But a critic might still usefully point out patterns of errors. Here a critic might tell the writer to look for repeated comma errors and typos when he gets to the final copy.

Writing Conferences

Writing conferences with your teacher are a major opportunity for you to improve your writing, so don't avoid them. In fact, seek them out. If your teacher doesn't require you to come for writing conferences, see if you can arrange one anyway.

In a writing conference, you can get suggestions for revising a rough draft or learn more about papers you have already done. Certainly any time you are confused by comments on your paper, talk with your teacher to get them clarified. Don't let all the time your teacher has put into writing comments go to waste; you need to follow up.

To make the most out of your conference time, consider the following suggestions:

BE PREPARED WITH YOUR OWN QUESTIONS AND REQUESTS.

If you can direct the conference toward what you need and want to know, it will be most helpful to you. So have a few questions ready, even written down, to make the most of conference time.

DON'T WORRY ABOUT A ROUGH DRAFT BEING ROUGH.

This may sound like a funny thing to mention, but many students expect teachers to look only at their final copies. If your rough draft is a mess, so what; read it to your teacher so she won't have to look at it. If it has major problems, don't apologize; you're having a writing conference so you can get help, after all.

> *We are all apprentices in a craft where no one ever becomes a master.*
> —ERNEST HEMINGWAY, *Simpson's Contemporary Quotations*

KEEP A PENCIL IN YOUR HAND.

Don't expect the teacher to start writing on your paper, but do stop and write down any suggestions or comments. You may well forget them later if you don't.

DON'T EXPECT TO REWRITE YOUR DRAFT DURING THE CONFERENCE.

A conference is meant to give you ideas to think about. If a section of your draft needs a better transition, you can play around with possibilities for a minute, but it is probably better to mark the spot with "needs transition" and come back to it later.

LOOK FOR THE BIG PICTURE.

Try to sum up loose ends before you leave. Time in most writing conferences runs out, but try not to leave with major questions or confusions in your head.

You can ask your teacher to sum up the two or three *major* suggestions he has for your draft or your writing. Or you could try to state what *major* revision ideas you have, based on the conference, to see if you are understanding each other. You don't have to leave feeling lost in details.

Whether your motivation is producing a better paper, furthering your development as a writer, getting a better grade, or all of these, writing conferences can provide you with expert advice. You just have to be ready to make the most of what a meeting with your instructor can offer you.

Chapter 19

Editing: The Final Polish

How Important Is Correctness?
What Standards of Correctness Do We Need?
Dealing with Errors
The Most Common and Unwanted Errors
Punctuation Problems
Spelling Problems
Usage and Grammar Problems

How Important Is Correctness?

We have said very little on the subject of correctness so far; in fact, we said that worrying about correctness when doing freewriting may be harmful to your writing. In the section on rough drafts, we said this was not the time to worry about errors either, except to note if you see a lot of one type of error. So why are we paying attention to errors *now*, when you are ready to type your paper for the last time? Because *now*, when you've fully worked out what you want to say and how to say it, is the time to work on surface errors.

Errors are important. Why? People have different answers to that question, but they boil down to three reasons:

1. Errors often confuse the reader. Most rules of punctuation and usage make meaning clear. Sure, your reader can go back and study what you intended to say and figure it out, but you don't want to shift the reader's attention from what you are saying and on to your errors.

2. Errors signal the writer's ignorance or carelessness. Maybe it's not fair, but when people notice that you've made little errors, the thought occurs to them, "What other kinds of errors is this writer making?" or "If this writer didn't bother to proofread, what else didn't she bother with?" Spots on your clothes at a job interview may signal incompetence to an employer, although the spots don't have anything to do with whether you are intelligent and reliable.

3. *Standard English* is the generally accepted way of speaking and writing. If you write with a slightly different usage, that is called a *dialect,* and many readers will consider these dialect difference as errors. It may be good to say in your neighborhood, "Ain't going," but you need to be aware that that "I am not going" is Standard English usage.

Is it fair that one dialect is called Standard English and favored over all the other dialects heard in America? In some ways, no—just as it was unfair that Latin was spoken in the English court of Henry VIII, so "common people" would be excluded. Sometimes people point out dialect errors to act superior, but there is a case to be made for Standard English. If you write in the same way as everyone else—in Standard English—the reader is not distracted from your main point by dialect differences, even if those differences are only momentarily confusing.

What Standards of Correctness Do We Need?

Just how correct does our writing have to be? is the next question. It's a question for each teacher and class and writer to answer. One composition teacher, Becky House, came up with this analogy for her students about how many errors are too many:

> Imagine you are going out on a special date to a fancy restaurant; you spend a lot of time and have fun just getting ready. You and your date both feel great when you find yourselves at a table with a beautiful view. As you study the menu, a fly comes by. You're surprised, but you just brush it away. As you order, the waiter has to brush a fly off his sleeve. When your drinks arrive, so do two more flies.
>
> How many times do flies have to come by before your evening is ruined?

In the same way, we might ask ourselves how many errors readers tolerate before they consider that a paper is "ruined." As you read others' papers, notice the effect errors have on you and figure out what your own standards are about errors.

> ### *Suggestions for Discussion and Writing*
>
> Here are some issues that you may want to look at as a class, so you understand what standards you, others in your class, and your teacher have.
>
> 1. How do you react, even unconsciously, when a paper has no errors? When it has two or three on a page? When there are ten or more errors per page?
>
> 2. Should only Standard English be acceptable in writing for college and business?
>
> 3. If you were teaching writing, how would you mark and grade errors on final drafts?
>
>   - Some teachers, for instance, mark and label every error.
>   - Others will underline each error but ask the reader to figure out what was wrong.
>   - Another approach is to mark the end of any line containing an error.
>   - And some feel it makes the most sense to mark only one or two *types* of errors.
>
> 4. What has helped you in the past to put that final polish and correctness on your papers?
>
> 5. How much help should students give one another when it comes to proofreading? Should they correct errors, just point out errors, or simply note that certain kinds of errors occur often without pointing them out?

Dealing with Errors

In dealing with all the errors we make, we can console ourselves with examples of the many fine communicators (like F. Scott Fitzgerald, Winston Churchill, John F. Kennedy, George Washington) who made many spelling errors. Making errors does not mean you are stupid, but unless you are famous, you still have to worry about your image and your errors.

However your instructor deals with errors, you may have to experiment to come up with the best system for yourself. Here are some principles that can be helpful:

REMEMBER: ERRORS ARE NOT ENDLESS.

If you tackle the errors you make one by one, you can conquer them.

SEE PATTERNS.

Suppose your paper contains 25 errors. If they are all marked in red, you may feel hopeless when the paper comes back to you. But if you notice that you are really making only four kinds of errors that repeat over and over, the situation is not so desperate. Anyone can learn to correct four kinds of errors.

STUDY THE ERRORS YOU DO MAKE.

Believe it or not, teachers do not live for the moment when they can take out their red pen and strike again and again at your paper. Marking errors takes a lot of time and is not done in a spirit of vengeance. Put your paper aside until you have time, or until you can work with a tutor or your teacher. Circle and correct each error. Then count the types of errors. Or you can keep a grammar notebook, the kind we show on page 463, where you record each error and then write the corrected version next to it.

LEARN TO PROOFREAD.

No one is asking you to love proofreading, but we all can learn some proofreading techniques that will improve the correctness of our papers. Here's a list of techniques for you to try out. Allow yourself at least a half hour, and have the discipline to do it.

1. *Read your paper aloud.* The results of this simple technique are amazing. Work on the habit of reading slowly so that you say only what is there on the page, not what you intended to say.

2. *Proofread for one kind of error at a time.* Choose one kind of error (for example, sentence fragments) and just look for that. Then choose another kind and proofread for that one. You probably aren't making that many kinds of errors, so this won't go on into infinity.

3. *Try proofreading backwards.* This is a trick professional proofreaders use to catch spelling errors. Reading backwards, you are certainly not going to get swept up in meaning and start skimming over spelling errors. It won't work for punctuation, of course.

4. *Make use of computers.* Spellers and grammar checking programs can be very helpful and can actually teach you about your errors.

5. *Have someone else proofread your paper.* This is something professional writers do. It is easier to spot someone else's errors because you see only what's on the paper, not what the writer intended to get on paper. You will also be learning if you note the errors others point out for you and make a record of them.

6. *Separate errors from ignorance.* Keep a record of the number of errors that were just careless slips—things you knew were wrong as soon as you saw them marked. Compare that number to the number of mistakes you made because you didn't know something was an error. This will tell you whether you need to spend more time proofreading or being tutored.

7. *Buy a good dictionary and grammar reference book.* You will need both of these all your life. Everyone occasionally has to look up some point about spelling or usage or punctuation to check on what is right.

The Most Common and Unwanted Errors

About 15 years ago a book about usage and punctuation came out with a title that said it all: *The Least You Need to Know About English,* by Teresa Glazier. Composition teachers and students alike want to spend the least amount of time they can on errors so that they can concentrate on what and how they want to write. Glazier gets down to the main points, and that's what we want to do here. Some interesting research by Robert Connors and Andrea Lunsford provides us with a list of the most frequently made errors by students and also a list of errors teachers mark most often (*College English,* December 1988, pp. 395 ff.). We've used their lists as the basis of our discussion.

What Connors's and Lunsford's research showed was that most teachers don't mark or notice every error. Types of errors that interfere with meaning make the reader work too hard to understand, and those are the errors that get marked a lot.

We won't be going over every rule here, just the essential ones for:

Punctuation

Spelling

Grammar and usage

Punctuation Problems

Punctuation marks communicate as much as words do. Readers rely on periods, or commas, or semicolons, without even thinking about them, to get your meaning.

Try life without punctuation for a moment:

> what is christmas in this country the old captain was saying its not the same as at home youre right its to see who can show off the most with presents and expensive presents there ought to be a law against it said joe in his imitation coarse voice frowning darkly yes there is nowhere the real feeling of christmas and all the color and so quiet music and bells and real happiness not here . . . its because everybody wants to beat the next one said joe thats the american way unless you have more than anybody else you have to feel ashamed of yourself oh you shouldnt talk like that joe said mathilda (William Carlos Williams, *White Mule*)

You probably got through that paragraph and understood it with effort. What punctuation marks did you miss the most?

Below is the same paragraph, but this time with the signals for paragraphs and sentences—indentions, periods, and capitals. Notice the difference in reading it.

What is christmas in this country? the old captain was saying. Its not the same as at home.

Youre right. It s to see who can show off the most with presents and expensive presents. There ought to be a law against it said joe in his imitation coarse voice frowning darkly.

Yes there is nowhere the real feeling of christmas and all the color and so quiet music and bells and real happiness not here.

Its because everybody wants to beat the next one said joe. Thats the American way. unless you have more than anybody else you have to feel ashamed of yourself.

Oh you shouldnt talk like that joe said mathilda.

The Basics of a Sentence: Marking off Complete Thoughts

Notice what a difference there is in reading the above paragraph when you know where one thought ends and the next begins. Marking off each complete thought is the signal we rely on most, and the error that teachers mark most often. The four main punctuation errors deal with our clearly marking off sentences or complete thoughts. You may know errors in signaling complete thoughts by the following names:

Sentence fragments

Run-on sentences

Comma splices

Comma missing after dependent clause

These all have to do with sending the reader a confusing signal about when one thought is over and the next is beginning.

Traditional grammar defines a sentence as having a subject and a verb in an independent clause. There are other ways to define a sentence, but the simplest way is to use the completeness test. Ask:

Does it sound complete?

Are you left waiting for the thought to be finished?

Practice Check: Recognizing Complete Sentences

Read these examples and see if you can tell which ones are sentences by whether they sound complete. Mark down the number if it is a complete thought and sentence.

1. The TV blew up.
2. Having been a great success on radio in the thirties.

3. If you wonder why "The Cosby Show" is one of the most popular shows of the 1980s.
4. How good really is "Sesame Street" at preparing children for school?
5. Geraldo who seems ready to take a whole show to talk about topics that would have been unthinkable on television even ten years ago.
6. Since the first beer commercials were integrated on TV in 1965 with jocks of different hues for the first time guzzling beer together in a bar booth.
7. Whether or not CNN is going to turn the world into a global village remains to be seen.
8. What a lousy movie.
9. Because the Nielsen ratings tell a sponsor how many homes are tuned in to their commercial.
10. Give me your honest reaction to "America's Funniest Home Videos."

The first, fourth, seventh, and tenth examples are complete sentences and can end with a period. Notice in example 1 how short a sentence can be. You may want to know more—Why *did* the TV blow up?—but the statement is complete. Examples 2, 3, 5, 6, and 9 should sound incomplete to you. Example 8 is a fragment—something you're likely to say or hear in conversation but does not conform to Standard English punctuation. Example 10 is a complete thought and sentence even though the subject—"You"—is understood and not written out. (The "you" that's understood in a request or order is the only time a sentence doesn't have to have a written subject.)

All the rest of the examples, even though some are very long, are not complete thoughts and can't stand alone.

Take a look at 3, 6 and 9; if you took away the first word, they would be complete sentences:

- *if* you wonder why "The Cosby Show" is one of the most popular shows of the 1980s.
- *since* the beer commercials were first integrated on TV in 1965 with jocks of different hues for the first time huddling together in a bar booth
- *because* the Nielsen ratings tell a sponsor how many homes are tuned into their commercial.

With "if," "since," and "because" beginning these examples, a complete sentence is changed into a dependent clause—one that has you waiting for or "depending" on more information to complete its meaning.

Because signaling when a thought is complete is so important, let's look at the most common sentence errors one by one. All are failures to signal a complete thought.

Sentence Fragments

Fragments confuse readers by leading them to think a thought is complete when it isn't.

> If you can imagine how hard it is to read fragments of sentences. Although you might adapt. Because you were eager to read whatever it was. Putting up with it but not liking it. Getting through it but taking forever. Which could get irritating. And get old real fast.

That paragraph probably made sense to you with some extra effort, but we are trained not to read in fragments, so they momentarily confuse and delay our reading.

Example: When people get picky about the spelling in my rough draft. I get mad. Because I only wanted them to look at my ideas.

Corrected: When people get picky about the spelling in my rough draft, I get mad because I only wanted them to look at my ideas.

The Basics of Fragments

When words that don't make a complete sentence are punctuated as a complete sentence, they form a fragment. A complete sentence could be one or two words, and a fragment could be thirty. But if it doesn't finish the idea it starts to state, it is still a fragment.

Before we set out to eliminate all fragments from the face of the earth, it is only honest to admit that you will find fragments in print. And they are accepted: in written dialogue, in ads and trendy writing in magazines, and in slang diction. If you can explain to your teacher why you want to use a fragment, then it may be all right to do so.

But generally the rule is: *Don't punctuate a fragment as a sentence.*

Practice Check: Converting Fragments

a. Rewrite the paragraph at the top of this page, turning each fragment into a complete sentence. (See answers, page 465.)
b. In groups of four or five, look for fragments that have occurred in your papers and turn each one into a complete sentence. This is the crucial test. Spotting your own fragments is the goal here, not being able to do fragment exercises well. (See answers on page 465.)

Comma Splices

In a comma splice, there are two complete thoughts or independent clauses that are separated only by a comma. Instead of a comma, you need to use a conjunction or period or semicolon to show where one thought finishes and the next begins.

Comma splice: Advertisements ignore rules of Standard English, they write whatever sounds catchy and looks good on the page.

Corrected: Advertisements ignore rules of Standard English; they write whatever sounds catchy and looks good on the page.

Comma splice: The rules of punctuation aren't sacred, they are harder to learn when you see fragments in ads all the time.

Corrected: The rules of punctuation aren't sacred, but they are harder to learn when you see fragments in ads all the time.

The Basics of Comma Splices

To correct a comma splice, you have to be able to recognize that two complete sentences have been separated by a comma. Cover up one of the complete thoughts and see if the other half will sound complete by itself. If so, you need to divide them by:

- Making them two sentences with a period and a capital letter.
- Putting a semicolon (;) where the first complete thought ends.
- Keeping the comma and adding a coordinating conjunction.

What is a coordinating conjunction? Frankly, it's easiest just to memorize the list:

and

but

or (nor)

for

yet

so

Practice Check: Correcting Comma Splices

a. Correct the comma splices in the following paragraph:

Commercialism is wrecking America, our cultural resources are dwindling, the very idea of *citizen* has become synonymous with *consumer.*

    The omnipresent signs of commercialism's stamp are so numerous that we are in danger of becoming oblivious to the obvious, ads are tucked in books, displayed on giant screens at sport events, projected from subway monitors, pumped into doctors' reception rooms, posted in public restrooms, inscribed on clothes, embedded in arcade games, zapped through fax machines, and emblazoned (thanks to food dyes) on hot dogs.

One hundred and thirty billion dollars is dumped annually into advertising, that's more money than the gross national product of our oil-rich ally Saudi Arabia.

There is the long-standing American ideal of simple and honest living, of moderation in the marketplace, frugality used to be a key word in America's civic vocabulary. Yet ever since World War II, we have allowed business people to exalt one value—consumption—to the near exclusion of all others, this treads on our moral and civic tradition like a bulldozer in a flower garden, in this one-value universe, the ideal of consumption too often obliterates other important social and environmental values. (Adapted from "Are We Consumers or Citizens?" Collins and Jacobson)

b. After correcting the paragraph, discuss with your group why you each chose to make the correction with a period, a semicolon, or a comma and coordinating conjunction.

c. Look for comma splices that have occurred in your papers and correct them. (See answers, page 465.)

Run-On or Fused Sentences

These errors are closely related to comma splices. The problem is the same: the writer fails to signal to the reader the end of one complete thought and the beginning of another—this time by omitting *all* punctuation at the sentence break. Here are some examples:

Run-on sentence: Ads today appear everywhere people consider it a privilege to wear shirts that advertise brands. You would think these T-shirts would be cheaper that's not the case just the reverse is true.

Corrected: Ads today appear everywhere; people consider it a privilege to wear shirts that advertise brands. You would think these T-shirts would be cheaper, but that's not the case; just the reverse is true.

The Basics of Run-On Sentences

Run-on sentences are corrected just like comma splices are because in both you have two complete thoughts and no signal to the reader about where one thought ends and the next begins. To correct run-on sentences, you need to:

- Identify where the break between the two thoughts is.
- Decide whether the two thoughts are best separated by a period and capital, a semicolon, or a comma and coordinating conjunction (and, but, or, nor [or], yet, so).

Practice Check: Correcting Run-On Sentences

a. Try correcting the run-on sentences in this passage:

In this one-value universe, the ideal of consumption too often obliterates other important social and environmental values, such as the following:

Psychological well-being: Our system of advertising purposefully promotes envy, creates anxiety, and fosters insecurity the tragic end product of this is kids killing kids for $100 name-brand sneakers.

Communal values: The soul of a community cannot thrive in a relentlessly commercial environment civic-mindedness is an alien concept to a people mesmerized by consumer goods. This is the "me only" world, the world where politicians feed the great promises of "no new taxes" in this world, public institutions that depend on government are forced to turn to business dollars to survive the resulting cost, of course, is the commercialization of schools, art museums, and non-profit organizations (Adapted from "Are We Consumers or Citizens?," ibid.)

b. Compare your corrections with those of others in your class. Why did you sometimes choose to mark the sentence break differently?

c. See if you can spot and correct the run-on sentences in another student's writing.

d. The true test: check over your own writing and see if you can spot and correct your own run-on sentences. (See answers, page 465.)

Comma Missing After Introductory Clause or Phrase

A writer needs to signal to the reader when an introductory or dependent clause ends and the real sentence starts. In fact, forgetting to do so is the most common error found in student papers. As you will see from the examples below, the introductory element cannot stand as a complete thought by itself. It needs a comma to set it off from the complete sentence that follows.

This same rule applies for introductory prepositional phrases, like "After the TV show" and "In 1918."

Missing comma: If a family has a television set in every room how close can their family life be?

Corrected: If a family has a TV in every room, how close can their family life be?

Missing comma: Because each one will be sitting alone facing the screen their lives and fantasy worlds will remain full of action and noise but lonely.

Corrected: Because each one will be sitting alone facing the screen, their lives and fantasy worlds will remain full of action and noise but lonely.

The Basics of Marking Introductory Dependent Clauses

The easiest way to figure out if you have started your sentence with a dependent clause is to learn the most common words that mark dependent clauses. If your sentence starts with one of these words, you need to mark the end of that clause with a comma:

after	although
as if	because
if	since
so that	unless
until	when

Practice Check: Punctuating Introductory Dependent Clauses

a. Correct the following passage:

> Even if some experts say that TV has weakened family ties. There may be important ways that TV strengthens families. Because not every family watches TV in the same way that generalization is just too big for me. If we didn't have TV broadcasting news and dramas in our home there are many things that families might never discuss that they do now. Without TV many controversial topics might have stayed buried. When you're sitting in a room and Geraldo is talking about homosexuality or AIDS or bulimia it is likely that someone will make a comment. Because one family member reacts the family discusses together something that never would have come up if the TV had not been on.

b. Write five sentences that begin with a dependent clause, punctuating them correctly.

c. Look at your own writing and underline any sentences that start with a dependent clause. Check to see that the comma is there to separate it from the main thought.

All the errors covered in our discussion of punctuation are about how to set off complete thoughts for the reader. Because these are among the twelve most commonly made and marked errors on students' papers, we thought the chart on page 427 summarizing how to punctuate complete thoughts or main clauses would be useful. It will also suggest ways to vary the kinds of sentences you use. (See answers, page 466.)

Punctuating Complete Thoughts

To avoid fragments and comma splices, we could, of course, just write sentences that contain one complete thought only and nothing else, but that would sound choppy after a while. So here are four ways to punctuate two complete thoughts when they *are* put together.

Here are the two complete thoughts:

1. Radio allows your mind to visualize.
2. I like it better than TV.

1. *Keep the ideas in separate sentences.* **Use a period.**
   I like radio better than TV. It allows your mind to visualize.

2. *Separate the two ideas, but suggest they are closely linked.* **Use a semicolon.**
   Radio allows your mind to visualize; I like it better than TV.
   Radio allows your mind to visualize; therefore, I like it better than TV.
   Note that the two ideas separated with a semicolon and a connecting word like "however, nevertheless, therefore, then, finally, or also" are punctuated with a semicolon and comma.

3. *Connect the two ideas with "and, but, or, for, so, or yet."* **Use a comma and a conjunction.**
   Radio allows your mind to visualize, so I like it better than TV.

4. *Turn one sentence into a dependent clause using "after, although, as if, because, if, since, so that, unless, until, or when."* **Use a subordinating conjunction and end the clause with a comma.**
   Since radio allows your mind to visualize, I like it better than TV.
   Radio allows your mind to visualize so that I like it better than TV.
   Note that no comma is used to mark the beginning of a dependent clause in the middle of a sentence because the dependent words—after although, because, before, since, if, so that, unless, when—do that.

Using Apostrophes Incorrectly

One more punctuation error—missing or misplaced apostrophes—is very common. Apostrophes are signs or symbols used to show missing letters or to indicate possession. Teachers and other readers notice its misuse or absence because an apostrophe can change meaning in a variety of ways.

Possession: the Dalmatian of William = William's Dalmatian

Missing letters: it is = it's

Plurals for letters: four A's

Plurals for numbers: three 2's

Apostrophe error: Vega is the second brightest star; it's magnitude is second only to that of Sirius.
Corrected: its magnitude . . .

Apostrophe error: Theyre going to order *Rolling Stone*.
Corrected: They're going to . . .

Apostrophe error: The books cover was far more lurid than what was inside.
Corrected: The book's cover . . .

Apostrophe error: I got three As and two Cs last term.
Corrected: I got three A's and two C's last term.

The Basics of Apostrophes

To Show Possession

There are two ways to show who or what something belongs to or is connected to:

the computer of Bill   Bill's computer

Very often we show possession by using an apostrophe because it sounds less formal.

The brother of Brendan, Henry   Brendan's brother, Henry

Rules for Forming the Possessive

Add *s*

> like July's heat
> men's volleyball

even when the word itself ends in *s,* and it looks odd:

> the business's bankruptcy
> Charles Dickens's novels

Exception 1: If the word is plural and ends in *s,* just add apostrophe and no *s.*

> books' covers
> foxes' lair
> ladies' man

Exception 2: Don't add apostrophe or *s* if you are using the possessive of the following pronouns:

> I—my, mine
> you—your, yours
> he—his
> her—hers, her

it—its
we—ours, our
they—their, theirs
who—whose

TO SIGNAL MISSING LETTERS

Whenever two words are run together or contracted to capture the informal way we speak, you need to signal with an apostrophe, in the right place, what letters are missing.

Informal	*More Formal*
I don't	I do not
she doesn't	she does not
we've	we have
they're	they are
it's	it is

For more on the correct use of *it's* and *they're*, see pp. 434–435.

TO SHOW THE PLURAL OF NUMBERS AND LETTERS

To show the plural of numbers and letters, add 's.

Example: For the sign, we'll need four *s*'s, four *i*'s, two *p*'s, and one *m*.

I got four A's and an F on my report card; four 0's for missing homework dropped me to an F in History.

Practice Check: Apostrophes

Rewrite the following phrases using apostrophes:

1. we do not
2. the magnitude of Vega
3. the broadcast of CNN
4. the plot of "As the World Turns"
5. she does not
6. the conclusion of the study
7. they are not
8. they are not (another way)
9. the choice of critics
10. the heroes of comics
11. the fuss of the boss
12. the end of it

13. we have
14. there is
15. the volume of the radios
16. the TV of women
17. the hat of the man
18. the basketball of the men

(See answers, page 466.)

Spelling Problems

Spelling problems are another whole category of mistakes that English teachers and professionals care about. People are quick to spot spelling errors, which can confuse meaning as well as distract the reader.

Life is not fair, so spelling correctly is effortless for some people and an endless struggle for others. Bad spellers were luckier in the sixteenth century because spelling was not yet standardized. Writers, even William Shakespeare, would spell the same word differently in the same passage and it was OK. But with the advent of dictionaries like Samuel Johnson's *Dictionary* in 1755, spelling became standardized, and it is no longer all right to write "rite" in three different ways.

For those of us whose spelling is triggered by our ears, it doesn't help that in English *to*, *too*, and *two* all sound the same. If you are not a natural speller, there are still ways to improve that won't take up all your free time. In the following we discuss some of them.

DECIDE THAT YOU WILL IMPROVE YOUR SPELLING.

Many people make the same spelling mistakes over and over simply because they believe that they can't change how they spell. Not true.

KEEP A LIST OF THE WORDS YOU MISSPELL.

This list will not go on into infinity, and it won't even be a dictionary. You may be amazed at how few words you misspell but how often they repeat.

BE WILLING TO LEARN SHORT LISTS OF WORDS YOU COMMONLY MISSPELL.

Although this sounds like what goes on in elementary school, learning a short list of words can still work in college. Collect a list of words that you commonly misspell and test yourself on them. If you learn just three words a week that you misspell often, you are eliminating hundreds of spelling mistakes.

Here are some of the words that teachers find themselves correcting most often:

a lot	all right	conscientious
necessary	occasion	separate

absence	argument	development
tragedy	truly	ninety
knowledge	prejudiced	privilege
forty	conscious	environment

USE GIMMICKS TO HELP YOU REMEMBER YOUR SPELLING DEMONS.

The best gimmicks are usually those you think up for yourself, but here are a few examples:

T*rage*dy puts us in a rage.

People with knowl*edge* have the edge.

If you can spell se*para*te, you are above par.

Pretty corny stuff, but if it helps you to remember these words, who cares?

LOOK FOR PATTERNS AND LEARN THE RULES THAT GO WITH THE MOST COMMON ERRORS YOU MAKE.

Most spelling errors fall into patterns, and sometimes learning a rule and a few exceptions can help you to spot and correct those mistakes quickly. Here are the most common patterns of errors and the rules that go with them.

Adding Suffixes

Suffixes are the letters added to the end of a word that change the meaning and use of the word.

Root   Suffix

live + ed   = lived

live + ly   = lively

live + able = livable

Rule 1. Drop the final vowel when

The word ends in a single vowel.

The final single vowel is preceded by a single consonant.

The suffix begins with a vowel.

So   agree + able = agreeable

and   advise + able = advisable

Rule 2. Double the final consonant when

The final syllable is accented. (It always is in single-syllable words.)

The final consonant is preceded by a single vowel.

let + ing = letting

un + stop + able = unstoppable

un + focus + ed = unfocused (accent is not on last syllable)

forgot + en = forgotten (accent shifts to last syllable)

Rule 3. Add *-ally* instead of *-ly* when

The word ends in *-ic*

logic + ly = logically

magic + ly = magically

There is an exception: *publicly.*

Rule 4. Change *y* to *i* when

The *y* is preceded by a consonant.

The suffix is not *-ing*.

party + ed = partied

party + ing = partying

occupy + ed = occupied

occupy + ing = occupying

Practice Check: Adding Suffixes

believe + ed =
hit + ing =
heat + ing =
party + ing =
write + ing =
tragic + ly =
fantastic + ly =
final + ly =
bombastic + ly =
plenty + ful =

(See answers, page 467.)

Adding Prefixes

Prefixes are those few letters that can be added *before* the root word to change the meaning.

The rule for prefixes. Just add the prefix, no matter how odd it looks

mis + spell = misspell

un + necessary = unnecessary

dis + satisfied = dissatisfied

Practice Check: Adding Prefixes

Spell the new word formed with the prefix.

    dis + assemble

    in   + accurate

    il   + logical

    un + natural

    in   + numerable

    mis + shapen

    mis + state

    dis + solve

    dis + associate

(See answers, page 467.)

Knowing When to Use ie or ei

Words like *receive* and *believe* are often misspelled. You can either memorize them one by one or learn this rule and some common exceptions.

    Rhyming: I before e, except after c. Examples: believe, relieve, achieve; conceive, deceive, perceive, receive.

    Notable exceptions: leisure; and science and its kin—conscience and conscientious; neighbor; weigh.

Practice Check: ei or ie

Decide whether the blank should be filled in with *ie* or *ei*.

1. he dec___ved her.
2. They were rel___ved of a great burden.
3. Advances in the sc___nes come from ideas that at first seem ill conc___ved.
4. L___sure is perc___ved as important in many countries where workers rec___ve many more paid holidays than in America. Here workers who want five weeks' vacation might be thought unconsc___tious.

(See answers, page 467.)

Commonly Confused Words

Sometimes using one word in place of another is a sign that you are stretching your vocabulary, so a few "wrong word" mistakes can be a good sign that you are reaching and developing as a writer. Teachers will note the errors because obviously they confuse meaning.

    The words here are commonly confused because they sound the same but mean something different. It is easy to see why they are confused in writing, especially by spellers who rely on their ears to spell. This mistake is the one most often marked by teachers.

Use a substitution test to correct the confusion. Replace the word with one that means the same thing and see if the sentence still makes sense.

- **accept** and **except**
  accept = to agree to, to receive

  Faulkner gave a brief, hurried, and magnificent speech when he accepted the Nobel Prize.

  except = not including, leaving out

  His taste in music extends to everything except Muzak.

Substitution test: Try replacing the word with *not including*. If the sentence still reads well, use *except*; if it does not, use *accept*.

- **affect** and **effect**
  affect = influenced by

  I was so affected by the movie that I had nightmares about bats.

  effect = (1) result (noun); (2) to accomplish or achieve (verb)

  The effect of the TV coverage of the homeless family was a job offer and a mobile home for that family, and many viewers were affected by the show. But the producers had hoped to do more and effect a change in policy.

Substitution test: Use *affect* if you can substitute the words *influence* or *influenced by* and the sentence still makes sense.

- **its** and **it's**
  This is the most commonly marked error on student papers. The pair is doubly confusing because the usual rule for making *it* show possession does not hold here.

  it's = it is

  It's a fine day.

  its = belonging to it

  The baby lost its bottle.

Substitution test: If you can substitute the phrase *it is* and the sentence makes sense, then use *it's*.

- **past** and **passed**
  past = a time before the present

  How much sense do we get of the past on TV?

  passed = moved by, successfully completed

My whole life passed in front of me when I thought I had not passed my driver's test.

Substitution test: This is a confusing one because *past* looks like the past tense of *to pass*. If you can substitute the word *moved* or *completed*, write *passed*.

- **personal** and **personnel**
  personnel = the group of people who work for an organization

  As personnel director, he had to interview all job applicants.

  personal = intimate or not public

  That's a personal matter that I would discuss with close friends.

Substitution test: If it makes sense when you substitute the word *intimate*, then use *personal*.

- **principal** and **principle**
  Although you may feel you have been working on this one since elementary school, it can still slip by you.
  principle = rule or moral

  This was one of the four principles she lived by.

  principal = head of a school; or an adjective meaning main or chief

  All the principal ideas came at the beginning of the principal's speech.

Substitution test: If you can substitute the word *rule*, use *principle*.

- **than** and **then**
  than = compared to

  He likes rap better than heavy metal.

  then = next or at that time

  Then they told us what life before radio was like, but we couldn't decide if life was better then.

Substitution test: Try substituting *next* or *at that time*. If it fits, you want *then*.

- **there** and **their** and **they're**
  These three words are *homonyms*, words that sound exactly the same. You can tell them apart by their meaning.
  their = belonging to them

  Their house was on fire.

  they're = they are

They're the best people I know.

there = in that place; or a general pronoun

There is no reason to go there again.

Substitution test: If you can substitute *they are,* then the contracted form *they're* is what you need. If the meaning is "belonging to them" and you can substitute that phrase, then use *their.* In all other cases, use *there.*

- **to** and **two** and **too**
  These are three more homonyms that you need to proofread for.
  two = the number 2

  I get two newspapers, so I can compare the coverage on different issues.

  too = (1) also; (2) very or overly

  She is too nice; she gets on my nerves.

  Are you going to watch that show, too?

  to = a preposition

  To is more complicated because it is both a preposition and a part of the infinitive.

  "To be or not to be?" is the question that Hamlet addresses to himself and to the audience.

  Substitution test: How do you avoid making errors with *two/too/to*? Again, try the substitution test. *Two* is easy: replace it with a number and see if it makes sense. If you can substitute the word *very* or *overly* or *also,* then you need to write *too.* All other cases are *to.*

  Thomas has two (2) sons.

  She is too (overly) nice; she gets on my nerves.

  Are you going to watch that show, too (also)?

  That show was too (very) funny.

  It's too (very) bad about your boombox being stolen.

- **whether** and **weather**
  These two words are easy to confuse when writing quickly, but the difference is clear.
  weather = the conditions outside

Call me strange, but I love hot, humid weather.

whether = if

The party doesn't depend on whether you show up.

Substitution test: If you can substitute *if*, use *whether*.

Practice Check: Spotting and Correcting Commonly Confused Words

a. Try filling in the correct word in the following paragraphs:

From whether/weather reports to/too/two the top news stories, the way the news is presented on TV affects/effects us. We might not want to accept/except how powerfully we are affected/effected, but its/it's undeniable. Although the producers are not in a conspiracy to force they're/there/their personal/personnel principals/principles on us, messages about values get through because of the very structure of the program.

   Whether/weather its/it's the too/to short, 40 second coverage of important stories or to/too/two many commercial interruptions, our personal/personnel reactions are effected/affected. We don't hang on to a story—even of a personnel/personal disaster—for longer than a minute, so how can we get involved? TV news, with its/it's high speed coverage, makes us passive and unmotivated to effect/affect change. There/they're/their may be reasons to say that people are better informed than/then ever before because of TV, but whether/weather they were so passive in the past/passed is another question.

b. Look over your papers and see which commonly confused words you have trouble with. Make corrections by testing out substitute words.

c. Try writing five sentences showing how to use the commonly confused words that you have trouble with.

(See answers, page 467.)

HYPHENATING WORDS CORRECTLY.

Make sure the hyphen comes at a syllable break. Syl-la-ble can be hyphenated in two places. But don't puzzle the reader by putting the hyphen in the middle of a syllable:

You can te-
ll that th-
is can mak-
e reading a l-
ot harder fo-
r the reade-
r.

If you are in doubt about where the syllable break comes, check your dictionary. It shows how the syllables divide for each word.

Usage and Grammar Problems

We've talked about errors in punctuation and in the spelling of words. There is another category of errors that is harder to define. Call it grammar or usage or syntax—all these words describe the way a whole language is put together and functions. Most native speakers know these rules unconsciously. They may not be able to explain them, but they rarely get them wrong.

Consider the following errors in grammar and you'll probably become aware of some rules you always get right and never think about.

"Dallas" goes off the air ten years ago.

This sentence violates our way of showing time. We have to change the verb "goes" to "went" to show past time. In some other languages "go," the verb, would not change; time is shown only through a phrase like "ten years ago."

Another example:

"Dallas" was a show that attracted millions of viewers
because "Dallas" was a sophisticated, high-powered soap opera.
Since "Dallas" was shown in the evening, men watched "Dallas," too.

This sounds odd because we usually use pronouns rather than repeat the same noun over and over. And standard usage requires those pronouns to agree in number with the nouns they stand in for. We can't say

"Dallas" were a show that attracted millions of viewers because they was a sophisticated, high-powered soap opera. Since it was shown in the evening, men watched "Dallas," too.

And we expect subjects of sentences, like "Dallas," to agree with the verb that goes with them. We have to say *"Dallas" was,* not *"Dallas" were.*

All of these errors are ones of grammar, usage, or syntax. And they are all about how we make meaning in small unconscious ways as we speak and write.

So, if this is part of the language and we are not learning it as a second language, why do we make usage errors? *There are reasons.*

The first is that language changes and so do grammar rules. What your teacher marks as an error today *may* be correct in another generation or two. Language is always in a state of change.

Second, although people can agree on what is Standard English, most people probably don't speak Standard English in their home or community. Call it home talk or dialect, but most of us speak variations of English that sound better to our friends and family and *are better among those people.* But speaking Standard English may serve you better in college, in business, or in public work, even if it would sound ridiculous in your own kitchen.

Fortunately, types of usage errors are not endless, although some of them do touch on deeply ingrained habits. We'll concentrate on the five most common ones:

- Subject-verb disagreement
- Pronoun-antecedent disagreement
- Tense shifts
- Shifts in point of view
- Vague pronoun reference

Subject-Verb Disagreement: Getting the Subject and Verb to Agree in Number

This is really a problem with inconsistency in number. A singular subject must have a singular verb. If the subject is singular and the verb is plural, the reader gets confused about how many people or things are involved.

Error: The cats in the ad *gobbles* up their dinner.
Correction: The cats (plural subject) in the ad *gobble* (plural verb) up their dinner.

Error: We *is* nowhere near the end of this lesson.
Correction: We (plural subject) *are* (plural verb) nowhere near the end of this lesson.

Error: Anybody *know* that there are fewer newspapers today than ever before.
Correction: Anybody (singular subject) *knows* (singular verb) that there are fewer newspapers today than ever before.

Error: Everybody *were* hoping that "MASH" would keep going.
Correction: Everybody (singular subject) *was* hoping (singular verb) that "MASH" would keep going.

In order to get your subject and verb to agree, you have to be able to find or identify subjects and verbs. The subject of a sentence usually comes first, but we'll start with the verb because once you have found it you can find the subject.

The *verb* can be more than one word, but it always conveys action or describes a state of being. You can also add *-ing* or *-ed* to the root of the verb so that it shows things happening at different times.

Some verb forms are so common that it helps to just know them: am, is, are, was, were, have, has, been, had, will and shall.

Examples of verbs: gave, will have gone, is, swam, is watching, had fallen, would have criticized, hope, are sitting.

The *subject* can be found by asking, "Who or what does the verb refer to?" of the verb. The subject will always be a noun or a pronoun referring to a person, place, thing or concept.

Examples of subjects: he, they, hopelessness, redness, democracy, mass media, Magic Johnson, courage, efforts.

See how you can find the subject and the verb in these sentences:

Teller wrote a *New York Times* editorial about violence in movies.

"Wrote" is the verb because it tells what happened; it also passes the test for a verb because you can change the way it shows time—write, will write, had written. You can't do that for any other word in the sentence.

To find the subject, ask "who or what wrote?" and you have the answer—Teller—and that's the subject.

The effects of violence in movies are controversial.

"Are" is the verb because it shows a state of being (and it is also one of the words listed above that always acts as a verb.)

Who or what "are"? The "effects" are. So that's the subject.

Practice Check: Find the Subject and Verb

Circle the subject and underline the verb in the following sentences:

1. Democracy comes in two forms.
2. It exists on a sheet of paper. The Constitution is one form of democracy.
3. Democracy lives if the country is run by the will of the people.
4. The people need to make decisions.
5. And these decisions need to be about important issues.
6. In America, not everyone votes.
7. Half of the possible voters usually stay home.
8. A president can win with only a quarter of the people voting for him.
9. Campaign issues and coverage are sometimes very trivial.

(See answers, page 468.)

The Basics of Getting Subject and Verb to Agree

To understand the basics of subject-verb agreement, you need to figure out why you are having trouble. It is likely to be for one of three reasons:

1. Clashes with your dialect. Your own version of non-Standard English may reverse this conventional pattern.

Standard English	*Example of a Dialect*
I am	I be or I is
you are	you is
he, she it is	he, she, it is
we are	we is
they are	they is

I want	I wants
you want	you want
he, she it wants	he, she or it want
we want	we wants
they want	they wants

Changing this pattern in speech is hard, but in writing, you can check each subject to make sure that it is the same number as the verb.

2. You might make a mistake and have the subject and verb suggest different numbers because a phrase comes between the subject and the verb and makes it harder to figure out what the subject is.

> Michael, *the man who never stopped going to the movies,* has (*not* have) the quick-cut style of the cinema when he talks.

> Which movie *of all the movies you have seen* comes (*not* come) the closest to capturing reality?

3. Certain words, such as *everyone, neither,* and *each,* sound plural but are actually considered singular in number. Watch out for intervening phrases that often make these words sound even more plural.

> Every one *of the people who drive drunk* is (*not* are) guilty of a crime.

> No one *of all the people who were drinking with them at the party* was (*not* were) sober enough to drive.

> Nothing *of all the errors in the world* galls (*not* gall) me more than people writing that instead of who.

When these words are the subjects of sentences, you need to have a singular form of the verb.

> Everyone is (*not* are) invited to come back tomorrow.

> Anybody plays (*not* play) basketball better than you do.

Our best advice is to learn the following list of words that sound plural but are singular:

Singular Indefinite Pronouns

every	someone	any	no	each
everyone	something	anyone	no one	neither
everything	somebody	anything	nothing	either
everybody		anybody	nobody	

Practice Check: Making Sure Subjects and Verbs Agree

Correct any errors in the following passages in subject-verb agreement.

> One important change in recent labor conditions are the increased reliance on part-time labor. A business or corporation save money when full-time position are divided up into part time ones. There is really two main reasons: lower wages are paid and health benefits is avoided. This mean profit go up.
>
> The worker who are just as likely to be a teacher, as a factory worker or fast food worker are hurt by this cost-cutting. Everybody in these positions who are working more than forty hours a week know she or he are not really part-time. And the taxpayer ends up paying some of the costs in increased welfare and medicaid payments. Americans who find themselves working two part-time jobs may work over forty hours a week and still falls below the federal poverty line and qualifies for welfare.

(See answers, page 468.)

Pronoun-Antecedent Disagreement: Getting Pronouns to Agree with Their Antecedents in Number

Antecedents are the words pronouns refer back to. For example, in the sentence "News bites are the brief quotes used in TV news coverage; they are getting shorter all the time," *News bites* is the antecedent and *they* is the pronoun that refers back to it. The same set of singular indefinite pronouns listed earlier is responsible for almost all errors of agreement between pronouns and their antecedents.

Error:	*Everybody* has trouble with *their* writing some of the time.
Corrected:	*Everybody* has trouble with *his* or *her* writing some of the time.
	[antecedent] [pronoun]
Better:	Since it's clumsy to write both his and her, and since it may sound sexist to leave one of them out, sometimes it's better to start with a plural subject that allows you to use the plural article:
	All writers have trouble with their writing some of the time.
	[antecedent] [pronoun]
Error:	Anybody who thinks writing is easy should have their head examined.
	(Notice the shift is again from singular to plural; this is the usual pattern of errors.)
Corrected:	Anybody who thinks writing is easy should have her (or his) head examined.
Better:	People who think writing is easy should have their heads examined.

Error: Somebody who is a professional writer can tell you they just work harder at writing than nonprofessional writers do.

Corrected: Somebody who is a professional writer can tell you she (or he or s/he) just works harder at it than others.

Better: Professional writers will tell you they just work harder at writing than others.

The Basics of Pronoun and Antecedent Agreement

You need to make sure you don't send the reader confusing messages about how many people or things are involved in a particular action.

Anybody (one) who (one or many) thinks (one) writing is (one) easy should have her (one) head (one) examined.

Looking at that simple sentence, you realize that seven out of eleven words convey number and they all have to agree. But almost all pronoun-antecedent errors involve those singular indefinite pronouns like none, anybody, or somebody that *sound* plural to us. So keep a look out for those words.

Practice Check: Spotting Pronoun-Antecedent Agreement Errors

a. Find and correct the errors in this passage.

What is everybody saying about journalists' coverage of wars? Well, really they are saying different things. Someone I talked to yesterday thought that the coverage of the Gulf War was fine; they didn't want journalists or missions to be put at risk by getting too close to the action. Someone else thought that if the government is running the war, they also may need to run the press coverage of it. Nobody examined what their ideas had to do with democracy. How can anybody say they think it is all right for the government not to report how many people are killed? But everyone should see that they need to know how many Americans or Iraqis are being killed if they are going to evaluate whether the war was worth it. Neither of my friends are ever going to speak to me again after the row this debate caused.

(See answers, page 468.)

b. Write five sentences beginning with everyone, someone, anyone, no one, everybody, somebody, anybody, nobody, each, neither, or either. Make sure the verb and any words that refer back to that pronoun agree with it.

c. Check your own writing for these same pronouns to make sure that words that refer back to them don't cause confusion about number.

Tense Shifts: Giving the Reader Confusing Signals About Time

All verbs suggest time, so you need to make sure that if you are talking about an event in the past, all verbs are in past form, unless you want to show a time change.

The most frequent errors in tense come up because writers forget the ending and rush on to the next word. Sometimes, too, a writer will start recalling an event and writing in the past, then get distracted and shift to the present without noticing the change.

Error: This year, I wanted to read a foreign newspaper at least once a week, but I got overwhelm with work and never found the time.

Correction: This year, I wanted to read a foreign newspaper once a week, but I got overwhelmed with work and never found the time.

Error: When I first came to college, I use to go home every weekend, but I don't any more.

Correction: When I first came to college, I used to go home every weekend, but I don't any more. (It is easy for most of us to forget the *-d* on *used* to because we don't hear it. But it *is* there.)

The Basics of Keeping Verb Tenses Consistent

Verb endings tell us the time frame or tense we are in. That is, they tell us whether the action in a sentence is in the past, present, or future. Often you can tell a story in the present or past tense, but once you choose the time frame your verbs need to be consistent.

(For help on figuring out which word is the verb, see pages 439–441.)

Practice Check: Finding and Correcting Confusing Verb Tenses

a. Clear up the confusion about verb tense in this passage.

People talk about yellow journalism as if it were a thing of the past. We all study in high school about how the dailies whipped up war fever for the Spanish-American war and sold copies by selling the war. That is in 1898, but how different is it today? In the last ten years our country goes to war three times: in Grenada, in Panama and in Iraq. Does the press promote those wars too? People still talked about how everyone is glued to TV watching the start of the Persian Gulf war. It is like a major movie. Dan Rather is there and headings like The Approaching Storm unfurled across the screen. My history teacher says it is as foolish as when people took their picnic baskets and couches and went to watch the battle outside of Washington during the Civil War.

b. Pair off with a partner and look over each other's papers to see if tense shifts occur where the writer does not intend to show a change in time.

(See answers, page 469.)

Shifts in Point of View: Making Clear Who's Talking to Whom

This confusion occurs most often when writers shift the way they think about their audience. The writer switches from saying "you" to "we" or to "one" without realizing it. Here are some examples:

Error: We all know that television is everywhere, but do you know its history? How many people know that the first regularly scheduled television began in Britain in 1936? Then one also needs to know that by 1939, RCA had an exhibition of television at the World's Fair in New York.

Correction: You may know that television is everywhere, but do you know its history? Do you know that the first regularly scheduled television began in Britain in 1936? Then you also may want to know that by 1939, RCA had an exhibition of television at the World's Fair in New York.

Correction: (more formal) One knows that television is everywhere but does one know its history? How many know that the first regularly scheduled television began in Britain in 1936? One also needs to know that by 1939, RCA had an exhibition of television at the World's Fair in New York. (Facts from Edward Jay Whetmore's *Mediamerica*.)

The Basics of Consistent Point of View

Writers need to be consistent in the way they address or think about their readers. If you start addressing the reader as "you," then you need to continue using "you" and not drift into a more impersonal "one" or "they."

Practice Check: Spotting and Correcting Shifts in Point of View

a. Try to spot and correct shifts in point of view in the following passage, which is also from *Mediamerica*:

> Perhaps one thinks of television as a phenomenon of the Fifties, but by the 1940's, we had the first application of a commercial broadcasting license by the Journal Company of Milwaukee [now WTMJ-TV]. You have sponsors beginning to buy TV time in 1944 during World War II, and does one realize that by the next year TV was so important that the FCC moved FM radio to another place on the band to make room for TV? Did you know that the color TV was demonstrated by CBS and NBC in 1946? So one notices that a lot had happened by 1951 because just as the Fifties were starting movie attendance was already declining in cities that had TV.

We think TV changed our lives drastically and it did. Politics and democracy changed because you watched them happen on TV, like the Army-McCarthy hearings in 1954 and the extensive coverage of the Eisenhower and Stevenson campaign in 1956. And one is exceptional if you missed seeing at least parts of the Nixon and Kennedy debate in 1960. (Information from Edward Jay Whetmore's *Mediamerica*.)

(See answers, page 469.)

b. Discuss why you choose to use "you" or "we" or "one." How does that choice change the paragraph?

c. Look for shifts in point of view in your own writing and correct them.

Vague Pronoun Reference: Making Clear Who or What Each Pronoun Refers To

Vague pronoun reference occurs when the reader can't figure out what word, thing, person, or idea a pronoun refers back to.

Error: The faculty didn't oppose TV's in college dorms in the sixties, and students liked TV, but *they* weren't *there* and *they* hadn't banned *them*.

Correction: The faculty didn't oppose TV's in college dorms in the sixties, and students liked TV, but still *TV's* weren't *in the dorms* and *the faculty* hadn't banned them.
(Here the vagueness and confusion are cleared up by replacing the pronoun with the word it refers to.)

Error: By the 1990s a TV is standard in every dorm room, and *they* watch a few hours a day. Sometimes students even schedule classes so they can still see their favorite soaps. *They* ought to do something about this because *it* shouldn't be just like any four years of your life.

Correction: By the 1990s, a TV is standard in every dorm room, and *students* watch a few hours a day. Sometimes they even schedule classes so they can still see their favorite soaps. *Faculty* should do something about this because *college* shouldn't be just like any four years of your life.
(Here, again, pronouns were replaced by the words they were referring to. Doing this can make us less sloppy in our thinking and make us more apt to listen critically to the generalizations we make by using "they" or "it.")

The Basics of Pronoun Reference

Make sure that when you use pronouns, especially "it" and "they," the reader will be clear exactly about what you are referring to. Generally, a reader assumes that the nearest person, place, thing, or idea mentioned is what is being referred back to by a pronoun.

Practice Check: Spotting and Correcting Confusion in Pronoun Reference

a. Edit the following paragraph to correct any confusion about pronoun reference.

> Whether TVs were in college dorms or not in the sixties, they were changed forever by the mass media. Maybe they didn't wear headsets and have the TV on in the background during the day, but ideas of what a woman or man did with their lives, what romance was like, what the world was like came just as much from it. It wasn't the only influence of TV. They were shaped by radio and movies too, and they didn't even realize it was happening.

b. Compare the way you edited the paragraph to the editing of others in your group. Can you come to any conclusions about what changes work best, and why?

c. With a partner look for examples of vague pronoun reference in your own writing and together figure out the best way of rephrasing for clarity.

(See answers, page 469.)

Chapter 20

Writing on the Spot

Five Ways to Avoid Panic
Typical Essay Questions

From the way this book is set up—with all the questions and readings—it may seem like we think you have a lifetime to write a paper, or at least two weeks. We do know that this is not always the case. So this chapter is about how to make the most of the five or fifteen or forty minutes you may have to write an essay in an examination. Even if you can't linger during an exam over invention exercises, organizing, or editing, you can still think about those phases of the writing process and you can avoid writing in a blind panic.

Five Ways to Avoid Panic: Writing Well on the Spot

1. READ THE ESSAY QUESTION AND EVEN OUTLINE YOUR ANSWER BEFORE YOU DO ANY SHORT-ANSWER OR MULTIPLE-CHOICE QUESTIONS

Your mind will unconsciously consider the question while you do other parts of the test. Even if this only gives you fifteen minutes of "unconscious thinking" time, that is a lot better than tackling the question cold. As you do the short-answer or multiple-choice part of the test, you may find information or get ideas that you want to use in the essay.

2. FIGURE OUT HOW MUCH TIME YOU SHOULD GIVE THE ESSAY

If an essay is worth 50 percent of a test, then it makes sense to spend about half the time on it. Here's one reasonable plan for a fifty-minute test.

   Section one: 20 multiple choice—40% of grade—20 minutes
   Section two: 5 I.D.s worth four points each—20% of grade—10 minutes
   Section three: essay question—40% of grade—20 minutes

3. **Spend as much time planning and reconsidering the essay as writing it**

Use about a quarter of the time to get your ideas together. Spend about half the time writing the essay and a quarter or less looking over the essay to make additions and corrections. For example, if you have one hour, spend fifteen minutes planning, thirty minutes writing, and the last fifteen minutes proofreading and editing.

This will help you avoid the panic, which may drive you to want to get some words down on paper right away. Resist. Have confidence and make a plan. Even if—worst-case scenario—you end up with an essay that is worth 50 percent of the test and have only five minutes left, you are probably much better off handing in an outline of your whole answer than the introduction to it.

Writing takes less time if you know where you are going. If you don't plan, you may leave out some good ideas or want to reorganize your whole answer when you are right in the middle of it.

4. **Leave space to revise**

Even in an examination, where there is usually little time for drastic changes and revisions, you can always go back, put in a new title, add or change supporting details. Leave space between each paragraph for these kinds of changes. Sometimes when you are writing on the spot, you may not figure out some key ideas until you are actually nearing the end of the essay. Read over your essay, then use the last paragraph for concluding statements to tie everything together.

5. **Study the question. Exactly what is it asking you to do?**

Figuring out what the question is asking you to do is vital. Analyze the question by underlining key phrases. You want to identify everything it is asking you to do. When you have figured out what the bare bones of the question are, you have also given yourself an outline.

There is information you can learn about types of essay questions, and we are going to turn to that now. You want to recognize easily what is being asked and you can do this by *recognizing patterns of questions and being alert to key words*.

Typical Essay Questions

1. **Questions that ask you to *recall* certain information**

Key words might be:

    Identify

    Define

    Explain

    List

    Describe

Examples

1. Explain what AM and FM mean.
2. Explain how radio waves are transmitted.
3. List three impacts television has had on American life.
4. Describe the important milestones in the development of radio.

2. QUESTIONS THAT ASK FOR YOUR *REACTION* OR *OPINION* AND *REASONS*.

Key words might be:

agree or disagree with a statement or quotation

give your opinion and explain your reasons for it

criticize

evaluate

discuss

Examples

1. "The point of TV is to round people up for the commercial." Discuss this claim with reference to your own viewing experiences.
2. What was your reaction to the character of Murphy in "Murphy Brown," and why did you react as you did?
3. How would you evaluate TV as a force for advocating nonviolence?
4. Discuss the treatment of the Rodney King trial by national TV news.

Even though this kind of question calls for your reaction or opinion, you will be graded on the way you support that opinion. The most likely format is *statement and support*. Make clear what your position is and then give your reasons to support that position. See pages 305 and 365 for more information on statement and support.

3. QUESTIONS THAT ASK YOU TO *MAKE CONNECTIONS* AND *SHOW RELATIONSHIPS*

The key words in the question will give you that clue you need to help you organize your ideas:

compare and contrast	*Caution:* Sometimes *compare* can mean to show differences *and* similarities. Make sure you know which your instructor means. (See pages 310 and 367 for ideas on how to organize comparison-contrast essays.)
apply	Illustrate a general idea or principle with specific examples.
synthesize	Bring together.

classify	Divide into groups or classes.
explain the cause of	Say why or how something happened.
explain the effects of	Say what the result of something is. (See pages 310 and 368 for information about how to organize cause-and-effect essays.)
analyze	Break down, take apart.

Examples

Compare the heroines of the movies *Working Girl* and *Norma Rae*. Which character presents a more positive role model, in your opinion? Use specific references to the two movies in your answer.

What effects does TV violence have on adult viewers?

What kinds of people are most frequently presented as "experts" on national television news? Support your claim with specific illustrations and examples.

All these questions ask you to break a subject down into its parts and then show how those parts relate to or connect with one another. Key words, such as *compare, classify, cause and effect*, suggest a standard form that can lead to a quick outline. (Look at Chapter 15, Organizing: Getting Your Ideas Together, to remind yourself about the way these questions can help you form an outline.)

Writing on the spot is different from writing a long paper because you have no extra time. But you can still use many of the same strategies so that you do the best work you can, even working against the clock.

Chapter 21

Making Gains for the Next Paper

It ain't over till it's over.
—YOGI BERRA

Writing Memos
Reading and Reacting to Grades and Comments
Keeping Records of Past Papers
Finale

When we get ready to hand a paper in, we may feel great or we may feel awful about the paper. But, generally, we are glad to get rid of it because our work is over. Or is it? In this chapter we suggest three ways of making gains for the next assignment. A few minutes spent just before you hand in your paper *and* when you get it back can help a lot.

Writing Memos: A Way of Getting Good Criticism from Your Instructor

On the principle that if you want something, you'd better ask for it, write a memo to your teacher with each paper you turn in. Some teachers require this. But even if your teachers don't, you will have let them know what you think about your paper and what you want to know about it. Keep these memos informal and do them almost like a freewriting, just recording what comes into your mind. Don't spend hours on a memo; ten minutes will do.

What to Put in a Memo

Below are questions that you can use as the basis of your memo and what it was like to write the paper.

a. What was it like to write this paper?
   To break down this question further, you could discuss . . .
   - What was hard or easy to write?
   - What were the biggest problems you had?
   - What activities or work in class or on your own helped or didn't help you?
   - What changes and revisions did you make?
   - What criticism did you use or reject? Why?
   - What would you do differently if you were writing this paper again?

b. How do *you* think your paper turned out?
   - What is your final reaction to the paper?
   - What problems do you think the paper still has?
   - What pleases you most about the paper?
   - How well do you think it addresses the audience?
   - What do you think of the beginning and ending?
   - How interesting are the ideas and/or the research?
   - How vividly are the experiences or anecdotes described?
   - How well focused is the paper?
   - How well organized is it?

c. What comments or advice do you most specifically want from your instructor?
   - What did you find most (or least) convincing about what was said in the paper?
   - What ideas did you find most interesting?
   - What feeling did you have when you finished this paper?
   - What is the biggest change needed?

What Gains Do You Get from Writing a Memo?

Bear in mind that you have spent only ten minutes writing your memo.

1. First off, if teachers have an idea how you see your paper, it is easier for them to give you the most useful comments.
2. Just writing a memo gets you to reflect, however briefly, on your own work. You will almost certainly come up with perceptions that help you.

3. If you are able to submit revisions of graded papers, these memos can ask for the kind of advice that will help you do a revision for a higher grade.
4. Memos can improve the teaching you get. It isn't all that easy for teachers to know what their students are getting out of a class. What you say in a memo can help put teachers in touch with what you and others in your class need.

So even if your writing teachers don't require memos, give them one! Taking the initiative will help you learn about your own writing and get better criticism and teaching.

Reading and Reacting to Grades and Comments

Some students look at the grade first when they get back a paper. They flip past summary comments and marginal notations and find "that letter." If it's the right sort of letter, sometimes they feel more like reading the accompanying comments. They may read them through several times and then pull the paper out later and read them again.

Or some students may get their papers back, those beautifully typed, clean, black and white papers they handed in, and join the cry of students past and present, and say, "He bled all over it!" or, "She made a mess of my paper!" Unless all the comments are glowing praise and the grade is an A, it is easy to resent people writing all over *your* writing. But evaluating your writing *is* their job.

Understanding more about the way teachers comment and grade, and why they comment and grade the way they do, may help you make more sense of your returned papers.

Suggestions for Discussion and Writing

Before you read the next section, take a few minutes to discuss, or write in your journals about, the teacher's view of grading papers.

1. If you were your teacher, how would you feel about starting to grade your latest assignment? What hopes and fears do you think teachers have as they grade and hand back a set of papers?
2. What do you think discourages teachers most in reading and commenting on papers? What might they find most rewarding?

Teachers' Views on Grading Papers

When teachers collect a set of papers, it usually means several hours of work for them, to be fitted into Saturday and Sunday afternoons or late evenings. In spite of all the work, students' papers are seldom boring. Reading them, teachers are learning about the people in their class, how their teaching is going, what people are learning about writing, and about the topics under discussion. These are the things that keep teachers interested in reading students' papers for years and years.

This is not to suggest that all teachers grade papers in the same way. What teachers do with the batch of papers they are about to read differs greatly. The following discusses these differences, some of which you may already have encountered.

Different Attitudes Toward Grading

Some teachers don't assign grades because they think it distracts students from focusing on comments and reactions to their writing. Some don't grade simply because they dislike reducing a complex reaction to a single letter—the one thing students will focus on but perhaps the thing that will tell least about how their writing is going.

Some teachers think that it is very helpful to students to have a grade as a measure of their progress from one paper to the next and to give them a clear summation of their overall evaluation of a paper.

A new method is portfolio grading, where your writing is reviewed and graded as a whole according to the amount of revision you did.

Different Approaches to Writing on Papers

Some teachers think that it is important to mark and label each surface error so that the student clearly understands the corrections to be made; others will only underline errors, reasoning that students learn best when they have to figure out what is wrong. Still other teachers will not mark *any* particular errors but will let the student know at the end if one kind of error recurs. There is controversy about how much the time and effort correcting and labeling each error for a student actually help the student in the long run.

Some teachers use a "holistic" approach. That is, they give a paper a quick reading, use their immediate overall impression to form a grade, and make very few comments on the paper. Teachers at the opposite end of the spectrum will spend half an hour or more on a paper, writing many marginal notes and noting all surface errors and writing an extensive summary comment.

Different Tones and Types of Comments

You've probably noticed that the range of tones in teachers' comments is as varied as teachers' personalities: removed, objective, very personal, funny, sarcastic, serious, positive, critical. You will soon get to know the scale your instructor operates on: from encouraging to the sarcastic. (If you don't like the tone, you can use your memos to try and change it.)

Some teachers focus on the technical aspects of a paper and provide a clear "points" system for you to follow. In fact, some will break a grade down into four criteria, like content, organization, style, and correctness, and give a grade or point for each. Others will operate more intuitively, giving you their personal reactions as a reader.

This discussion of differences could go on, but we think it shows that teachers do have particular rationales behind their method of grading papers. The main point is that when you get your paper back from your instructor, you should think of it as part of a dialogue:

1. Feel free to question comments and grades.
2. Use your memos to ask for specific types of criticism in the future.
3. Feel free to ask for a conference to get more explanation.

> *Suggestions for Discussion and Writing*
>
> Freewrite about or discuss with your fellow students the business of giving and getting grades.
>
> 1. What ideal grading or nongrading system would you put into place?
> 2. Discuss the kinds of comments and grading that have helped you the most and the ones that have helped you the least.

Keeping Records of Past Papers

Students often ask teachers to explain a series of grades in a course—why they keep getting all C's, or why their grades go up and down. Your record keeping may help to explain what would otherwise be a cryptic series of letters. Record keeping should also help you to generalize about your work, to say what you're good at and what you need to work on. On pages 461–464 are four different ways of keeping records of what happened in your papers so that you can learn more about your writing.

Finale

So, as Yogi Berra said, "It ain't over till it's over." You can learn as much from a paper after you've written it and after you get it back from your instructor as you did while actually writing it. And we hope that after using this book you will feel that working on your writing is satisfying.

When I say writing, O believe me it is rewriting that I have chiefly in mind.
—R.L. STEVENSON

Good writing takes place at intersections, at what you might call knots, at place where society is snarled or knotted up.
—MARGARET ATWOOD, *Shoptalk*, DONALD MURRAY

Student: Mr. Quinn, are you trying to tell us that writing is just work?
Quinn: That's it. You got it.
—DANIEL QUINN, AUTHOR OF *Ishmael*

APPENDIXES

A. Record Forms for Making Gains on Your Writing

FORM A
THINKING ABOUT STRENGTHS AND WEAKNESSES

Use this form to record your view of your paper's strengths and weaknesses. Then add your instructor's views. You can then discuss significant differences in views with your instructor, in a conference or in a memo.

Major strengths of this paper   **Major weaknesses of this paper**

Your view

Instructor's view

FORM B
USING CATEGORIES TO EVALUATE

Use this form to compare your view of specific parts of your paper (or categories for evaluation) with your instructor's.

How you rate this paper (and why)   **How your teacher rates this paper (and why)**

Focus

Content

Organization

Style

Surface errors

FORM C
KEEPING A GRAMMAR NOTEBOOK

Some teachers feel that there is no better way to work on surface errors than to record each error and put the correction in a column right next to it. This routine takes time, but it can help you to learn some basic rules that you may have missed in previous English classes. Some instructors may link this activity with handbook sections, and simply give you handbook section numbers on your papers to lead you to the right grammar rule.

Error	Correction	Type
Although the USA is violent.	Although the USA is violent, it is not as violent as people believe.	Fragment

FORM D
PORTFOLIO ASSESSMENT

Put all your finished drafts together in a portfolio. Then use the form below to think about your writing as a whole. Have two other students in the class fill out these forms on your work, too.

1. Give your overall impression of all the writing.

Describe and evaluate all the papers in these specific ways:

2. *Focus:* being able to narrow a topic and carry that focus through the whole paper

3. *Development:* might include supplying examples, facts, details, statistics; considering different points of views and possibilities; and pursuing a question, theme, or topic in depth

4. *Organization:* being able to signal to the reader the overall plan; signaling transitions; choosing a framework

5. *Style:* sentence style, tone, voice, humor, diction

6. *Audience:* adapting the paper to an audience, planning beginnings and endings

7. *Correctness:* patterns of errors, problems proofing, using correct source note form

8. What is this writer's (or your) greatest strength?

9. What would you advise this writer to work on? (Or what change is your writing most in need of?)

B. Answers to Practice Checks

Converting Fragments, page 422

There are a number of ways fragments can be turned into complete sentences. This is one example:

> If you can, imagine how hard it is to read fragments. You might adapt because you were eager to read whatever it was. You would put up with it but not like it, and you would find getting through it would take forever. This could get irritating and old real fast.

Correcting Comma Splices, pages 423–424

(Other answers are possible.)
Commercialism is wrecking America; our cultural resources are dwindling. The very idea of *citizen* has become synonymous with *consumer.*

The omnipresent signs of commercialism's stamp are so numerous that we are in danger of becoming oblivious to the obvious. Ads are tucked in books, displayed on giant screens at sport events, projected from subway monitors, pumped into doctors' reception rooms, posted in public restrooms, inscribed on clothes, embedded in arcade games, zapped through fax machines, and emblazoned (thanks to food dyes) on hot dogs.

One hundred and thirty billion dollars is dumped annually into advertising, and that's more money than the gross national product of our oil-rich ally Saudi Arabia.

There is the long-standing American ideal of simple and honest living, of moderation in the marketplace; frugality used to be a key word in America's civic vocabulary. Yet ever since World War II, we have allowed business people to exalt one value—consumption—to the near exclusion of all others. This treads on our moral and civic tradition like a bulldozer in a flower garden. In this one-value universe, the ideal of consumption too often obliterates other important social and environmental values.

Correcting Run-On Sentences, page 425

(Other answers are possible.)
In this one-value universe, the ideal of consumption too often obliterates other important social and environmental values, such as the following:

Psychological well-being: Our system of advertising purposefully promotes envy, creates anxiety, and fosters insecurity. The tragic end product of this is kids killing kids for $100 name-brand sneakers.

Communal values: The soul of a community cannot thrive in a relentlessly commercial environment. Civic-mindedness is an alien concept to a people mesmerized by consumer goods. This is the "me only" world, the world where politicians feed the great promises of "no new taxes." In this world, public institutions that depend on government are forced to turn to business dollars to survive; the resulting cost, of course, is the commercialization of schools, art museums, and non-profit organizations.

Punctuating Introductory Dependent Clauses, page 426

Even if some experts say that TV has weakened family ties, there may be important ways that TV strengthens families. Because not every family watches TV in the same way, that generalization is just too big for me. If we didn't have TV broadcasting news and dramas in our home, there are many things that families might never discuss that they do now. Without TV many controversial topics might have stayed buried. When you're sitting in a room and Geraldo is talking about homosexuality or AIDS or bulimia, it is likely that someone will make a comment. Because one family member reacts, the family discusses together something that never would have come up if the TV had not been on.

Apostrophes, pages 429–430

1. we don't
2. Vega's magnitude
3. CNN's broadcast
4. "As the World Turn"'s plot
5. she doesn't
6. study's conclusion
7. they're not
8. they aren't
9. critics' choice
10. comics' heroes
11. boss's fuss
12. its end
13. we've
14. there's
15. radio's volume
16. TV's women
17. man's hat
18. men's basketball

Adding Suffixes, page 432

believed
hitting
heating
partying
writing

tragically
fantastically
finally
bombastically
plentiful

Adding Prefixes, page 433

disassemble
inaccurate
illogical
unnatural
innumerable

misshapen
misstate
dissolve
disassociate

ei or *ie*, page 433

1. He dec*ei*ved her.
2. They were rel*ie*ved of a great burden.
3. Advances in the sc*ie*nces come from ideas that at first seem ill conc*ei*ved.
4. L*ei*sure is perc*ei*ved as important in many countries where workers rec*ei*ve many more paid holidays than in America. Here workers who want five weeks vacation might be thought unconsc*ie*ntious.

Spotting and Correcting Commonly Confused Words, page 437

From *weather* reports *to* the top news stories, the way the news is presented on TV *affects* us. We might not want to *accept* how powerfully we are *affected*, but *it's* undeniable. Although the producers are not in a conspiracy to force *their personal principles* on us, messages about values get through because of the very structure of the program.

Whether it's the *too* short, 40 second coverage of important stories or *too* many commercial interruptions, our *personal* reactions are *affected*. We don't hang on to a story—even of a *personal* disaster—for longer than a minute, so how can we get involved? TV news with *its* high speed coverage, makes us passive and unmotivated to *effect* change. *There* may be reasons to say that people are better informed *than* ever before because of TV, but *whether* they were so passive in the *past* is another question.

Find the Subject and Verb, page 440

Subject	Verb
1. Democracy	comes
2. It	exists
Constitution	is
3. Democracy	lives
country	is
4. people	need
5. decisions	need
6. everyone	votes
7. Half	stay
8. president	can win
9. issues and coverage	are

Making Sure Subjects and Verbs Agree, page 442

One important *change* in recent labor conditions *is* the increased reliance on part-time labor. A business or *corporation saves* money when full-time *positions are divided* up into part-time ones. There *are* really two main *reasons*: lower *wages are paid* and health *benefits are avoided. This means profits go* up.

The *worker*, who *is* just as likely to be a teacher as a factory worker or fast food worker, *is* hurt by this cost-cutting. *Everybody* in these positions who *works* more than forty hours a week knows *she or he is* not really part-time. And the *taxpayer ends* up paying some of the costs in increased welfare and medicaid payments. *Americans* who *find* themselves working two part-time jobs *may work* over forty hours a week and still *fall* below the federal poverty line and *qualify* for welfare.

Spotting Pronoun-Antecedent Agreement Errors, page 443

What is everybody saying about journalists' coverage of wars? Well, really they are saying different things. *Someone* I talked to yesterday thought that the coverage of the Gulf War was fine; she didn't want journalists or missions to be put at risk by getting too close to the action. Someone else thought that if the *government* is running the war, *it* also may need to run the press coverage of it. *Nobody* examined what *his or her* ideas had to do with democracy. How can *anybody* say *she* thinks it is all right for the government not to report how many people are killed? But *everyone* should see that *he* needs to know how many Americans or Iraqis are being killed if *he* is going to evaluate whether the war was worth it. Neither of my friends is ever going to speak to me again after the row this debate caused.

Finding and Correcting Verb Tenses, page 444

People *talk* about yellow journalism as if *it were* a thing of the past. We all *studied* in high school about how the dailies *whipped* up war fever for the Spanish-American war and *sold* copies by selling the war. That *was* in 1898, but how different *is* it today? In the last ten years our country *has gone* to war three times: in Grenada, in Panama and in Iraq. *Does* the press *promote* those wars too? People still *talk* about how everyone *was glued* to TV watching the start of the Persian Gulf war. It was like a major movie. Dan Rather was there and headings like "The Approaching Storm" unfurled across the screen. My history teacher said it was as foolish as when people took their picnic baskets and couches and went to watch the battle outside of Washington during the Civil War.

Spotting and Correcting Shifts in Point of View, pages 445–446

This is one sample "you." Remember there are several ways to correct shifts in point of view. Perhaps you think of television as a phenomenon of the Fifties, but by the 1940's, we had the first application of a commercial broadcasting license by the Journal Company of Milwaukee [now WTMJ-TV]. Sponsors began to buy TV time in 1944 during World War II, and do you realize that by the next year TV was so important that the FCC moved FM radio to another place on the band to make room for TV? Did you know that the color TV was demonstrated by CBS and NBC in 1946? So you notice that a lot had happened by 1951 because just as the Fifties were starting movie attendance was already declining in cities that had TV.

You think TV changed your life drastically and it did. Politics and democracy changed because you watched them happen on TV, like the Army-McCarthy hearings in 1954 and the extensive coverage of the Eisenhower and Stevenson campaign in 1956. And you are exceptional if you missed seeing at least parts of the Nixon and Kennedy debate in 1960.

Information from Edward Jay Whetmore's *Mediamerica*.

Spotting and Correcting Confusion in Pronoun Reference, page 447

Whether TVs were in college dorms or not in the sixties, those dorms were changed forever by the mass media. Maybe students didn't wear headsets and have the TV on in the background during the day, but ideas of what a woman or man did with their lives, what romance was like, what the world was like, came just as much from TV. It wasn't only the influence of TV. Students were shaped by radio and movies too, and they didn't even realize it was happening.

Acknowledgments

Text Credits

Drawing by R. Chast; © 1987 The New Yorker Magazine, Inc. Used by permission. Page 492.

Copyright © 1989 by The New York Times Co. Reprinted by permission. Page 501A.

Drawing by Lorenz; © 1991 The New Yorker Magazine, Inc. Used by permission. Page 506A.

Arthur Asa Berger, *Media Analysis Technique*, pp. 135–138, copyright © 1982 by Sage Publications, Inc. Reprinted by permission of Sage Publications, Inc. Page 512C.

European Industrial Relations Review, Published by Industrial Relations Services, Eclipse Group Ltd. 18–20 Highbury Place, London N5 12P, England. Used by permission. Page 77.

From Earl Babbie, *Practice of Social Research*, Third Edition. Copyright © 1983. Used by permission of Wadsworth Publishing Co. Page 512.

Brent Staples writes editorials for the New York Times and is author of the memoir, "Parallel Time: Growing Up In Black and White." This essay appeared in Ms. Magazine in 1986. Page 105.

From Clyde Kluckhohn, *Mirror for Man: The Relation of Anthropology to Modern Life*. Copyright © 1949. Reprinted by permission. Page 15.

Fellowship (November/December 1994), the magazine of the Fellowship of Reconciliation, Box 271, Nyack, NY 10960. Reprinted by permission. Page 19.

"Teenage Truths & Tribulations: Degrassi Junior High & Beverly Hills 90210," by Marie-Claire Simonetti, Journal of Popular Film and Television, Spring 1994, pp. 38–42. Reprinted with permission of the Helen Dwight Reid Educational Foundation. Published by Heldref Publications, 1319 Eighteenth St., N. W., Washington, D. C. Page 25.

"Sex, Lies & Advertising," by Gloria Steinem, *Ms. Magazine*, July/August, 1990. Reprinted by permission of the author. Page 32.

"Family Life," from *The Plug-in Drug*, Revised Edition by Marie Winn. Copyright © 1977, 1985 by Marie Winn Miller. Used by permission of Viking Penguin, a division of Penguin Books USA Inc. Page 41.

Copyright © 1991 by The New York Times Co. Reprinted by permission. Page 47.

"Don't Ask, Don't Tell: What You Didn't Hear on the 6 O' Clock News," by Craig McLaughlin, *The Independent Weekly*, May 4, 1994, pp.7–10. This story was edited and adapted for *The Independent Weekly* by senior writer Barry Yeoman. Copyright © 1994. Reprinted by permission. Page 50.

"Television Power and American Values," by William Lee Miller, *The Search for a Value Consensus*, Rockefeller Foundation Working Papers, September 1978. William Lee Miller is a Thomas C. Sorensen Professor of Political and Social Thought at The University of Virginia. Reprinted by permission of The Rockefeller Foundation and the author. Page 56.

Reprinted by permission of Neal Gabler. Copyright © 1991 by Neal Gabler. All rights reserved. Page 56.

Copyright © 1989, The Boston Globe Newspaper Co./Washington Post Writers group. Reprinted with permission. Page 83.

Reprinted from *Columbia Journalism Review*, January/February 1993. Copyright © 1993 by Columbia Journalism Review. Page 88.

"Working Class Heroes No More," by Barbara Ehrenreich, *Harper's Magazine*, December 1989, pp. 25–26. Reprinted by permission of the author. Page 96.

From *Working* by Studs Terkel. Copyright © 1972, 1974 by Studs Terkel. Reprinted by permission of Pantheon Books, a division of Random House, Inc. Page 102.

"The Price of Success," from *Fire in the Belly* by Sam Keen. Copyright © 1991 by Sam Keen. Used by permission of Bantam, a division of Bantam Doubleday Dell Publishing Group, Inc. Page 115.

Reprinted from *Columbia Journalism Review*, January/February 1993. Copyright © by Columbia Journalism Review. Page 88.

Copyright © 1988 Peggy McIntosh. Permission to copy must be obtained from Peggy McIntosh, Wellesley College, MA (617) 283-2520. Longer version also available. Page 133.

"The Media's Image of Arabs," by Jack G. Shaheen, *Newsweek*, February 29, 1988, p.10. reprinted by permission of the author. Page 140.

"TV's Black World Turns—But Stays Unreal," by Henry Louis Gates, Jr. Originally published in *The New York Times*, section 2, November 12, 1989. Copyright © 1989 by Henry Louis Gates, Jr. Reprinted by permission of the author. Page 150.

"Portrayals of Latinos In and By the Media," by Debra Gersh, *Editor and Publisher*, July 31, 1993. Reprinted by permission. Page 156.

Fox Butterfield is a National Correspondent for The New York Times and author of "All God's Children: The Bosket Family and the American Tradition of Violence." Reprinted with permission from Parade, copyright © 1990. Page 163.

Copyright © 1989 Christian Century Foundation. Reprinted by permission from the October 25, 1989 issue of the Christian Century. Page 179.

From *The Brain: The Last Frontier* by Richard Restak. Copyright © 1979 by Richard M. Restak. Used by permission of Doubleday, a division of Bantam Doubleday Dell Publishing Group, Inc. Page 184.

From Herb Goldberg, *The Hazards of Being Male: Surviving the Myth of Masculine Privilege*, pp. 1–7. Copyright © 1976. Reprinted by permission of Sanford J. Greenburger Associates, agent for the author. Page 189.

Lindsay Van Gelder, *Ms. Magazine*, April 1980. Reprinted by permission of the author. Page 197.

The following is reprinted from *Ain't I Woman* with permission from the publisher, South End Press, 116 Saint Botolph Street, Boston, MA 02115. Page 201.

Reprinted from *USA Today* magazine November copyright © 1991 by the Society for the Advancement of Education. Page 207.

Copyright © 1994 by The New York Times Co. Reprinted by permission. Page 225.

Reprinted with permission from Parade, copyright © 1991. Page 230.

Reprinted with permission from *In These Times*, a bi-weekly news magazine published in Chicago. Page 235.

"Sports For Sale" by D. Klatell and N. Marcus, from *Sports For Sale: Television, Money, and the Fans*, edited by David Klatell, et al. Copyright © 1988 by D. Klatell, et. al. Used by permission of Oxford University Press, Inc. Page 239.

From *I Know Why the Caged Bird Sings* by Maya Angelou. Copyright © 1969 by Maya Angelou. Reprinted by permission of Random House, Inc. Page 245.

Material is reprinted from Coakley JJ: Sport in Society: Issues and Controversies, Fourth Edition, 1990 St. Louis, Mosby-Year Book, Inc. Page 251.

Reprinted with permission from Parade, copyright © 1991, and the author. Page 230.

Used by permission of the Institute for Social Research. Page 263.

Reprinted with permission from *The American Prospect*, Summer 1995. © New Prospect, Inc. Page 263.

From George Henderson, (ed.), *America's Other Children: Public Schools Outside Suburbia*. Copyright © 1971. Used by permission of the publisher, University of Oklahoma Press. Page 268.

From *World Hunger: Twelve Myths* by Frances Moore Lappé and Joseph Collins. Copyright © 1986 by The Institute for Food and Development policy. Used by permission of Grove/Atlantic, Inc. Page 275.

From *In the Absence of the Sacred*, by Jerry Mander. Copyright © 1991 Jerry Mander. Reprinted with permission of Sierra Club Books. Page 280.

"Hunger in Africa: A Story Untold until Too Late," by Jane Hunter and Steve Askin, *Extra!*, July/August 1991, pp. 8–10. Reprinted with permission of the authors. Page 284.

"A Society Without Poverty" by Katherine Van Wormer, *Social Work*, Vol. 39 (3), May 1994, pp. 324–327. Copyright © 1994, National Association of Social Workers, Inc. Page 289.

Reprinted from *Columbia Journalism Review*, July/August 1992. Copyright © 1992 by Columbia Journalism Review. Page 296.

Reprinted with permission from *The American Prospect*, Summer 1995. © New Prospect, Inc. Page 263.

Copyright © 1992 by The New York Times Co. Reprinted by permission. Page 309.

Reprinted with permission from *In These Times*, a bi-weekly news magazine published in Chicago. Page 317.

Women's Action for New Directions, Education Fund Board. Reprinted by permission of the author. Page 325.

Copyright © 1992 by The New York Times Co. Reprinted by permission. Page 329.

Reprinted with permission. © Stephen King. All rights reserved. Originally appeared in *Playboy* magazine. Page 335.

Reprinted with permission from the January 1983 Reader's Digest. Copyright © 1982 by The Reader's Digest Association, Inc. Page 340.

Reprinted with permission from *The Washington Monthly*. Copyright by The Washington Monthly Company, 1611 Connecticut Ave., N. W., Washington, D. C. 20009 (202) 462-0128. Page 375.

Excerpted from *Fair Arguments for the Elimination of Television*, by Jerry Mander, published by Quill: New York. Copyright © 1978 Jerry Mander. Reprinted by permission of the author. Page 375.

"Are Today's Kids Detached From Nature?" adapted from *Childhood's Future*. Copyright © 1990 by Richard Louv. As published in Utne Reader 1991. Reprinted by permission of Houghton Mifflin Co. All rights reserved. Page 366.

"Seeing" from *Pilgrim at Tinker Creek* by Annie Dillard. Copyright © 1974 by Annie Dillard. Reprinted by permission of HarperCollins Publishers, Inc. Page 385.

"Technology Is the Answer (But What Was the Question?)" by Amory B. Lovins from *Living in the Environment*, Eighth Edition, edited by G. Tyler Miller, pp.71–73. Copyright © 1994. Used by permission of Wadsworth Publishing Co.

Source: "The Media and Misinformation," by Susan McDonald. Originally appeared in *Friends of the Earth* newsmagazine, September 1993, pp. 6–7. Reprinted by permission of the author. Page 397.

Art and Photo Credits

Page 13: photo courtesy of Playing With Time, Inc.; **14:** © 1996 Torand. All rights reserved. Produced under license by Houghton Mifflin Company; **33:** © Horacio Cardo; **67:** © Ferinando Scianna / Magnum Photos, Inc.; **122:** © Jamie Tanaka; **170:** Wide World Photos; **175:** "Hoop Dreams." Copyright © 1994, Fine Line Features. All rights reserved. Photo appears courtesy of Fine Line Productions, Inc.; **211:** © 1996 Tom Tomorrow; **295:** © 1996 Andrew Toos; **317:** Drawing by R. Chast; © 1987 *The New Yorker Magazine*, Inc.; **331:** Drawing by Lorenz; © 1991 *The New Yorker Magazine*, Inc.

Index

Angelou, Maya, *Joe Louis*, 182
Are Today's Kids Detached from Nature?, Richard Louv, 271
Aufderheide, Patricia, *Outside Shot*, 173

Battered Justice, Joan Meier, 257
Black Women and Feminism, bell hooks, 147
Blackfeet Chief, *Our Land Is More Valuable Than Your Money*, 282
Butterfield, Fox, *Why They Excel*, 118

Can We End Media Bias Against Gays,? Craig Davidson, 151
Coakley, Jay J., *Media, Sports and Gender*, 185
Covering the Cops, Jon Katz, 64
The Cruel Logic of Teenage Violence, William O'Brien, 9
Customs, Clyde Kluckhohn, 6

Davidson Craig, *Can We End Media Bias Against Gays?*, 151
Dillard, Annie, *Seeing*, 283
Don't Ask, Don't Tell: What You Didn't Hear on the Six O'Clock News, Craig McLaughlin and Barry Yeoman, 35
A Driving Fear, Ellen Goodman, 62

The Effects of Television on Family Life, Marie Winn, 29
Ehrenreich, Barbara, *Working-Class Heroes No More*, 72

Freedom of Speech for the Wealthy, Jerry Mander, 207
From Mary to Murphy, Victoria A. Rebeck, 129

Gabler, Neal, *Now Playing: Real Life, the Movie*, 46
Gates, Henry Louis, Jr., *TV's Black World Turns—But Stays Unreal*, 109
Gersh, Debra, *Portrayals of Latinos in and by the Media*, 114
Get to the Root of Violence: Militarism, Jean Prokopow, 241

Goldberg, Herb, *In Harness: The Male Condition*, 138
Goodman, Ellen, *A Driving Fear*, 62
The Great Person-Hole Cover Debate, Lindsy Van Gelder, 144

hooks, bell, *Black Women and Feminism*, 147
Hunger in Africa: A Story Untold Until Too Late, Jane Hunter and Steve Askin, 210
Hunter, Jane, and Steve Askin, *Hunger in Africa: A Story Untold Until Too Late*, 210

In Harness: The Male Condition, Herb Goldberg, 138

Joe Louis, Maya Angelou, 182
Just Walk on By: A Black Man Ponders His Power to Alter Public Space, Brent Staples, 105

Katz, Jon, *Covering the Cops*, 64
Keen, Sam, *The Price of Success*, 85
King, Stephen, *Why We Crave Horror Movies*, 249
Klatell, David, and Norman Marcus, *What We Are Watching: The View from the Couch*, 177
Kluckhohn, Clyde, *Customs*, 6

Lappé, Frances Moore, and Joseph Collins, *There's Simply Not Enough Food*, 202
Let's Stop Glorifying Bullies, José Chegui Torres, 169
Louv, Richard *Are Today's Kids Detached from Nature?*, 271
Lovins, Amory B., *Technology Is the Answer (But What Was the Question?)*, 286

McDonald, Susan, *The Media and Misinformation*, 291
McIntosh, Peggy, *White Privilege: Unpacking the Invisible Knapsack*, 96
McLaughlin, Craig, and Barry Yeoman, *Don't Ask, Don't Tell: What You Didn't Hear on the Six O'Clock News*, 35
Males, Mike, *Public Enemy Number One?*, 234
Mander, Jerry, *Freedom of Speech for the Wealthy*, 207

Mander, Jerry, *TV's Capture of the Mind*, 278
The Media and Misinformation, Susan McDonald, 291
Media, Sports and Gender, Jay J. Coakley, 185
The Media's Image of Arabs, Jack G. Shaheen, 102
Meier, Joan, *Battered Justice*, 257
Methvin, Eugene H., *TV Violence: The Shocking New Evidence*, 252
Miller, William Lee, *Television Power and American Values*, 43
My Young Men Shall Never Work, Chief Smohalla, 83

Now Playing: Real Life, the Movie, Neal Gabler, 46

O'Brien, William, *The Cruel Logic of Teenage Violence*, 9
On Rap, Symbolism and Fear, Jon Pareles, 243
The Other Differences Between Boys and Girls, Richard M. Restak, 133
Our Land Is More Valuable Than Your Money, Blackfeet Chief, 282
Outside Shot, Patricia Aufderheide, 173

Pareles, Jon, *On Rap, Symbolism and Fear*, 243
Parker, Jo Goodwin, *What is Poverty?*, 198
Portrayals of Latinos in and by the Media, Debra Gersh, 114
The Price of Success, Sam Keen, 85
Prokopow, Jean, *Get to the Root of Violence: Militarism*, 241
Public Enemy Number One?, Mike Males, 234

Rebeck, Victoria A., *From Mary to Murphy*, 129
Reed, Ishmael, *Tuning Out Network Bias*, 32
Restak, Richard M., *The Other Differences Between Boys and Girls*, 133
Rhoden, William C., *Strong in the Blood but Perhaps Not in the Future*, 165

Seeing, Annie Dillard, 283
Sex, Lies, and Advertising, Gloria Steinem, 21
Shaheen, Jack G., *The Media's Image of Arabs*, 102
Shirley, Carol Bradley, *Where Have You Been?*, 224
Simonetti, Marie-Claire, *Teenage Truths and Tribulations Across Cultures: Degrassi Junior High and Beverly Hills 90210*, 12

Smohalla, Chief, *My Young Men Shall Never Work*, 83
A Society Without Poverty, Katherine van Wormer, 217
Staples, Brent, *Just Walk on By: A Black Man Ponders His Power to Alter Public Space*, 105
Steinem, Gloria, *Sex, Lies, and Advertising*, 21
Strong in the Blood but Perhaps Not in the Future, William C. Rhoden, 165

Technology Is the Answer (But What Was the Question?), Amory B. Lovins, 286
Teenage Truths and Tribulations Across Cultures: Degrassi Junior High and Beverly Hills 90210, Marie-Claire Simonetti, 12
Television Power and American Values, William Lee Miller, 43
Terkel, Studs, *Who Built the Pyramids?*, 76
There's Simply Not Enough Food, Frances Moore Lappé and Joseph Collins, 202
Torres, José Chegui, *Let's Stop Glorifying Bullies*, 169
Tuning Out Network Bias, Ishmael Reed, 32
TV Violence: The Shocking New Evidence, Eugene H. Methvin, 252
TV's Black World Turns—But Stays Unreal, Henry Louis Gates, Jr., 109
TV's Capture of the Mind, Jerry Mander, 278

Van Gelder, Lindsy, *The Great Person-Hole Cover Debate*, 144
van Wormer, Katherine, *A Society Without Poverty*, 217

What Is Poverty? Jo Goodwin Parker, 198
What We Are Watching: The View from the Couch, David Klatell and Norman Marcus, 177
Where Have You Been? Carol Bradley Shirley, 224
White Privilege: Unpacking the Invisible Knapsack, Peggy McIntosh, 96
Who Built the Pyramids? Studs Terkel, 76
Why They Excel, Fox Butterfield, 118
Why We Crave Horror Movies, Stephen King, 249
Winn, Marie, *The Effects of Television on Family Life*, 29
Working-Class Heroes No More, Barbara Ehrenreich, 72